POLICING CYBERSPACE

Law Enforcement and Forensics in the Digital Age

FIRST EDITION

Matthew J. Dolliver and Diana S. Dolliver
University of Alabama – Tuscaloosa

Bassim Hamadeh, CEO and Publisher
Michael Simpson, Vice President of Acquisitions
Jamie Giganti, Senior Managing Editor
Jess Busch, Graphic Design Supervisor
Zina Craft, Senior Field Acquisitions Editor
Gem Rabanera, Project Editor
Elizabeth Rowe, Licensing Coordinator
Claire Yee and Allie Kiekhofer, Interior Designers

First published in the United States of America in 2016 by Cognella, Inc.

Printed in the United States of America

ISBN: 978-1-63487-146-4 (pbk) / 978-1-63487-147-1 (br)

www.cognella.com 800-200-3908

Contents

DEDICATION

To our family, friends, and students.

ACKNOWLEDGMENTS

This book could not have happened without the support of our enthusiastic graduate and undergraduate students. We'd like to thank the Criminal Justice graduate students at the University of Alabama for their hard work over the past year in vetting and analyzing materials for this edition. We are also grateful to Katie Love for her contributions to this project, not only in the form of writing, but also for her time and countless hours of assistance without hesitation.

-M.J.D.

-D.S.D.

CHAPTER 1

Introduction to Cyber-Based Crimes and Policing

It is no secret that technology has changed the way humans interact in the twenty-first century. Conversations that once took place primarily in face-to-face settings or by handwritten letters are now being conducted in new, electronic media characterized by emoticons, texting shorthand, apps, and hashtags. Instead of getting our daily news primarily from printed newspapers, we turn to online social media outlets. The lightning speed with which news is disseminated around the world is enough to catch anyone's breath—at least anyone who is old enough to remember the days before computers became central to our daily lives. Now, there are new generations who are not familiar with life before the Internet; these generations expect global news at the touch of a button (even buttons are outdated now!), are not impressed by the electronic world, and have little knowledge of how to use that strange writing utensil the older people call a "pencil."

While the world adapts to this new electronic age, we cannot forget that police departments and other law enforcement entities in the United States and around the globe have also had to adapt. Police have had to adapt by receiving computer-based training whenever a new database is introduced to the department that may store information or search through criminal records. They have had to adapt by learning how to properly collect, store, and forensically analyze digital evidence (e.g., iPhones, computers, apps). Importantly, law enforcement officers have had to adapt to investigating law violations that now take place online (e.g., selling illegal goods) or crimes that are solely cyber-based (e.g., hacking, phishing). The electronic age has impacted the larger policing culture, how law enforcement agencies communicate and coordinate with one another, and the qualities sought after in police recruits. The cyber world has impacted how police visualize crime in neighborhoods, the capabilities of less-than-lethal weapons carried by police, and the way police interact with their local communities. However, laws and technologies available to police have not necessarily kept pace with the rapidity of general advancements in technologies available to the public. Unified definitions (legal or otherwise) of "cyberspace" or "cybercrime," or what might constitute either, do not exist. Up to this point, law enforcement officers have had to adapt to the investigative challenges presented by cyberspace while also tactfully navigating a legal system that, in many regards, has yet to catch up.

Also similarly impacted by the ushering in of the electronic age is the field of criminology. For a century, criminologists have studied all matters of crime and delinquency, developing theories to explain ranges of related phenomena. For example, age-graded informal social control theory (Sampson and Laub, 1993) examines events over the course of individuals' lives to better understand involvement in (or desistance from) engaging in crime and delinquency. Institutional anomie theory examines macro-level impacts of both culture and social institutions on aggregated crime rates (Messner and Rosenfeld, 1994). Bentham (1789) and Beccaria (1963[1764]) first introduced the idea that perhaps criminals are no different from non-criminals, suggesting that everyone makes rational choices about which behaviors (criminal or not) to engage in. Biological and biosocial theories later countered this assumption, claiming that offenders *do* differ from non-offenders, and that differences can be found within the interaction of our biological composition and our social environment (though traditional biological theories examine only biological characteristics) (e.g., Goring, 1913; Mednick et al., 1982; Raine, 1993; Rocque, Welsh, and Raine, 2012; Sheldon, 1949). So, amongst these theoretical arguments (and many more), where does the Internet fit in to the explanation of crime? Does the Internet simply provide an additional virtual "place" for crimes to take place, or are there motivating factors unique to the cyber world that are driving forces shaping criminality? Criminologists have just recently begun to address these questions, some of which are discussed within the readings in this chapter.

This chapter serves as an introduction to the topics of cyber-based crimes and cyber-related police investigations in the criminological context.

The first reading, by Osterburg and Ward (2010), introduces numerous aspects of cybercrimes and cyber-related terms, including the increasing range, scope, and detrimental effect of cybercrimes, the importance of specialized investigators (a.k.a. cyber-detectives), the fragile nature of electronic evidence, and the significance of proper investigative procedural methods, among others. Various legal issues unique to cybercrime that complicate and impede criminal investigations (such as Fourth Amendment concerns regarding an individual's right to privacy in the search and seizure of electronic evidence) are discussed, as are the legal differences between searching home and workplace computers, internet service providers, social networking sites, and websites. A summary of basic procedures and recommendations (such as protecting technological evidence, familiarizing oneself with some technological aptitude, following appropriate jurisdictional procedures, and keeping detailed records for criminal court trials) for any investigator dealing with cybercrime are described and emphasized. Several types of common cybercriminal activities are briefly described, and information regarding each is provided. These commonly encountered illegal activities include child exploitation and child pornography, stalking and harassment, economically driven crimes, hacking, drug trafficking, and cyberterrorism. Recommendations from the National Institute of Justice (NIJ) Guide for how to appropriately document an electronic crime scene are listed. The use of computer technology in criminal investigations continues to lag behind the evolution of its advancement despite the valued innovation and sophistication computers provide to criminal investigations (e.g., development of automated fingerprint identification systems [AFISs], Chicago's CLEAR program, and the FBI's Rapid Start Teams). At the end of this reading, a detailed list of names and descriptions of online resources available to investigators to aid them in investigations is given.

The second reading in this chapter, from the United Nations Office on Drugs and Crime (UNODC, 2013), outlines the increasing challenge cybercrime presents to the monitoring and prevention of domestic and international criminal activity. Due to the increasingly global nature of Internet connectivity, along with underlying factors such as economic and socio-economic influences, the risk and threat of cybercrime steadily growing and evolving is serious and evident. From information gathered from responding participant countries, this reading posits that, despite challenges in the empirical measurement of cybercrime, media reports (e.g., global news references to cybercrime) and law enforcement officials' observations of levels of cybercrime reflect the consensus that instances of cybercrime are a growing concern. After discussing the relatively undefinable nature of the word "cybercrime" and its surrounding concepts and categories, a non-comprehensive core list of fourteen cybercriminal acts are proposed to outline the general description of the term "cybercrime." These acts are further broken down into three categories: acts against the confidentiality, integrity and availability of computer data or systems; computer-related acts for personal or financial gain or harm; and computer content-related acts. Overall, this reading provides an introduction to the term "cybercrime" and its related categories and concepts while also initiating a discussion of the current state of cybercrime issues and a prediction of how future global Internet connectivity growth will impact cybercriminal activity.

The third reading in this chapter, also written by Osterburg and Ward (2010), provides a general overview of the role of a criminal investigator. Eight crucial responsibilities of an investigator are listed and subsequently explored in detail, and include identifying the perpetrator or eliminating a suspect as the perpetrator, locating and apprehending the perpetrator, and testifying effectively as a witness in court. Then various desirable and advantageous abilities and qualifications of potential investigators are discussed. A history of criminal investigations is given, including: accounts of post-industrial revolution "thief catchers"; Jonathan Wild and his rogue law enforcement tactics; the earliest police institutions in England, France, and the United States; and the establishment of the Department of Justice in 1870, among others. After the brief historical description of criminal investigations, the shift in investigations from brutal interrogative methods to the development and use of forensic identification methods (such as fingerprinting, bloodstain identification, and firearm identification) are described. The advent and utility of crime laboratories are stressed, as is the development of forensic medicine, one branch of forensic science. Lastly, the evolution of criminal investigations due to various technological advancements is addressed, and the role and efficacy that technology plays in criminal investigations is emphasized.

The final reading in this chapter, written by Kyung-shick Choi (2010) draws from the field of criminology by discussing two victimization theories (routine activities theory and lifestyle exposure theory) in order to investigate cybercrime through the criminological lens. This reading also considers how potential variables like demographic features, geographic locations, and lifestyle differences may contribute to cyber-victimization. First, routine activities theory (the idea that the convergence of motivated offenders, suitable targets, and the absence of capable guardians leads to criminal activity), along with the factors of spatiality and temporality in the theory, are redefined to coincide with the new expanded dimensions of cyberspace. The three major concepts of routine activities theory (i.e., motivated offenders, suitable targets, and the absence of capable guardians) are then discussed in terms of what these concepts mean in cyberspace rather than in a physical space. Next, lifestyle exposure theory (the argument that criminal victimization results from one's daily interactions or "routine daily activities," including work and errands along with one's race, gender, and income) is applied to lifestyles maintained in cyberspace. These two theoretical perspectives are presented together, with routine activities theory acting as an expansion of lifestyle exposure theory in an attempt to explain cybercrime victimization. With these two theories in mind, a conceptual model of cybercrime victimization is hypothesized, arguing that one's online lifestyle and capable guardianship directly influences victimization.

KEY WORDS FOUND IN THIS PART

- Computer/information system
- Computer/information program
- Computer data/information
- Encryption
- Pinging or spamming
- Virus
- Cracking
- IP Spoofing
- Trap and trace device
- Computer Emergency Response Team (CERT)
- *Modus operandi*
- Routine Activities Theory
- Lifestyle Exposure Theory
- Hackers

READING ONE

The Investigator

BY JAMES W. OSTERBURG AND RICHARD H. WARD

The role and responsibilities of the criminal investigator have changed dramatically over the past 10 years, largely as a result of changes in technology, the law, the media, and new forms of communication—such as the Internet, cellular telephones, and imaging. Perhaps most important has been the changing role of the investigator as a specialist, educated and trained to be knowledgeable about complex systems, societal differences, and organizational theory.

This chapter addresses the general framework associated with being a criminal investigator: the functional aspects of the job, necessary skills, tools of the trade, and the criteria necessary for success in what can be a challenging and rewarding career. Like most professional occupations, criminal investigation encompasses a historical framework that continues to evolve through new techniques and technology, as well as research. Thus, a brief description of the history of investigating crime is included in this chapter. The one thing that has not changed radically over time has been the definition of criminal investigation.

Criminal Investigation Defined

The investigation of crime encompasses "the collection of information and evidence for identifying, apprehending, and convicting suspected offenders," or in the words of Professor Ralph Turner, a pioneer in the field, "the reconstruction of a past event."[1,2] In essence, the responsibilities of the investigator include the following:

1. Determine whether a crime has been committed.
2. Decide if the crime was committed within the investigator's jurisdiction.
3. Discover all facts pertaining to the complaint.
    a. Gather and preserve physical evidence.
    b. Develop and follow up all clues.
4. Recover stolen property.
5. Identify the perpetrator or eliminate a suspect as the perpetrator.
6. Locate and apprehend the perpetrator.
7. Aid in the prosecution of the offender by providing evidence of guilt that is admissible in court.
8. Testify effectively as a witness in court.

The date and time when each responsibility was carried out should be recorded. Being unable to answer confidently "when" a task was carried out affords defense counsel the opportunity to cast doubt on the investigator's capability. If a witness repeatedly responds to the question "At what time did you do________?" with "I don't remember" or "as best as I can recall," defense counsel will use this technique to impugn a witness's competence.

Determine if a Crime Has Been Committed

Determining whether a crime has been committed necessitates an understanding of the criminal law and the elements of each criminal act. For this reason the investigator should have in his or her possession copies of the penal and case law of the state or jurisdiction. The jurisdiction of federal investigators may be broader in some cases, but it is limited by legislation, and state and local investigators should be familiar with the crimes over which federal statutes may apply.

Ideally, an investigator should have digital copies of the various legal texts on a personal computer, making it easy to identify and answer questions. In more complex cases, such as cybercrime or fraud, the investigator may contact the state prosecutor, district attorney, or

U.S. Attorney. In rare cases in which it is determined that a crime has not been committed, or the issue is one for a civil court, law enforcement personnel do not have responsibility.

Verify Jurisdiction

If a crime is not within the investigator's jurisdiction, there is no responsibility for its investigation, but the complainant may need to be referred to the proper authority. Occasionally a crime is committed on the border line of two jurisdictions or involves more than one jurisdiction. Depending on whether it has the potential for publicity (especially a high-profile case), it affords the chance to make a "good arrest," or it is inherently interesting or important, an investigator will seek to retain authority over the case, remain involved in it; otherwise, talk the other jurisdiction into accepting it.

When two investigators have concurrent jurisdiction, the issue of who will handle the case becomes complicated. Cases such as terrorism, cross-border fraud or Internet crime, illegal immigration, drug trafficking, and other multiple-jurisdiction criminal activity may involve joint investigative activities, and may require clarification by legal authority (such as a U.S. Attorney or local prosecuting authority—district, city, or county attorney). In other cases, such as serial murder in multiple jurisdictions, the place where the suspect is apprehended (for the crime in that jurisdiction will usually have the right to prosecute). In those cases in which there may be federal as well as state jurisdiction (such as bank robbery), the U.S. Attorney has the first right of refusal, and relatively minor cases may be prosecuted at a local level.

Discover All Facts and Collect Physical Evidence

The facts available to the first officer to arrive at a crime scene are provided by the victim or complainant and any eyewitness(es). Except in departments with programs in place for managing criminal investigations (see Chapter 12), they will be communicated to the detective dispatched to investigate the crime. He or she may decide to verify and pursue all of them, or to home in on specific details. At the outset, the investigator should develop a preliminary record that addresses the following points:

- When?
- Where?
- Who?
- What?

- How?
- Why?

In addition, the detective will collect any physical evidence, or arrange for its collection (preferably by an evidence technician) and examination in the appropriate crime laboratory. Depending on the kind of information provided, immediate follow-up might be required or the investigator may have to await laboratory results. In either event, it is essential at this point to follow through on any clue that holds promise for the identification of the perpetrator, and promptly exploit it.

Keeping in mind that information and records may be called into question during a later court case, the investigator must take care to prepare a comprehensive record of the crime scene, using notes, photographs, sketches, and in some cases video and voice recording. Care must be taken not to rely on memory, which has shown to be notoriously unreliable in many cases. Statements of victims, witnesses, and suspects should be recorded accurately and verbatim where possible.

In longer investigations, the use of records is more likely to contribute to the solution. If the victim furnishes the suspect's name to the detective, the case may be solved promptly. Then the chief problem is proving that the particular individual did in fact commit the crime. If the identity of the perpetrator must be developed, the effort required is much greater and, for certain crimes, often not successful. When it is, there comes a point not unlike that reached in solving a jigsaw puzzle: when the crucial piece is found, those remaining quickly fall into place.

Recover Stolen Property

The description and identification of stolen property is an important aspect of an investigation, and may later be critical in establishing ownership. Stolen property may turn up at a pawn shop, in the hands of secondhand dealers, or for sale on the Internet. The ability to establish makes and models, serial numbers, or other distinguishing characteristics of an item can contribute to a successful investigation. Pawn shops are common locations for stolen property to turn up, and the investigator should be familiar with record keeping and reports of these locations.

Identify the Perpetrator

Identifying the perpetrator is, of course, the primary goal of a criminal investigation, but the ability to bring a suspect to justice also depends on the evidence necessary for conviction.

This may take many forms, including physical evidence linking the suspect to the scene (fingerprints, blood, DNA, toolmarks); possession of evidence from the scene (property, fibers, hair); physical identification (tattoos, deformities, physical descriptors); and eyewitness descriptions, which, incidentally, have proven to be highly unreliable when the suspect is not known to victims or witnesses. *Modus operandi*, or method of operation, is also an important consideration.

In addition to the identification of the perpetrator from records, physical evidence, and eyewitnesses, the value of motive must be examined. Certain crimes, such as burglary, robbery, and rape, seem to have a universal motive; others, such as homicide, arson, and assault, have what might be called "particularized motives," because they often relate victim to criminal. Once established, it would be practical to develop a short list of persons who might have a particularized motive; then, if the investigator considers who had the opportunity and the temperament to carry out the crime, one or perhaps a few suspects may remain on the list. When physical evidence is available, as it often is in these crimes, this extends the possibility of a solution beyond what can be accomplished by interrogation alone.

Locate and Apprehend the Perpetrator

When people who know the perpetrator are unwilling or unable to provide an address or a clue to his or her whereabouts (should the suspect be elusive or have escaped), records may provide the information. (See Chapters 5 and 7, which discuss the value and utilization of records.) When the suspect is located, apprehension seldom presents difficulties; if it does, a raid may be called for. Planning and staging a raid require coordination, but this is essentially a police function rather than an investigative one. Owing, however, to several raids that received worldwide attention and, to some extent, had a deleterious impact on all law enforcement agencies, it is important to consider these events.

Aid the Prosecution by Providing Evidence of Guilt Admissible in Court

Largely as a result of plea bargaining, only a few cases that are investigated and solved eventually go to trial, but the detective must operate on the assumption that each will be tried. This necessitates that the investigator follow correct procedures in conducting the investigation, and not assume that the perpetrator will plead guilty and plea bargain, or assume that other evidence will carry the case.

Because such a large number of cases are plea bargained, the number of times an investigator may actually testify in a trial may be quite low. Problems concerning physical evidence can arise needlessly when it is presumed that a case will involve plea bargaining. One example is of a major city detective who had handled 75 burglary cases and none had gone to trial (each defendant having pleaded guilty to a reduced charge). Based on this experience, and because the suspect had confessed verbally, the detective believed that it was but a needless exercise to submit the physical evidence to the laboratory. Unfortunately, the prisoner was allowed to be placed in a police station cell wearing the incriminating evidence; once there, he ripped incriminating crepe shoe soles into pieces and flushed them down the toilet. He then repudiated the confession and demanded a trial.

Testify Effectively as a Witness in Court

Although few people are comfortable when called to the witness stand, the experienced investigator who has testified often can appear jaded. Yet testimony is effective only when it is credible. When sincerity, knowledge of the facts, and impartiality are projected, credibility is established. In all events, it is helpful that the investigator be familiar with the rules of evidence and the pitfalls of cross-examination (see Chapter 15).

Attributes Desirable in an Investigator

Abilities and Skills

The attributes that enable a person to be an accomplished investigator are many, including three important areas:

1. the ability, both physical and mental, to conduct an inquiry
2. the knowledge and training necessary to handle complex investigations
3. those skills necessary to reach the intended objectives.

Abilities	Related Skills
Conduct a proper crime scene search for physical evidence.	Know how to recognize, collect, and preserve physical evidence. Know the varieties of *modus operandi.* Be familiar with contemporary collection and recording techniques.
Question complainants, witnesses, and suspects.	Know how to use interviewing techniques. Know interrogation methods. Have a knowledge of local street jargon, and if pertinent, any foreign language spoken in the community. Be sensitive to the constitutional and civil rights of all: rich or poor, witness or suspect. Have a developed sense of mind-set.
Develop and follow up clues.	Know sources of records and how to check them. Know how to cultivate and use informants. Know how to conduct surveillances. Know how to check pawn shops, secondhand dealers, Internet sites, and the like.
Prepare written reports of case activity as it develops.	Have knowledge and skill in English, and a second language when possible.
Obtain legal search warrants based on evidence of probable cause.	Know how to use departmental and court forms to secure a search warrant.
Conduct raids, possibly under adverse conditions.	Know the techniques of cover and concealment.
Act with initiative, as the fluidity of the (raid) situation demands.	Acquire skill in silent communication. Use teamwork—within and between agencies.
Apprehend violators in a lawful manner.	Acquire a working knowledge of applicable laws, departmental rules, and regulations. Know about the use of handcuffs and the various types of firearms and other weapons that may be used, especially with regard to legal restrictions. Know proper search and seizure techniques and electronic intercept procedures used for suspects, houses, and automobiles.
Assist prosecuting attorney in presentation to the grand jury or trial court.	Know how to prepare clear, comprehensive reports. Know how to serve subpoenas, when necessary. Know how to have witnesses available or willing to appear on notice.
Appear as a witness in court.	Testify effectively in court. Know how to serve subpoenas, when necessary. Know how to have witnesses available or willing to appear on notice.

Qualifications of Mind, Personality, Attitude, and Knowledge

The following list of traits, which are desirable and help to qualify an individual for investigative work, was developed through classroom discussions (including many detectives who were students) and by conferring with police administrators interested in the topic of qualifications.

1. Intelligence and reasoning ability.
   An above-average score on an accepted intelligence test.
   Ability to analyze and interrelate a large number of facts.
   Ability to use advanced computer programs related to investigation.
2. Curiosity and imagination.
   Taking nothing for granted.
   Skepticism of the obvious.
   A sense of the unusual: anything out of place or not in keeping with the norm.
   An inquisitive mind.
   A suspicious nature with respect to the behavior of people.
   A sense of awareness.
   Insight.
   A flair for detective work.
3. Observation and memory.
   All five senses are intact and functioning.
   The investigator is alert and attentive.
4. Knowledge of life and people.
   Includes all strata of society; especially necessary to deal with the heterogeneous population of large cities. Also helpful: common sense, an outgoing personality, a spirit of cooperativeness, emotional stability, and some acting ability for role-playing.
5. Possession of technical "know-how."
   Implies training and knowledge of statutory and case law, as well as in the recognition, collection, preservation, and investigative value of physical evidence. It is important to be widely read and willing to keep up with current research and writing in the field.
6. Perseverance, "stick-to-itiveness," and energy.
   Many who wish to become detectives believe the job involves a glamorous life style, but the ability to be indefatigable, survive boredom, and keep energy in reserve to carry on, is more realistic.
7. Ability to recognize and control bias and prejudice in one's self and on the job.

Owing to bias and prejudice, for example, there may be a preconceived idea as to the perpetrator. Other truths may be ignored, such as: a chronic complainant can have a legitimate grievance; a prostitute can be raped; etc.

8. Sensitivity to people's feelings; acts with discretion and tact; respects a confidence.
9. The honesty and courage to withstand temptation and corruption.
10. When testifying, is not overzealous and does not commit perjury.
11. Miscellaneous characteristics:

    Physically fit appearance, report-writing skills, awareness of good public relations as a future source of cooperation and information.

Some police administrators believe that the traditional means of selecting detectives—written and oral examinations—have proved to be unsatisfactory:

> Prepared written examinations have not proved predictive in the selection of outstanding candidates for the position of investigator ... . No theoretical foundation exists for the oral board portion of the current testing process, other than a belief in its content validity.[3]

It is suggested that future performance can be gauged by an individual's "past work product." Further, good prospects must be recruited—not merely a fallout of the hiring process. Selection should include such considerations as: computer literacy, superior analytical capability, and good communication and reading skills.[4] Another prerequisite is education.

> ... [The] most important requirement is education. Study after study produces the same conclusions: that college educated people make better law enforcement officers.[5]

The National Institute of Justice published the results of a more comprehensive study of the detective selection process. In the Foreword, James K. Stewart wrote:

> ... managers and line personnel alike could identify some officers who were much better investigators than others. Studies bear out their observation: a small proportion of officers in any department is responsible for the majority of cases that successfully result in convictions.[6]

The concept of "past work product" is again endorsed as a predictor of success, yet criminal justice researchers have paid scant attention to the problem of detective selection, despite the impact of crime on the quality of life in communities across the nation.

Origins of Criminal Investigation

The concept of criminal investigation can be traced back thousands of years, to early times in China and Asia, as well as the Middle East, where agents of government used a great many legal, as well as illegal approaches (most notably torture) as a means of identifying transgressors of public order.

From a Western perspective, the Industrial Revolution in Europe drew many from the peasant classes in the countryside to larger towns and cities, resulting in burgeoning crime waves, forcing governments to move beyond the traditional night watches and use of the military to maintain order.[7] In England, the so-called "thief catchers" were frequently drawn from elements of the underworld. The rank and file of the recruits constituted a distinct breed, but two clear-cut differences in motivation set some apart from others. One kind were hirelings; with mercenary motives, they would play both sides of the street. The other kind were social climbers who, in order to move into respectable society, would incriminate their confederates.

An example of the former may be found in eighteenth-century England where Jonathan Wild personified the old saying, "Set a thief to catch a thief" (see Figure 1.1). Wild was well-acquainted with London's riffraff, having operated a brothel that served as headquarters for the gang of thieves and cut-throats under his tight control. Simultaneously, he was the public servant doing undercover work for the authorities. A rogue on the grand scale, Wild was both law enforcer and law breaker. He soon realized, however, that there was more profit to be made arranging for the return of stolen goods than for its disposal at the stiff discounts taken by the fence. Therefore, throughout the period he worked for the authorities, he was actually a receiver of stolen goods posing as the recoverer of lost property—the middle man exacting his cut while protecting the criminals in his employ. Even today, there are resemblances between his fictitious "Lost Property Office" and the "no questions asked" practices of individuals (even of some insurance companies) when stolen property, such as valuable jewelry and priceless paintings, is ransomed.

Metropolitan Police, New Scotland Yard, London

Figure 1.1 Jonathan Wild.

The earliest police in England worked only at night. First known as the "Watch of London," and later as the "Old Charleys," they were paid by the inhabitants in the vicinity of the watchman's box from which they regularly made the rounds of their beat. These parish constables had been appointed in 1253; they lasted until 1829 in London. About 20 years after Jonathan

Wild was hanged, novelist Henry Fielding (who wrote about Wild's exploits in a genial, tolerant vein) accepted an appointment as a London Magistrate. Taking his call to the bar seriously, Fielding was promptly embroiled in the sorry state of England's penal codes and its administration of justice (see Figure 1.2). The new magistrate tried to deal with the rising crime rate by enlarging the scope of the government's crime-fighting methods and assigning to his court a few parish constables, who had been accustomed to night watchman duties, to perform some criminal investigative functions. They came to be successful "thief-takers," owing to the use of informants and their close ties with the underworld. First called "Mr. Fielding's People," they later came to be known as the "Bow Street Runners" (see Figure 1.3). Unofficial and unpaid, the constables wore no uniforms and were ranked directly under the magistrate, who had to fight for their fair share of the reward moneys for apprehending criminals.

Metropolitan Police, New Scotland Yard, London

Figure 1.2 Henry Fielding.

Metropolitan Police, New Scotland Yard, London

Figure 1.3 One of "Mr. Fielding's People," who came after the "Old Charleys," and were later known as the "Bow Street Runners." They covered all of London, yet were never greater than 10 in number.

When the public finally became aware of their goings-on, the Bow Street Runners were perceived as thief-takers of the Jonathan Wild mold. Inevitably, abuses followed hard upon their close ties with the underworld, resulting in widespread criticism and loss of public trust. Then, around 1790, a staff of trained detectives was established, known as the "Runners." Officially recognized and paid, they were plainclothesmen who wore no uniforms and coexisted with the constables until the passage of the Metropolitan Police Act in 1829. The constables were replaced by a professional police force of 1,000 men, the "Runners" lasting another 10 years until the passage of the Metropolitan Police Act and Metropolitan Police Courts Act of 1839.[8] The members of this first professional force, organized by Sir Robert Peel (Britain's Home Secretary), were called the "Peelers" (see Figure 1.4); later and up until the present, they became known as the "Bobbies."

en.wikipedia.org

Figure 1.4 A member of the professional police force organized by Sir Robert Peel. Initially referred to as "Peelers," they later came to be known as "Bobbies."

About a decade later, a small number of full-time plainclothes officers had become an integral part of the new force. Because it was quartered in the Scotland Yard, an ancient structure that once protected Scottish kings and royal visitors, the police force in general and the detective force in particular were dubbed with that name.

In the early nineteenth century, French authorities also sought out convicted criminals to do undercover work. A notorious example of the thief-turned-informer, Francois Eugene Vidocq quickly set an enviable arrest and conviction record for the Paris police (see Figure 1.5). Throughout 1812 the high crime rate in Paris continued and Vidocq's suggestion to establish a plainclothes bureau was finally adopted. The Brigade de la Sûreté, created by the Ministry of Police, would function in all of the city's districts and report directly to the Prefect (the head of the Paris police force). Then Vidocq, the thief-turned-informer-turned-detective, became chief of this cohort of ex-convicts.

Meanwhile, in the United States, Thomas Byrnes was appointed detective bureau chief for the New York Police Department. His stewardship in 1880 exemplifies this gradual shift in direction—from one who consorted with criminals to one who was first and foremost a policeman. But just as the Bow Street Runners' close ties with the underworld were unethical, so were Byrnes's. With his coterie of informers, and his system of singling out which criminals to prosecute and which to tolerate—a system almost as corrupt as that of Jonathan Wild (who actually set up, or framed, his own confederates)—this chief of detectives, like Wild, gave the impression that crime was under control. One of Theodore Roosevelt's first acts upon assuming the post of President of the Board of Police Commissioners in 1895 was to force Byrnes out.

Metropolitan Police, New Scotland Yard, London

Figure 1.5 Francoise Eugene Vidocq.

Because federal laws also needed to be enforced, the Department of Justice was created by Congress in 1870. The investigative forces of the federal government consisted largely of the Treasury Department's

Secret Service and Bureau of Customs, together with the U.S. Postal Inspection Service. All were essentially ad hoc agencies with restricted jurisdictions. The next year, limited funds were appropriated for the newly formed Department of Justice; its mandate, the detection and prosecution of federal crimes. As investigators it employed part-time outsiders, some Pinkerton detectives, paid informers, political patronage workers, and occasionally agents borrowed from the Secret Service and other units. This practice continued for 30 years, until the administration of President Theodore Roosevelt in 1901. Among the many concerns of this conservationist, activist, reformer president were the "public be damned" attitude of big business and its flouting of the Sherman Antitrust Act. The effort to make it subservient to law and government was evident from the angry force of Roosevelt's speeches about the large-scale thefts of public lands in the western states; he was advancing the new idea that natural resources should be held in trust. Subsequently, two politicians (a senator and a congressman, both from Oregon) were convicted for "conspiracy to defraud the United States out of public lands." A historic investigation, it was accomplished with borrowed Secret Service agents.

> Roosevelt's administration called "The attention of Congress ... to the anomaly that the Department of Justice has ... no permanent detective force under its immediate control ... it seems obvious that the Department ... ought to have a means of ... enforcement subject to its own call; a Department of Justice with no force of permanent police in any form under its control is assuredly not fully equipped for its work."[9]

Not only did Congress ignore the request, it retaliated by initiating an inquiry into the Justice Department's habit of employing the investigative forces of other federal agencies. Indeed, just before adjournment, Congress amended an appropriation bill to expressly forbid the department's use of Secret Service or other agents. Roosevelt's response to the challenge was characteristically quick. Rather than accede to a continual hamstringing of the new department, his attorney general established an investigative unit within the Department of Justice soon after Congress adjourned. Named "The Bureau of Investigation" a short time later, the unit was to report only to the attorney general.

Two of the men who directed this unit formerly had been in command of the Secret Service. President Harding's appointee, the director since 1921, was replaced by another former Secret Service head, William J. Burns. Burns, however, was responsible for bringing Gaston B. Means, a man of unsavory reputation, into the Bureau. It was not long before the new agent was suspended for such unethical deals as selling departmental reports to underworld figures and offering to fix federal cases. The Attorney General suspended Means; quietly, Burns brought him back, ostensibly because of Means's underworld contacts. Under such stewardship, needless to say, the prestige of the Bureau declined; it sank even further when Harding's attorney general used the agency to frame a senator. This scandal, among the many others in Harding's administration, brought about the appointment of a new attorney general when, upon the sudden death of the president in 1923, Calvin Coolidge was catapulted into office.

President Coolidge did not equivocate about replacing Harding's corrupt cabinet members. The first decision of Harlan Fiske Stone, the new Attorney General (later Chief Justice of the Supreme Court,) was to demand Burns's resignation and offer the directorship to a 29-year-old attorney in the Justice Department. J. Edgar Hoover accepted the post, but only under certain conditions. The first applied to the Bureau's personnel practice: it must be divorced from politics, cease to be a catch-all for political hacks, and base appointments on merit. The director's authority was the subject of his second condition: he must have full control over hiring and firing (with promotion solely on proven ability), and be responsible only to the attorney general. Appointed to clean up the scandals, Stone not only agreed, he asserted that J. Edgar Hoover would not be allowed to take the job under any other conditions.

The sweeping powers given the new director brought a radical improvement in personnel quality. Although such sweeping authority was certainly necessary to effect change, the seeds of disaster accompanied it nonetheless. As Lord Acton's aphorism aptly warns, "Power tends to corrupt, and absolute power corrupts absolutely." It should not be unexpected, therefore, that absolute power corrupted once more. Toward the close of Hoover's distinguished 48-year regime, some investigative practices were viewed critically, first by a senate committee, and then by the press. What should be surprising is that the far greater excesses proposed were not countenanced. Indeed, they were rejected by the director.[10]

Of all the executive departments of government, those having the power to investigate crime represent a potential threat to freedom. In a democracy, therefore, civilian supervision of the exercise of such power is crucial.

Shift in Investigative Methods

When formally organized police departments came into being in response to crime conditions, the use of informers as the main staple in the investigative cupboard was supplemented by the use of interrogation, though the methods permitted to secure confessions varied widely from country to country. In the United States in 1931, the Wickersham Commission (appointed by President Herbert Hoover) employed the term "third degree" to characterize the extraction of confessions accompanied by brute force. It was, said the report, a widespread, almost universal police practice. Then the Supreme Court began to apply the provisions of the Bill of Rights to the states. Its judicial decisions, together with the potential offered by the application of science to the examination of physical evidence, brought an end to brutal methods of interrogation.

Europe was well ahead of the States in recognizing that potential. In 1893, Hans Gross, an Austrian who might be called the father of forensic investigation, wrote a monumental treatise so advanced for its time that it was unmatched for decades. *Handbuch fur Untersuchungsrichter* when translated became *Criminal Investigation.* At about the same time in England, Sir Francis Galton's landmark book, *Fingerprints,* was published (in 1892). It led to the identification of criminals based on fingerprint evidence found at the crime scene. The marks or visible evidence left on an object by a person's fingers had long been observed, but such observations lacked any understanding of the intrinsic value of a human fingerprint. A somewhat similar situation prevailed with respect to bloodstain evidence. For a long time it could not be proved that a suspected stain was in fact blood; when it could, its presence would be explained by alleging the source to be that of a chicken or other animal. Prior to 1901, such allegations could neither be proved nor disproved; then, a German, Paul Uhlenhuth, discovered the precipitin test for distinguishing human blood from animal blood. In the field of firearms identification, it was not until 1923 that Calvin Goddard, an American, developed (with others) the comparison microscope; it helped to determine whether a particular gun fired a bullet or cartridge found at a crime scene.

en.wikipedia.org

Figure 1.6 Sir Francis Galton wrote about the technique identifying common patterns in fingerprints and devising a classification system.

These scientific developments, when applied to the examination of physical evidence, pointed to the need for properly equipped crime laboratories. In 1910 the first police laboratory was established by Edmond Locard in Lyon, France. In the United States it ultimately led, in the mid-1920s to early 1930s, to the installation of crime laboratories in a few of the larger cities. In Washington, DC, one was established in the Bureau of Investigation (renamed the Federal Bureau of Investigation in 1935). The expansion of crime laboratories proceeded slowly: by 1968, there still were none within the borders of 17 (mostly western) states. The availability of Law Enforcement Assistance Administration (LEAA) funds, however, soon permitted each state to install a crime laboratory. In California, a university program in criminalistics (a term coined by Hans Gross), coupled with strong support from the law enforcement community, led to the greatest proliferation of county laboratories in this country. With his research contributions and leadership of the program at the University of California, Professor Paul L. Kirk must be viewed as one of the few major figures in the field of criminalistics. In the Midwest, another major figure, Professor Ralph F. Turner, integrated criminalistics with the teaching of criminal investigation at Michigan State University's strong police/law enforcement program, turning out criminalists to serve that area of the country.

In the 1970s research was undertaken that examined the proficiency of crime laboratories in the United States in examining common types of physical evidence: bloodstains, bullets and cartridge cases, controlled substances, latent fingerprints, hair, glass, paint, and other types of evidence. Many laboratories did not perform well; they made errors in identifying substances and in determining if two or more objects/evidence shared a common origin. This research continues to this day (Collaborative Testing Services), and proficiency testing has become an integral part of most crime laboratory quality assurance procedures. It is one way in which laboratories attempt to ensure their examiners' routine work is of the highest quality. Most laboratories in the nation seek to meet accreditation standards that are sponsored by the American Society of Crime Laboratory Directors.

Although the nation's crime laboratories have made dramatic improvements over the years, problems persist. Many of the problems are the result of laboratories being placed within law enforcement organizations that either do not devote adequate resources to these enterprises or pressure scientists to provide them with results that match their conclusions. Laboratories must have the resources to examine evidence in a timely manner and to hire personnel that possess the equipment, training, and research opportunities to ensure quality scientific work. Even though the science is progressing, there are still individuals within certain laboratories who lack proper scientific credentials. Laboratories must also be independent operations that are allowed to pursue investigations of evidence without interference and are free to report results—even if they show a prime suspect is uninvolved in the crime. There have been many instances brought to the public's attention in recent years in which forensic examiners have been too eager to assist police investigators and have cut corners or compromised high scientific standards.

Forensic medicine, the other main branch of forensic science, developed outside the control of police agencies. For this reason and because it otherwise contributes to the general well-being, forensic medicine evolved sooner and grew more quickly, remaining well ahead of criminalistics. This was the state of affairs until the 1960s when both branches benefited from the infusion of federal funds. Just the same, forensic medicine and its subdivisions are largely, but not exclusively, concerned with homicide; their use within the totality of criminal investigation is more limited than is that of criminalistics. Owing to the importance attached to homicide, however, forensic medicine is of vital significance to the criminal investigator.

The field of forensic medicine has evolved through ongoing research and by the move away from the "coroner" system that involved autopsies conducted by medical doctors with little experience in handling suspicious deaths. Today, most medical examiners are schooled in pathology and devote their full time to the profession.

Trends in Investigation

The influences of developments in transportation (the automobile), communications (telephone, radio, computers), and forensic science changed the practice of criminal investigation over the past century. The rapid pace of more recent modifications in virtually all aspects of American society have contributed directly to the many changes in law enforcement, not the least of which have been in the area of investigating crime. It has been more than 40 years since publication of the President's Crime Commission Report in 1968, and the infusion of billions of federal, state, and local funds to the criminal justice system. Policing has changed dramatically, due in no small part to higher education, training, and research. Improved management, salaries, and professionalism have characterized much of the past two decades.

The following chapters address the many aspects of conducting a criminal investigation, but it is important to recognize that as society changes it is incumbent on the investigator to stay abreast of this impact on policing. As sophisticated information systems become prevalent, the long-term implications are indicated by the proposed (but disputed) reforms of the investigative process suggested by Greenwood and Petersilia: "Increase the use of information processing systems in lieu of investigators."[11]

Although technology is now commonly used in police work, its ultimate contribution is only beginning to be realized. Sophisticated electronic information systems are having a major effect on case investigations: helping the detective cull a quantity of data efficiently and effectively; providing clues and identifying potential suspects; making it possible to prepare reports quickly and assemble evidence for presentation in court. Present technology allows for the transfer of photographs, fingerprints, and other forms of visual information through networks. Technology makes it possible for an investigator to carry a small "notebook" computer containing thousands of pages of information that can be called up and utilized. For example, "mug shot" presentations can now be utilized in the field.

On the international level, the need for enhanced computer systems increases as the world becomes smaller owing to rapid global travel. Computerized databases are critical in combating terrorism and fraud. INTERPOL, the International Police Organization, acknowledged this by significantly upgrading its computer systems. The United Nations also views the goal of worldwide computerization as crucial. Indeed, large criminal syndicates and those involved in "enterprise crime" are in many respects much further ahead in their use of computer technology than are many law enforcement agencies. The use of artificial intelligence is also being adapted to criminal investigation,

The scrutiny of the criminal investigation process by police administrators, researchers, and scholars has also been important. A serious dialogue between practitioners and researchers is a valuable result of such scrutiny.[12] Research across the spectrum of the behavioral and information sciences holds great promise for improvement in the investigative function.

Notes

1. Elinor Ostrum, Roger B. Parks, and Gordon P. Whitaker, *Patterns of Metropolitan Policing* (Cambridge, MA: Ballinger, 1978), 131.
2. Ralph F. Turner, personal communication, 1987.
3. Frank Adams, "Selecting Successful Investigative Candidates," *The Police Chief*, 61:7, 12–14 (July 1994), 12.
4. Ibid., 12, 14.
5. Ibid., 14.
6. Bernard Cohen and Jan Chaiken, *Investigators Who Perform Well* (Washington, DC: U.S. Department of Justice, September 1987), iii.
7. Henry Fielding, *Jonathan Wild*, ed. by David Nokes (New York: Penguin Books, 1982), 8.
8. R.L. Jones, "Back to the Bow Street Runners," *Police Journal*, 63:3 (1990), 246–248.
9. D. Whitehead, *The FBI Story* (New York: Random House, 1956), 19.
10. W.C. Sullivan with Bill Brown, *The Bureau: My Thirty Years in Hoover's FBI* (New York: Norton, 1979), 205–217, 251–257.
11. Peter Greenwood and Joan Petersilia, *The Criminal Investigative Process, Vol. I: Summary and Policy Implications* (Santa Monica, CA: RAND, 1975), 30.
12. National Institute of Law Enforcement and Criminal Justice, *The Criminal Investigation Process: A Dialogue on Research Findings* (Washington, DC: U.S. Government Printing Office, 1977).

Supplemental Readings

Amidon, H.T. "Law Enforcement: From the Beginning to the English Bobby." *Journal of Police Science and Administration*, 5:3 (1977), 355–367.

Anon. *Investigators Who Perform Well*. Washington, DC: U.S. Department of Justice, National Institute of Justice, 1987.

Berman, Jay S. *Police Administration and Progressive Reform: Theodore Roosevelt as Police Commissioner of New York*. Westport, CT: Greenwood Press, 1987.

Defoe, Daniel. Introduction and notes to "The True and Genuine Account of the Life and Actions of the Late Jonathan Wild." Pages 225–227 in *Jonathan Wild*, by Henry Fielding, edited by David Nokes. New York: Penguin Books, 1982.

Edwards, Samuel. *The Vidocq Dossier: The Story of the World's First Detective*. Boston: Houghton-Mifflin, 1977.

Ericson, Richard V. *Making Crime: A Study of Detective Work.* Toronto: Butterworth, 1984.

Hopkins, Ernest Jerome. *Our Lawless Police.* New York: Viking Press, 1931; New York: Da Capo Press, 1971.

Joy, Peter A., and Kevin McMunigal. "Ethics." *Criminal Justice,* 20:4 (2006), 50–52.

Mones, Paul. *Stalking Justice: The Dramatic True Story of the Detective Who First Used DNA Testing to Catch a Serial Killer.* New York: Pocket Books, 1995.

National Commission on Law Observance and Enforcement. *Report on Lawlessness in Law Enforcement.* Washington, DC: U.S. Government Printing Office, 1931. [Report No. 11 of the Wickersham Commission appointed by President Herbert Hoover in 1929.]

Roth, Mitchel P. *Crime and Punishment: A History of the Criminal Justice System.* Belmont, CA: Thomson Wadsworth, 2005.

Thorwald, Jurgen. *The Century of the Detective.* New York: Harcourt, Brace & World, 1965.

Thorwald, Jurgen. *Crime and Science.* New York: Harcourt, Brace & World, 1967.

Credits

1. Fig. 1.1. "Jonathan Wild," http://commons.wikimedia.org/wiki/File:Ticket_for_the_execution_of_Jonathan_Wild.jpg. Copyright in the Public Domain.
2. Fig. 1.2. "Henry Fielding circa 1743 etching from Jonathan Wild the Great," http://commons.wikimedia.org/wiki/File:Henry_Fielding_c_1743_etching_from_Jonathan_Wild_the_Great.jpg. Copyright in the Public Domain.
3. Fig. 1.3. Robert Dighton, "Bow Street Runner, John Townsend," http://www.npg.org.uk/collections/search/portraitLarge/mw63945/John-Townsend-The-Towns-end. Copyright in the Public Domain.
4. Fig. 1.4. "Robert Peel," http://commons.wikimedia.org/wiki/File:Robert_Peel.jpg. Copyright in the Public Domain.
5. Fig. 1.5. Marie Gabriel Coignet, "Eugène François Vidocq," http://commons.wikimedia.org/wiki/File:Vidocq.jpg. Copyright in the Public Domain.
6. Fig. 1.6. "Francis Galton," http://commons.wikimedia.org/wiki/File:Francis_Galton_1850s.jpg. Copyright in the Public Domain.

READING TWO

Connectivity and Cybercrime

BY UNODC REPORT

This Chapter examines the effect of the global connectivity revolution on cybercrime and identifies cybercrime as a growing contemporary challenge driven by a range of underlying socio-economic factors. It considers definitions of cybercrime and finds that while certain definitions are required for 'core' cybercrime acts, the aggregate concept is not well suited as a legal term of art.

The Global Connectivity Revolution

KEY RESULTS

- In 2011, more than one third of the world's total population had access to the internet
- Over 60 per cent of all internet users are in developing countries, with 45 per cent of all internet users below the age of 25 years
- It is estimated that mobile broadband subscriptions will approach 70 per cent of the world's total population by 2017
- The number of networked devices (the 'internet of things') are estimated to outnumber people by six to one, transforming current conceptions of the internet
- In the future hyper-connected society, it is hard to imagine a 'computer crime', and perhaps any crime, that does not involve electronic evidence linked with internet protocol (IP) connectivity

In 2011, at least 2.3 billion people—equivalent to more than one third of the world's total population—had access to the internet. Developed countries enjoy higher levels of internet access (70 per cent) than developing countries (24 per cent). However, the absolute number of internet users in developing countries already far outnumbers that in developed countries. Some 62 per cent of all internet users were in developing countries in 2011.

In both developed and developing countries, more younger people are online than older people. Some 45 per cent of the world's internet users are below the age of 25 years[1]—a demographic that also broadly corresponds with an age group often at special risk of criminal offending.[2]

The Growth of Mobile Internet Access

Almost 1.2 billion mobile broadband subscriptions exist globally. This is twice as many as fixed-line broadband subscriptions, and corresponds to around 16 per cent of the global population.[3] In 2009, the volume of global mobile data traffic overtook the volume of mobile voice traffic. Global mobile data traffic in 2011 was some four times greater than mobile voice traffic.[4]

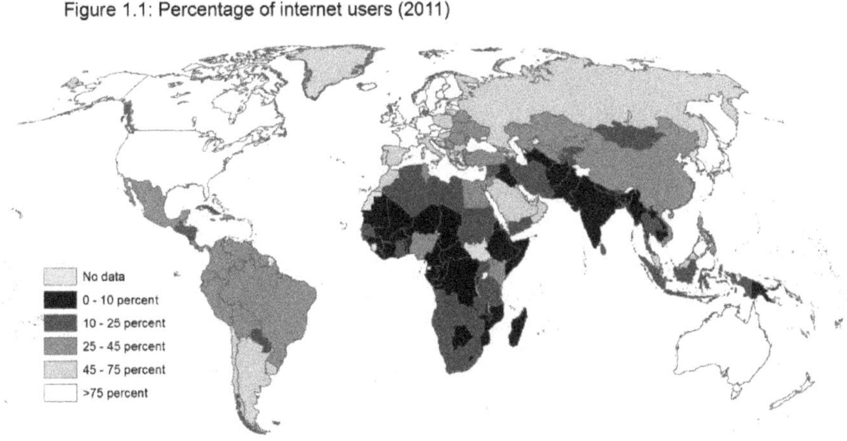

Figure 2.1 Percentage of internet users (2011).
Source: World Telecommunication/ICT Indicators 2012.

Africa and the Arab states show especially high ratios of mobile broadband to fixed broadband, reflecting the launch of high-speed 3G+ mobile networks and services in those regions, coupled with the growth in handheld devices, including smartphones and tablet computers. By 2017, GSM/EDGE[5] mobile technology is expected to cover more than 90 per cent of the world's population, with 85 per cent of the population accessing WCDMA/HSPA[6] mobile technology, at speeds of up to 2Mb per second. Forecasts suggest that the number of mobile broadband subscriptions will reach five billion by the year 2017. In 2011, the number of networked *devices*—the so-called 'internet of

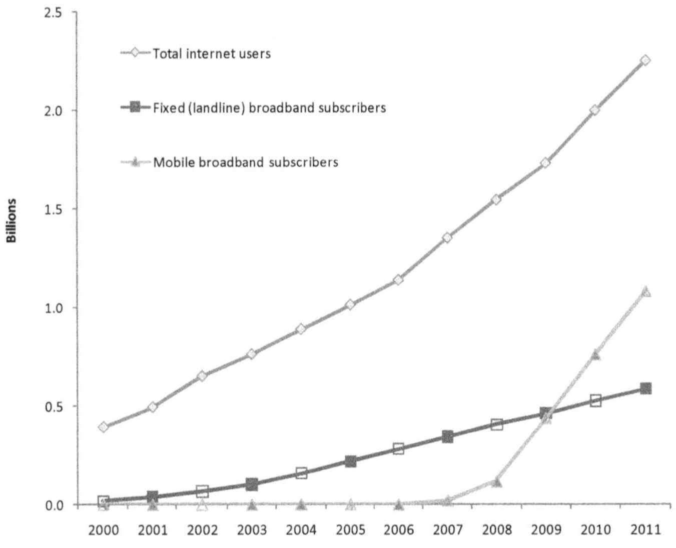

Figure 2.2 Global internet connectivity 2000–2011
Source: ITU World Telecommunication ITC Indicators 2012

things'—overtook the total global population. By 2020, the number of connected devices may outnumber connected people by six to one, potentially transforming current conceptions of the internet.[7] Whereas connected persons currently have at least one or both of two devices connected to the internet (typically a computer and smartphone), this could rise to seven devices by 2015.[8] In the 'internet of things,' objects such as household appliances, vehicles, power and water meters, medicines or even personal belongings such as clothes, will be capable of being assigned an IP address, and of identifying themselves and communicating using technology such as RFID and NFC.[9]

The Persisting Digital Divide

Disparities in internet access are vividly illustrated by mapping the geo-location of global IP addresses. This provides a reasonable approximation of the geographic reach of the internet. While IP address density largely follows global population density, a number of populated locations in developing countries show sparse internet connection availability. Gaps in Southern and Eastern Asia, Central America, and Africa, in particular, exemplify the present digital divide. As of mid-2012, some 341 million people in sub-Saharan Africa live beyond a 50km range of a terrestrial fibre-optic network—a number greater than the population of the United States of America.[10]

As noted by the Broadband Commission for Digital Development established by ITU and UNESCO, regions not connected to the internet miss its unprecedented potential for economic opportunity and social welfare. The World Bank estimates that a 10 per cent increase in

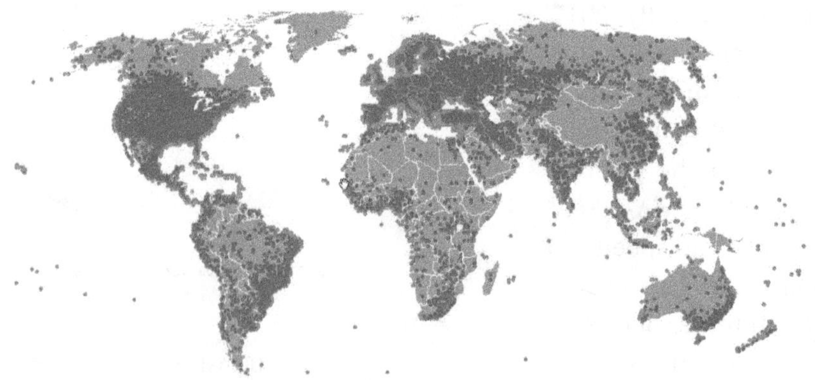

Figure 2.3 IP geolocation (2012).
Source: UNODC elaboration of MaxMind GeoCityLite.

broadband penetration would yield, on average, a 1.38 per cent increase in GDP growth in low and middle income countries.[11] Mobile broadband has been found to have a higher impact on GDP growth than fixed broadband through the reduction of inefficiencies.[12] Beyond economic growth, the internet enables access to vital services for the most remote, including education, healthcare, and e-governance.

The Role of the Private Sector

A significant proportion of internet infrastructure is owned and operated by the private sector. Internet access requires a 'passive' infrastructure layer of trenches, ducts, optical fibre, mobile base stations, and satellite hardware. It also requires an 'active' infrastructure layer of electronic equipment, and a 'service' layer of content services and applications.[13] Large global ISPs, such as AT&T, NTT Communications, Sprint, Telefonica, and Verizon, own or lease high capacity inter- and intra-continental fibre optic transport (the internet *backbone*) as well as other core internet infrastructure, such as switches and routers. ISP networks are connected both bilaterally, and at concentrated points (known as *internet exchange points*, or IXPs). Major networks negotiate *peering agreements* among themselves, whereby each agrees to carry the other's traffic—this allows them to provide fast global connections to their clients. They also carry paid-for data for non-peering networks. Mobile telephone operators and local ISPs own or manage the network of radio cells and local cables that bring the internet the 'last kilometre' from server to handheld and desktop devices. Annex Four to this Study contains further details about internet infrastructure.

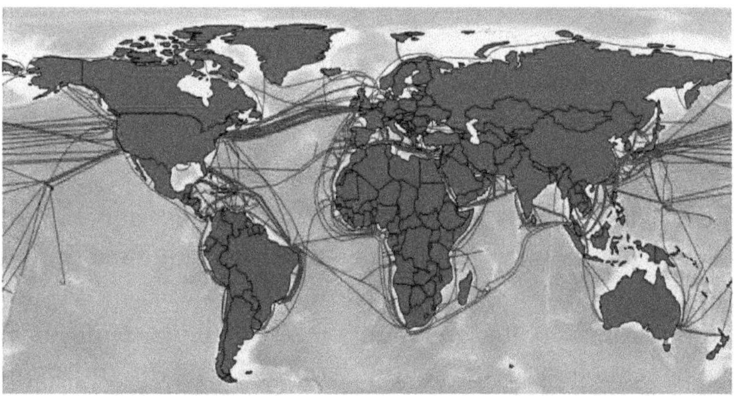

Figure 2.4 Global submarine cables.
Source: UNODC elaboration of data from http://www.cablemap.info/

As global operators seek to build broad business bases, and to maximize efficiency and returns on infrastructure investment, recent years have seen a convergence of traditionally distinct information technologies, communication technologies, and web services.[14] Telecommunications networks are evolving into all-IP data networks, with standardized products and simpler interconnectivity. Increased cloud storage and computing will enable the same services and user content to be delivered to any user device, whether a mobile phone, desktop or tablet computer.[15]

IP technology generally reduces the cost of commercial network operations. However, the cost of international bandwidth can still vary enormously, depending upon the elasticities of supply and demand. Until, for example, the ACE (Africa Coast to Europe) submarine cable becomes fully operational, countries in Western Africa remain burdened with some of the highest internet connectivity costs in the world, due to exclusive reliance on commercial satellite bandwidth.[16]

As an infrastructure, the internet's growth can be compared to the development of roads, railways, and electricity, which are dependent on private sector investment, construction and maintenance, but regulated and incentivized by national governments. At the same time, the internet is often regarded as more private-sector led. Working with the private sector, governments can offer public sector policy leadership and facilitate growth of the internet through direct investment in infrastructure and services, by putting in place policies that promote competition and remove investment barriers, and by providing incentives to enterprises that deploy internet services.

Contemporary Cybercrime

KEY RESULTS

- Computer-related crime is a long-established phenomenon, but the growth of global connectivity is inseparably tied to the development of contemporary cybercrime
- Today's cybercrime activities focus on utilizing *globalized* information communication technology for committing criminal acts with *transnational* reach
- Some cybercrime is committed using stand-alone or closed computer systems, although much less frequently

In addition to its socio-economic benefits, there is no doubt that computer technology and the internet—just as with other means enhancing capabilities of human interaction—can be used for criminal activity. While computer-related crime, or computer crime, is a comparatively long-established phenomenon, the growth of global connectivity is inherent to contemporary cybercrime.

Computer-related acts including physical damage to computer systems and stored data;[17] unauthorized use of computer systems and the manipulation of electronic data;[18] computer-related fraud;[19] and software piracy[20] have been recognized as criminal offences since the 1960s.

In 1994, the United Nations Manual on the Prevention and Control of Computer Related Crime noted that fraud by computer manipulation; computer forgery; damage to or modifications of computer data or programs; unauthorized access to computer systems and service; and unauthorized reproduction of legally protected computer programs were common types of computer crime.[21]

While such acts were often considered local crimes concerning stand-alone or closed systems, the *international* dimension of computer crime and related criminal legislation was recognized as early as 1979. A presentation on computer fraud at the Third INTERPOL Symposium on International Fraud, held from 11 to 13 December 1979, emphasized that '*the nature of computer crime is international, because of the steadily increasing communications by telephones, satellites etc., between the different countries.*'[22]

The core concept at the heart of today's cybercrime remains exactly that—the idea that converging *globalized* information communication technology may be used for committing criminal acts, with *transnational* reach.

These acts may include all of the computer-related crimes listed above, in addition to many others, such as those related to computer or internet content,[23] or computer-related acts for personal or financial gain.[24] As set out in this Chapter, this Study does not 'define' contemporary cybercrime as such. It rather describes it as a list of acts which constitute cybercrime. Nonetheless, it is clear that the focus is on the misuse of ICT from a *global perspective*. More than half of responding countries, for example, reported that between 50 and 100 per cent of cybercrime acts encountered by the police involve a *transnational* element.[25] Respondents referred to cybercrime as a *'global phenomenon'* and noted that *'online communication invariably involves international or transnational dimensions.'*[26]

Placing the focus on global connectivity does not exclude crimes involving stand-alone or closed computer systems from the scope of cybercrime.[27] Interestingly, while law enforcement officials in developed countries typically identified a high proportion of cybercrime with a transnational element, those in developing countries tended to identify a much lower proportion—fewer than 10 per cent in some cases.[28] On the one hand, this may indicate that cybercrime perpetrators in developing countries focus more on domestic victims and (possibly, stand-alone) computer systems. On the other, it may also be the case that, due to capacity challenges, law enforcement in developing countries less frequently identify, or engage with, foreign service providers or potential victims linked with national cases.

Nonetheless, the reality of global connectivity must be considered as a central element to contemporary cybercrime and, in particular, the cybercrime of tomorrow. As cyberspace and IP traffic grows,[29] as traffic from wireless devices exceeds traffic from wired devices, and as more internet traffic originates from non-PC devices, it may become hard to imagine a 'computer' crime without the fact of IP connectivity. The particularly personal nature of mobile devices, and the emergence of IP-connected household or personal effects, means that electronic data and transmissions could even be generated by, or become integral to, almost every human action—whether legal or illegal.

Cybercrime As a Growing Challenge

KEY RESULTS

- Because of the difficulties arising when trying to define and identify cybercrime, cross-nationally comparative statistics on cybercrime are much rarer than for other crime types
- At the global level, law enforcement respondents to the Study perceive increasing levels of cybercrime, as both individual offenders and organized criminal groups exploit new opportunities, driven by profit and personal gain
- Cybercrime is advancing in the focus of the public due to increased media reporting of cybercrime cases, cybersecurity issues and other cyber-related news
- Criminological theories and socio-economic approaches offer possible explanations for the recent growth in cybercrime activities
- In many countries across all regions, the explosion in global connectivity has come at a time of economic and demographic transformations, with rising income disparities, tightened private sector spending, and reduced financial liquidity

The increasing ubiquity of global connectivity presents a serious risk that rates of cybercrime will increase. While reliable statistics are hard to obtain, many country respondents to the Study questionnaire indicated that cybercrime is a growing challenge—a plausible viewpoint given underlying criminological and socio-economic factors. One responding country from Europe, for example, noted that: '*Relying upon research and statistics provided mostly by the private sector or the academia, it is commonly agreed upon that cybercrime acts are increasing dramatically, with a limited powers to control it.*'[30] In the 2010 Salvador Declaration on Comprehensive Strategies for Global Challenges, annexed to General Assembly resolution 65/230, it was noted that the '*development of information and communications technologies and the increasing use of the Internet create new opportunities for offenders and facilitate the growth of crime.*'[31]

Due to significant challenges in the measurement of cybercrime, cross-nationally comparative statistics on cybercrime are much rarer than for other crime types.[32] Annex Two to this Study examines current methodological approaches to measuring cybercrime, and presents some of the few available statistics.

In the past five years in particular, the issue of cybercrime has come prominently to the forefront of public discussion, including in developing countries. A search of global news wires for the terms 'cybercrime' and 'homicide', in the six official United Nations languages, reveals a significant relative growth in the frequency of global news references to cybercrime, as compared with references to homicide. Between the years 2005 and 2012, references to cybercrime have increased by up to 600 per cent, compared with around 80 per cent in the case of references to homicide.[33] Such measurements are not directly related to underlying cybercrime acts. Nonetheless, they can reflect general global 'activity' concerning cybercrime—including media reporting on government initiatives and counter measures.

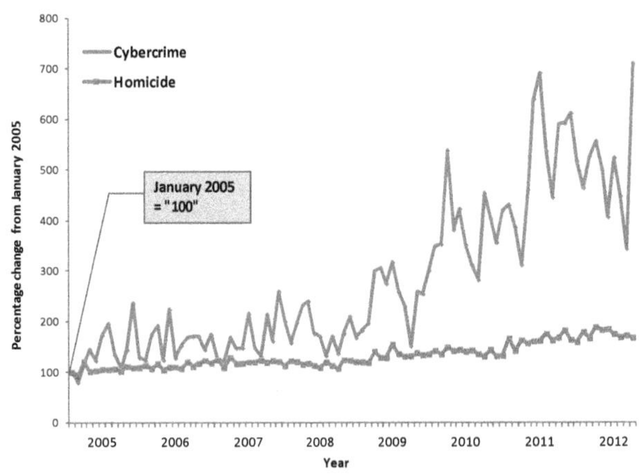

Figure 2.2 Relative frequency of global news reports 2005–2012.
Source: UNODC calculations from Dow Jones Factiva.

The views of law enforcement officials also reflect a consensus that levels of cybercrime are increasing. When asked about cybercrime trends observed in their own country over the past five years, all law enforcement officials in 18 countries in Africa, and the Americas responded that cybercrime was either

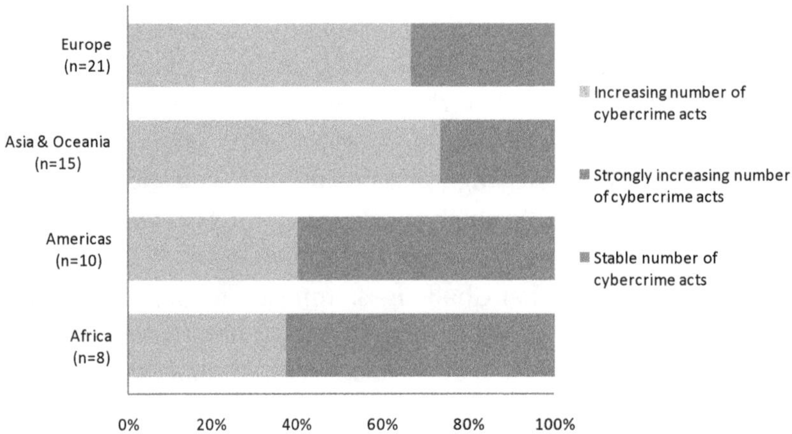

Figure 2.6 Cybercrime trends observed by law enforcement 2007–2011.
Source: Study cybercrime questionnaire. Q84 (n = 54).

increasing or strongly increasing.[34] Law enforcement officials in Europe and Asia and Oceania tended to view cybercrime as increasing, rather than strongly increasing; and a small number of countries in Europe were of the view that the phenomenon was stable.[35]

Law enforcement officials referred to a range of cybercrime acts as increasing, including computer-related fraud and identity theft; computer-related production, distribution or possession of child pornography; phishing attempts; and illegal access to computer systems, including hacking. Increasing levels of cybercrime are attributed by law enforcement officials in part to a growing capability in the area of anonymity techniques when using ICT, as well as the growing commercialization of computer misuse tools. Chapter Two (The global picture) further analyses information provided by states and the private sector on trends in and threats from specific cybercrime acts.

Underlying Factors: Criminological and Socio-Economic Approaches

From a criminological perspective, the suggestion that ICT and the increasing use of the internet create new opportunities for offenders and facilitates the growth of crime is highly plausible. While a number of different criminological theories are applicable, the fact that cybercrime represents *'a new and distinctive format of crime,'*[36] creates challenges to predicting developments, and to its prevention, by the application of general crime theories.[37]

One key proposition is that the emergence of 'cyberspace' creates new phenomena that are notably distinct from the (mere) existence of computer systems themselves, and the direct opportunities for crime that computers present. Within cyberspace, persons may show differences between their conforming (legal) and nonconforming (illegal) behaviour as compared with their behaviour in the physical world. Persons may, for example, commit crimes in cyberspace that they would not otherwise commit in physical space due to their status and position. In addition, identity flexibility, dissociative anonymity and a lack of deterrence factors may provide incentives for criminal behaviour in cyberspace.[38]

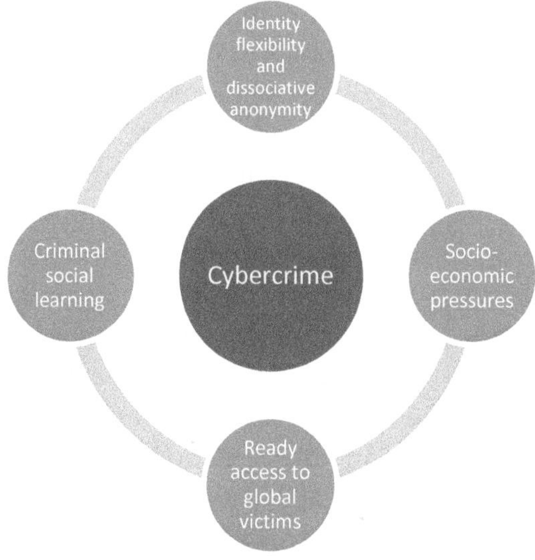

Figure 2.7 Possible underlying factors linked to increases in cybercrime.

Routine activity theory (RAT)[39] may also provide insight into underlying drivers of cybercrime. RAT proposes that crime risk increases upon the convergence of: (i) a motivated offender, (ii) a suitable target, and (iii) the absence of a capable guardian.[40] In the case of cybercrime, large numbers of suitable targets may emerge through increasing time spent online, and the use of online services such as banking, shopping and file sharing—making users prone to phishing attacks or fraud.[41] The emergence of online social networks, including Twitter and Facebook, also provides a ready supply of millions of potential scam or fraud victims. Where users have not restricted communication settings to enable only interaction with their private network of 'friends,' such networks can enable accessibility of a large number of potential victims all at once. Persons also tend to organize their social networking profiles according to their interests and location, which enables criminals to target victims with specific modes of behaviour or backgrounds. Such 'guardian' measures that do exist, such as anti-virus programmes and a (comparatively small) risk of law enforcement action, can be insufficient to deter a perpetrator motivated by the lure of significant profit.

Research also highlights that the general theory of crime concerning reduced self-control and a preparedness to assume risk for short-term gains, may apply to acts that can be facilitated or enhanced by electronic communications and the internet. In addition, individuals exposed online to cyber criminal models and peers may themselves be more likely to engage in cybercrime.[42] This 'social-learning' theory may have particular application when it comes to cybercrime, as offenders often need to learn specific computer techniques and procedures.[43] Social learning theory and the general theory of crime interact, in that persons with reduced self-control may actively seek out similar others and coalesce in virtual environments in the same way as in the real world. In cyberspace this process can occur in a significantly reduced timeframe, and with much broader geographic reach.

Online connectivity and peer-learning is likely central to the engagement of organized criminal groups in cyber criminality. Online 'carding' or 'carder' forums for the exchange of stolen credit card details are one such example. 'Carder' forums have often commenced with a 'swarm' structure with no obvious chain of command as cyber perpetrators seek out one another and 'meet' online for exchange of knowledge and the provision of criminal services. Forums later evolve into more controlled 'hub'-like operations with higher degrees of criminal organization.[44] The use of social networking sites can also enable forms of social 'outreach' and connectivity between individuals and criminal groups.[45]

Another underlying development that may contribute to driving cybercrime levels is the emergence of global connectivity in the context of world economic and demographic transformations. By 2050, the world will experience a near doubling of the urban population to 6.2 billion—70 per cent of the projected world population of 8.9 billion.[46] The World Economic Forum Global Risks Report 2012 cites severe income disparity and chronic fiscal imbalances as two of the top five global risks in the year 2012.[47] Gallup polling data from 2011 reveal that, globally, people perceive their living standards to be falling—a discontent exacerbated by stark income disparities.[48] UNODC research shows that economic factors play an important role in the evolution of crime trends. Out of a total of 15 countries examined, statistical modelling suggested some overall association between economic changes and three conventional crime types in 12 countries.[49]

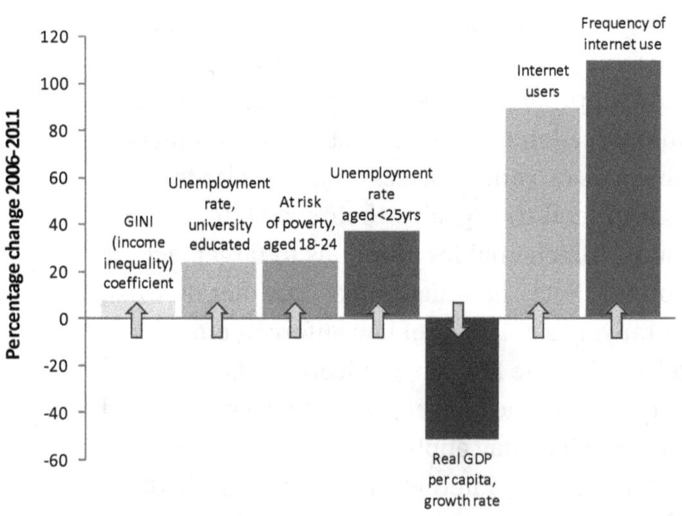

Figure 2.8 Socio-economic changes and frequency of internet use in one Eastern European country 2006–2011
Source: Eurostat and ITU World Telecommunication ICT Indicators 2012

Socio-economic factors may also play an important role in increases in cybercrime. Pressure on private sector enterprises to cut spending and to reduce staffing levels can lead, for example, to reductions in security, and to opportunities for exploitation of ICT weaknesses.[50] As firms are forced to hire in outside or temporary contractors, or employees become disgruntled by lower wages and fear of job loss, the risk both of lone criminal actions and influence by organized criminal groups over company 'insiders' may increase.[51] Some cybersecurity companies have expressed concern that former employees who have been made redundant pose one a possible threat during periods of economic downturn.[52] Increasingly large numbers of unemployed or underemployed graduate students with computing skills have also been reported to offer potential new resources for organized crime.[53]

The role of socio-economic factors in cybercrime is not limited to the developed world. Rather, it is equally applicable in the developing country context. In one country in Western Africa, for example, studies on the socio-demographic characteristics of *yahooboys*[54] show that many are university students who view online fraud as a means of economic sustenance.[55] Unemployment, in particular, is identified as a crucial factor luring youths to *yahooboyism*.[56] Studies in another country in Africa similarly highlight that '*Sakawa*' boys engaged in internet fraud frequently justify their activities as being the only way that they can survive in the absence of employment.[57]

The contemporary growth of cybercrime is important due to its impact and threat on multiple levels. Asked about the threat of cybercrime, law enforcement officials referred to a range of impacts. These included the fact that some cybercrime acts, such as online fraud and identity-theft, represent a threat because they are very common, producing an aggregate impact from the volume of offending and cumulative effects. Chapter Two (The global picture) of this Study examines the extent of the financial impact of cybercrime on individuals and companies. Such acts may also generate resources for organized criminal groups that may be used to support further crimes. Other cybercrime acts, such as the creation of illegal computer-misuse tools, may be quite rare, but pose a significant threat because individual incidents may cause great harm. A third category includes offences which cause harm to individuals, such as the creation and online dissemination of child pornography.[58]

Describing Cybercrime

KEY RESULTS

- 'Definitions' of cybercrime mostly depend upon the purpose of using the term
- A limited number of acts against the confidentiality, integrity and availability of computer data or systems represent the core of cybercrime
- Computer-related acts for personal or financial gain or harm, including forms of identity-related crime, and computer content-related acts do not lend themselves easily to efforts to arrive at legal definitions of the aggregate term
- Certain definitions are required for the core of cybercrime acts. However, a 'definition' of cybercrime is not as relevant for other purposes, such as defining the scope of specialized investigative and international cooperation powers, which are better focused on electronic evidence for any crime, rather than a broad, artificial 'cybercrime' construct

A comprehensive Study on cybercrime must be clear on the range of acts that are included in the term. The word 'cybercrime' itself is not amenable to a single definition, and is likely best considered as a *collection* of acts or conduct, rather than one single act. Nonetheless, the basic content of the term can be described—at least for the purposes of this Study—by a non-exhaustive list of acts that constitute cybercrime. These acts can, in turn, be organized into categories based on the material offence object and *modus operandi*.

The Term 'Cybercrime'

Numerous academic works have attempted to define 'cybercrime.'[59] National legislation, however, does not appear concerned with a strict definition of the word. Out of almost 200 items of national legislation cited by countries in response to the Study questionnaire, fewer than five per cent used the word 'cybercrime' in the title or scope of legislative provisions.[60] Rather, legislation more commonly referred to *'computer crimes,'*[61] *'electronic communications,'*[62] *'information technologies,'*[63] or *'high-tech crime.'*[64] In practice, many of these pieces of legislation created criminal offences that are included in the concept of cybercrime, such as unauthorized access to a computer system, or interference with a computer system or data. Where national legislation did specifically use cybercrime in the title of an act or section (such as 'Cybercrime Act'), the definitional section of the legislation rarely included a definition for the word 'cybercrime.'[65] When the term 'cybercrime' *was* included as a legal definition, a common approach was to define it simply as *'the crimes referred to in this law.'*[66]

In a similar manner, very few international or regional legal instruments define cybercrime. Neither the Council of Europe Cybercrime Convention, the League of Arab States Convention, nor the Draft African Union Convention, for example, contain a definition of cybercrime for the purposes of the instrument. The Commonwealth of Independent States Agreement, without using the term 'cybercrime,'[67] defines an 'offence relating to computer information' as a *'criminal act of which the target is computer information.'*[68] Similarly, the Shanghai Cooperation Organization Agreement defines 'information offences' as *'the use of information resources and (or) the impact on them in the informational sphere for illegal purposes.'*[69]

The definitional approaches apparent from national, international and regional instruments inform the method adopted by this Study. The Study does not seek to 'define' cybercrime *per se*. Rather, it identifies a list, or 'basket,' of acts which could constitute cybercrime. This has the advantage of placing the focus on careful description of the precise conduct to be criminalized. As such, the word 'cybercrime' itself may be better *not* considered as a legal term of art.[70] It is notable that this is equivalent to the approach adopted by international instruments such as the United Nations Convention against Corruption.[71] This instrument does not define 'corruption,' but rather obliges States Parties to criminalize a specific set of conduct which can be more effectively described.[72] 'Cybercrime' is therefore best considered as a *collection* of acts or conduct.

Describing Surrounding Concepts

It is also instructive to examine descriptions of surrounding concepts, such as 'computer,' 'computer system,' 'data' and 'information.' Their meaning is inherent to understanding the objects and/or protected legal interests which cybercrime acts concern. A review of international and regional instruments shows two main approaches: (i) terminology based on 'computer' data or system; and (ii) terminology based on 'information' data or system.[73] Analysis of the elements of the definitions, however, suggests that the terms might be considered as largely interchangeable. The figure shows common elements from these definitions. While nomenclature varies, a number of core concepts are consistent.

Computer/information system

- Device [or interconnected devices] which [pursuant to a computer/information program] perform(s) [[automatic] processing of computer data/information] [logical/arithmetic/storage functions] [including computer data/information stored/processed/retrieved/transmitted by the computer/information system] [including any communications facility or equipment] [including the internet]

Computer/information program

- Instructions [in machine readable form] that [enable a computer/information system to [process computer data/information] [perform a function/operation]] [can be executed by a computer/information system]

Computer data/information

- Representation of facts/information/concepts [in a machine readable form] [suitable for processing by a computer/information program [or a computer/information system]] [including a computer/information program]

The core feature of legal descriptions of 'computer', 'computer system' or 'information system', for example, is that the device must be 'capable of processing computer data or information.'[74] Some approaches specify that the processing must be 'automatic,' or 'high speed,' or 'pursuant to a program.'[75] Some approaches extend the definition to devices that store or transmit and receive computer data or information.[76] Others include within the definition the computer data that is processed by the system.[77] Where the term 'computer system' or 'information system' excludes data stored in the system or in other storage devices, these are often handled separately in the substantive legal provisions of the instrument.[78] While some instruments define both 'computer' and 'computer system,' the latter normally includes the former, and the context of the use of both terms in the instrument suggests that no meaningful difference arises in practice.[79] Other instruments define both 'computer network' and 'computer system.'[80] Again, it is possible that the latter includes the former, and there does not appear to be a distinguishable difference in use within the instrument itself.

International and regional cybercrime legal instruments are predominantly 'technology-neutral' in their text. They do not specifically list devices that might be considered as computer systems or information systems. In most contexts, this approach is considered good practice, insofar as it mitigates the risk of new technologies falling outside of legal provisions and the need for continuous updating of legislation.[81] Based on the core concept of processing computer data or information, it is likely that provisions typically apply to devices such as mainframe and computer servers, desktop personal computers, laptop computers, smartphones, tablet devices, and on-board computers in transport and machinery, as well as multimedia devices such as printers, MP3 players, digital cameras, and gaming machines.[82] Under the concept of 'processing computer data or information,' it is strongly arguable that any device, such as a wireless or fixed router, that connects to the internet is also included. Storage devices such as hard disk drives, USB memory sticks or flash cards may or may not strictly be part of the 'computer system' or 'information system.' But, where they are not, they can still be relevant objects through separate legal provisions.

Only one international or regional instrument attempts a 'lower technology' limit on the description of a computer system—stating that the term does not include an *'automated typewriter or typesetter, a portable hand held calculator, or other similar device.'*[83] As the world moves towards an 'internet of things' and nano-computing, descriptions such as 'computer system' or 'information system' will likely need to be interpreted as encompassing a greater range of devices.[84] In principle, however, the core concept of 'automated processing of information' would likely be sufficiently flexible to include, for instance, a monitoring and control smart chip with NFC and IP connectivity, built into a household appliance.

'Computer data' or 'computer information' is commonly described as a *'representation of facts, information or concepts that can be read, processed, or stored by a computer.'* Some approaches clarify that this includes a computer program.[85] Others are silent on the point. The difference between the formulations 'machine-readable' and 'can be read, processed or stored by a computer system (or information system)' is likely of a semantic nature only. In practice, computer data or information likely includes data or information stored on physical storage media (such as hard disk drives, USB memory sticks or flash cards), data or information stored in the memory of a computer system or information system, data or information transmissions (whether wired, optical, or radio frequency), and physical displays of data or information, such as in printout form or on a device screen.

While recognizing the use of different approaches to terminology, this Study makes use of the terms 'computer system' and 'computer data,' which it treats as equivalent to 'information system' and 'computer information.'

Categories of Cybercrime

While the term 'cybercrime' is not amenable to a single description, the question arises whether cybercrime objectives, features, or *modus operandi* can be identified in general terms, rather than (or in addition to) by reference to a list of individual cybercrime acts. As noted above, one example of this approach is found in the Commonwealth of Independent States Agreement, which describes an *'offence relating to computer information'* as a *'criminal act of which the target is computer information.'*[86] The Shanghai Cooperation Organization Agreement (more broadly) describes *'information offences'* as *'the use of information resources and (or) the impact on them in the informational sphere for illegal purposes.'* The Council of Europe Cybercrime Convention—although not by way of defined terms—uses broad criminalization headings, including *'offences against the confidentiality, integrity and availability of computer data and systems,' 'computer-related offences'* and *'content-related offences.'*[87] The Draft African Union Convention similarly uses criminalization chapter headings that make a distinction between *'offences specific to information and communication technologies'* and *'adapting certain offences to information and communication technologies.'*[88]

It is clear from these approaches that a number of general features could be used to describe cybercrime acts. One approach is to focus on the material offence *object*—that is, on the person, thing, or value against which the offence is directed.[89] This approach is seen in the Commonwealth of Independent States Agreement (where the offence object is computer information) and also in Title One of the substantive criminal law chapter of the Council of Europe Cybercrime Convention (where the objects are computer data or computer systems). Another approach is to consider whether computer systems or information systems form an integral part of the *modus operandi* of the offence.[90] This approach is also seen in Titles Two, Three and Four of the substantive criminal law chapter of the Council of Europe Cybercrime Convention, as well as in the Shanghai Cooperation Organization Agreement, and the Draft African Union Convention. Identifying possible cybercrime offence objects and *modus operandi* does not describe cybercrime acts in their entirety, but it can provide a number of useful general categories into which acts may be broadly classified.

Some international or regional instruments concern cybercrime only in the narrower conception of the computer system or data as the offence object.[91] Others address a broader range of offences, including acts where the offence object is a person or value, rather than a computer system or data—but where a computer system or information system is nonetheless an integral part of the *modus operandi* of the offence.[92] Chapter Four (Criminalization) examines the specific acts criminalized by such instruments in detail. While not all international or regional instruments use a broad conception of cybercrime, the approach taken by this Study aims to be as comprehensive as possible. It thus makes use of a wide list of cybercrime act descriptions, broadly organized in three categories based on the offence object and *modus operandi*. Due to the use of two methods of classification, some degree of overlap may exist between the categories.

Acts Constituting Cybercrime

The figure below proposes 14 acts that may constitute cybercrime, organized in three broad categories. Annex One to this Study provides a more detailed description for each act. This list of acts was also used in the questionnaire sent to states, private sector entities, and intergovernmental and academic organizations for information gathering for the Study.[93] The purpose of the list is to introduce a tentative set of acts that may be included in the term 'cybercrime,' with a view to establishing a basis for analysis throughout the Study. The list is not intended to be exhaustive. In addition, the terms used—and the accompanying descriptions in Annex One—are not intended to represent legal definitions. Rather, they are broad 'act descriptions' that may be used as a starting point for analysis and discussion. While this Study does not 'define' cybercrime (either with a definition attached to the term itself, or by a 'definitive' list of acts), the conduct listed may nonetheless be considered as the basic content for the meaning of the term, at least for the purposes of this Study.[94]

It should be noted, at this stage, that the ubiquity of the internet and personal computer devices means that computer systems or computer data can be ancillary—at least in developed countries—to almost any

Acts against the confidentiality, integrity and availability of computer data or systems

- Illegal access to a computer system
- Illegal access, interception or acquisition of computer data
- Illegal interference with a computer system or computer data
- Production, distribution or possession of computer misuse tools
- Breach of privacy or data protection measures

Computer-related acts for personal or financial gain or harm

- Computer-related fraud or forgery
- Computer-related identity offences
- Computer-related copyright or trademark offences
- Sending or controlling sending of Spam
- Computer-related acts causing personal harm
- Computer-related solicitation or 'grooming' of children

Computer content-related acts

- Computer-related acts involving hate speech
- Computer-related production, distribution or possession of child pornography
- Computer-related acts in support of terrorism offences

criminal offence. Closely related to cybercrime therefore, but conceptually distinct, is the domain of electronic evidence. The collection and presentation of electronic evidence is integral to the investigation and prosecution of cybercrime. Increasingly this is also the case for conventional crimes such as robbery, theft, or burglary, as well as for forms of organized crime. Computerized telephone records, emails, IP connection logs, SMS messages, mobile telephone address books, and computer files may all contain evidence of the location, motive, crime scene presence, or criminal involvement of a suspect in almost any form of crime.

'Operation Aurora'

In 2010, a series of online attacks were reported by several high-profile software companies, and, ultimately, breaches were recorded at a large search engine firm. Using a zero-day vulnerability in a web browser, the attackers created a tunnel into an internal network via employees' compromised workstations, and gained access to e-mail accounts and inadequately secured source code repositories.

The same year, users of a social networking site received e-mails from a fake account with links to a fictitious new login system appearing to be from the company, with the victim's username already entered in the login system. Users' credentials would then be compromised, and the infected host could potentially become a member of the ZeuS botnet.

Source: Trustwave. 2011. SpiderLabs Global Security Report.

Acts Against the Confidentiality, Integrity and Availability of Computer Data or Systems

The core list of cybercrime acts have as their object a computer system or computer data. Basic actions include unauthorized access, interception, acquisition, or interference with a computer system or data. Chapter Four (Criminalization) examines these further, both from a sample of national laws, and from international and regional instruments. These acts may be committed using many different *modus operandi*. Illegal access to a computer system, for example, may consist of the unauthorized use of a discovered password, or remote access using exploit software.[95] The latter may also constitute interference with computer data and/or a computer system. Individual acts can thus show a degree of overlap across offence 'baskets.' The first category also includes acts related to tools that can be used to carry out acts against computer systems or data.[96] Finally, the category includes criminal acts related to the (mis)handling of computer data in accordance with specified requirements.

Computer-Related Acts for Personal or Financial Gain or Harm

The second category focuses on acts for which the use of a computer system is inherent to the *modus operandi*. The object of such acts differs. In the case of computer-related fraud, the object may be considered as the economic property targeted. In the case of computer-related copyright or trademark offences, the offence object may be considered as the protected intellectual property right. In the case of computer-related acts causing personal harm, such as the use of a computer system to harass, bully, threaten, stalk or to cause fear or intimidation of an individual, or 'grooming' of a child, the offence object may be regarded as the individual targeted.

The '*Gozi*' virus

In early 2013, three European men were charged by North American prosecutors with the creation and distribution of a computer virus that infected more than a million computers worldwide, enabling them to access personal bank information and steal at least 50 million dollars in the period between 2005 and 2011. The virus was introduced in Europe and spread to North America, where it also infected computers belonging to national agencies. Extradition proceedings against two of the accused are under way. The case is said to be '*one of the most financially destructive yet seen*.'

Soure: http://www.fbi.gov/

The view that a diverse range of acts with different material offence objects can nonetheless be considered 'cybercrime' is supported by preliminary work on the development of a framework for an international classification of crimes for statistical purposes. Work by the Conference of European Statisticians notes that acts of 'cybercrime' could be recorded, for statistical purposes, by the use of an 'attribute tag' that would indicate the 'computer-facilitation' of a particular act within a (full) crime classification system. Such a 'tag' could apply, in principle, to computer-facilitated acts falling anywhere within the larger crime classification system—whether acts against the person, acts against property, or acts against public order or authority.[97]

A challenge concerning 'computer-related' cybercrime acts is that the category risks being expanded to include a broad range of otherwise 'offline' crimes, when committed with the use or help of a computer system. The question of whether this type of act should be considered 'cybercrime' remains somewhat open. While some international or regional instruments are limited to a comparatively few number of computer-related offences, others are expansive. The Council of Europe Cybercrime Convention, for example, covers (from this category) computer-related forgery and computer-related fraud alone.[98] In contrast, the League of Arab States Model Law contains criminal provisions on the use of a computer system for forgery, threats, blackmail, appropriating moveable property or a deed through fraudulent use of a name, unlawfully obtaining the numbers or particulars of a credit card, unlawfully benefiting from communication services, establishing an (internet) site with the intention of trafficking in human beings, narcotic drugs or psychotropic substances, and transferring illicit funds or disguising their illicit origin.[99]

Another act that may fit into this category—and, in contrast to those acts previously discussed, is exclusively cyber-related—is the sending and controlling of the sending of spam.[100] While the sending of spam is prohibited by all internet service providers, it is not universally criminalized by countries. Chapter Four (Criminalization) examines this area further.

Computer Content-Related Acts

The final category of cybercrime acts concerns computer content—the words, images, sounds and representations transmitted or stored by computer systems, including the internet. The material offence object in content-related offences is often a person, an identifiable group of persons, or a widely held value or belief. In the same way as the second category, these acts could in principle be committed 'offline,' as well as through the use of computer systems. Nonetheless, many international and regional cybercrime instruments include specific provisions on computer content.[101] One argument for the inclusion of content-related acts within the term 'cybercrime' is that computer systems, including the internet, have fundamentally altered the scope and reach of dissemination of information.[102]

The possession or dissemination of a range of content expressed via computer systems may be considered as criminal conduct by countries. In this respect, it is important to note that, in addition to the principle of state sovereignty, a key starting point enshrined in international human rights treaties is the right to freedom of opinion and expression.[103] From this starting point, international law *permits* certain necessary restrictions as provided for by law.[104] International law further *obliges* states to prohibit certain exceptional types of expression, including child pornography, direct and public incitement to commit genocide, forms of hate speech, and incitement to terrorism.[105] Chapter Four (Criminalization) examines national, international and regional approaches to the criminalization of computer content, including from an international human rights law perspective, in detail.

Computer-related acts in support of terrorism offences are included in the content-related cybercrime category. The recent UNODC publication 'The use of the Internet for terrorist purposes'[106] observes that computer systems may be used for a range of acts that promote and support terrorism. These include propaganda (including recruitment, radicalization and incitement to terrorism); financing; training; planning (including through secret communication and open-source information); execution; and cyberattacks.[107] The questionnaire used for information gathering for this Study referred directly to computer-related incitement to terrorism, terrorist financing offences and terrorist planning offences.[108] As such, this Study concerns only on the computer *content* aspect of terrorism offences and excludes the threat of cyberattacks by terrorist organizations from the scope of the analysis—an approach equivalent to that of the UNODC publication on the use of the internet for terrorist purposes.

Other Cybercrime Acts

The list of 14 cybercrime acts is not exhaustive. During information gathering for the Study, countries were invited to identify other acts that they considered to also constitute cybercrime.[109] Responses included *'computer-related tools for facilitating illegal acts related to financial instruments and means of payment'*; *'online gambling'*; *'use of an information technology device for the purposes of trafficking in persons'*; *'computer-related drug trafficking'*; *'computer-related extortion'*; *'trafficking in passwords'*; and *'access to classified information.'*[110] In all of these cases, respondents said that the act was

Conspiracy for preparation of a terrorist act

In May 2012, a Western European court sentenced one of its nationals to five years of imprisonment for participation in a criminal conspiracy for the preparation of a terrorist act. At trial, the prosecution presented dozens of decrypted e-mail communications of jihadist content, which were, among others, sent to the website of the President of the country, and traced back to a member of a globally operating extremist group. A preservation order enabled the authorities to identify communication between the extremist group's member and extremist websites, including a website with the stated goal of hosting and disseminating the extremist group's documents, audio and video recordings, statements from warlords and suicide attackers and the materials of other extremist groups. This indicated that the defendant actively performed, *inter alia*, the translation, encryption, compression and password-protection of pro-jihadist materials, which he then uploaded and circulated via the internet; and taking concrete steps to provide financial support to extremist group, including through the attempted use of PayPal and other virtual payment systems. The court found the required sufficient evidence to demonstrate that the defendant had provided not merely intellectual support, but also direct logistical support to a clearly identified terrorist plan.

Source: UNODC. 2012. Use of the internet for terrorist purposes.

covered by cyber-specific legislation—indicating the centrality of the use of computer systems or data to the act.

In some of these cases, the act may be considered as a specialized form or variation of one of the cybercrime acts already listed. Use or possession of computer-related tools for financial offences, for example, may be covered by the broad act of computer-related fraud or forgery.[111] Access to classified information may be a subset of illegal access to computer data in general. Trafficking in passwords is covered by some computer misuse tool provisions.[112]

Other acts, such as computer-related extortion,[113] raise the challenge of the inclusion (or non-inclusion) of offline crimes that have, to varying extents, migrated online—a point discussed briefly in the context of computer-related acts for personal or financial gain or harm.

The internet and illicit drug sales

Since the mid-1990s, the internet has increasingly been used by drug traffickers to sell illicit drugs or the chemical precursors required to manufacture such drugs. At the same time, illegal internet pharmacies advertise illicit sales in prescription medicines, including substances under international control, to the general public. These substances are controlled under the three international drug control treaties and include opioid analgesics, central nervous system stimulants, tranquillizers and other psychoactive substances. Many pharmaceuticals offered for sale in this way are either diverted from the licit market or are counterfeit or fraudulent—constituting a danger to the health of consumers. The fact that illegal internet pharmacies conduct their operations from all regions of the world and are able to relocate their business easily when a website is closed down means that taking effective measures in this area is essential.

In 2009, the International Narcotics Control Board (INCB) published 'Guidelines for Governments on Preventing the Illegal Sale of Internationally Controlled Substances through the Internet.' These Guidelines highlight the importance of: empowering appropriate authorities to investigate and take legal action against internet pharmacies and other websites, that are used in the illegal sale of internationally controlled substances; prohibiting shipment by mail of internationally controlled substances and ensuring that such shipments are intercepted; and establishing standards of good professional practice for the provision of pharmaceutical services via the internet.

As noted by a number of responding countries, a general principle is frequently that *'what is illegal offline, is also illegal online.'*[114] In many cases, criminal laws regulating offline conduct can also be applied to online versions of the same conduct. Thus, countries have, for example, interpreted existing conventional laws to cover computer-related extortion,[115] or the use of computer systems to facilitate trafficking in persons.[116] National legal practice in this respect is examined further in Chapter Four (Criminalization).

One approach may be to include in a description of 'cybercrime' only those acts where the use of a computer system is strictly integral to fundamentally altering the scope or nature of the otherwise 'offline' act.[117] Drawing the line here is extremely challenging. Is it appropriate to argue, for example, that the use of computer systems is fundamentally a 'game-changer' when it comes to the nature and extent of consumer fraud, but not for trafficking in narcotic drugs? Is the use of online financial services to conceal the origin of criminal profit[118] significantly different from traditional financial transactions to require the definition of a separate offence of computer-related money-laundering? To some extent, the list of 14 acts presented in this Study represents an attempt to distil contemporary practice in terms of those acts that are commonly spoken of as 'cybercrime.'

Other acts referred to by countries, in particular online gambling, are not consistently criminalized across countries. The act of gambling through the internet is allowed in many countries, but is prohibited directly or indirectly in other countries.[119] Irrespective of its legal status, internet gambling sites may frequently be the subject or object of computer-related fraud or computer data interception or interference.[120] Within the general term 'online gambling,' a distinction is sometimes made between the internet as a mere communication medium—akin to remote telecommunication gambling on a physical world event—and the case of a 'virtual' casino in which the player has no means of verifying the results of the game.[121] The latter, in particular, is often seen as distinct from offline gambling, due to its potential for compulsive engagement, fraud,[122] and abuse by minors. In accordance with the principle of national sovereignty, at least one regional approach recognizes the right for countries to set the objectives of their policy on betting and gambling according to their own scale of values and to define proportionate restrictive measures.[123] The inclusion of online gambling in a general description of cybercrime may thus face challenges concerning the universality of its criminalization.

Discussion

It is notable that responding countries did not identify a large range of conduct outside of the 14 cybercrime acts listed in the Study questionnaire. Some degree of consensus may therefore exist on at least a core of conduct included in the term 'cybercrime.'

Nonetheless, as discussed in this Study, the determination of whether it is necessary to include specific conduct in a description of 'cybercrime' depends, to a large extent, on the *purpose* of using the term 'cybercrime' in the first place.

From the international legal perspective, the content of the term is particularly relevant when it comes to agreements for international cooperation. One feature of international and regional cybercrime instruments, for example, is the inclusion of specialized investigative powers not usually found in non-cyber specific instruments.[124] States parties to instruments agree to make such powers available to other States parties through mutual legal assistance requests. While some instruments have a broad scope that enables the use of such powers for the gathering of electronic evidence for *any* criminal offence,[125] others limit the scope of international cooperation and investigative powers to 'cybercrime', or 'offences relating to computer information.'[126] In the international sphere, conceptions of 'cybercrime' may thus have implications for the availability of investigative powers and access to extraterritorial electronic evidence. Chapter Seven (International cooperation) examines this area in detail.

As the world moves towards universal internet access, it may be that conceptions of cybercrime will need to operate on a number of levels: specific and detailed in the case of the definition of certain individual cybercrime acts, but sufficiently broad to ensure that investigative powers and international cooperation mechanisms can be applied, with effective safeguards, to the continued migration of offline crime to online variants.

Notes

1. International Telecommunication Union, 2012. *Measuring the Information Society, and World Telecommunication/ICT Indicators Database.* See also Moore, R., Guntupalli, N.T., and Lee, T., 2010. Parental regulation and online activities: Examining factors that influence a youth's potential to become a victim of online harassment. *International Journal of Cyber Criminology,* 4(1&2):685–698.
2. European Commission, 2012. *Special Eurobarometer 390: Cyber Security Report.* See also Fawn, T. and Paternoster, R., 2011. Cybercrime Victimization: An examination of individual and situational level factors. *International Journal of Cyber Criminology,* 5(1):773–793, 782.
3. International Telecommunication Union, 2012. *Measuring the Information Society, and World Telecommunication/ICT Indicators Database.*
4. Ericsson, 2012. *Traffic and Market Report.*
5. Global System for Mobile Communications/Enhanced Data rates for GSM Evolution, or EGPRS.

6. Wideband Code Division Multiple Access/High Speed Packet Access.
7. International Telecommunication Union, 2012. *The State of Broadband 2012: Achieving Digital Inclusion For All.*
8. European Commission, 2012. *Digital Agenda: Commission consults on rules for wirelessly connected devices—the 'Internet of Things.'* Available at: http://ec.europa.eu/yourvoice/ipm/forms/dispatch?form=IoTGovernance
9. Radio-frequency identification and Near field communication.
10. Commonwealth Telecommunications Organisation, 2012. *The Socio-Economic Impact of Broadband in sub-Saharan Africa: The Satellite Advantage.*
11. World Bank, 2009. *Information and Communications for Development: Extending Reach and Increasing Impact.*
12. World Bank, 2012. *Information and Communications for Development: Maximizing Mobile.*
13. International Telecommunication Union, 2012. *The State of Broadband 2012: Achieving Digital Inclusion For All.*
14. World Economic Forum, 2012. *The Global Information Technology Report 2012: Living in a Hyperconnected World.*
15. Commonwealth Telecommunications Organisation, 2012. *The Socio-Economic Impact of Broadband in sub-Saharan Africa: The Satellite Advantage.*
16. World Economic Forum, 2012. *The Global Information Technology Report 2012: Living in a Hyperconnected World.*
17. Regarding related challenges, see Slivka, R.T., and Darrow, J.W., 1975. Methods and Problems in Computer Security. *Rutgers Journal of Computers and Law,* 5:217.
18. United States Congress, 1977. *Bill S.1766, The Federal Computer Systems Protection Act,* 95th Congress, 1st Session., 123 Cong. Rec. 20, 953 (1977).
19. Glyn, E.A., 1983. Computer Abuse: The Emerging Crime and the Need for Legislation. *Fordham Urban Law Journal,* 12(1):73–101.
20. Schmidt, W.E., 1981. Legal Proprietary Interests in Computer Programs: The American Experience. *Jurimetrics Journal,* 21:345.
21. United Nations, 1994. *UN Manual on the Prevention and Control of Computer Related Crime.*
22. INTERPOL, 1979. *Third INTERPOL Symposium on International Fraud,* Paris 11–13 December 1979.
23. Including computer-related acts involving racism or xenophobia, or computer-related production, distribution, or possession of child pornography.
24. Including computer-related identity offences, and computer-related copyright and trademark offences.
25. Study cybercrime questionnaire. Q83.
26. *Ibid.*
27. Some approaches hold that cybercrime is narrower than 'computer-related' crime, insofar as cybercrime is said to require the involvement of a computer *network*—thereby excluding crimes committed using a stand-alone computer system. While focusing on the feature of connectivity, this Study does not strictly

exclude stand-alone or closed computer systems from the scope of cybercrime. Thus, the term 'cybercrime' is used to describe a range of offences including traditional computer crimes, as well as network crimes.

28. Study cybercrime questionnaire. Q83.
29. In 2016 the gigabyte equivalent of all movies ever made will cross global IP networks every 3 minutes. Cisco, 2012. *Cisco Visual Networking Index, 2011-2016.*
30. Study cybercrime questionnaire. Q84.
31. *Salvador Declaration on Comprehensive Strategies for Global Challenges,* annex to United Nations General Assembly Resolution A/Res/65/230 on the *Twelfth United Nations Congress on Crime Prevention and Criminal Justice,* 1 April 2011, para.39.
32. United Nations Statistical Commission, 2012. *National Institute of Statistics and Geography of Mexico Report on Crime Statistics.* Note by the Secretary General E/CN.3/2012/3, 6 December 2011.
33. UNODC calculations from Dow Jones Factiva.
34. Study cybercrime questionnaire. Q84. Due to variable preparation and release times for official statistics, this may refer to the time period of 2007 to 2011 or 2006 to 2010 ('the last five years').
35. *Ibid.*
36. Yar, M., 2005. The novelty of 'cybercrime': An assessment in light of routine activity theory. *European Journal of Criminology,* 2(4):407-427.
37. Koops, B.J., 2010. The Internet and its Opportunities for Crime. *In:* Herzog-Evans, M., (ed.) *Transnational Criminology Manual.* Nijmegen, Netherlands: WLP, pp.735-754.
38. Jaishankar. K., 2011. Expanding Cyber Criminology with an Avant-Garde Anthology. *In:* Jaishankar, K., (ed.) *Cyber Criminology: Exploring Internet Crimes and Criminal Behaviour.* Boca Raton, FL: CRC Press, Taylor & Francis Group.
39. Kigerl, A., 2012. Routine Activity Theory and the Determinants of High Cybercrime Countries. *Social Science Computer Review,* 30(4):470-486, 470.
40. *Ibid.*
41. For an overview and further references, see *ibid.* p.473; Hutchings, A., Hennessey, H., 2009. Routine activity theory and phishing victimization: Who got caught in the 'net'? *Current Issues in Criminal Justice,* 20(3):433-451; Pratt, T.C., Holtfreter, K., Reisig, M.D., 2010. Routine online activity and internet fraud targeting: Extending the generality of routine activity theory. *Journal of Research in Crime and Delinquency,* 47(3):267-296.
42. Holt, T.J., Burruss, G.W., Bossler, A.M., 2010. Social Learning and Cyber Deviance: Examining the Importance of a Full Social Learning Model in the Virtual World. *Journal of Crime and Justice,* 33(2):31-61.
43. Skinner, W.F., Fream, A.M., 1997. A Social Learning Theory Analysis of Computer Crime among College Students. *Journal of Research in Crime and Delinquency,* 34(4):495-518.
44. BAE Systems Detica and John Grieve Centre for Policing and Security, London Metropolitan University, 2012. *Organised Crime in the Digital Age.*
45. A number of Twitter feeds, for example, either purport to represent individuals associated with hacking groups such as Anonymous or Lulzsec, or the organizations themselves.

46. World Economic Forum, 2011. *Outlook on the Global Agenda 2011.*
47. World Economic Forum, 2012. *Global Risk Report 2012.*
48. *Ibid*, citing Credit Suisse Research Institute, 2011. *Global Wealth Report 2011.*
49. UNODC, 2011. *Monitoring the Impact of Economic Crisis on Crime.*
50. BAE Systems Detica and John Grieve Centre for Policing and Security, London Metropolitan University, 2012. *Organised Crime in the Digital Age.*
51. *Ibid.*
52. McAfee, 2009. *Unsecured Economies: Protecting Vital Information.*
53. BAE Systems Detica and John Grieve Centre for Policing and Security, London Metropolitan University, 2012. *Organised Crime in the Digital Age.*
54. The sub-culture of '*yahooboys*' describes youths, especially those living in cities, who make use of the internet for acts of computer-related fraud, phishing and scamming. Adeniran, A.I., 2011. Café Culture and Heresy of Yahooboyism. *In:* Jaishankar, K., (ed.) *Cyber Criminology: Exploring Internet Crimes and Criminal Behaviour.* Boca Raton, FL: CRC Press, Taylor & Francis Group.
55. Adeniran, A.I., 2008. The Internet and Emergence of Yahooboys sub-Culture. *International Journal of Cyber Criminology*, 2 (2):368–381; and Aransiola, J.O., Asindemade, S.O., 2011. Understanding Cybercrime Perpetrators and the Strategies They Employ. *Cyberpsychology, Behaviour and Social Networking*, 14(12):759.
56. *Ibid.*
57. Warner, J., 2011. Understanding Cybercrime: A View from Below. *International Journal of Cyber Criminology*, 5(1):736–749.
58. Study cybercrime questionnaire. Q81.
59. Among various others, International Telecommunication Union, 2011. *Understanding Cybercrime: A Guide for Developing Countries*; Explanatory Report to the Council of Europe Cybercrime Convention, ETS No. 185; Pocar, F., 2004. New challenges for international rules against cyber-crime. *European Journal on Criminal Policy and Research,* 10(1):27–37; Wall, D.S., 2007. *Cybercrime: The Transformation of Crime in the Information Age.* Cambridge: Polity Press.
60. Study cybercrime questionnaire. Q12.
61. See, for example, Malaysia, Computer Crimes Act 1997; Sri Lanka, Computer Crime Act 2007; Sudan, Computer Crimes Act 2007.
62. See, for example, Albania, Electronic Communications in the Republic of Albania, Law no. 9918 2008; France, Code des postes et des communications électroniques (version consolidée) 2012; Tonga, Communications Act 2000.
63. See, for example, India, The Information Technology Act 2000; Saudi Arabia, IT Criminal Act 2007; Bolivarian Republic of Venezuela, Ley Especial contra los Delitos Informáticos 2001; Vietnam, Law on Information Technology 2007.
64. See, for example, Serbia, Law on Organization and Competence of Government Authorities for Combating High-Tech Crime 2010.

65. See, for example, Botswana, Cybercrime and Computer Related Crimes Act 2007; Bulgaria, Chapter 9, Criminal Code SG No. 92/2002; Cambodia, Draft Cybercrime Law 2012; Jamaica, Cybercrimes Act 2010; Namibia, Computer Misuse and Cybercrime Act 2003; Senegal, Law No. 2008-11 on Cybercrime 2008.
66. See for example, Oman, Royal Decree No 12/2011 issuing the Cybercrime Law; Philippines, Cybercrime Prevention Act 2012.
67. The original agreement is in Russian language and uses the term 'преступление в сфере компьютерной информации,' rather than the contemporary equivalent to 'cybercrime': 'киберпреступности.'
68. Commonwealth of Independent States Agreement, Art. 1(a).
69. Shanghai Cooperation Organization Agreement, Annex 1.
70. See also International Telecommunication Union, 2011. *Understanding Cybercrime: A guide for Developing Countries.*
71. United Nations. 2004. *Convention against Corruption.*
72. *Ibid.*, Arts. 15 et seq.
73. The Council of Europe Cybercrime Convention and the Commonwealth Model Law make use of the terms 'computer system' and 'computer data.' The Draft African Union Convention uses 'computer system' and 'computerized data.' The EU Decision on Attacks against Information Systems makes use of 'information system' and 'computer data.' The League of Arab States Convention makes use of 'information system' and 'data,' and the Commonwealth of Independent States Agreement uses 'computer information.'
74. See, for example, Council of Europe Cybercrime Convention, Art. 1.
75. See, for example, COMESA Draft Model Bill, Art.1 and ITU/CARICOM/CTU Model Legislative Texts, Art. 3.
76. Draft African Union Convention, Part III, Section 1, Art. III-1(6).
77. EU Decision on Attacks against Information Systems, Art. 1(a).
78. See, for example, Council of Europe Cybercrime Convention, Art. 19, procedural power for competent authorities to search or similarly access (a) a computer system or part of it and computer data stored therein; and (b) a computer-data storage medium in which computer data may be stored.
79. COMESA Draft Model Bill, Part 1, Art. 1(b) and (e).
80. League of Arab States Convention, Art. 2(5) and (6).
81. See, for example, Explanatory Report to the Council of Europe Cybercrime Convention, ETS No. 185.
82. A Guidance Note of the Council of Europe Cybercrime Convention Committee (T-CY) also reaches the conclusion that the definition of 'computer system' in Article 1(a) of the Council of Europe Cybercrime Convention covers developing forms of technology that go beyond traditional mainframe or desktop computer systems, such as modern mobile phones, smart phones, PDAs, tablets or similar. See Council of Europe. 2012. T-CY Guidance Note 1 on the notion of 'computer system.' T-CY (2012) 21, 14 November 2012.
83. COMESA Draft Model Bill, Part 1, Art. 1(b).
84. For a review of potential developments and regulatory challenges associated with the internet of things see European Union, 2009. Communication from the Commission to the European Parliament, the Council, the European Economic and Social Committee and the Committee of the Regions. *Internet of Things—An Action Plan for Europe.* COM (2009) 278 Final, 18 June 2009.

85. Council of Europe Cybercrime Convention, Art. 1(b).
86. Commonwealth of Independent States Agreement, Art. 1(a).
87. Council of Europe Cybercrime Convention, Titles 1, 2, and 3.
88. Draft African Union Convention, Part III, Chapter V, Section II, Chapters 1 and 2.
89. Those comprise offences against the confidentiality, integrity and availability of data and computer systems. See Calderoni, F., 2010. The European legal framework on cybercrime: striving for an effective implementation. *Crime, Law, and Social Change,* 54(5):339–357.
90. Podgor, E.S., 2002. International computer fraud: A paradigm for limiting national jurisdiction. *U.C. Davis Law Review*, 35(2):267–317, 273 et seq.
91. EU Decision on Attacks against Information Systems and Commonwealth of Independent States Agreement.
92. For instance, ECOWAS Draft Directive, Art. 17 (Facilitation of access of minors to child pornography, documents, sound or pornographic representation). See also Pocar, F., 2004. New challenges for international rules against cyber-crime. *European Journal on Criminal Policy and Research,* 10(1):27–37.
93. The draft questionnaire for information gathering was developed initially by the Secretariat based on the list of topics for inclusion in the Study approved by the expert group on cybercrime (contained in *Report of the open-ended intergovernmental expert group on the comprehensive Study of the problem of cybercrime* (E/CN.15/2011/19)). The draft questionnaire, including a first draft of cybercrime act descriptions, was sent to all countries for comment in 2011. Following incorporation by the Secretariat of comments received, the final questionnaire, including the list of acts presented here, was approved by the Bureau of the Expert Group on Cybercrime at its meeting on 19 January 2012.
94. In response to comments from countries, a number of amendments have been made to the list of acts presented in this Chapter, compared to that used in the Study questionnaire. In the Study questionnaire, the second category was entitled 'Computer-related acts for personal or financial gain.' This has been amended to 'Computer-related acts for personal or financial gain or harm.' In the Study questionnaire, the third category was entitled 'Specific computer-related acts.' This has been amended to 'Computer content-related acts.' The items 'Computer-related acts causing personal harm' and 'Computer-related solicitation or 'grooming' of children' have been moved from the third category to the second category. In addition, the questionnaire contained the item 'Computer-related acts involving racism or xenophobia.' This has been amended to the broader category 'Computer-related acts involving hate speech.'
95. United Nations, 1994. *UN Manual on the Prevention and Control of Computer Related Crime.*
96. Examples include Low orbit ion cannon (LOIC), sKyWIper and the ZeuS banking malware.
97. See United Nations Economic Commission for Europe, Conference of European Statisticians. *Principles and Framework for an International Classification of Crimes for Statistical Purposes.* ECE/CES/BUR/2011/NOV/8/Add.1. 11 October 2011.
98. Council of Europe Cybercrime Convention, Arts. 7 and 8.
99. League of Arab States Model Law, Articles 4, 9–12, and 17–19.

100. Sending or controlling sending of spam refers to acts involving the use of a computer system to send out messages to a large number of recipients without authorization or request. See Annex One (Act descriptions).
101. See Council of Europe Cybercrime Convention, Art. 9; League of Arab States Convention, Art. 12 et seq.; and ITU/CARICOM/CTU Model Legislative Texts, Section II, among others.
102. Marcus, R.L., 2008. The impact of computers on the legal profession: Evolution or revolution? *Northwestern University Law Review,* 102(4):1827–1868.
103. UDHR, Art. 19; ICCPR Art. 19; ECHR, Art. 9; ACHR Art. 13; ACHPR Art. 9.
104. Cassese, A., 2005. *International Law*. 2nd ed. Oxford: Oxford University Press. p.53. and pp.59 et seq.
105. United Nations General Assembly, 2011. *Promotion and protection of the right to freedom of opinion and expression. Report of the Special Rapporteur on the promotion and protection of the right to freedom of opinion and expression.* A/66/290. 10 August 2011.
106. UNODC, 2012. *The Use of the Internet for Terrorist Purposes.* Available at https://www.unodc.org/documents/frontpage/Use_of_Internet_for_Terrorist_Purposes.pdf
107. *Ibid.*
108. Study cybercrime questionnaire. Act Descriptions section. See also Annex One (Act descriptions).
109. Study cybercrime questionnaire. Q39.
110. *Ibid.*
111. Some countries, for example, include the act of 'possession of articles for use in frauds' within fraud criminal offences.
112. Computer passwords, access codes or similar data were not explicitly included in the act description for the item 'Production, distribution or possession of computer misuse tools' used in the Study questionnaire, leading some countries to identify this conduct as an additional act.
113. In addition to use of computer systems to communicate extortion-related threats, computer-related extortion can be associated with unauthorized interference with computer systems or data, such as demands for money linked to DDoS attacks.
114. Study cybercrime questionnaire. Q39.
115. See, for example, Landgericht Düsseldorf, Germany. 3 KLs 1/11, 22 March 2011, in which the accused was convicted of extortion and computer sabotage against online betting sites through the hired services of a botnet.
116. UN.GIFT, 2008. *The Vienna Forum to fight Human Trafficking. Background Paper for 017 Workshop: Technology and Human Trafficking.* Available at: http://www.unodc.org/documents/human-trafficking/2008/BP017TechnologyandHumanTrafficking.pdf The UNODC trafficking in persons database also includes a number of cases involving the use of placement of online advertisements, https://www.unodc.org/cld/index.jspx For further information, please see also https://www.unodc.org/unodc/en/human-trafficking/what-is-human-trafficking.html?ref=menuside
117. This may be applied, for instance, in terms of sexual abuse of children, when images created by offenders 'offline' are subsequently shared 'online' with networks of like-minded individuals—the additional acts

of distributing, receiving and collecting the material 'online' are new criminal offences. An overview of this exemplified scenario and further examples can be found in: UK Home Office, 2010. *Cyber Crime Strategy*. p.45.

118. Council of Europe Committee of Experts on the Evaluation of Anti-Money Laundering Measures and the Financing of Terrorism (MONEYVAL), 2012. *Criminal money flows on the Internet: methods, trends and multi-stakeholder counteraction.*
119. Fidelie, L.W., 2008. Internet Gambling: Innocent Activity or Cybercrime? *International Journal of Cyber Criminology*, 3(1):476–491; Yee Fen, H., 2011. Online Gaming: The State of Play in Singapore. *Singapore Academy of Law Journal*, 23:74.
120. See, for example, McMullan, J.L., Rege, A., 2010. Online Crime and Internet Gambling. *Journal of Gambling Issues*, 24:54–85.
121. Pereira de Sena, P., 2008. Internet Gambling Prohibition in Hong Kong: Law and Policy. *Hong Kong Law Journal*, 38(2):453–492.
122. See for example, European Court of Justice, *Sporting Exchange Ltd v Minister van Justitie*, Case C-203/08. para 34: *'Because of the lack of direct contact between consumer and operator, games of chance accessible via the internet involve different and more substantial risks of fraud by operators compared with the traditional market for such games.'*
123. *Ibid.* para 28.
124. Such powers include orders for stored computer data, real time collection of computer data, and expedited preservation of computer data. See, for instance, Draft African Union Convention, COMESA Draft Model Bill, Commonwealth Model Law, Council of Europe Cybercrime Convention, and League of Arab States Convention.
125. See, for example, Council of Europe Cybercrime Convention and League of Arab States Convention.
126. See, for example, Commonwealth of Independent States Agreement and Draft African Union Convention.

Credits

1. Copyright © MaxMind, Inc. (CC BY-SA 3.0) at http://dev.maxmind.com/geoip/legacy/geolite/.

Computers and Technological Crime

BY JAMES W. OSTERBURG, AND RICHARD H. WARD

Introduction

Rapid increases in technology, including computers, cell phones, data storage, digital imagery, and other forms of information technology (IT), have had a major impact on domestic and international communication, global business practices, and social interaction. With these changes have also come new forms of criminality, commonly referred to as *cybercrime* or *cyberterrorism*. The expansions of these relatively new forms of crime, some of which have been in existence for decades, have resulted in more specialized aspects of criminal investigation. In addition to the more traditional role of the detective, the emergence of crime and intelligence analysts has increased dramatically, and today virtually all federal agencies and larger police departments employ analysts, many of whom work directly with field operatives.

On the national level, the Federal Bureau of Investigation, the Department of Homeland Security, and the Central Intelligence Agency employ analysts as part of the criminal investigative process. The concept of predictive policing is based on the premise that information collected in many forms provides the basis for using technology to develop intelligence that can be used in the field to combat crime. The full impact of technology-related crime has yet to be realized, largely because criminals introduce new schemes and methods to avoid detection on an ongoing basis.

This chapter addresses some of the more common types of computer and technological crime, and some of the more troublesome types of criminal activity that cut across borders and jurisdictions using various forms technology. At the outset it should be recognized that law enforcement continues to increase its use of computers, software, and information technology. Criminal investigation has been enhanced considerably through the use of commercial programs involving relational databases, mapping, artificial intelligence, and criminal profiling. The result has been the development of a new type of investigator, sometimes referred to as a *cyberdetective*. These specialists bring a new dimension to the field of crime investigation, and like advances in forensic science, their contributions are becoming increasing important. Unfortunately, in many ways it is safe to say that law enforcement continues to be behind the curve in knowledge of technological related crime.

Cybercriminal activity, which includes crimes related to terrorism, generally falls into three categories:

- Cases in which technology is integral to commission of a crime (electronic fraud, money laundering, child pornography).
- Cases in which the technology is used to commit a crime (identity theft, computer sabotage, theft of privileged information).
- Cases in which technology is used as an incidental aspect of a crime (data and image storage, Internet and cellular communication).[1]

Today more than 75 percent of the homes in America have at least one computer, and a new generation of technology-savvy individuals has arrived. Overall, a small percentage use IT for criminal purposes, but because of the power of the Internet and today's technology, their impact can be much greater than that of more traditional criminals. Some of the more common types of crime using information technology with which an investigator should be familiar include:

- Child pornography and exploitation
- Economic related fraud
- Electronic stalking and harassment (cyberstalking)

- Extortion
- Gambling
- Identity theft
- Illegal drug activity
- Intellectual property crimes
- Mail and wire fraud
- Money laundering
- Prostitution
- Software theft
- Telecommunications fraud
- Terrorism
- Transporting stolen property
- Data theft
- Electronic sabotage

The National Institute of Justice's *Electronic Crime Scene Investigation: A Guide for First Responders* is an important publication that should be of interest to all investigators.[2] Some of the material for this chapter was culled from this NIJ guide, as well as other publications. This chapter focuses on IT from the crime perspective, and in relation to its use by law enforcement.

Cybercrime: Information Technology and Criminal Activity

It is virtually impossible to determine the monetary amounts of various types of IT crime, but costs and losses easily run into billions of dollars and may be close to reaching a trillion dollars. Consider, for example, such high-volume crimes as child pornography and identity theft. These are just two types of crime that cross national and international borders and involve thousands of individuals, both as perpetrators and victims.

The U.S. National Consumers League (NCL) data in 2007 indicated that the total losses of Internet fraud amounted to $17,508,480, and the most frequent schemes were fake checks (29%), general merchandise (23%), auction (13%), Nigerian advance fee loans (11%), lotteries (7%), phishing (3%), advance fee loans (3%), friendship and sweetheart swindles, (1%), and Internet access services (1%).[3]

In fact, these reported numbers are quite low according to many experts, who note that many victims fail to report Internet fraud because of the embarrassment associated with being scammed. In addition, some large companies and corporations do not report cybercrime and cyber attacks because they may fear customer lack of confidence, or do not wish to draw attention to the vulnerability of their system.

In his research on Internet fraud, T.J. Chung identified the following types:

- Identity theft
- Credit card fraud
- On-line auction fraud
- Short firm fraud
- Advance fee fraud
- Direct investment fraud
- Drug sale scams
- Prize/sweepstakes fraud
- Social engineering and internet fraud[4]

There was a time when it was generally possible to profile cybercriminals, but this has changed over the past decade. Profiling in this area is now related more to the type of technological crime than to a specific set of criteria. For example, individuals involved in economic fraud are more likely to be older than those involved in "hacking" or software piracy; child pornographers cut across international dimensions that may involve persons from two or more countries; identity theft is usually an individual criminal activity; and terrorist web sites may involve numerous persons. Enterprise and organized crime groups have taken to the use of various forms of technology to elude detection and foster communication.

Investigations following the September 11, 2001, terrorist attacks in the United States and the foiled attack in England in August 2006 revealed a global computer network used by terrorists to communicate, as well as the use of computers to gather information about targets and to do research on everything from bombs to building layouts and air transport vulnerabilities.

Emerging databases and search engines on the Internet enable individuals to gather information on virtually any subject, including biographical data on millions of individuals. For instance, the Google search engine has integrated several public information databases into its basic search capabilities. For instance, anyone can now enter a Vehicle Identification Number (VIN) into the search engine and get free a basic report on the history of the vehicle from CarFax.com.

As the amount of public information about individuals has increased, the availability of inexpensive, portable storage capacity has also increased. For instance, today it is possible to carry gigabytes of information on a storage device the size of a pack of chewing gum. These portable storage devices allow a person to carry as much as 16,000 pictures (at 500KB each) or more than 100,000 pages of text in their pocket, plugging it into a computer only when needed.

The most popular of these devices are the so-called flash drives because they allow users to transport up to eight gigabytes of data that can be plugged into any computer (Windows or Macintosh) without restrictions of computer ownership or permissions.

Cell phone technology has also increased to the point at which it is possible to take, store, and send images, access the Internet, and perform many of the functions that once required a computer. Handheld personal digital assistants (PDAs), electronic organizers, iPods and iPads, and memory cards may also be used to store information that may be of interest to investigators (see Figure 3.1).

Figure 3.1 A personal digital assistant (PDA), a handheld computer that can store large amounts of data that may be of interest to the investigator.

Additionally, smart cards and other small devices may contain their own microprocessors that enable a card to hold and change information, such as fund balances (known as debit cards). Removable storage devices come in many different forms, ranging from the early floppy disks, to zip disks, CDs and DVDs, and tape drives, to name a few.

A further complicating factor in cases involving various forms of electronic technology involves case preparation and the presentation of evidence for court. Because this is a relatively new area in which law breakers frequently know more about the technology than investigators or the courts, there is the increasing problem of not being able to present a case that can be understood by a jury. Everything from initial investigations to the collection, presentation, and admissibility of evidence is important.

Electronic evidence is, by its very nature, fragile. It can be altered, damaged, or destroyed by improper handling or improper examination. For this reason, special precautions should be taken to document, collect, preserve, and examine this type of evidence. Failure to do so may render it unusable or lead to an inaccurate conclusion.[5]

Systemic Components

At the heart of virtually all information technology lies a computer system or central processing unit (CPU). Generally, these systems contain a data storage component and a "hard" drive that is programmed to run the system. The computing power of today's technology is enormous, enabling the user to run a broad range of programs, commonly referred to as software, in conjunction with the hard drive.

The computer contains a number of files that are connected to different types of software, such as word processing, spreadsheets, databases, e-mail, or web sites. Some of these programs, such as dictionaries and directories, may not be alterable, whereas user-created files are developed by the user and generally prove to be the most valuable from an investigative standpoint. One of the major exceptions involves downloaded images or documents that may be used in developing a *prima facie* case, such as for child pornography.

Some of the more important files that an investigator should be familiar with include:

- Address books
- Audio or video files
- Bookmarks
- Calendars
- Databases
- Documents or correspondence files
- E-mail files
- Favorite sites
- Images and graphics
- Indexes
- Spreadsheets
- Voicemail
- Social networking accounts

Moreover, the development of high-quality peripheral devices, such as scanners and printers, has increased opportunities for the criminal element to perform further illicit activities, including counterfeiting, various types of fraud, child pornography, and identity theft.

Legal Issues

In many ways investigation involving various forms of technology, especially computers and the Internet, are complicated by a myriad of legal issues, court decisions, and policy issues of organizations. Because case law in this area is relatively new, there are times when the investigator may be operating in uncharted territory, or may come up against newly designed computer programs or criminal activities. Further, because many of the laws and policies may be based on individual state laws, they may not be applicable from one state to another. For this reason, when in doubt, the investigator should consult with appropriate legal counsel.

On the federal level, there has been a steady stream of decisions by circuit courts that serve to give better clarification to the procedures that must be followed by investigators. Generally, a search warrant is required to conduct an investigation of a computer's contents or to gather information from an Internet source (e-mail or Internet service providers—ISPs). A suspect may give permission for an investigator to conduct a search of his or her computer, but it is advisable to get this permission in writing. Courts have become more involved in Fourth Amendment issues related to the search and seizure of computers and data culled from ISPs.[6]

The search of a computer or other electronic device is generally developed from search warrants in other more traditional contexts, with Fourth Amendment guarantees that protect a person from unreasonable searches and seizures being an important consideration. The highest privacy interest is attached to private dwellings.[7]

In searches and seizures of computers and other forms of electronic storage, the investigator is generally required to establish probable cause to obtain a warrant. This includes reasonable grounds to believe that the data to be seized actually exists and will provide evidence of a crime; the location of what will be searched, and a reasonably detailed description of the information or data that will be retrieved.[8]

The primary issue in computer-related cases centers on an individual's right to privacy regarding information stored in a computer or other device. Locations from which information can be obtained include:

- The home
- The workplace
- Personal computers and other portable devices
- Social networking sites (e.g., Facebook, MySpace, LinkedIn)
- Internet service providers (ISPs)
- Chat rooms
- Web sites
- External storage devices

Home Computers

As indicated above, home computers and other personal and portable devices fall under the purview of the Fourth Amendment of the U.S. Constitution, which protects citizens from unreasonable searches and seizures. A search warrant requires permission to gain entry to the residence or portable devices in possession of a suspect. As noted, the warrant must include a statement as to what technological equipment (computers, storage devices, cameras, printers, etc.) is to be searched, what is to be sought, and why the warrant is requested. The investigator must show probable cause for the search, which may be based on a variety of circumstances, such as prior knowledge based on the experience of the investigator; the past criminal record of the suspect; or information provided by informants and victims. There is no reasonable expectation of privacy when the information was openly available, where the device has been stolen, where control of the device was given to another person, or where the individual owner loses control of the device.[9] In cases in which the home or computer may be shared by another person, the other person may give permission to search the computer, but not access to password-protected files.[10]

Workplace Computers

Workplace searches present a somewhat different issue, and it has been held that an employee does not necessarily have a right to the expectation of privacy.[11] However, in determining an individual's expectation of privacy, Stephen W. Cogar suggests that the following questions should be considered:

- Is the employee's office shared?
- Is the hard drive password-protected?
- Is the computer physically locked?
- Is the office locked, and if so, who has access?
- Can the files be accessed remotely through a network program?
- Is there an employee policy in place regarding computer usage that states that files can be searched or monitored?
- Is the policy enforced uniformly?
- Is there evidence that the employee was aware of the policy?
- Is software used to monitor computer use, and are employees aware of the practice?
- Do work stations contain a message when the computer is accessed that the computer can be monitored?[12]

In many instances, employees may contend that they were not aware of company policy, which may negate permission given by the employer to conduct a search. For this reason it is advisable to seek a search warrant whenever possible.

Internet Service Providers

When a suspect may be anonymous, using a screen name or other form of e-mail address, the best source of identification is likely to be an ISP, such as America OnLine (AOL); Comcast, Earthlink, Windstream, and so on. Although the content of information may be protected under the Fourth Amendment, the Courts have held that the identity of the subscriber is not protected. However, a number of recent cases in which the government has sought to obtain information from Internet providers, specifically in terrorism-related cases, have sparked debate, and it is likely that the issue will be addressed by the Supreme Court in the future.

While under certain circumstances a person may have an expectation of privacy in content information, a person does not have an interest in the account information given to the ISP in order to establish an e-mail account. This is considered non-content information.[13] This includes: name; billing address; and home, work, and fax telephone numbers. The Stored Wire and Electronic Communication and Transactional Records (SWECTRA) Act requires ISPs to disclose non-content information to the law enforcement community pursuant to legal authorization.[14] The Cyber Security Enhancement Act of 2003, which is part of the Homeland Security Act of 2002, "makes it easier for police agencies to obtain investigative information from Internet service providers (ISPs) and shields from lawsuits ISPs who hand over user information to law enforcement officers without a warrant."[15]

Cases involving terrorism investigations permit disclosure of more non-content information than is permissible in other types of criminal investigations. The USA PATRIOT Act "can force the disclosure of a subscriber's name; address; local and long distance telephone connection records, or records of session times and duration, length of service (including start date and types of service utilized; telephone or instrument number or other subscriber number or identity, including any temporary assigned network address; and means and source of payment for such service of a subscriber)."[16]

Chat Rooms and Social Networking

One of the most common forms of communication today is the use of a number of computers and cell phone–based Internet social networks that have changed in large measure the way Americans relate to each other. Twitter (a free social networking service that enables users to send and read messages known as "tweets," which are text-based posts of up to 140 characters); text messaging; social networking sites such as Facebook, MySpace, and LinkedIn; and Internet "chat rooms" have made it possible to exchange photos and other data even on a hand-held cell phone. These methods of communication have become commonplace in the United States and most other developed and developing countries. The emerging capabilities of computers make a broad range of opportunities available to users, including access to relatively fine mapping technology, relational databases, sophisticated statistical and analytical tools, and access to thousands of web sites.

The many advantages notwithstanding, the potential for utilizing these technological advances for criminal purposes represents a challenge for law enforcement. Two of the more common investigative approaches include identifying pedophiles and child molesters, and investigations of child pornographic images on web sites and in the possession of individuals.

"Sting" operations by police departments, in which investigators communicate with suspected pedophiles who are trying to lure children into illicit relationships, have become commonplace in a number of state and local agencies.

> Child pornography and individuals who possess pictures or video (collectively "images") that are sexually exploitative of children represent one of the darkest sides of the Internet. Investigating and prosecuting child pornography cases inevitably involves more than just the evidence that certain images were found on a computer used by the defendant ...
>
> Child pornography investigations often involve people who are quite knowledgeable about technology, computers, and the Internet. They trade images with other collectors within their own towns and around the world using, for example, Web sites, file sharing, e-mail, buddy lists, password protected files, or *encryption** (emphasis in original).[17]

With the growth of social networking sites (e.g., MySpace) on which many youngsters post revealing or sexually explicit photographs, the problem has become more complex, and some sites have agreed to remove individuals who have a criminal record involving children from access. Later in this chapter, we address the investigation of child exploitation.

Web Sites

Today there are thousands of web sites, making it possible to gather information on almost any subject. Some of these are nothing more than propaganda sites, devoted to fostering ideological positions, racism, ethnic hate, and dissatisfaction with the government. Free speech protects these sites, and many of them draw a fine line between what is legal and what is illegal. The fact that an individual visits a web site is not a crime, and an investigator must take care in how such information is used. In cases involving pedophiles, the fact that they subscribed to or visited web sites may serve as circumstantial evidence when a sex crime is involved.

* Encryption refers to any procedure used in cryptography to convert plain text into cipher-text so as to prevent anyone but the intended recipient from reading the data.

A number of federal agencies monitor the web sites of suspected violent groups, largely as a means of keeping track of potential criminal activity. However, it should be noted that care must be taken in attempting to develop cases based on information from a site. Web sites also serve as one of the largest libraries in the world, providing not only information about people, places, and things. Many web sites may also be targets for hackers trying to disrupt an organization.

Investigating High-Tech and IT Crime

A thorough discussion of investigative methods involving high-tech crime is beyond the scope of this chapter, but it is important to have a basic understanding of the type of crimes that an investigator may come across. Because computers have become so common in everyday life, it is important to recognize that a vast amount of information can be obtained from what appears to be normal record-keeping. This may include address and telephone records, bank account records, e-mail transactions between suspects, and other personal data.

The Computer Crime and Intellectual Property Section of the U.S. Department of Justice and the specialized computer investigation units of the Federal Bureau of Investigation are available to assist local law enforcement in technology-related investigations. The investigator facing a crime scene involving computers should protect the area and call for a component service technician. However, there may be situations in which this is impossible. For example, if a computer virus has been introduced, or a self-destruct system implanted by an "intruder," it may be necessary to take preliminary action to preserve the equipment. (See Box 3.1 for available guides from the National Institute of Justice (NIJ) on Internet Digital Evidence.)

In other cases, the investigator may be seizing or protecting a computer that has been or is being used in the commission of a crime. In such cases, the suspect may have

Box 3.1: NIJ Guides On Digital Evidence

Electronic Crime Scene Investigation: A Guide for First Responders:
http//www.ojp.usdoj.gov/nij/pubs-sum/187736.htm

Forensic Examination of Digital Evidence:
A Guide for Law Enforcement:
http://www.ojp.usdoj.gov/nij/pubs-sum/199408.htm

Investigations Involving the Internet and Computer Networks:
http://www.ojp.usdoj.gov/nij/pubs-sum/210798.htm

built systems into the computer designed to destroy the evidence necessary for proving that a crime has been committed using the equipment. Thus, the investigator must have some basic familiarization with the types of criminal activity he or she might encounter, how they are generally carried out, and the procedures necessary for the safeguarding of evidence and preliminary investigations. The investigator should also be familiar with those agencies or organizations that might also be able to assist in such investigations. A number of federal agencies, such as the FBI and the Secret Service, now have cybercrime experts located in major field offices.

Because cybercrime and other forms of high-technology crime may involve multiple jurisdictions, or involve a federal offense, it is important to communicate with appropriate agencies or organizations early in the process. For example, fraud involving interstate communication by electronic communication is likely to fall under the jurisdiction of the U.S. Postal Service. The use of a computer to transmit child pornography—much of which actually originates abroad—may involve multiple jurisdictions. The Immigration and Customs Enforcement (ICE) agency can be of assistance in crimes carried out in the United States as well as other countries.

It is extremely important that a detailed record be kept of all actions taken during the investigation. This may prove helpful when it is necessary to reconstruct events or design a particular strategy and may be very important when such cases reach the trial stage.

At the outset, the investigator must be extremely careful not to destroy evidence that may be on a computer, a disk, or other electronic storage mechanism. Sophisticated criminals using computers are likely to use passwords or other program methods that are designed to erase data if not properly accessed. It may be possible, though, for experts to recover data that appears to have been erased. Thus, unless an investigator is thoroughly familiar with this type of investigation, it is best to leave the equipment untouched until an expert can be called. One should not turn the computer off or on or ask the suspect to assist unless an expert is present.

Most experts agree that training and education of investigators must increasingly include a basic knowledge of computers and how they can be used in criminal activities. In many cases, the investigator will have to rely on the victim to explain how a crime was carried out, and what damages may be attributed to the offender. The investigator, frequently in cooperation with legal counsel, will be faced with determining what crime took place and the legal standards and jurisdiction that are involved.

Of the crimes that are predominantly carried out using various forms of technology, child pornography and exploitation, electronic and economic fraud, identity theft, and gambling are quite common. The following illustrations and case studies provide an overview of the more common methods employed.

Child Exploitation

The Internet has become a notorious tool for pedophiles, child pornographers, and other child sex abusers. ICE, the Postal Inspection Service, and the FBI generally investigate international providers. Depending on how information comes to authorities, either federal, state, and local law enforcement may handle local investigations of users. Users of child pornography may also be pedophiles who are active in recruiting children for photos or using chat rooms to entice children to meet them.

A growing number of states have expanded or initiated child exploitation units, which usually include a computer specialist who is familiar with the methods used by suspects who make contact with young people through chat rooms as a means of luring victims to a prearranged location. When a parent or other person makes a complaint, the investigator should be thoroughly familiar with local laws relating to solicitation of a minor. Generally, it must be proved that the suspect was aware that the individual was a minor and in most cases it will be necessary to prove that something more than a meeting was planned. For this reason, it is important to obtain prior communications. If a meeting is arranged, it must be proved that the suspect was actually going to make contact and that a positive identification of the suspect has been made.

The Cook County Sheriff's Department in Illinois and the Texas Attorney General's criminal investigation unit have been successful in drawing out numerous pedophiles who believed they were communicating with a minor. One key to success has been the ability to establish and build cases that have not been viewed as entrapment. Generally, by studying the ways in which young people communicate on the Internet, law enforcement agents have been successful in getting the suspect to communicate freely. When arrested, the suspect is frequently found to have other incriminating material in his or her residence.

The U.S. Postal Inspection Service has stopped about 500 child molesters and been involved in the conviction of more than 250 persons for child sexual exploitation since 1997. Their research indicates a high correlation between child molesters and people involved in selling, purchasing, and trading child pornography. The Postal Inspection Service is an excellent source for assistance in cases involving the Internet or mail.[18]

In 2003, the Supreme Court held that sex offenders' photos and other information, such as an address, may be posted on the Internet as a means of providing citizens with information about potential threats.[19] At least 35 states provide this information. Such databases may also prove to be a good tool for investigators to develop suspects. However, care should be taken in jumping to conclusions, as well as making decisions to conduct interviews.

Stalking and Harassment

A more common problem for local law enforcement is the use of the computer to stalk or harass individuals. In most cases, the sender is most likely to be anonymous. The prior section on legal aspects outlines the procedures involved in gaining access to the identity of an individual who is using the computer or telephone for illegal purposes.

A year-long study in 2006 of stalking victims found that about 25 percent of stalking suspects used e-mail (83%) or instant messaging (35%), and about 75 percent of the victims knew the stalker in some capacity. Overall, more than three million people over the age of 18 were stalking victims. Stalking was defined as "a course of conduct that would cause a reasonable person to feel fear." More than one in four stalking victims reported that some form of cyberstalking was used:

> Electronic monitoring was used to stalk 1 in 13 victims. Video or digital cameras were equally likely as listening devices or bugs to be used to electronically monitor victims (46% and 42%). Global positioning systems (GPS) technology comprised about a tenth of the electronic monitoring of stalking victims.[20]

Of the 3.4 million victims surveyed, 278,580 sustained injuries in attacks, including 38,590 (13.9%) victims who were raped or sexually assaulted, 52,080 who were seriously injured, and 276,440 who suffered minor or other injuries. A weapon was used in 138,630 attacks. The majority of offenders (64%) were between the ages of 18 and 29, and the majority of the victims were between the ages of 21 and 39 (71%).[21]

Economic Crimes—Fraud, Embezzlement, and Identity Theft

There are a great many types of economic-related fraud, including business fraud and embezzlement, perhaps the largest of which was the Enron case in Texas, which involved a broad range of criminal activities. A major component of this scheme involved computer usage for money transfers and communication. The sale of products that are not delivered as well as misrepresentation by sellers has become a growing problem, and investigations may involve multiple jurisdictions and countries.

Keeping transactions within the computer allows the suspect to destroy information rapidly. However, in many cases, transactions may have been sent to one or more other computers or organizations with which the suspect is conducting business. Further, with the development of small storage devices that can hold enormous amounts of data, it will be increasingly common for criminals to maintain suspect records separate from the computer.

One of the more common types of electronic fraud involves the use of stolen or forged credit cards. Despite efforts by companies to create "safer" credit cards using photos and fingerprints, this problem continues to grow, due in some measure to the ability to purchase products and services over the Internet. Identity theft is one of the fastest-growing crimes in the United States. Criminals use a variety of means to secure information. They then use this information to commit fraudulent purchases, acquire other forms of false identification, receive large cash advances, and establish fraudulent lines of credit in the forms of loans and other credit cards.

A number of schemes involving telecommunications fraud have arisen with the increase in the number of cell phones available throughout the world. Each type of telecommunications offering, from voice to wireless data, is vulnerable For instance, through fraudulent access to networks, perpetrators can avoid paying for wireless service, steal and resell long-distance minutes, hijack a network device to send unsolicited commercial e-mail or pornographic spam to unsuspecting end users, or use stolen cell phones to make large numbers of calls.

Additionally, a number of organized crime groups, frequently with international connections, have developed sophisticated fraudulent credit card rings. Investigations of these types of activities must be handled quickly because perpetrators are likely to move frequently to avoid apprehension. Unfortunately, in many cases, the victim whose number or card has been stolen is not aware of the crime until he or she receives a statement.

On a higher level, fraudulent wire transfers, bank fraud, telecommunications fraud, and money laundering have also become commonplace. In many instances, the illegal activities are carried out across borders and will involve multiple jurisdictions. Electronic funds transfers have made it possible for individuals to move funds to off-shore accounts, to gain entry illegally into funding institutions and make transfers, and to embezzle large amounts of money. Section 2314 of Title 18 of the U.S. Code makes it illegal to transport interstate computer data[22] and stolen computer hardware worth at least $5,000.[23]

Economic espionage has also become a major problem. Although relatively little attention is paid by law enforcement to the issue of economic espionage, patent or intellectual property infringement, or the stealing of trade secrets, this is an area in which the amount of criminal activity has been growing steadily. In many cases, the companies being victimized are unaware of the problem or do not have procedures for reporting or investigating such activities. Estimates of annual misappropriations and fraud (frequently committed by trusted employees) of U.S. companies amount to more than $250 billion. Although statutes differ by states, the elements of computer fraud make it unlawful for any person to:

- Use a computer or computer network,
- Without authority, and
- With the intent to: (a) obtain property or services by false pretenses; (b) embezzle or commit larceny; or (c) convert the property of another.[24]

Computer Hacking/Cracking and Sabotage

One of the more pervasive illegal uses of the computer is hacking or cracking, which generally involves entering a computer system illegally or without knowledge of the victim. The term *hacker* generally refers to individuals who enter computer systems illegally; the term *cracker* is used more often to describe a person who attempts to destroy, change, or steal programs or information. Often undertaken as what hackers refer to as an "intellectual challenge," the practice has become a major problem in both the public and private sectors. A growing number of individuals and "clubs" throughout the world have been involved in developing methods to break codes or find ways to enter a system, and they have frequently been successful in "crashing" web sites, altering information, and introducing viruses.

According to one report, Russian hackers obtained American identities and software developed by Microsoft as part of their attack on Georgia during the five-day conflict in 2008 between the two countries. This was the first time cyber-attacks were known to have coincided with a military campaign. According to the report, the attacks, using social networking sites such as Twitter and Facebook, disabled 20 web sites, including those of the Georgian President, the defense minister, the National Bank of Georgia, and major news outlets.[25]

Table 3.1 defines some of the terms involved in economic-related criminal activity. "A number of states criminalize the dissemination of viruses, worms and other forms of malware [malicious software]. Many of these prohibitions target the dissemination of a 'computer contaminant.' 'Computer contaminant' is defined as encompassing viruses, worms and other harmful programs."[26]

Professional crackers are involved in garnering classified or sensitive information that they can sell to others. In recent years, governments have also been involved in using the computer to steal or pass information. Investigations of this nature require sophisticated knowledge of the computer and should not be attempted without consulting a technical advisor.

Closely related to hacking is computer sabotage, which may involve the actions of a disgruntled employee to destroy an employers' database or make an external attack on a computer database.

Table 3.1 Computer Terminology

Clipper chip	A computer chip for encryption as a means of protecting computerized information.
Encryption	A means of protecting communication and electronic commerce. Can be used by organized crime or terrorist groups to conceal illegal activities.
Logic Bomb	A virus that is dormant until a particular time (which can be days, months, or years) or when a particular command is entered in the computer.
Pinging or Spamming	A form of vandalism, or sabotaging, that involves bombarding an e-mail address with thousands of messages using automatic remailer tools.
Remailer	A program that makes it possible to send thousands of messages to an e-mail address.
Trapdoor	A means for bypassing the security controls of a computer mainframe system (usually installed by programmers to permit then to enter the system to check when things go wrong).
Trojan Horse	Software embedded in a popular and trusted computer software program (maybe unknown to the user) that is stealing secrets, modifying the database, or deleting specific items of information. It is not usually considered a virus because it does not replicate itself and does not spread.
Virus	A program designed to attach itself to a file, reproduce, and spread from one file to another, destroying data, displaying an irritating message, or otherwise disrupting computer operations.
Worm	Software that works its way through a single computer system or a network, changing and destroying data or codes.
Packet Sniffer	A program that examines all traffic on a section of network to find passwords, credit card numbers, and other information of value.
SATAN	A security loophole analysis program designed for use by system administrators (and abused by electronic intruders) to detect insecure systems.
File Infector	Computer viruses that attach to program files and spread when the program is executed.
Boot Sector Virus	A computer virus that infects the sectors on a disk that contain the data a computer uses during the boot process. This type of virus does not require a program to spread, and may cause the destruction of all data on a drive.
Macro Virus	A computer virus that infects the automatic command execution capabilities (macros) of productivity software. Macro viruses are typically attached to documents and spreadsheets.
Cracking	The process of trying to overcome a security measure.
Black Hat	A term used to describe a hacker who has the intention of causing damage or stealing information.
Crackers	People who break into a computer system with intent to damage files or steal data, or who are driven to hack highly secure systems.

Table 3.1 Computer Terminology (*Contiuned*)

Denial of Service Attack	An attack that causes the targeted system to be unable to fulfill its intended function.
IP Spoofing	An attack whereby the attacker disguises himself or herself as another user by means of a false IP network address.
Letterbomb	An e-mail containing live data intended to cause damage to the recipient's computer.
Malware	A term for malicious software.
Phreaking	When a person hacks telephone systems, usually for the purpose of making free phone call.
Phracking	When a person combines phone phreaking with computer hacking.
Trap and Trace Device	A device used to record the telephone numbers dialed by a specific telephone.
War Dialer	Software designed to detect dial-in access to computer systems.
Computer Emergency Response Team (CERT)	An organization that collects and distributes information about security breaches.
Firewall	A device designed to enforce the boundary between two or more networks, limiting access.
Keystroke Monitoring	The process of recording every character typed by a computer user on a keyboard.
Pretty Good Privacy (PGP)	A freeware program designed to encrypt e-mail.
Warez	Slang for pirated software.

Illegal Drug Activity

Drug traffickers have taken to using the Internet for distribution of drugs, communicating between groups, and keeping records of transactions. Organized crime groups have developed sophisticated methods for the transfer of funds to other countries or offshore accounts, frequently by establishing electronic business "fronts" or by "purchasing" high-cost items with illegal cash and then "selling" the items abroad as a means of recovering the cash.

Terrorism

Although this subject is covered in more detail in Chapter 22, it is important to recognize that terrorist groups use the Internet as a primary means of communication. They also use the Internet to gather information about individuals, possible targets, and ways of making explosives or other weapons.

Computer Crime Investigation and the Electronic Crime Scene

There are a number of considerations that should be observed when dealing with a high-tech crime scene. The National Institute of Justice (NIJ) Guide stresses the importance of documentation in detail. The following steps are recommended:

- Observe and document the physical scene, such as the position of the mouse and the location of components relative to each other (e.g., a mouse on the left side of the computer may indicate a left-handed user).
- Document the condition and location of the computer system, including power status of the computer (on, off, or in sleep mode). Most computers have status lights that indicate the computer is on. Likewise, if fan noise is heard, the system is probably on. Furthermore, if the computer system is warm, that may also indicate that it is on or was recently turned off.
- Identify and document related electronic components that will not be collected.
- Photograph the entire scene to create a visual record as noted by the first responder. The complete room should be recorded with 360 degrees of coverage, when possible.
- Photograph the front of the computer as well as the monitor screen and other components. Also take written notes on what appears on the monitor screen. Active programs may require videotaping or more extensive documentation of monitor screen activity.[27]

The computer has come of age in law enforcement as departments and other agencies develop applications through which this technology can benefit the field. In many cases, the technology and the application software—the programs used to handle and manipulate the data—exist in various forms but require modification for law enforcement purposes. In other cases, software is available (frequently through hardware vendors) that has been designed specifically for police work. Included in this category are programs ranging from relatively simple data-storage programs to extremely complex systems for tasks such as imaging (for storing photographic images on the computer) and optical scanning (for storing fingerprints for later retrieval).

In the field of criminal investigation, the computer has not yet come close to the potential it offers as an investigative tool. Although one reason for this is a lack of sufficient funding, other considerations also limit computer utilization—for example, concern about the right to privacy, a lack of trained technicians, and an entrenched resistance by officers who have little understanding of the computer's capabilities.

Nevertheless, as a new generation of computer-literate personnel moves into the law enforcement profession, there is likely to be a growing trend toward acceptance. Many federal agencies have begun to develop and adopt computer-based systems that go far beyond mere data storage and retrieval. The Federal Bureau of Investigation, for example, will virtually revamp its computer system in the first decade of the twenty-first century. A number of police departments—including those in Chicago, Los Angeles, and Houston—have invested millions of dollars in automated fingerprint identification systems (AFISs) and are seeing their value in the investigative function. Illustrative of this potential value is a case involving a forcible rape in which a latent fingerprint was lifted from the handbag of the victim. Fingerprint analysis provided no suspects. However, more than a year later, a suspect arrested in a burglary was surprised to learn that, despite the passage of time, his prints identified him as the rapist. (At the time of the rape, he had been too young to be fingerprinted, despite his long record as a juvenile offender.) This illustrates the capability of technology to solve what in all likelihood would have remained an unsolved case.

Figure 3.2 International cooperation through expanded computer networks continues to grow. Representatives of the Attorney General's office in Sri Lanka participate in a training program at the Office of International Criminal Justice at the University of Illinois at Chicago with Officer Thomas Moran.

Computers also are being used for developing crime patterns (see Figure 3.2); for sophisticated data manipulation using a concept known as "artificial intelligence," and, with imaging, for storing online mug shots of suspects and photographs of stolen artwork or other valuable collections.

Perhaps the greatest innovation in programming software in the past decade has been the development of relational databases, and linking and geospatial programs for law enforcement purposes. A relational database makes it possible to combine a large number of individual databases into a system that makes it possible to link a broad range of disparate variables for search and profiling purposes. The Chicago Police Department's CLEAR program makes it possible to link millions of records from different sources (including other police departments) to provide a powerful tool for investigators. The program utilizes artificial intelligence, photographs, images, and geographic mapping in addition to text-based records. Some of these include:

- Nickname database.
- MO file.
- Informants file.
- Business locator index with emergency telephone numbers for business owners.
- Case file indicating which cases are assigned to which investigator.
- Skills index listing the names of those who can assist with specific needs, such as language skills, scuba divers, technicians, etc.
- Intelligence file offering a source for various bits of information that can be pieced together to form a clearer picture of suspects or crime patterns. (This file, which usually requires the expertise of an analyst or other individual familiar with the technology, represents one of the more significant changes appearing in the field of criminal investigation.)
- Stolen property files.
- Building layouts and schematics.
- Tattoo files.
- Gang symbols and descriptors.
- Motor vehicle records.
- Victimization files.

The FBI utilizes Rapid Start Teams, which are teams of experienced investigators and technical experts who can quickly load information from hundreds of leads and investigative tips into a database to assist in major case investigations. Established in 1995, the Rapid Start Team gained notoriety in major crisis incidents including the Oklahoma City Bombing in 1995, the Atlanta Olympics Bombing in 1996, and the 9/11 attacks in 2001. Rapid Start Teams are also available for child abduction cases and other major cases.

On an individual basis, investigators can use PCs, laptops, or PDAs to maintain their own data sources, address and telephone files, case information, and for numerous other applications.

If a picture is worth a thousand words, imaging technology offers immense possibilities. One of the most obvious uses today is through computer-based identification kits, which make it possible to prepare a composite of a suspect relatively easily. However, the quality and color of newer monitors and systems make it possible to have a four-color, instant-access mug shot book readily available. Indeed, coupled with search technology, the investigators can feed in information on *modus operandi*, physical descriptors, type of victim, and so on, to call up groups and individuals in various categories for the victim to view on the scene.

Electronic surveillance takes many forms, and is being used more frequently in terrorism and organized crime investigations. Some of these, most of which require a court order, include:

- Telephone wiretap
- Electronic intercept of oral conversation
- Voice paging
- Digital display paging
- Cellular telephone intercepts
- Pen register
- Internet or computer communications intercept

Information technology offers investigators one of the most important advances in law enforcement, and is a major new area of development. Most federal agencies and many police departments are now employing crime analysts, specialists schooled in this technology who can serve as an important source of support to field investigators. Additionally, there are also a great number of sources on the Internet that are available to investigators, including but not limited to:

- *American Society for Industrial Security, International*—Private organization providing training and information on matters related to industrial security (http://www.asisonline.org/).
- *Center for Education and Research in Information Assurance and Security (CERIAS)*—One of the world's leading centers for research and education in areas of information security that are crucial to the protection of critical computing and communication infrastructure, CERIAS is unique among such national centers in its multidisciplinary approach to problems such as intrusion detection and network security (http://www.cerias.purdue.edu/).
- *CERT Coordination Center (CERT/CC)*—Located at the Software Engineering Institute (SEI) at Carnegie Mellon University, it is charged with coordinating communication among experts during security emergencies and to help prevent future incidents (http://www.cert.org).
- *FinCEN*—The U.S. Treasury Department maintains a financial center (FINCEN) that provides information and technical assistance in the area of financial crime (http://www.fincen.gov/).

- *Forum of Incident Response and Security Teams (FIRST)*—A consortium of computer security incident response teams from government, commercial, and academic organizations, FIRST aims to foster cooperation and coordination in incident prevention, to prompt rapid reaction to incidents, and to promote information sharing among members and the community at large (http://www.first.org).
- *InfraGard*—A partnership between private Industry and the U.S. government (represented by the FBI), the InfraGard initiative was developed to encourage the exchange or information by the government and the private-sector members about securing the nation's electronic infrastructure (http://www.infragard.net/).
- *Internet Crime Complaint Center (IC3)*—A partnership between the FBI, the National White Collar Crime Center (NW3C), and the Bureau of Justice Assistance to serve as a means to receive Internet-related criminal complaints and to further research, develop, and refer the criminal complaints to federal, state, local, or international law enforcement and/or regulatory agencies for any investigation they deem to be appropriate (http://www.ic3. gov/about/default.aspx).
- *INTERPOL*—The International Police Organization now has field offices in each of the 50 states. Queries within states should be made through a local office when possible. INTERPOL can be of assistance in cases involving individuals from other countries (http://www.interpol.int).
- *National Vulnerability Database (NVD)*—The U.S. government repository of standards-based vulnerability management data. This data enables automation of vulnerability management, security measurement, and compliance (http://nvd.nist.gov/).
- *U.S. Computer Emergency Readiness Team (US-CERT)*—A team charged with providing response support and defense against cyber attacks for the Federal Civil Executive Branch and information sharing and collaboration with state and local government, industry, and international partners (http://www.us-cert.gov/).
- *U.S. Department of Justice Computer Crime and Intellectual Property Section (CCIPS)*—A division of lawyers who focus exclusively on the issues raised by computer and intellectual property crime. Section attorneys advise federal prosecutors and law enforcement agents; comment upon and propose legislation; coordinate international efforts to combat computer crime; litigate cases; and train all law enforcement groups. Other areas of expertise possessed by commerce, hacker investigations, and intellectual property crimes (http://www.usdoj.gov/criminal/cybercrime/index.html).
- *U.S. Postal Inspection Service*—Provides a broad range of information and investigative assistance in crimes involving the mail and Internet (http:// www.usps.gov/postal inspectors).

Notes

1. Susan W. Brenner, "Defining Cybercrime: A Review of State and Federal Law." In Ralph D. Clifford, ed. (2006). *Cybercrime: The Investigation, Prosecution and Defense of a Computer Related Crime*, 2nd ed. (Durham, NC: Carolina Academic Press).
2. U.S. Department of Justice, *Electronic Crime Scene Investigation: A Guide for First Responders* (Washington, DC: National Institute of Justice, July 2001). See http://www.ncjrs.gov/pdffiles1/nij/187736.pdf.
3. Tae J. Chung, "Policing Internet Fraud: A Study of the Tensions Between Private and Public Models of Policing Fraudulent Activity in Cyberspace with Particular Focus on South Korea and Special Reference to the United Kingdom and the United States." Unpublished dissertation, The University of Leeds School of Law, Leeds, UK (December 2008), 64.
4. Ibid., 51–54.
5. Supra note 1, 2.
6. Stephen W. Cogar, "Obtaining Admissible Evidence from Computers and Internet Service Providers." *FBI Law Enforcement Bulletin* (Washington, DC: U.S. Department of Justice, 2003), 11.
7. *Welsh v. Wisconsin,* 466 U.S. 740, 748 (1984); Ivan Orton, "The Investigation and Prosecution of a Cybercrime." In Ralph D. Clifford, ed., *Cybercrime: The Investigation, Prosecution and Defense of a Computer Related Crime*, 2nd ed. (Durham, NC: Carolina Academic Press, 2006), 126.
8. Donald Resseguie, *Computer Searches and Seizure,* 48 Clev. St. L. Rev. 185 (2000).
9. Rolando V. del Carmen and Jeffery T. Walker, *Briefs of Leading Cases in Law Enforcement*, 7th ed. (Newark, NJ: LexisNexis Matthew Bender, 2008), 69–79.
10. *Trulock v. Freeh*, 275 F.3d 391(4th Cir. 2001).
11. *United States v. Simons*, 206 F.3d 392 (4th Cir. 2000).
12. Cogar, loc. cit.
13. *United States v. Hambrick*, 225 F.3d 656 (4th Cir. 2000).
14. Cogar, 14.
15. Frank Schmalleger, *Criminal Law Today: An Introduction to Capstone Cases*, 3rd ed. (Upper Saddle River, NJ: Pearson/Prentice Hall, 2006), 411.
16. Cogar, 15.
17. U.S. Department of Justice, Office of Justice Programs, "Digital Evidence in the Courtroom: A Guide for Law Enforcement and Prosecutors" (Washington, DC: National Institute of Justice, 2007), 53.
18. See the web site of the U.S. Postal Inspection Service at http://www.usps.com/postalinspectors/.
19. Rolando V. del Carmen, Susan E. Ritter, and Betsy A. Witt, *Briefs of Leading Cases in Corrections*, 5th ed. (Newark, NJ: LexisNexis Matthew Bender, 2008), 340–341.
20. Katrina Baum, Shannon Catalano, Michael Rand, and Kristina Rose, *Stalking Victimization in the United States* (Washington, DC: U.S. Department of Justice, Bureau of Justice Statistics , 2009), 1–3
21. Ibid.
22. *United States v. Farraj*, 211 F.Supp. 2d 479 (S.D.N.Y. 2002).

23. Brenner, 54.
24. Schmalleger, 418.
25. Siobhan Gorman, "Deciphering Cyber Attacks," *The Wall Street Journal*, (August 18, 2009), 11.
26. Brenner, 84.
27. Supra note 2.

Supplemental Readings

Blitzer, Herbert L., Karen Stein-Ferguson, and Jeffrey Huang. *Understanding Forensic Digital Imaging.* Boston: Academic Press, 2008.

Casey, Eoghan, ed. *Handbook of Computer Crime Investigation: Forensic Tools and Technology.* San Diego: Academic Press, 2002.

Clifford, Ralph D., ed. *Cybercrime: The Investigation, Prosecution and Defense of a Computer Related Crime*, 2nd ed. Durham, NC: Carolina Academic Press, 2006.

Kovacich, Gerald L., and Andy Jones. *High Technology Crime Investigator's Handbook: Establishing and Managing a High-technology Crime Prevention Program.* Boston: Butterworth-Heinemann/ Elsevier, 2006.

Moore, Robert. *Cybercrime: Investigating High-Technology Computer Crime.* Newark, NJ: LexisNexis Matthew Bender, 2005.

U.S. Department of Justice. *Electronic Crime Scene Investigation: A Guide for First Responder*, 2nd ed. Washington, DC: National Institute of Justice, 2008.

Credits

1. Copyright © Stefano Palazzo (CC BY-SA 3.0) at http://commons.wikimedia.org/wiki/File:PalmTX.jpg.

Computer Crime Victimization and Criminological Perspectives

BY KYUNG-SHICK CHOI

Although cybercrime has rapidly evolved and become a significant criminological issue, research reveals that academia has developed a few significant empirical assessments regarding computer-crime victimization and the potential contribution to this victimization by online users' characteristics combined with their lack of computer security components. Therefore, the main purpose of this chapter is to discuss two traditional victimization theories, routine activities theory (Cohen & Felson, 1979) and lifestyle-exposure (Hindelang, Gottfredson, & Garofalo, 1978) theory, and their potential application to computer-crime victimization by examining the theoretical core concepts within these theories. Arguably, these two theories are actually one theory, with Hindelang et al.'s (1978) theory being expanded upon by Cohen and Felson in 1979. These two theories have been, individually, widely applied to various crimes, as discussed below, and they have attempted to tie primary causations of victimization to demographic factors, geographic difference, and traits of lifestyle.

Routine Activities Theory and Nature of Cyberspace

In 1979, Cohen and Felson proposed their routine activities theory,which focuses mainly on opportunities for criminal events. Cohen and Felson posited that there are three major tenets that primarily affect criminal victimization. The main tenets are (a) motivated offenders, (b) suitable targets, and (c) the absence of capable guardians against a violation (Cohen & Felson, 1979; Cohen, Felson, & Land, 1980; Felson, 1986, 1988; Kennedy & Forde, 1990; Massey, Krohn, & Bonati, 1989; Miethe, Stafford, & Long, 1987; Roneck & Maier, 1991; Sherman, Gartin, & Buerger, 1989). The researchers argued that crime is likely to occur via the convergence of the three tenets. In other words, lack of any of the suggested tenets will be sufficiently capable to prevent a crime occurrence (Cohen & Felson). Other criminologists, namely Akers (2004) and Osgood et al. (1996) noted that routine activities theory suggests that most crimes are associated with the nature of an individual's daily routines based on sociological interrelationships; thus, illustrating that crime is based on situational factors which enable the criminal opportunities.

Yar (2005) applied the routine activities theory core concepts and "aetiological schema" to computer crime in cyberspace (p. 1). Even though Yar's study does not provide an empirical assessment, it guides the current project to construct an optimum measurement strategy by clearly defining new conceptual definitions in computer crime and traits of cyberspace that reflect the core concepts of routine activities theory. Therefore, this section will focus on two phases that reflect Yar's (2005) research. In the first phase, spatiality and temporality in cyberspace are presented, while comparing these items to crimes in the physical world. In the second phase, the major tenets of routine activities are presented via the application of computer crime.

Spatiality and Temporality in Cyberspace

Cohen and Felson (1979) emphasized the importance of "the spatial and temporal structure of routine legal activities" that facilitates an interpretation of how criminals take opportunities to transfer their criminal inclinations into criminal acts (p. 592). In other words, an individual's daily activities in a social situation produce certain conditions or opportunities for motivated offenders to commit criminal acts. Utilizing burglary as an example, frequent social activities away from home can facilitate increasing criminal opportunity, as the absence of a capable guardian at home is likely to make household property a suitable target (Garofalo, 1987).

Indeed, many studies support the likelihood of property crime victimization as being associated with frequent absences from the home (Corrado et al., 1980; Gottfredson, 1984; Sampson & Wooldredge, 1987; Smith, 1982). Routine activities theorists also argue that crime victimization can be determined by a "proximity to high concentrations of potential offenders" (p. 596; see Lynch 1987; Cohen et al., 1981; Miethe & Meier, 1990). However, the important question is how to link from these concepts in the physical world to computer-crime victimization in cyberspace.

In order to apply the concept of routine activities to the computer-crime issue, cyber-spatial and cyber-temporal structures need to be defined. Cyberspace or online activities consist of Web sites hosted by digital communities ("chat rooms," "classrooms," "cafes," etc.) that link together via the World Wide Web (Adams, 1998, p. 88–89). The significant difference between physical-space and cyberspace is that, unlike a physical location, cyberspace is not limited to distance, proximity, and physical separation (Yar, 2005). Mitchell (1995) referred to cyberspace and its environment as "antispatial" (p. 8). Stalder (1998) also asserted that the cyber environment is composed of a zero-distance dimension. Clicking a digital icon in cyberspace takes an online user everywhere and anywhere. Thus, the mobility of offenders in cyberspace far exceeds the mobility of offenders in the physical world. Although it has been proposed that the mobility rules of the physical world would not apply in the world of cyberspace (Dodge & Kichin, 2001; Yar, 2005), this would only necessarily apply in dealing with the weight or physical bulk of the target.

Examining social context factors in both physical and cyber-spatial structures is crucial because social environments interact with the traits of spatiality, and this association can provide criminal opportunities. In the physical world, numerous studies suggest that social context factors have a substantial influence on crime victimization. The National Crime Survey and British Crime Survey have consistently indicated that demographic factors such as age, race, and marital status are associated with general crime victimization (Cohen et al., 1981; Gottfredson, 1984, 1986; Laub, 1990). Cohen and Cantor (1980) specifically found that the demographic characteristics associated with a typical larceny victimization include "a family income of $20,000 or more a year, sixteen through twenty-nine year olds, people who live alone, and persons who are unemployed" (p. 140). Mustaine and Tewksbury (1998) examined minor and major theft victimization among college students and found that the victims' demographic factors, types of social activities, level of self-protective efforts, neighborhood environments (level of noise), and the participation in illegitimate behaviors (threats with a weapon) have a strong influence on the level of both minor and major theft victimization risk.

Bernburg and Thorlindsson (2001) expanded routine activity theory, referring to it as "differential social relations," by mainly focusing on social context that addresses situational motivation and opportunity. The study was based on cross-sectional data from a national survey of Icelandic adolescents. Bernburg and Thorlindsson (2001) found that a routine activities indicator, "unstructured peer interaction in the absence of authority figures," is positively associated with deviant behaviors (violent behavior and property offense), and the association between the routine activities indicator and deviant behavior is significantly accounted for by social contextual factors (pp. 546–547).

Cyberspace also shares a common social environment with the physical world. Castells (2002) asserted that cyberspace is oriented from the social and international environment in our society and reflects the "real world" of socioeconomic and cultural dimensions (p. 203). In other words, cyberspace is "real space'" that is closely correlated to the physical world. Internet users can view diverse Web pages everyday as a part of their routine activities in relation to their different needs. Online users with different demographic backgrounds may visit different types of Web sites based on their different interests and, thus, the compilation of a cyber-community can be distinguished by its members' interests in cyberspace (Castells, 2002).

In addition, even though there are no limitations on physical distance in order to connect another place in cyberspace, Internet users usually find a popular Web site (i.e., Ebay, MSN, AOL, Myspace.com) that has a higher density of Internet connections than other domains via a search engine (i.e. Google, Yahoo). Therefore, a higher density of Internet connection may indicate the proximity of computer criminals and computer-crime victims (Yar, 2005). In fact, computer victimization occurrences can be seen in many social networking Web sites.

In terms of the concept of temporarily, routine activities theory assumes that a crime event occurs in a particular place *at a particular time,* which indicates the importance of a clear temporal sequence and order for a crime to occur. Cohen and Felson (1979) asserted that "the coordination of an offender's rhythms with those of a victim" facilitates a convergence of a potential offender and a target (p. 590). In Cohen and Felson's proposition, crime occurrences in particular places may be applicable to a study of computer-crime victimization because computer criminals often search suitable targets in certain social networking sites where online users are populated (Piazza, 2006). However, their proposition of a particular time does not seem to match with the temporal structure of cyberspace. The uniqueness of the temporal structure of cyberspace is that computer users and crime offenders are globally populated because the World Wide Web does not limit time zones and is fully available to anyone at anytime for access (Yar, 2005). Thus, it is almost impossible to estimate the number of computer criminals that are engaging in crimes at any specific point in time. However, just as is noted in routine activities theory, it is assumed that there is always a motivated offender waiting for the opportunity to commit a criminal act.

Three Core Concepts: Routine Activities Theory

Motivated Offender: Computer Criminal

The routine activities theoretical perspective suggests that there will always be a sufficient supply of crime motivation, and motivated offenders are a given situational factor (Cohen & Felson, 1979). This project accepts Cohen and Felson's assumption that there will always be motivated offenders. Therefore, the new computer-crime victimization model will not test this specific element, but it is important to explain the computer criminals' motivations and why the existence of motivated offenders in cyberspace is a given situation in this research.

The Internet has allowed certain people to find new and innovative ways to commit traditional crimes. These people are called "hackers." The term "hacker" was originated from a tradition of creating attention-seeking pranks (called "hacks") at the Massachusetts Institute for Technology (MIT) in the 1950s and 1960s (Wark, 2010). Hacking was achieved among computer enthusiasts for recognition via improvements or modifications to each other's programming code (Wark). Hackers form computer clubs and user groups, circulate newsletters, attend trade shows, and even have their own conventions. More recently, the term has changed to have negative connotations, referring to those who use computers for illegal, unauthorized, or disruptive activities (Knetzger and Muraski, 2009). In order to emphasize this difference, some use the term "cracker" to refer to the latter and "hacker" as it originally was used (Wark, 2010).

Britz (2004) described hackers as people who view and use computers as toolkits of exploration and exploitation. In fact, there has been very little research on the way how they truly operate in cyberspace. Holt (2009) argues that hackers have become engaged in various criminal activities such as cyber terrorism and organized crime but the prevalence of these criminal groups within hacker subculture is unknown.

Hoffer and Straub's (1989) study of the motivations of computer abusers indicated that 34.1% of the hackers abuse computer systems for their personal gain, 26% of hackers do so for fun and entertainment purposes, 11.4% of the hackers intentionally attack computer systems, and 28.4% of the hackers misuse computer systems due to ethical ignorance. According to the 2004 Australian Computer Crime and Security Survey (2005), 52% of respondents from the survey believed that the primary motive of the computer criminals was "unsolicited malicious damage" against their organization, while other respondents believed that the computer criminals are motivated by "the possibility of illicit financial gains or commercially motivated sabotage" (pp. 14–15).

Computer criminals use computers, and telecommunications links, as a potentially dangerous and costly deviant behavior, partially for the purpose of breaking into various computer systems (Britz, 2004). They also steal valuable information, software, phone services, credit card numbers, and digital cash. They pass along and even sell their services and techniques to others, including organized crime organizations (Britz, 2004). In cyberspace, motivated computer criminals are online to find the suitable targets (online users), who connect to the Internet without taking precautions or using computer security software (Britz, 2004).

Thus, in cyberspace, motivated offenders and suitable targets collide frequently. Grabosky (2000) lists the most evident motivations of computer criminals as "greed, lust, power, revenge, adventure, and the desire to taste 'forbidden fruit'" (p. 2). After an Internet Technology employee is fired from a company, the angered employee may retaliate by shutting down the company's computer systems. Computer criminals, like "cyber-punks," want to try hacking to have fun, and they like to feel in control over others' computer systems (Britz, 2004). After getting caught by authorities, they often claim that they were just curious. In addition, "crackers" implant a malicious virus to a computer system, or take valuable files which may contain customer information such as credit card numbers or social security numbers (Britz, 2004). They can then sell or illegally use the information, thus posing a threat to corporate security and personal privacy (Rosenblatt, 1996).

Parker (1998) also described computer criminals' motives as greed, need, and the inability of recognizing the harm towards computer-crime victims. In addition, Parker (1998) asserts that computer criminals tend to utilize "the Robin Hood syndrome" as their justification for committing crimes. Therefore, following Cohen and Felson's (1979) theoretical assumption in terms of motivated offenders, the suggested various research also speculates that motivated offenders are a given situational factor. This is due to the fact that computer criminals, with various motivations, are available in cyberspace. Thus, one of routine activity theory's tenets, motivated offenders, nicely matches with motivated computer criminals.

Suitable Target in Cyberspace

The second tenet, a "suitable target" refers to a person or an item that may influence the criminal propensity to commit crime (Cohen, Kluegel, & Land, 1981; Felson, 1998). So, theoretically, the desirability of any given person or any given item could be the subject of a potential perpetuator (Cohen et al., 1981; Felson, 1998). However, crime victimization is mostly determined by the accessibility dimension, which links to the level of capable guardianship, regardless of the target desirability (Cohen et al., 1981; Yar, 2005).

Felson (1998), in an extension to the theory, presented four different target suitability measures based on the potential offender's viewpoint. Felson referred to the offender's perception of the *value* of target to likely offender, the *inertia* of the target to likely offender, the *visibility* of the target to likely offender, and the *access* to easily exit from the offense location (commonly referred to as VIVA). First, the valuation of targets becomes complicated in computer crime because the complexity is associated with the offender's motivation or purpose to commit computer crime (Yar, 2005). Even though Hoffer and Starub's research (1989) and the 2004 Australian Computer Crime and Security Survey briefly delineate a computer criminal's motivation (for malicious intent, personal pleasure, personal gain, etc.) toward computer-crime victims, it is difficult to conclude that the research reflects the true estimate of the computer criminal's motivation. This is due to the fact that the survey respondents, company employees, do not represent the pool of the computer criminal population. In fact, many criticisms on computer crime related quantitative and qualitative research are driven from lack of "generalizable data" based on computer-crime incidents against private victims in quantitative research, and small sample sizes in qualitative research that may draw biased outcomes (Moitra, 2005).

However, research indicates that one of clearest computer criminals' targets are individuals, or an organization, from whom they seek to obtain digital property. This is because cyberspace is formed by digital codes that contain digital information and digital property (Yar, 2005). Digital property such as business Web sites and personal Web sites can also be vandalized by computer criminals, or the criminals can steal important personal information such as social security numbers or credit cards numbers (Yar, 2005). Thus, the targets in cyberspace can experience a wide range of offenses committed against them including trespass, theft, cyber stalking, or vandalism based on the potential offender's intent (see Bernburg & Thorlindsson, 2001; Birkbeck & LaFree, 1993; Yar, 2005).

The second measure of VIVA, the inertia of crime targets, is an important criterion in target suitability. Inertia and suitability have an inverse relationship; a higher level of the inertial resistance is likely to weaken the level of the target suitability (Yar, 2005). In human-to-human confrontations, it may be more difficult for the offender to commit a violent crime against a physically stronger target (Felson 1998; Felson 1996). Comparatively, in cyberspace, the level of inertia of crime targets may be affected by "the volume of data" if the computer criminals have limited computer systems such as a very low capacity in their hard drive, their memories, or their CPUs (Yar, 2005). However, overall, the inertia of a crime target in cyberspace is relatively weaker than the physical world because the cost of computers is becoming affordable and the development of technology constantly helps computer criminals equip themselves with more efficient tools, such as high-speed Internet and external hard drives, to commit computer crimes.

The third measure of VIVA, the visibility of crime targets, has a positive association with target suitability (Bennett, 1991; Felson, 1998; Yar 2005). That is, the level of target visibility increases the crime target suitability. Since most computer-crime targets in cyberspace are intangible, consisting of digital information, it would be difficult to conceptualize its visibility (Yar, 2005). However, computer criminals gain the digital information from online users through various toolkits they can use in cyberspace, such as I.P. Trackers or Password Sniffers. Therefore, the gained valuable digital information such as credit card information, personal documentation, or passwords, is observable via a computer monitor. Such information can then be transformed to a hard copy via a printer. Thus, computer-crime targets are "globally visible" to computer criminals in cyberspace (Yar, 2005).

The fourth measure of VIVA, accessibility, has a positive correlation with target suitability. Felson (1998) defined accessibility as the "ability of an offender to get to the target and then get away from the scene of crime" (p. 58). The IC3 2004 Internet Crime Report (2005) indicated that one of the most significant problems in investigating and prosecuting computer crime is that "the offender and victim may be located anywhere worldwide" (p. 13). In fact, the Internet provides criminals with vast opportunities to locate an abundance of victims at a minimum cost, because computer criminals use computers to cross national and international boundaries electronically to victimize online users (Kubic, 2001).

In addition, the sophistication of computer criminal acts, by the criminals utilizing anonymous re-mailers, encryption devices, and accessing third-party systems to commit an offense for the original target, makes it difficult for law enforcement agencies to apprehend and prosecute the offenders (Grabosky 2000; Grabosky & Smith 2001; Furnell, 2002; Yar, 2005). Thus, anonymity and sophistication of computer criminal techniques in cyberspace strengthens the level of accessibility that provides computer criminals with the ability to get away in cyberspace.

In sum, the application of VIVA to cyberspace indicates that target suitability in cyberspace is a fully given situation. When an online user accesses the Internet, personal information in his or her computer naturally carries valuable information into cyberspace that attracts computer criminals. In addition, if computer criminals have sufficiently capable computer systems, the inertia of the crime target becomes almost weightless in cyberspace. The nature of visibility and accessibility within the cyber-environment also allows the motivated cyber-offenders to detect crime targets and commit offenses from anywhere in the world. Therefore, the current project speculates that within the three Routine Activities theoretical components, the most viable tenet that can control the level of computer-crime victimization is the level of capable guardianship.

Capable Guardianship in Cyberspace

In the third tenet of routine activities theory, an absence of capable guardianship, a guardian can simply be a person who can protect the suitable target (Eck & Weisburd, 1995). Guardianship can be defined in three categories: formal social control, informal social control, and target-hardening activities (Cohen, Kluegel, & Land, 1981). First, formal social control agents would be the criminal justice system, which plays important roles in reducing crime (Cohen et al., 1981). Examples of these formal social controls would be the police, the courts, and the correctional system.

In cyberspace, computer crime is likely to occur when online users have an absence of formal capable guardians. Law enforcement agencies contribute formal social control against criminals to protect prospective victims (Grabosky, 2000). Tiernan (2000) argued that primary difficulties in prosecuting computer criminals arise because much of the property involved is intangible and does not match well with traditional criminal statutes such as larceny or theft. This problem weakens the reliability of formal social control agents and is compounded by the increasing number of computer criminals who have been able to access both private and public computer systems, sometimes with disastrous results (Tieran, 2000).

As stated earlier, formal social control agencies have increasingly acknowledged the need to stress new priorities and promote innovative crime prevention strategies designed to counter the advent and continued growth of computer crimes (Taylor, et. al, 2006). Even though federal agencies have guided law enforcement efforts against computer crime, most state and local law enforcement officers still lack knowledge concerning the processing of computer data and related evidence which would be necessary for effective computer-crime investigations (Taylor, et. al, 2006). Hinduja (2009) argues that that the lack of resources and failure of dissimilation of updated technology and training within local and state enforcement agencies are significant impediments to combat against the catalyst of new forms of computer-related crime. Specialized forces to patrol cyberspace are very limited, and they seem to face an extreme difficulty in building a strong formal guardianship for online users (Grabosky, 2000; Grabosky & Smith, 2001). In addition, computer criminals are able to commit crime from any geographic location, and they target victims from all over the world (Kowalski, 2002). Furthermore, the rapid development of technology allows a computer criminal's identity to be concealed by using various computer programs, some of which are mentioned above, which make it very difficult to identify a suspect (Grabosky, 2000).

The 2005 FBI Computer Crime Survey (2006) revealed that computer-crime victims tend not to report incidents to law enforcement agencies for various reasons. The survey found that 23% of the respondents believed that law enforcement would not take any action against the crime, and an equal ratio of respondents believed that law enforcement does not have the ability to help prevent computer crime. The findings also indicate that the computer-crime victims are less likely to contact law enforcement agencies for assistance because of a lack of faith in the criminal justice system.

In the physical world, examples of informal social control agents would be parents, teachers, friends, and security personnel (e.g., see Eck, 1995; Felson, 1986). Informal social control involves groups of citizens and individuals who can increase the surveillance and protection function (Cohen, Kluegel, & Land, 1981). In cyberspace, informal social guardians range from "private network administrators and systems security staff" to "ordinary online citizens" (Yar, 2005, p. 423). Even though criminal justice policies have been slowly geared toward computer-crime initiatives to increase public awareness, by relying upon "self-regulation, codes-of-conduct or etiquettes, monitoring groups (against for example, child pornography), and cooperative measures by private and semi-public groups" in order to minimize computer crime, these initiatives are not yet fully viable (Moitra, 2005).

In other words, similar to formal social control, informal social control agents are not actively operative in our cyber society. In addition, it is almost impossible for both formal and informal social control agents to maintain existing effective guardianship since computer criminals have acquired "the ease of offender mobility and the temporal irregularity of cyber-spatial activities" (Yar, 2005, p. 423). Thus, the current study posits that both formal and informal social control agents have little impact on computer-crime victimization.

The last category of capable guardianship, target hardening, is associated with activities through physical security such as lighting on areas, using locks, alarms, and barriers which are good examples to reduce the incidence of property crime in the physical world (Tseloni et al., 2004). Various literatures support that increasing the level of target-hardening activities via physical security is likely to decrease victimization risk (Chatterton & Frenz, 1994; Clarke, 1992, 1995; Clarke & Homel, 1997; Laycock, 1985, 1991; Poyner, 1991; Tilley, 1993; Webb & Laycock, 1992). In cyberspace, physical security can be equivalent to computer security with a digital-capable guardian being the most crucial component to protect the computer systems from computer criminals.

Even though technology has generated many serious cybercrimes, it has also created defense systems, so called computer security, to reduce the opportunity to commit computer-related crimes. The failure of an individual to equip their personal computer with computer security, which can enhance the level of capable guardianship in cyberspace, can potentially lead to online victimization. Indeed, the absence of computer security significantly weakens the guardianship and facilitates computer criminals in committing crimes. Thus, this digital guardian, installed computer security, is likely to be one of the most crucial elements of a viable capable guardianship in cyberspace.

When computers are tied to modems or cables, a whole new avenue to potential attack is opened. Simple password protections become insufficient for users demanding tight security (Denning, 1999). Computer security programs, such as anti-hacking software programs, protect the systems against an online attack. The threat is reduced on the mainframe computer because of software incorporated to prevent one user from harming another user's computer by accidental or illegal access. Thus, today many corporations and computer users install software such as firewalls, antivirus, and antispyware programs, to protect computer systems against hackers. In addition, biometric devices such as fingerprint or voice recognition technology and retinal imaging enhance the protection against unauthorized access to information systems (Denning, 1999).

Unfortunately, computer security is never absolute and the only secure computer is one that has no contact with the outside world (Denning, 1999). In other words, the computer system will never be completely secured, so it is impossible to remove the opportunity for computer criminals to commit crimes. However, computer users can minimize the criminal opportunity by installing computer security, so they can hinder criminals from penetrating their computer systems. Thus, the current project includes installed computer security as the crucial key element of a capable guardian, from the perspective of routine activities Theory, which is transposable into the new computer-crime victimization model.

Target Suitability Revisited: Lifestyle-Exposure Theory

In 1978, Hindelang, Gottfredson, and Garofalo developed the lifestyle exposure model which focuses on the victims' daily social interactions, rather than concentrating on the characteristics of individual offenders or individual causal variables. Lifestyle-exposure theory holds that criminal victimization results from the daily living patterns of the victims (Goldstein, 1994; Kennedy & Ford, 1990). Hindelang et al. (1978) defined lifestyle as "routine daily activities" including "vocational activities (work, school, keeping house, etc.) and leisure activities" (p. 241). The current project interest in lifestyle-exposure theory is to assess online lifestyles by examining the individual's online vocational activities and leisure activities that may contribute to computer-crime victimization. This section briefly introduces the concepts of the original lifestyle-exposure theory. Then, the lifestyle-exposure theory is applied to online lifestyles, such as vocational activities and leisure activities in cyberspace, online risk-taking behavior, and properly maintaining installed computer security systems.

Hindelang et al. (1978) posited that the lifestyles of individuals are determined by "differences in role expectations, structural constraints, and individual and subcultural adaptations" (p. 245). In the first phase of the lifestyle exposure theoretical model, Hindelang et al. (1978) discussed how role expectations and social structure create constraints. They conceptualized "role expectation" as expected behaviors that are corresponded to cultural norms, which link with the individuals' "achieved and ascribed statuses" (Hindelang et al., p. 242). Hindelang et al. argued that an individual's age and gender are substantially associated with role expectations, because certain age and gender differences are expected to follow normative roles in American society. The researchers defined "structural constraints" as "limitations on behavioral options" which constantly deploy conflicts to individuals by corresponding with "the economic, familial, educational, and legal orders" (Hindelang, et al., p. 242). Research by Kennedy and Forde (1990) found that personal variables associated with the lifestyle, such as age, sex, marital status, family income, and race, significantly influence daily activities and the level of criminal victimization risk. The study also suggests that lifestyle factors significantly reflect the individuals' amount of exposure time in places associated with victimization risk (Kennedy & Forde, 1990).

An adaptation process occurs when individuals or groups initiate gaining knowledge of skills and attitudes in order to manage the constraints associated with role expectations and social structure. This process develops some individual traits, including the individual's attitudes and beliefs. In the course of continuing these processes, the individuals modify their attitudes and beliefs, and these learned traits naturally become a part of the daily routine behavioral patterns (Hindelang et al., 1978). In the second phase of the model, differential lifestyle patterns are associated with "role expectations, structural constraints, and individual and subcultural adaptations (Hindelang et al.).

Hindelang et al. (1978) addressed the importance of the relationship between victimization and vocational and leisure activities. Vocational and leisure activities are the daily activities that are central to a person's life. These lifestyle activities are predictive of personal interactions with others as formal roles. Hindelang et al. asserted that lifestyle and exposure to the level of victimization risk are directly related in the model. Moreover, Hindelang et al. (1978) suggested that association, which refers to the level of personal relationships within individuals who share common interests, is another factor that indirectly links exposure to personal victimization. In other words, personal associations increase level of the exposure to individual victimization.

So, how can we define lifestyle activities in cyberspace? Like the physical world, in cyberspace, online users have online daily activities, such as checking e-mail, seeking information, purchasing items, socializing with friends, and obtaining online entertainment, which are becoming a major portion of the users' lives. Through online activities in cyberspace, people can constantly interact with others via various online tools, such as e-mail and electronic messengers, and create their own online lifestyle by engaging in various online communities based on their particular interests, such as cyber-cafés, clubs, and bulletin boards.

However, online lifestyles can result in a catastrophic event for online users. For instance, on May 3, 2000, many online users received and opened an e-mail from significant others, coworkers, or government officials with the subject line "ILOVEYOU" without sensing that the email was one of the most malicious viruses ever experienced by Internet users. The ILOVEOU virus was a fast-infecting virus that changed window registry settings and then e-mailed copies of itself to everyone in the original victim's Microsoft Outlook Express address book. Thus, clicking on the icon activated the virus. The virus then forwarded itself via e-mail to each address contained in the affected computer's Outlook address book (Winston Salem Journal, 2000).

Even though there was no clearly discernable, actual amount of monetary damage from the ILOVEYOU virus, the worldwide monetary damage due to the virus infection was estimated at between $4 billion to $10 billion, all occurring during a mere couple of days (Winston Salem Journal, 2000). This disastrous case clearly indicates that the Internet has become one of the most significant communication tools by combining online vocational and leisure activities into one method of "mail, telephone, and mass media" in cyberspace (Britz, 2004). The case presented above also illuminates that as digital necessity, in the form of going online, is becoming an increasing part of more peoples' lifestyles it is a crucial lifestyle activity that could also carry with it a very great threat to our personal lives.

Lifestyle-exposure theory attempts to estimate the "differences in the risks of violent victimization across social groups" (Meier et al., 1993, p. 466). It has been applied to various types of crime, and it has succeeded in various ways in explaining the causes of victimization (Meier et al., 1993). Gover (2004) tested victimization theories by utilizing a public high-school student population in South Carolina. This study suggested that the effects of social interaction indirectly influence violent victimization in dating relationships (Gover, 2004). Key factors were measured through risk-taking behaviors such as drug abuse, alcohol abuse, driving under the influence, and a promiscuous sexual lifestyle (Gover, 2004). The concept of risk taking factors can be applied to cyberspace.

In cyberspace, computer criminals attract online users through fraudulent schemes. In many hacking incidents, computer criminals typically attract a victim, and thus their computer systems, by offering free computer software, free MP3 music downloads, or free movie downloads. Various types of software such as Trojan horses, logic bombs, and time bombs are designed to threaten computer security, and many computer criminals use those viruses and worms by placing hidden virus codes in these free programs. Thus, clicking on an icon without precaution in social networking places in cyberspace can contribute to computer-crime victimization. According to the 2005 FBI Computer Crime Survey (2006), "the virus, worm, and Trojan category" was rated as the highest category of financial loss, which is a rate over three times larger than any other category (p. 10).

Like routine activities theory, life-exposure theory asserts that differential lifestyle patterns involve the likelihood of being in certain locations at certain times and having contact with people with certain characteristics. Thus, the occurrence of criminal victimization relies on "high risk times, places, and people" (Hindelang et al, 1978, p. 245). As noted in the routine activities theory section, temporality is not absolutely necessary in cyberspace because there is no time zone in cyberspace (Yar, 2005).

However, this proposed research argues that visiting certain locations in cyberspace may have a correlation with computer-crime victimization. In other words, specific lifestyle patterns directly link with "differences in exposure to situations that have a high victimization risk" (Hindelang et al, 1978, p. 245). Miethe and Meier (1990) asserted that physical proximity to perpetrators and the level of exposure is statistically associated with risky environment based on burglary, personal theft, and assault victimization cases. Their research used data from the British Crime Survey (Miethe & Meier, 1990). Kennedy and Forde (1990) also indicated that criminal victimization is not a random occurrence, but is strongly associated with certain geographic locations.

Computer criminals search for suitable victims in cyberspace. Online users congregate based on their interests, and they socialize with others in cyberspace. Piazza (2006) stated that computer users' information can be easily sent to hackers by simply clicking a pop-up window in "social networking sites" such as free download places and online bulletin boards when a hacker plants a malicious JavaScript code on these Web sites (p. 54). High levels of network activity on a particular site and search engine tools can guide offenders to popular Web sites in cyberspace (Yar, 2005). These popular Web sites become a sort of shopping mall for offenders, as they cause a multitude of potential victims to congregate in one localized area, thus enabling the offenders to shop for their potential targets.

In addition, properly maintaining installed computer security is a crucial factor in terms of online vocational activities. If an online user connects to the Internet without properly updating computer security, and visits the delinquent Web sites planted with computer viruses, it maximizes the risk of computer-crime victimization. Thus, the project also hypothesizes that those online users, who frequently visit the delinquent Web sites without precaution and neglect regularly updating installed computer security programs, have a high likelihood of experiencing computer-crime victimization.

Potential Theoretical Expansion

Both routine activities theory and lifestyle-exposure theory are widely applied to explain various criminal victimizations. In general, most studies found fairly strong support for both victimization theories with predatory and property crimes. Even though the two theories are empirically supported in the criminological research, the major critique resides in the failure of these theories to specify testable propositions regarding certain offenders' and victims' conditions, as such specification would allow for more accurate predictions of crime (Meier & Miethe, 1993). In addition, little research has been empirically tested on individual computer-crime victimization.

Moreover, it is proffered here that routine activities theory is simply an expansion of the lifestyle-exposure theory espoused by Hindelang et al. in 1978. In other words, routine activities theory is really a theoretical expansion of lifestyle-exposure theory, as it adopts the main tenet in lifestyle-exposure theory, the individual's vocational and leisure activities. It appears that Cohen and Felson (1979) absorbed this tenet into what they call their suitable target tenet, and then add a motivated offender and a lack of capable guardianship. It is posited here that an individual's vocational and leisure activities are what makes him or her a suitable target. Even Cohen and Felson (1979) acknowledged this point. Cohen and Felson (1979) asserted that the individuals' lifestyles reflect the individuals' routine activities such as social interaction, social activities, "the timing of work, schooling, and leisure" (p. 591). These activities, in turn, create the level of target suitability that a motivated offender assigns to that particular target.

Thus, routine activities theory shares more than an important common theme with the lifestyle variable from lifestyle-exposure theory; it has actually incorporated this tenet and added the additional tenets of capable guardianship and motivated offender. This is akin to what Akers (1985) acknowledged that he did with Sutherland's (1947) differential association theory when he developed his social learning theory. Akers (1985) noted that he simply incorporated that theory into his theory by expanding upon the already existent differential association theory tenets. Hence, it is suggested here that these two theories, routine activities theory and lifestyle-exposure theory, are not two separate theories, but that routine activities theory is simply an expansion of lifestyle-exposure theory. Therefore, this study will apply routine activities theory while acknowledging that lifestyle-expansion theory provides a more complete explanation of the "suitable target" tenet found in routine activities theory.

From the routine activities theoretical perspective, one of three tenets, capable guardian, contributes to the new computer-crime victimization model in this project. This project assumes that motivated offenders and suitable targets are given situational factors. In cyberspace, pools of motivated computer criminals can find suitable targets in the form of online users who connect to the Internet without precaution or without equipping adequate computer security. The routine activities approach would lead to the practical application of situational computer-crime prevention measures by changing the conditions and circumstances.

This project finds that the most feasible method of preventing computer-crime victimization that can be adapted from routine activities theory is a target-hardening strategy. This is accomplished in the form of up-to-date, adequate computer security equipment. A target-hardening approach via computer security will make it more difficult for computer criminals to commit computer crimes in cyberspace. Since the operation of formal social control agents in cyberspace is very limited, establishing a viable target-hardening strategy can be made via equipping adequate computer security in the computer system. It is also of note that the individual can also increase the target-hardening strategy by updating and maintaining this computer security. However, updating and maintaining this computer security equates to the lifestyle choices made by the individual. Regardless of whether the person properly updates and maintains the computer security, the fact remains that equipping the computer with computer security is a crucial component in reducing computer criminal opportunities in the new theoretical model.

General research on the lifestyle-exposure theory is limited in explaining computer-crime victimization, but supportive of the new theoretical computer-crime victimization model. Although studies associated with lifestyle-exposure theory have not focused on computer-crime victimization, a victimology perspective based on a personal lifestyle measure under lifestyle-exposure theory is appropriate and useful for understanding computer-crime victimization. This is because the gist of the lifestyle-exposure theory is that different lifestyles expose individuals to different levels of risk of victimization. Thus, one of the research interests is to estimate the level of target suitability by measuring risk-taking factors that potentially contribute to computer-crime victimization. The project assumes that online users, who are willing to visit unknown Web sites or download Web sites in order to gain free MP 3 files or free software programs, or who click on icons without precaution, are likely to be victimized by computer criminals. In other words, the levels of online vocational and leisure activities produce greater or lesser opportunities for computer-crime victimization. Numerous findings support that lifestyle factors play significant roles in individual crime victimization in the physical world. This project hypothesizes that the level of online lifestyle activities would contribute to the potential for computer-crime victimization.

Hindelang et al. (1978) suggest that "vocational activities and leisure activities" are the most crucial components in a lifestyle which have a direct impact on exposure to the level of victimization risk. Here, the specific tenets from lifestyle-exposure theory, as expanded upon by routine activities theory, addressed herein as the online lifestyle activities measure, will be presented as an important theoretical component. In routine activities theory, Felson (1998) stated that target suitability is likely to reflect four main criteria: the value of crime target, the inertia of crime target, the physical visibility of crime target, and the accessibility of crime target (VIVA). This statement is a crucial point, which is compatible with the main lifestyle exposure theoretical perspective that explains why online users become suitable targets by computer criminals. It is the vocational and leisure activities that translate into the level of target suitability ascribed to Felson's (1998) VIVA assessment.

Mustain and Tewksbury (1998) argued that people who engage in delinquent lifestyle activities are likely to become suitable targets "because of their anticipated lack of willingness to mobilize the legal system" (p. 836). More importantly, the victims tend to neglect their risk of victimization by failing to inspect themselves regarding "where you are, what your behaviors are, and what you are doing to protect yourself" (Mustain & Tewksbury, p. 852). This study is designed to follow Mustain and Tewksbury's statement above.

The model is tested using SEM and is followed by a presentation of the research methods used in this study. The model actually consists of what is commonly referred to as two distinct theories, Cohen and Felson's (1979) routine activities theory and Hindelang et al.'s (1978) lifestyle-exposure theory. However, as shown above, routine activities theory is an expansion of lifestyle-exposure theory. Thus, routine activities theory's major concept, the target-hardening strategy, is represented by digital-capable guardianship. Hindelang et al.'s lifestyle-exposure theory's core concept, vocation and leisure activities, which is proffered here represents a more detailed explanation of the suitable target tenet in routine activities theory, is represented here by online lifestyle. This is done to estimate computer-crime victimization. The conceptual model posits that digital-capable guardianship and online lifestyle directly influence computer-crime victimization. This project also posits that convergence of the two variables has an interaction effect that contributes to a direct impact on computer-crime victimization.

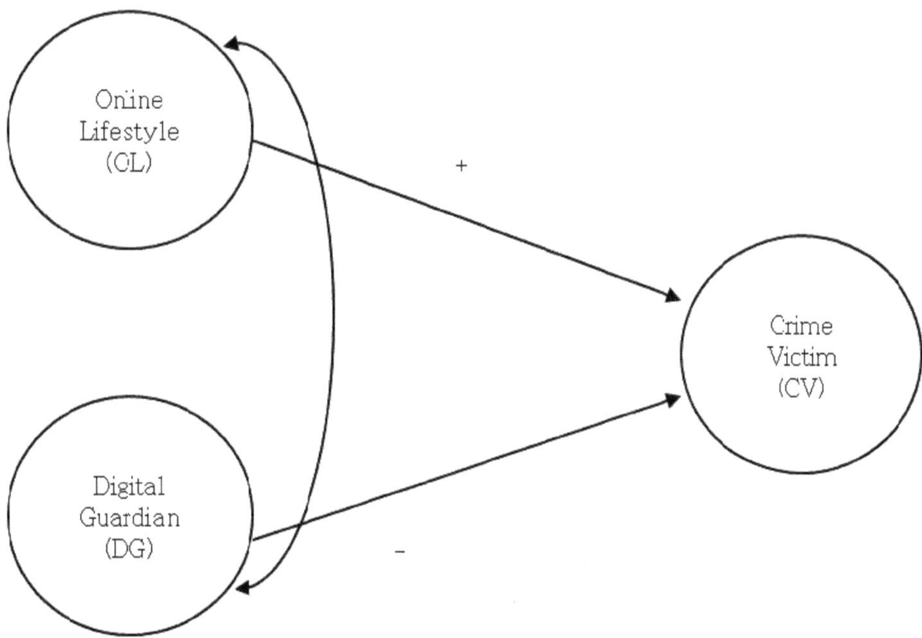

Figure 4.1 The conceptual model for computer-crime victimization.

CHAPTER 1

Conclusion, References, and Review

Increased cyber-connectivity worldwide has brought the global to the local, with rapid advancements in technology constantly impacting and shaping our daily lives. This includes the lives and careers of both law enforcement and criminological researchers, two populations tasked with addressing, studying, analyzing, and predicting crime-related phenomena. As the introductory chapter to *Cybercrime, Cyber Forensics, and Cyber Policing: Law Enforcement Investigations and Forensic Science in the Digital Age*, this chapter familiarized readers with cybercrime terms and concepts as well as criminological perspectives on cybercrime, and offered an introduction to cyber-related police investigations.

More specifically, this chapter began by introducing numerous aspects of cybercrimes, to include tools used by online criminals to facilitate their activities and terms applied to such activities (e.g., encryption, hacking, spoofing, cracking, logic bombs, viruses, worms, PGP). Also introduced briefly were law enforcement concerns regarding potential Fourth Amendment violations related to cyber criminal investigations (an issue that will be revisited in greater detail in Chapter Four of this book) and technologies available to police to aid their investigations (e.g., AFIS and CODIS).

Common types of cybercrimes (including child pornography, drug trafficking, identity theft, and hacking, with some mention of cyberterrorism) were also discussed throughout the readings in this chapter. As the UNODC (2013) emphasized, the risk and threat of cybercrime continuing to grow and evolve is very serious and evident, and one that is in the forefront of international concerns. New cyber dimensions have been added to traditional criminal investigation procedures. With each passing week, new challenges arise for law enforcement and researchers as new forms of cybercrime develop, and individuals engaged in illegal online acts continue to stay one step ahead of investigators. The next chapter discusses some of these challenges directly related to digital evidence and digital forensic methods and procedures.

References

Beccaria, Cesar. *Of crimes and punishments*. Translated with an introduction by Henry Paolucci. New York: Macmillan, 1963 (1764).

Bentham, Jeremy. *An introduction to the principles of morals and legislation*. Oxford England: Clarendon Press, 1789.

Goring, Charles. *The English convict: a statistical study*. Montclair, NJ: Patterson Smith, 1913. Reprint, Montclair: Patterson Smith, 1972.

Mednick, S.A., J. Volavka, W.F. Gabrielli, and T. Itil, "EEG as a predictor of antisocial Behavior," *Criminology* 19 (1982): 219–231.

Messner, Steven and R. Rosenfeld. *Crime and the American Dream (1st ed)*. Belmont, CA: Wadsworth, 1994.

Raine, Adrian. *The psychopathology of crime: criminal behavior as a clinical disorder*. San Diego: Academic.

Rocque, Michael, B.C. Welsh, and A. Raine, "Biosocial criminology and modern crime Prevention," *The Journal of Criminal Justice*. 40, no.4 (2012): 306–312.

Sampson, Robert and J.H. Laub. *Crime in the making: pathways and turning points through life*. Cambridge, MA: Harvard University Press, 1993.

Sheldon, William. *Varieties of delinquent youth: an introduction to constitutional patriarchy*. Oxford England: Harper, 1949.

United Nations Office on Drugs and Crime (UNODC). *Comprehensive Study on Cybercrime*. New York: United Nations Publication, 2013.

Chapter 1 Review

SECTION A

Choose the best match from the list below. Answers are listed at the back of the book.

1. _____ Virus
2. _____ *Modus operandi*
3. _____ Cracking
4. _____ Hackers
5. _____ Lifestyle Exposure Theory
6. _____ IP Spoofing
7. _____ Pinging or spamming
8. _____ Trap and trace device
9. _____ Encryption
10. _____ Routine Activities Theory

A. Hindelang, Gottfredson, and Garofalo's (1978) theory that criminal victimization results from the daily living patterns of the victims. This theory focuses on the victims' daily social interactions, rather than concentrating on the characteristics of individual offenders or individual causal variables.

B. A form of vandalism, or sabotaging, that involves bombarding an e-mail address with thousands of messages using automatic remailer tools.

C. A means of protecting communication and electronic commerce. Can be used by organized crime or terrorist groups to conceal illegal activities.

D. A device used to record the telephone numbers dialed by a specific phone.

E. Method of operation.

F. A program designed to attach itself to a file, reproduce, and spread from one file to another, destroying data, displaying an irritating message, or otherwise disrupting computer operations.

G. Originally a term for attention-seeking pranksters at MIT in the 1950s and 1960s, but has since come to be defined as individuals who use computers for illegal, unauthorized, or disruptive activities.

H. Cohen and Felson's (1979) theory that crime is likely to occur via the convergence of three tenets: motivated offenders, suitable targets, and the absence of capable guardians.

I. An attack whereby the attacker disguises himself or herself as another user by means of a false IP network address.

J. The process of trying to overcome a security measure.

SECTION B

Discussion questions. Answer these questions given the context of the readings in the chapter.

1. The UNODC report stated that the word "cybercrime" "... is not amenable to a single definition, and is likely best considered as a collection of acts or conduct, rather than one single act." Do you agree with this argument? Is it possible to come up with one universal definition that all countries can use? If not, is it possible to develop one single definition that all entities in the United States can use? Why or why not?

2. The UNODC report discussed fourteen cybercrime acts. Do you believe this list to be comprehensive? Given the readings in this chapter, would you add or remove anything to or from this list? Why or why not?

While the previous chapter introduced broad topics under the "cybercrime" and "police investigations" umbrellas, this chapter takes a closer look at two very important elements in cyber-related police investigations: digital evidence and digital forensics. Digital evidence references information and data of value to an investigation that is stored on, received, or transmitted by an electronic device. In other words, digital evidence is the evidence collected by law enforcement officials investigating cybercrime cases or traditional cases involving some form of technology. Digital forensics refers to the branch of forensic science concerned with the recovery and investigation of material found in digital and computer systems. Here, trained investigators and laboratory technicians use digital forensic methods to glean information from digital evidence in criminal investigations. This information may tell investigators more about the person who owns the technology or the people associated with the person in question, and investigators may even be able to place the individuals or technology at the crime scene.

One issue unique to cybercrime investigations is the crime scene itself. If you live in Alabama and hackers living in Massachusetts obtain your personal information and steal your identity, where is the crime scene? Is it your personal computer in Alabama? Is it the computer of the hackers? Is it both? The notion of a "digital crime scene" has further complicated modern policing and has left victims of cybercrime at a loss about which authorities to alert. Now, the victim and the perpetrator can be thousands of miles apart *during* the commission of the crime; concepts of "local" and "global" converge. In this scenario, multiple state jurisdictions are involved, which requires either additional cooperation between multiple local and state agencies or the engagement of federal law enforcement in the investigation (depending on the circumstances of each case). Having multiple agencies involved requires cooperation and coordination of forensic analysis of the digital evidence, a feat that in and of itself presents its own (legal and investigative) complications. Regardless, it cannot be emphasized enough how digital evidence commonly stretches across multiple jurisdictions and plays a key role in multiple digital crime scenes.

Digital evidence differs from physical evidence and constitutes an incredibly broad array of items limited only by the imagination. Hardware—consisting of (for instance) computers, thumb drives, or phones themselves—falls under the physical evidence umbrella; investigators can dust these objects for fingerprints, they can be physically picked up and moved, and, if damaged, parts of these objects may be left behind at a physical location. These are devices that house digital evidence, and can also include GPS devices, digital video recorders, gaming systems capable of storing data (e.g., Xbox), and digital music players (Cohen, 2007). Digital evidence, however, cannot be physically touched, held, or dusted for fingerprints. Digital evidence is the information and the data taken from these physical, technological objects, and can be either content-based digital evidence or non-content-based. "Content-based" refers to the fact that it is the digital *content* that is illegal to possess, sell, or buy, while "non-content-based" refers to illegal digital movements or actions. Evidence of content-based cybercrimes includes examples such as pictures of child pornography stored on a person's computer, digital lists of illegally obtained Social Security and credit card numbers, and electronic ledgers from illegal transactions. These are pictures or content that can be emailed, bought, and sold online. When the police are investigating a person suspected of engaging in these digital content-based crimes, digital forensic methods will be applied to the suspect's computer, mobile phone, and any other device that might store the illegal content. For investigative purposes, it is generally easier for the police to connect individuals to content-based cybercrimes than non-content-based.

However, not all cybercrimes involve content-based evidence. For instance, hackers' obtaining unauthorized access to databases, websites, or secured networks is considered non-content-based, because it is the act of online trespassing that is illegal. Likewise, while illicit drugs are bought and sold online, buyers cannot have the physical heroin emailed to them. These types of cybercrimes are often more challenging for police to investigate than content-based, because it is much harder to identify, for instance, the source of the hack: that is, aside from what computer was used in the process of hacking, where in the world was the hacker located? How can investigators be sure of the identity of the person behind the computer who initiated the hack (absent a camera capturing the moment or catching the person in the act)? In reality, many cybercrimes are composed of both content- and non-content-based digital evidence. In the hacking scenario, it is plausible that the hacker simply wanted unauthorized access to a secured network with no intentions of recording or copying information. However, often hackers (and other cybercriminals) will duplicate such information after cyber-trespassing and store it on their personal computers or other electronic devices, thus also creating content-based digital evidence.

With this in mind, this chapter examines various forms of digital evidence and national guidelines in the United States for forensically analyzing such evidence, and closes with a comparative analysis of assorted international approaches to handling digital evidence among a variety of different criminal justice systems around the world. The first reading in this chapter was produced by the National Forensic Science Technology Center in 2013, and provides a basic understanding of what digital evidence entails, how and when digital evidence can be used to aid an investigation, who can properly conduct an examination of digital evidence, and what the proper procedures are for procuring, maintaining, and examining digital evidence. After describing the uses of the three most common categories of electronic devices from which digital evidence is collected (i.e., the Internet, computers, and mobile devices), the article describes the purpose and relevance of digital evidence in a criminal investigation. Although qualifications are not standardized and there are numerous legal and procedural restrictions (e.g., jurisdictional, privacy, and encryption issues), Certified Digital Media Examiners (DME) can inspect digital evidence such as text messages, photographs, and cellular locations, and can use the evidence gathered to corroborate an ongoing criminal investigation; this evidence could eventually be submitted in court. This guide also outlines the basic necessary procedural steps for collecting various forms of digital evidence from crime scenes, transporting the materials, and analyzing the data once it has arrived in the forensic laboratory. Finally, this reading presents some common misconceptions about digital evidence, and concludes by discussing three standards used to guide evidence and expert witness admissibility in court: the *Frye* Standard,

Federal Rules of Evidence Rule 702, and the *Daubert* Standard.

The second reading in this chapter, written by Tim Grant (2010), opens with two illustrative examples highlighting the value and capability of forensic linguistics as it pertains to criminal investigations; however, this capability is subsequently called into question for its lack of empirically measurable efficiency. First, the reading gives a detailed explanation of an analysis of the cognitivist and stylistic theories of idiolect (a "distinct and individual version of language" as defined the linguistic analyst Martin Coulthard), followed by a discussion of the two major theories of idiolect and their differing abilities to explicate authorial reliability and individuality. Then, a need for a unified theory is emphasized—a unified theory that combines the cognitivist approach's ability to explain the production of certain linguistic features with the stylistic approach's ability to explain individual differences in linguistic patterns. This reading argues in favor of using forensic psychology and the principle of case linkage. Arguments are also made for using behavioral analysis in order to aid criminal investigations, thus enhancing the quantifiable nature of forensic linguistics to distinguish between an independent event and a series of related crimes.

The third and final reading comes from the UNODC's (2013) comprehensive study on cybercrime. Electronic evidence is becoming increasingly important to all stages of criminal proceedings, from the commission of a crime to the admissibility of electronic evidence in court, and this reading highlights the role and procedure of using electronic evidence in criminal justice systems around the world. Types of electronic evidence and the importance of evidence continuity, or chain-of-custody, are described first, followed by a discussion of various types of digital forensics (including computer forensics, mobile device forensics, and network forensics) and forensic techniques used to gain access to and protect the evidence stored inside various devices. From the countries which responded to the study's questionnaire, divergent results regarding the capacity of law enforcement of various countries to handle electronic evidence are revealed, and numerous challenges of electronic evidence (which include a lack of resources, deficiency of technical specialists, encryption complications, cloud computing difficulties, and legal obstacles) are presented and discussed. These challenges all constitute serious problems for the analysis of electronic evidence and the successful prosecution of the offender. In addition to related challenges that law enforcement faces, this reading discusses various challenges endured by prosecutors. Figures and statistics are provided to show the results from the responding countries' questionnaires regarding suspect-to-offense ratios, attrition rates of cybercrime cases, organizational and court structure for prosecuting cybercrime cases, technical capabilities of law enforcement and prosecutors, and various categories regarding training for prosecutors. The reading concludes by discussing areas of technical assistance involved in criminal investigations requested and received by the participating countries, and by calling for long-term sustainable assistance that would aid in building stronger capabilities for both law enforcement and prosecutorial authorities to combat cybercrime worldwide.

KEY WORDS FOUND IN THIS PART

- Digital evidence
- Digital forensics
- Forensic linguistics
- Hash/Hash values
- Cloud computing
- Forensic wipe
- Source code
- "Bit-for-bit" copy
- Write-blocker
- "Data carving"/"file carving"

A Simplified Guide to Digital Evidence

BY NATIONAL FORENSIC SCIENCE TECHNOLOGY CENTER

Introduction to Digital Evidence

Digital devices are everywhere in today's world, helping people communicate locally and globally with ease. Most people immediately think of computers, cell phones and the Internet as the only sources for digital evidence, but any piece of technology that processes information can be used in a criminal way. For example, hand-held games can carry encoded messages between criminals and even newer household appliances, such as a refrigerator with a built-in TV, could be used to store, view and share illegal images. The important thing to know is that responders need to be able to recognize and properly seize potential digital evidence.

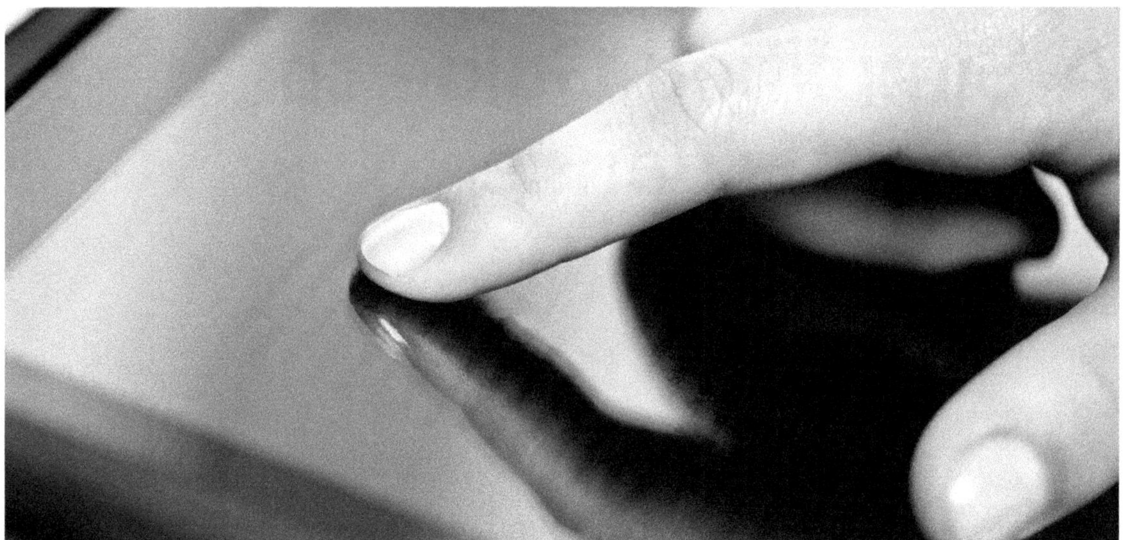

Digital evidence is defined as information and data of value to an investigation that is stored on, received or transmitted by an electronic device[1]. This evidence can be acquired when electronic devices are seized and secured for examination. Digital evidence:

- Is latent (hidden), like fingerprints or DNA evidence
- Crosses jurisdictional borders quickly and easily
- Can be altered, damaged or destroyed with little effort
- Can be time sensitive

There are many sources of digital evidence, but for the purposes of this publication, the topic is divided into three major forensic categories of devices where evidence can be found: Internet-based, stand-alone computers or devices, and mobile devices. These areas tend to have different evidence-gathering processes, tools and concerns, and different types of crimes tend to lend themselves to one device or the other.

The Principles of Digital Evidence

Information that is stored electronically is said to be 'digital' because it has been broken down into digits; binary units of ones (1) and zeros (0), that are saved and retrieved using a set of instructions called software or code. Any kind of information—photographs, words, spreadsheets—can be created and saved using these types of instructions. Finding and exploiting evidence saved in this way is a growing area of forensics and constantly changes as the technology evolves.

Internet: The launch of the Internet or World Wide Web in the mid 1990's truly ushered in the 'age of access.' For the first time, individuals outside the academic world could use it to connect with others (and their computers) in a brand new way. The Internet opened up access to a world of information and resources, but also provided a highway for the traffic of illegal images, information and espionage.

Because of the global access to information and to other computers, criminals are able to use this access to hack into financial and communications systems, major corporations and government networks to steal money, identities and information, or to sabotage systems. One of the biggest challenges in Internet crime is for investigators, laboratory and technical personnel to understand how the process works and to stay closely engaged with advances in software and tracking technologies.

How it works: Any computer that connects to an Internet Service Provider (ISP) becomes part of the ISP's network, whether it is a single computer or part of a local area network (LAN) at a work place. Each ISP connects to another network, and so on. In this way, the Internet is literally a web of networks where information can be sent and received to any point on the web from any other point. This global collection of networks has no 'owner' or overall controlling network, so it operates like a community with all the pros and cons you might find in any other community.

Computers: In the late 1970s, employees at the Flagler Dog Track in Florida used a computer to create and print fraudulent winning tickets. This prompted Florida to enact the first computer crime law, the Florida Computer Crimes Act, which declared un-authorized use of computing facilities a crime. Federal laws followed in 1984.

Computer crimes continue to be a growing problem in both the public and private sector. A single computer can contain evidence of criminal activity carried out on the web, or the criminal use can be contained in the computer itself, such as pornography, copyright infringement, extortion, counterfeiting and much more. Digital evidence is located on the computer's hard drive and peripheral equipment, including removable media such as thumb drives and CD-ROM discs.

Mobile devices: Although handheld voice transmission devices using radio transmission have been in use since the 1940s (the Walkie- Talkie), the first version of what we would now call a cell phone was not developed until the 1980s. Cell phone use around the world skyrocketed in the 1990s and hit 4.6 billion cell subscriptions by the end of 2009. Cell phone and wireless technology has expanded to include many types of mobile devices such as tablet computers and hand-held video games.

Once used only for voice communications, today's cell phones are also used to take digital photos and movies, send instant messages, browse the web and perform many of the same tasks as a computer. Mobile devices allow criminals to engage in an ever-growing variety of activities and the devices keep track of every move and message. It is this tracking capability that turns mobile devices into key evidence in many cases.

Why and When is Digital Evidence Used?

Digital evidence may come into play in any serious criminal investigation such as murder, rape, stalking, car-jacking, burglary, child abuse or exploitation, counterfeiting, extortion, gambling, piracy, property crimes and terrorism. Pre- and post-crime information is most relevant, for example, if a criminal was using an online program like Google Maps™ or street view to case a property before a crime; or posting stolen items for sale on Craigslist or E-Bay®; or communicating via text-message with accomplices to plan a crime or threaten a person. Some crimes can be committed entirely through digital means, such as computer hacking, economic fraud or identity theft.

In any of these situations, an electronic trail of information is left behind for a savvy investigation team to recognize, seize and exploit. As with any evidence-gathering, following proper procedures is crucial and will yield the most valuable data. Not following proper procedures can result in lost or damaged evidence, or rendering it inadmissible in court.

How It's Done

Evidence that May be Gathered Digitally

Computer documents, emails, text and instant messages, transactions, images and Internet histories are examples of information that can be gathered from electronic devices and used very effectively as evidence. For example, mobile devices use online-based based backup systems, also known as the 'cloud,' that provide forensic investigators with access to text messages and pictures taken from a particular phone. These systems keep an average of 1,000–1,500 or more of the last text messages sent to and received from that phone.

In addition, many mobile devices store information about the locations where the device traveled and when it was there. To gain this knowledge, investigators can access an average of the last 200 cell locations accessed by a mobile device. Satellite navigation systems and satellite radios in cars can provide similar information. Even photos posted to social media such as Facebook may contain location information. Photos taken with a Global Positioning System (GPS)-enabled device contain file data that shows when and exactly where a photo was taken. By gaining a subpoena for a particular mobile device account, investigators can collect a great deal of history related to a device and the person using it.

Who Conducts the Analysis

According to the National Institute of Justice (**http://www.nij.gov/nij/topics/forensics/evidence/digital/investigati ve-tools/welcome.htm**), "Digital evidence should be examined only by those trained specifically for that purpose." With the wide variety of electronic devices in use today and the speed with which they change, keeping up can be very difficult for local law enforcement. Many agencies do not have a digital evidence expert on hand and, if they do, the officer might be a specialist in cell phones but not social media or bank fraud. A detective may be able to log onto e-Bay® and look for stolen property but may be unable to capture cell phone text message histories and could destroy evidence just by trying. Many take an interest in the area and learn what they can, but there is no single path to digital evidence expertise—qualifications and certifications are not standardized across the country. Incorporation of digital seizure techniques is becoming more widespread in first responder training.

Certified Digital Media Examiners are investigators who have the education, training and experience to properly exploit this sensitive evidence. That said, there is no single certifying body, and certification programs can contain different courses of study. Generally speaking, these professionals have demonstrated core competencies in pre-examination procedures and legal issues, media assessment and analysis, data recovery, specific analysis of recovered data, documentation and reporting, and presentation of findings. While certification of examiners is not required in most agencies, it is becoming a widely valued asset and the numbers of certified examiners will increase. Vendor-neutral (not software based, but theory- and process-based) certification is offered through the Digital Forensics Certification Board (DFCB), an independent certifying organization for digital evidence examiners, the National Computer Forensics Academy at the High Tech Crime Institute and some colleges.

Most states have at least one laboratory or section for digital forensics and a variety of task forces including Internet Crimes Against Children (ICAC), Joint Terrorism Task Force (JTTF), and Narcotics and Property Crimes.

These forces comprise officers with specialized training, including search, seizure and exploitation of digital evidence as it pertains to their area of expertise. Agencies and investigators must work together to ensure the highest level of security and evidence handling is used. In the United States, the FBI can provide assistance in some specialty areas.

How Digital Devices are Collected

On the scene: As anyone who has dropped a cell phone in a lake or had their computer damaged in a move or a thunderstorm knows, digitally stored information is very sensitive and easily lost. There are general best practices, developed by organizations like SWGDE and NIJ, to properly seize devices and computers. Once the scene has been secured and legal authority to seize the evidence has been confirmed, devices can be collected. Any passwords, codes or PINs should be gathered from the individuals involved, if possible, and associated chargers, cables, peripherals, and manuals should be collected. Thumb drives, cell phones, hard drives and the like are examined using different tools and techniques, and this is most often done in a specialized laboratory.

First responders need to take special care with digital devices in addition to normal evidence collection procedures to prevent exposure to things like extreme temperatures, static electricity and moisture.

Seizing Mobile Devices

Devices should be turned off immediately and batteries removed, if possible. Turning off the phone preserves cell tower location information and call logs, and prevents the phone from being used, which could change the data on the phone. In addition, if the device remains on, remote destruction commands could be used without the investigator's knowledge. Some phones have an automatic tier to turn on the phone for updates, which could compromise data, so battery removal is optimal.

If the device cannot be turned off, then it must be isolated from its cell tower by placing it in a Faraday bag or other blocking material, set to airplane mode, or the Wi-Fi, Bluetooth or other communications system must be disabled. Digital devices should be placed in antistatic packaging such as paper bags or envelopes and cardboard boxes. Plastic should be avoided as it can convey static electricity or allow a buildup of condensation or humidity.

In emergency or life threatening situations, information from the phone can be removed and saved at the scene, but great care must be taken in the documentation of the action and the preservation of the data.

When sending digital devices to the laboratory, the investigator must indicate the type of information being sought, for instance phone numbers and call histories from a cell phone, emails, documents and messages from a computer, or images on a tablet.

Seizing Stand Alone Computers and Equipment: To prevent the alteration of digital evidence during collection, first responders should first document any activity on the computer, components, or devices by taking a photograph and recording any information on the screen. Responders may move a mouse (without pressing buttons or moving the wheel) to determine if something is on the screen. If the computer is on, calling on a computer forensic expert is highly recommended as connections to criminal activity may be lost by turning off the computer. If a computer is on but is running destructive software (formatting, deleting, removing or wiping information), power to the computer should be disconnected immediately to preserve whatever is left on the machine.

Office environments provide a challenging collection situation due to networking, potential loss of evidence and liabilities to the agency outside of the criminal investigation. For instance, if a server is turned off during seizure that is providing a service to outside customers, the loss of service to the customer may be very damaging. In addition, office equipment that could contain evidence such as copiers, scanners, security cameras, facsimile machines, pagers and caller ID units should be collected.

Computers that are off may be collected into evidence as per usual agency digital evidence procedures.

How and Where the Analysis is Performed

Exploiting data in the laboratory: Once the digital evidence has been sent to the laboratory, a qualified analyst will take the following steps to retrieve and analyze data:

1. **Prevent contamination:** It is easy to understand cross contamination in a DNA laboratory or at the crime scene, but digital evidence has similar issues which must be prevented by the collection officer. Prior to analyzing digital evidence, an image or work copy of the original storage device is created. When collecting data from a suspect device, the copy must be stored on another form of media to keep the original pristine. Analysts must use 'clean' storage media to prevent contamination—or the introduction of data from another source. For example, if the analyst was to put a copy of the suspect device on a CD that already contained information, that information might be analyzed as though it had been on the suspect device. Although digital storage media such as thumb drives and data cards are reusable, simply erasing the data and replacing it with new evidence is not sufficient. The destination storage unit must be new or, if reused, it must be forensically 'wiped' prior to use. This removes all content, known and unknown, from the media.
2. **Isolate Wireless Devices:** Cell phones and other wireless devices should be initially examined in an isolation chamber, if available. This prevents connection to any networks and keeps evidence as pristine as possible. The Faraday bag can be opened inside the chamber and the device can be exploited, including phone information, Federal Communications Commission (FCC) information, SIM cards, etc. The device can be connected to analysis software from within the chamber. If an agency does not have an isolation chamber, investigators will typically place the device in a Faraday bag and switch the phone to airplane mode to prevent reception.
3. **Install write-blocking software:** To prevent any change to the data on the device or media, the analyst will install a block on the working copy so that data may be viewed but nothing can be changed or added.

4. **Select extraction methods:** Once the working copy is created, the analyst will determine the make and model of the device and select extraction software designed to most completely 'parse the data,' or view its contents.
5. **Submit device or original media for traditional evidence examination:** When the data has been removed, the device is sent back into evidence. There may be DNA, trace, fingerprint, or other evidence that may be obtained from it and the digital analyst can now work without it.
6. **Proceed with investigation:** At this point, the analyst will use the selected software to view data. The analyst will be able to see all the files on the drive, can see if areas are hidden and may even be able to restore organization of files allowing hidden areas to be viewed. Deleted files are also visible, as long as they haven't been over-written by new data. Partially deleted files can be of value as well.

Files on a computer or other device are not the only evidence that can be gathered. The analyst may have to work beyond the hardware to find evidence that resides on the Internet including chat rooms, instant messaging, websites and other networks of participants or information. By using the system of Internet addresses, email header information, time stamps on messaging and other encrypted data, the analyst can piece together strings of interactions that provide a picture of activity.

FAQs

What Kind of Results can be Expected From Analysis of Digital Evidence?

If evidence collection and analysis is conducted properly, examiners can secure information that can support criminal activity claims through dialog or message exchange, images and documents. The examiner will generally provide all the supporting documentation, highlighting relevant information, but also a report detailing what was done to extract the data. As with evidence of other types, chain of custody and proper collection and extraction techniques are critical to the credibility of evidence and must be thoroughly documented.

What are the Limitations Regarding the Evidence that can be Gained from Digital Devices?

Investigative limitations are primarily due to encryption and proprietary systems that require decoding before data can even be accessed. Unlike what is portrayed on popular television crime shows, decoding an encrypted password can take a very long time, even with sophisticated software.

There are both legal and technical limitations in this area of investigation. Laws governing processing and prosecution are different from state to state. Digital crime can easily cross jurisdictions, making standardization an increasingly critical law enforcement issue.

Data ownership can be an issue as well. In a recent ruling in Colorado, the holder of a password was compelled to divulge the password, but in doing so did not have to admit knowledge or ownership of the data protected by the password[1]. This is akin to a landlord being able to unlock a rental apartment with no responsibility for what might be inside the unit. In this case, it would still be up to the investigator to tie the two together.

Wiretapping laws can also come into play particularly with regard to mobile phone seizure. Intercepting a call without a court order violates an expectation of privacy. Even after a phone has been seized, any calls or messages received by that phone cannot be used as the holders of the phone (law enforcement) are not the intended recipient.

Privacy laws and issues are the most limiting areas of search. Without proper authority to search or seize electronics, the information contained on the device may not be used. Internet and personal device privacy laws can be confusing. In addition, people's understanding of privacy tends to be generational—younger people tend to believe they should have access to information freely but that their movements and communications are inherently private; older users tend to understand that their movements and communications can be tracked and have a lesser expectation of privacy. Today there has been no major case law to clearly define new limits in the United States.

In the United Kingdom examiners usually follow guidelines issued by the Association of Chief Police Officers (**http://www.acpo.police.uk/**) (ACPO) for the authentication and integrity of evidence. The guidelines consist of four principles:

1. No action taken by law enforcement agencies or their agents should change data held on a computer or storage media which may subsequently be relied upon in court.
2. In exceptional circumstances, where a person finds it necessary to access original data held on a computer or on storage media, that person must be competent to do so and be able to give evidence explaining the relevance and the implications of their actions.
3. An audit trail or other record of all processes applied to computer based electronic evidence should be created and preserved. An independent third party should be able to examine those processes and achieve the same result.
4. The person in charge of the investigation (the case officer) has overall responsibility for ensuring that the law and these principles are adhered to.

These guidelines are widely accepted in courts of England and Scotland, but they do not constitute a legal requirement and their use is voluntary.

How is Quality Control and Assurance Performed?

Quality control and assurance is similar to other forensic specialties in that the laboratory must have and follow guidelines in addition to the responders and analysts. SWGDE brings together organizations actively engaged in the field of digital and multimedia evidence in the U.S. and other countries to foster communication and cooperation as well as to ensure quality and consistency within the forensic community. Practices have been cited by the European Network Forensic Science Institute—Forensic Information Technology Working Group (ENFSI-FITWG) and in publications.

According to SWGDE's Minimum Requirements for Quality Assurance in the Processing of Digital and Multimedia Evidence (**http://www.swgde.org/documents/current-documents/2010-05-15 SWGDE Min Req for QA in Proc Digital Multimedia Evidence_v1.pdf**), Digital Evidence Laboratories (DEL) must have and follow a written Quality Management System (QMS) that is documented in a Quality Manual (QM). The QMS is similar to those in other types of forensic laboratories in that it defines structure, responsibilities, procedures, processes, and resources sound and error-free work and documentation.

To ensure the most accurate analysis of evidence, the management of forensic laboratories puts in place policies and procedures that govern facilities and equipment, methods and procedures, and analyst qualifications and training. Depending on the state in which it operates, a crime laboratory may be required to achieve accreditation to verify that it meets quality standards. There are two internationally recognized accrediting programs focused on forensic laboratories: The American Society of Crime Laboratory Directors Laboratory Accreditation Board (**http://www.ascld-lab.org**) and ANSI-ASQ National Accreditation Board / FQS (**http://www.forquality.org**).

What Information does the Report Include and How are the Results Interpreted?

Like other forms of evidence, digital evidence must remain pristine and unaltered. In a courtroom, text messages would most likely be shared on the actual phone or digital device, but other evidence might be printed out, such as a string of emails or email headers.

```
Received: from SERVERNAME-Exch1.place.com ([172.16.102.10]) by SERVERNAME-exch1
 ([172.16.102.10]) with mapi; Mon, 27 Feb 2012 09:53:10 -0500
Content-Type: application/ms-tnef; name="winmail.dat"
Content-Transfer-Encoding: binary
From: Bad Guy  Bad.Guy@place.com
To: Worse Guy worse.guy@place.com
Date: Mon, 27 Feb 2012 09:53:09 -0500
Subject: Here's the plan
Thread-Topic: Here's the plan
Thread-Index: Acz1X4VRzKScTInUTWSTqYrRhGJhqg==
Message-ID: <2E95727AD62F534E9A60644CAB99079D011790B7E201@servername-exch1>
Accept-Language: en-US
Content-Language: en-US
X-MS-Has-Attach:
X-MS-Exchange-Organization-SCL: -1
X-MS-TNEF-Correlator: <2E95727AD62F534E9A60644CAB99079D011790B7E201@server-exch1>
MIME-Version: 1.0
```

Sample email header showing the path and timing of the message.

This can show a track record of information exchange, and the "hash value", also referred to as a checksum, hash code or hashes, is the mark of authenticity and must be present and explained to courtroom participants.

Results	
Original text	forensic science
Original bytes	66:6f:72:65:6e:73:69:63:20:73:63:69:65:6e:63:65 (length=16)
Adler32	36890654
CRC32	65b2a252
Haval	ec53e6b5a3315da4ac3fab83ec9f8f7a
MD2	e27cc4e242c05896e7e1b4be08159724
MD4	1fd5241554970223a34acae2b9de2cef
MD5	769aaa196bf49c716c905b4b91d6d94c
RipeMD128	32d26d2b1b10c3adbf292b66da8b766f
RipeMD160	3aee598566cb9cecff5dda2968646 3c1aa91848c
SHA-1	a728a136e1fbfafef6205e423423c62efd9fd12f
SHA-256	02d0779148771712a27d93ed92b5240c041a8c6a048ab9078cb1d83610e82df7
SHA-384	40b63414a5c7ef4f6c53d5915521fec4d8e83c46a2e864c7535923502a130c6a3f6e1d1e56eba05654bc22a9229c4f2e
SHA-512	146a6257bb58b4305f00ec92d41edb419efb9b60373f302c5edf0107dfca6eba86548d1276870a0b3572c231a6f513fae2befcae68f2f3db0b3590ff930d9dcf
Tiger	2cb2b89ca649f106d72d14e565df217245967b30695 38b61
Whirlpool	89f0f8e2403a13cc12057071503a7b7a7d9734811869df0c6e859826c0f35c2de611af7bcf77e6c63e6e5c9581c7e9b80e1589752a3f4c9f64a38237f75e96be

Hash values calculated for the text string "forensic science". Each line contains the search term value calculated using the unique algorithm in the left hand column.

A hash value is the result of a calculation (hash algorithm) performed on a string of text, electronic file or entire hard drive contents. Hash values are used to identify and filter duplicate files (i.e. email, attachments, and loose files) from a given source and verify that a forensic image or clone was captured successfully. For example, a hash function performed on a suspect's hard drive should generate a hash value report that exactly match the report generated by using the same algorithm on the hard drive's image, typically created by the laboratory for use in the investigation.

Hash values are a reliable, fast, and a secure way to compare the contents of individual files and media. Whether it is a single text file containing a phone number or five terabytes of data on a server, calculating hash values is an invaluable process for evidence verification in electronic discovery and computer forensics.

Once verified, the information pulled from the files can be shown in the courtroom, such as photos or emails. In addition, email headers, showing the path and timing emails took to get from source to destination could be displayed.

Are There Any Misconceptions or Anything Else About Digital Evidence that Might be Important to the Non-Scientist?

There are a number of common misperceptions about the retrieval and usefulness of digital evidence, including:

Anything on a hard drive or other electronic media can always be retrieved. This is incorrect as over-written or damaged files, or physical damage to the media can render it unreadable. Highly specialized laboratories with clean rooms may be able to examine hard drive components and reconstruct data, but this process is very laborious and extremely expensive.

Decrypting a password is quick and easy, with the right software. With the increasing complexity of passwords including capitals, numbers, symbols and password length, there are billions of potential passwords. Decryption can take a great deal of time, up to a year in somc cascs, using system resources and holding up investigations. Gathering passwords from those involved in a case is much more efficient and should be done whenever possible.

Any digital image can be refined to high definition quality. Images can be very useful for investigations, but a low resolution image is made by capturing fewer bits of data (pixels) than higher resolution photos. Pixels that are not there in the first place cannot be refined.

Investigators can look at digital evidence at the crime scene or any time. Just looking at a file list does not damage the evidence. It is crucial to note that opening, viewing or clicking on files can severely damage forensic information because it can change the last access date of a file or a piece of hardware. This changes the profile and can be considered tampering with evidence or even render it completely inadmissible. Only investigators with the proper tools and training should be viewing and retrieving evidence.

First responder training lags behind advancements in electronics. Without regular updates to their training, responders may not be aware of what new digital devices might be in use and subject to collection. For example, there should be an awareness that thumb drives and SD cards can be easily removed and discarded by a suspect in the course of an encounter with law enforcement.

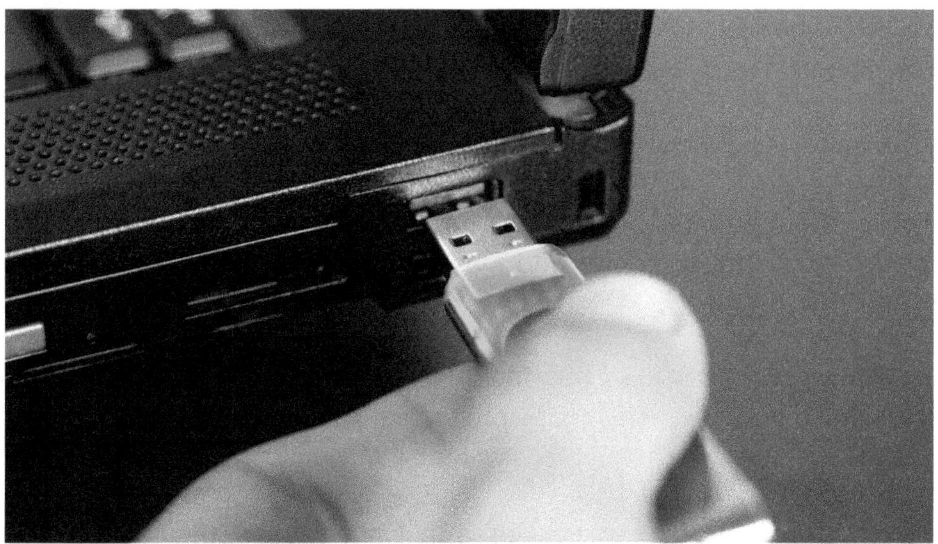

Common Terms

Common terminology is critical in the digital evidence world. The Scientific Working Group on Digital Evidence (SWGDE) in collaboration with the Scientific Working Group on Imaging Technology (SWGIT) has developed and continuously maintains a glossary of terms used within the digital and multimedia disciplines. SWGDE has used ASTM International, a recognized standards organization, to establish international acceptance of terminology. SWGDE/SWGIT's full glossary is available online:
(**http://www.swgde.org/documents/current-documents/SWGDE SWGIT Combined Glossary V2.5.pdf**)

Some common terms include:

Cloud Computing—software, applications and digital storage that is accessed on the Internet through a web browser or desktop or mobile app. The software and user's data are stored on servers at a remote location.

Data—Information in analog or digital form that can be transmitted or processed.

Data Extraction—A process that identifies and recovers information that may not be immediately apparent.

Encryption—procedure that converts plain text into symbols to prevent anyone but the intended recipient from understanding the message.

File Format—The structure by which data is organized in a file.

Forensic Wipe—A verifiable procedure for sanitizing a defined area of digital media by overwriting each byte with a known value; this process prevents cross-contamination of data.

Handheld (Mobile) Devices—Handheld devices are portable data storage devices that provide communications, digital photography, navigation systems, entertainment, data storage, and personal information management.

Hash or Hash Value—Numerical values that represent a string of text (search term), generated by hashing functions (algorithms). Hash values are used to query large sums of data such as databases or hard drives for specific terms. In forensics, hash values are also used to substantiate the integrity of digital evidence and/or for inclusion and exclusion comparisons against known value sets.

Log File—A record of actions, events, and related data.

Media—Objects on which data can be stored. Includes hard drives, thumb drives, CD/DVD, floppy discs, SIM cards from mobile devices, memory cards for cameras, etc.

Metadata—Data, frequently embedded within a file, that describes a file or directory, which can include the locations where the content is stored, dates and times, application specific information, and permissions. Examples: Email headers and website source code contain metadata.

Partition—User defined section of electronic media. Partitions can be used to separate and hide information on a hard drive.

Source Code—The instructions written in a programming language used to build a computer program.

Work Copy—A copy or duplicate of a recording or data that can be used for subsequent processing and/or analysis. Also called an image.

Write Block/Write Protect—Hardware and/or software methods of preventing modification of content on a media storage unit like a CD or thumb drive.

Resources & References

You can learn more about this topic at the websites and publications listed below.

Resources

ELECTRONIC CRIME SCENE INVESTIGATION: A GUIDE FOR FIRST RESPONDERS, SECOND EDITION, **http://www.nij.gov/pubs-sum/219941.htm**

BEST PRACTICES FOR SEIZING ELECTRONIC EVIDENCE: A POCKET GUIDE FOR FIRST RESPONDERS, V.3, DHS/Secret Service **http://publicintelligence.net/u-s-secret-service-best-practices-for- seizing-electronic-evidence/**

DIGITAL EVIDENCE IN THE COURTROOM: A GUIDE FOR LAW ENFORCEMENT AND PROSECUTORS, **http://www.nij.gov/pubs-sum/211314.htm**

FORENSIC EXAMINATION OF DIGITAL EVIDENCE: A GUIDE FOR LAW ENFORCEMENT **http://www.ojp.usdoj.gov/nij/pubs-sum/199408.htm**

ELECTRONIC CRIME PREVENTION CENTER OF EXCELLENCE **http://www.ectcoe.net/**

NATIONAL INSTITUTE OF JUSTICE **http://www.nij.gov/topics/forensics/evidence/digital/welcome.htm**

SCIENTIFIC WORKING GROUP DIGITAL EVIDENCE **http://www.swgde.org/**

References

ELECTRONIC CRIME SCENE INVESTIGATION: A GUIDE FOR FIRST RESPONDERS, 2ND ED, 2008. Department of Justice, Office of Justice Programs, National Institute of Justice. **http://www.nij.gov/pubs-sum/219941.htm** (accessed July 5, 2012).

DIGITAL EVIDENCE AND FORENSICS, 2010. Department of Justice, Office of Justice Programs, National Institute of Justice. **http://www.nij.gov/topics/forensics/evidence/digital/welcome.htm** (accessed July 5, 2012).

U.S. Secret Service, BEST PRACTICES FOR SEIZING ELECTRONIC EVIDENCE: A POCKET GUIDE FOR FIRST RESPONDERS, Version 3, 2006. Public Intelligence.net. **http://publicintelligence.net/u-s-secret-service-best- practices-for-seizing-electronic-evidence/** (accessed July 5, 2012).

DIGITAL EVIDENCE IN THE COURTROOM: A GUIDE FOR LAW ENFORCEMENT AND PROSECUTORS, 2007. Department of Justice, Office of Justice Programs, National Institute of Justice. **http://www.nij.gov/pubs-sum/211314.htm** (accessed July 5, 2012).

FORENSIC EXAMINATION OF DIGITAL EVIDENCE: A GUIDE FOR LAW ENFORCEMENT, 2004. Department of Justice, Office of Justice Programs, National Institute of Justice. **http://www.ojp.usdoj.gov/nij/pubssum/199408.htm** (accessed July 5, 2012).

Scientific Working Group Digital Evidence. **http://www.swgde.org/** (accessed July 5, 2012).

Acknowledgements

The authors wish to thank the following for their invaluable contributions to this forensic guide:

Stephen Pearson, *Managing Partner*, High Tech Crime Institute Group

Chris Hendry *Crime Lab Analyst in Computer Evidence Recovery*, Florida Department of Law Enforcement, Florida Computer Crime Center Tallahassee

Dagmar Spencer, *Research and Training specialist*, Florida Department of Law Enforcement, Florida Computer Crime Center Tallahassee

Alastair Ross, *Director*, National Institute of Forensic Science at Australia New Zealand Policing Advisory Agency

Forensic Evidence Admissibility and Expert Witnesses

How or why some scientific evidence or expert witnesses are allowed to be presented in court and some are not can be confusing to the casual observer or a layperson reading about a case in the media. However, there is significant precedent that guides the way these decisions are made. Our discussion here will briefly outline the three major sources that currently guide evidence and testimony admissibility.

The *Frye* Standard—Scientific Evidence and the Principle of General Acceptance

In 1923, in *Frye v. United States*[1], the District of Columbia Court rejected the scientific validity of the lie detector (polygraph) because the technology did not have significant general acceptance at that time. The court gave a guideline for determining the admissibility of scientific examinations:

> *Just when a scientific principle or discovery crosses the line between the experimental and demonstrable stages is difficult to define. Somewhere in this twilight zone the evidential force of the principle must be recognized, and while the courts will go a long way in admitting experimental testimony deduced from a well-recognized scientific principle or discovery, the thing from which the deduction is made must be* **sufficiently established to have gained general acceptance** *in the particular field in which it belongs.*

Essentially, to apply the "*Frye* Standard" a court had to decide if the procedure, technique or principles in question were generally accepted by a meaningful proportion of the relevant scientific community. This standard prevailed in the federal courts and some states for many years.

Federal Rules of Evidence, Rule 702

In 1975, more than a half-century after *Frye* was decided, the Federal Rules of Evidence were adopted for litigation in federal courts. They included rules on expert testimony. Their alternative to the *Frye* Standard came to be used more broadly because it did not strictly require general acceptance and was seen to be more flexible.

The first version of Federal Rule of Evidence 702 provided that a witness who is qualified as an expert by knowledge, skill, experience, training, or education may testify in the form of an opinion or otherwise if:

a. the expert's scientific, technical, or other specialized knowledge will help the trier of fact to understand the evidence or to determine a fact in issue;
b. the testimony is based on sufficient facts or data;
c. the testimony is the product of reliable principles and methods; and
d. the expert has reliably applied the principles and methods to the facts of the case.

While the states are allowed to adopt their own rules, most have adopted or modified the Federal rules, including those covering expert testimony.

In a 1993 case, *Daubert v. Merrell Dow Pharmaceuticals, Inc.,* the United States Supreme Court held that the Federal Rules of Evidence, and in particular Fed. R. Evid. 702, superseded *Frye's* "general acceptance" test.

The *Daubert* Standard—Court Acceptance of Expert Testimony

In *Daubert* and later cases[2], the Court explained that the federal standard includes general acceptance, but also looks at the science and its application. Trial judges are the final arbiter or "gatekeeper" on admissibility of evidence and acceptance of a witness as an expert within their own courtrooms.

In deciding if the science and the expert in question should be permitted, the judge should consider:

- What is the basic theory and has it been tested?
- Are there standards controlling the technique?
- Has the theory or technique been subjected to peer review and publication?
- What is the known or potential error rate?
- Is there general acceptance of the theory?
- Has the expert adequately accounted for alternative explanations?

- Has the expert unjustifiably extrapolated from an accepted premise to an unfounded conclusion?

The *Daubert* Court also observed that concerns over shaky evidence could be handled through vigorous cross-examination, presentation of contrary evidence and careful instruction on the burden of proof.

In many states, scientific expert testimony is now subject to this *Daubert* standard. But some states still use a modification of the *Frye* standard.

Who can Serve as an Expert Forensic Science Witness at Court?

Over the years, evidence presented at trial has grown increasingly difficult for the average juror to understand. By calling on an expert witness who can discuss complex evidence or testing in an easy-to-understand manner, trial lawyers can better present their cases and jurors can be better equipped to weigh the evidence. But this brings up additional difficult questions. How does the court define whether a person is an expert? What qualifications must they meet to provide their opinion in a court of law?

These questions, too, are addressed in **Fed. R. Evid. 702**. It only allows experts "qualified ... by knowledge, skill, experience, training, or education." To be considered a true expert in any field generally requires a significant level of training and experience. The various forensic disciplines follow different training plans, but most include in-house training, assessments and practical exams, and continuing education. Oral presentation practice, including moot court experience (simulated courtroom proceeding), is very helpful in preparing examiners for questioning in a trial.

Normally, the individual that issued the laboratory report would serve as the expert at court. By issuing a report, that individual takes responsibility for the analysis. This person could be a supervisor or technical leader, but doesn't necessarily need to be the one who did the analysis. The opposition may also call in experts to refute this testimony, and both witnesses are subject to the standard in use by that court (*Frye, Daubert,* Fed. R. Evid 702) regarding their expertise.

Each court can accept any person as an expert, and there have been instances where individuals who lack proper training and background have been declared experts. When necessary, the opponent can question potential witnesses in an attempt to show that they do not have applicable expertise and are not qualified to testify on the topic. The admissibility decision is left to the judge.

Additional Resources

Publications:

Saferstein, Richard. CRIMINALISTICS: AN INTRODUCTION TO FORENSIC SCIENCE, Pearson Education, Inc., Upper Saddle River, NJ (2007).

McClure, David. Report: Focus Group on Scientific and Forensic Evidence in the Courtroom (online), 2007, **https://www.ncjrs.gov/pdffiles1/nij/grants/220692.pdf** (accessed July 19, 2012)

Acknowledgements

The authors wish to thank the following for their invaluable contributions to this guide:

Robin Whitley, *Chief Deputy*, Appellate Division, Denver District Attorney's Office, Second Judicial District

Debra Figarelli, *DNA Technical Manager*, National Forensic Science Technology Center, Inc.

About This Project

This project was developed and designed by the National Forensic Science Technology Center (NFSTC) under a cooperative agreement from the Bureau of Justice Assistance (BJA), award #2009-D1-BX-K028. Neither the U.S. Department of Justice nor any of its components operate, control, are responsible for, or necessarily endorse, the contents herein.

National Forensic Science Technology Center®
NFSTC *Science Serving Justice*®
7881 114th Avenue North Largo,
Florida 33773
(727) 549-6067 info@nfstc.org

Notes

1. *United States vs. Fricosu*, 247 10 (Colorado 2012)
2. 293 Fed. 1013 (1923)
3. The "Daubert Trilogy" of cases is: Daubert V. Merrell dow pharmaceuticals, general electric co. V. Joiner and kumho tire co. V. Carmichael.

Credits

1. Copyright © Depositphotos/elenathewise.
2. Copyright © Depositphotos/BrianAJackson.
3. Copyright © Depositphotos/simpson33.
4. Copyright © Depositphotos/bloomua.
5. Copyright © Depositphotos/maxpro.
6. Copyright © Depositphotos/yupiramos.

Text Messaging Forensics

Txt 4n6: Idiolect Free Authorship Analysis?

BY TIM GRANT

Introduction

Danielle Jones disappeared on 18 June 2001; she has not been seen since and her body has never been found. Within hours of her disappearance two text messages were sent from her phone which, the police suspected, might have be written by her Uncle, Stuart Campbell. In the first case of its type to reach the UK courts, Malcolm Coulthard offered a linguistic analysis which showed that the messages were unlikely to have been written by Danielle. Stuart Campbell was convicted of Danielle's murder on the 19 December 2002 at least in part because of the linguistic evidence. In a parallel case, Jenny Nicholl disappeared on 30 June 2005. Once more Malcolm Coulthard was able to offer a linguistic analysis suggesting that she was unlikely to have texted the final messages sent from her phone and that her lover, David Hodgson, was one of a small group of possible authors. Hodgson was convicted of Jenny's murder on 19 February 2008.

Further evidence of the potential utility of forensic linguistics in the examination of text messages was provided in 2007 when I was given permission to carry out a survey of mobile telephone seizures by the Northamptonshire Police, a medium-sized semi-rural force, located in the East Midlands of the UK and covering about 900 square miles and a population of 640,000. The police in the UK have powers to seize mobile phones and the information they obtain ranges from the location of the phone at any particular time, to the call record and details of the SMS text messages sent and received. I was given access to all 186 phones seized during a three-month period, from which a total of some 10,000 text messages were recovered. Further analysis of the case files showed that for only twelve of these phones was there any suspicion that the owner had not sent all of the messages. Perhaps unsurprisingly in none of the cases was a forensic linguist employed to resolve these potential disputes. However, the degree of actual and potential investigative interest in the authorship of text messages appears to be growing and this raises some very real theoretical and methodological problems, not least whether such short and fragmentary texts are amenable to any form of authorship analysis.

Coulthard makes the strong claim that

> The linguist approaches the problem of questioned authorship from the theoretical position that every native speaker has their own distinct and individual version of the language they speak and write, their own idiolect, and ... this idiolect will manifest itself through distinctive and idiosyncratic choices in texts.
>
> (Coulthard 2004: 432)

Even if the first claim here, that every speaker has their own idiolect, can be sustained, there is no necessary implication from it that an individual's idiolect will be measurable in every text produced by that person, whatever its length. It would be perfectly rational to hold Coulthard's view and to also hold that a substantial and varied body of text would be required before manifest idiolectal features became noticeable or measurable. Coulthard's working definition of the idiolect as a 'distinct and individual version of language' only becomes useful to the authorship analyst if an idiolectal feature repeats itself, either within one text or across several texts by the same author. In the context of text messaging it may be that individual messages are considered too short to allow the possibility of idiolectal analysis, but conversely it may be possible to analyse idiolect in text messages by examining many messages written by the same individual. Further to this, although Coulthard claims his definition to be a 'theoretical position', a distinction must be made between observation and theory. On the one hand, there is the observation of features which might comprise an idiolect, that is to say idiolectal analysis requires an empirical study which produces evidence of consistency and distinctiveness. On the other hand, a linguistic theory of idiolect is required, which would provide explanation of any empirical evidence. The analysis of authorship may depend conceptually on theories of idiolect as distinctive versions of language but practically and methodologically authorship analysis depends on the facility to detect consistent patterns of language use. If consistent patterns can be detected, then the next step will be to determine how distinctive any such patterns are. Practical authorship analysis may depend less on a strong theory of idiolect than on the simple detection of consistency and the determination of distinctiveness.

The principal theoretical question this chapter addresses is whether authorship analysis can be valid as the mere detection of degrees of consistency and the determination of degrees of distinctiveness, or whether in its practical application it must rest implicitly or explicitly on a particular and strong theory of idiolect. Consistency and distinctiveness may, of themselves, be evidence that an idiolect exists, but they do not constitute an explanatory theory of idiolect. In this theoretical sense, authorship analysis based only on consistency and distinctiveness can be considered idiolect free, or at least idiolect light. Below, following a theoretical discussion of different theories of idiolect and their explanatory usefulness, a method will be demonstrated that measures consistency and distinctiveness in text messaging authorship analysis. The chapter then concludes with a discussion of whether such an analysis in fact depends upon or requires the practitioner to subscribe to a theory of idiolect, and whether one particular theory of idiolect has advantages over any other.

Authorship Analysis and Theories of the Linguistic Individual

Current work in forensic authorship analysis has tended to polarise between those who argue that work on authorship requires a strong understanding of the cognitive mechanisms of textual production on the one hand (Chaski 2001; Howald 2009), and on the other those who believe a stylistic understanding of language production is sufficient to explain authorial consistency and distinctiveness (McMenamin 2001). This debate has proved important in the United States Court system. Howald (2009) supporting Chaski's (2001) position, argues that stylistic approaches to authorship analysis are theoretically weak and therefore should fail the legal admissibility tests applied by the American courts. Some of this debate seems to rest on alternative conceptions of the idea of the linguistic individual and indeed on different theories of idiolect.

Cognitivist Theories of Idiolect

A set of theories of idiolect (which I shall refer to as cognitivist theories) suggest that individual language production is largely determined by linguistic competence. Competence is conceptualised here as the cognitive capacity of an individual to produce language and as such is reflected in linguistic performance. If one holds a cognitivist view of the linguistic individual then one good approach for authorship analysis involves trying to measure their cognitive capacity. Such approaches analyse particular aspects of language which are well explained by cognitive models of language production; aspects such as syntactic complexity or measures of the mental lexicon. It is possible in a general sense to measure such features and demonstrate variation between authors and groups. For example, quantitative and computational linguists can, at least with longer texts, describe mathematically, features of individuals' language production in terms of word frequency distributions (Baayen 2001; Holmes 1998; Grant 2007) syntactic structures (Chaski 2001; Spassova and Grant 2008) and other observable markers of authorship. The successful employment of these approaches in the resolution of authorship attribution problems does in fact depend upon, and thus demonstrate, degrees of consistency and distinctiveness. However, the cognitivist theories of language production upon which these approaches rest do not of themselves explain consistency within an author's textual production, nor distinctiveness between any two authors. To have a well worked out theory of language production is different in this sense from having an explanatorily strong theory of idiolect. A theory of idiolect must provide an explanation as to why one individual's production is consistent across texts, and must also explain why that individual's language is distinctive as compared with that of other individuals. Cognitivist theories may be better at explaining consistency within an individual's textual production but it is more difficult to elaborate cognitive explanations of distinctiveness between individuals. In describing language production systems cognitivist theorists tend to assume minimal individual differences or assume that differences between individuals are relatively uninteresting.

A good example of this cognitivist reduction in interest in individual linguistic variation is Chomsky's move from his earlier interest in the dichotomy between competence and performance to his later, allied but distinct theoretical dichotomy between internal and external language; *L-I* and *L-E,* respectively (Chomsky 1985). Theories of language competence can incorporate the possibility of variation between individuals, however, the more recent dichotomy between *L-I* and *L-E* holds less explanatory power in this respect. In these theories, theoretical primacy is given to understanding individual internal language capacity, *L-I,* rather than the less essential *L-E,* where distinctions between natural languages and their variants are seen as rather uninteresting. The research focus is not on differences between different individuals' *L-I* (arguably there are none) but rather on what is common to all individuals in *L-I.* This theoretical work is one of the foundations for the development of cognitive science in the late 1980s and early 1990s and cognitive science has in turn informed the more recent biologically focused project of cognitive neuroscience. Where cognitive linguists proposed information processing models or architectures for language production the neuroscientists looked to realise these models in terms of particular brain locations and processes.

In order to understand the implications of this to forensic work, we need to trace a brief history of an area where cognitive psychologists and neuroscientists have made some progress in explaining just one small part of language production. One such area is child language acquisition and a small part of this literature focuses on the way children learn irregular past tense verbs which is sometimes said to demonstrate a U-shaped learning curve. Initially children produce these irregular forms accurately, for example, English 'went' as a past tense for 'go' and 'was' for 'is.' In the next stage of learning, however, children appear to unlearn these verb forms now creating errors such as 'goed' or 'wented.' This stage represents the 'dip' in the U-shaped learning curve. In the final stage of learning, representing a rise out of the learning curve dip, children's performance improves again and they begin to use the correct forms for irregular past tense verbs again.

Beretta *et al.* (2003) examined alternative cognitive models attempting to explain this U-shaped learning curve. Some cognitive models propose a rule-based system whereby the first language learner produces regular verbs using a *stem+ed* production model and there is also an entirely separate part of the model devoted to simply memorising the small number of irregular verbs (e.g. Pinker and Ullman 2002). This type of model is referred to as a '*rules plus memory model*' and it is argued that the developmental interaction between these two elements can explain the U-shaped learning curve. A less recent and entirely different model, based on neural networks, is provided by Rumelhart and McClelland (1986) who argue that associative learning alone can account for the U-shaped learning curve. Their model contains only a single processing network and is unified in the sense that regular and irregular forms are learnt in a single system.

These two models both appear to accurately explain the observable data but at this stage in the historical development of the field, they both faced the same reasonable criticism; this is that although each model was conceived to be consistent with experimental results, there is no strong sense in which they could have claimed to be real. That is to say, neither model could claim to be related either to the biological foundations of language production, or to the social reality of language use. Choosing between two models which are both consistent with the available experimental data is entirely arbitrary. The solution to this problem came with the development of brain imaging techniques over the last ten years. This has made real the understanding that there are very specific brain locations through which different aspects of language are produced. In the case of learning past tense verbs, Beretta *et al.* (2003) report the discovery that the production of regular and irregular verbs actually occurs at two separate brain locations. This new evidence can provide a reason for choosing Pinker's rules plus memory model over Rumelhart and McClelland's associative model with its implication of a single structure.

Developments such as these in cognitive neuroscience have important implications for discussions of idiolect which in turn, are important for work in authorship analysis. With regard to idiolect, the main implication is that, just as we as a species share biological structures, so too we share brain structures in language production. The general focus of cognitive neuroscience is not on variation between individuals, but on shared commonalities. If I as a speaker of English have two neurological structures for the production of past tense verbs then so too will you. Adopting a cognitive view of language production tends to make the explanation of idiolectal variation more difficult rather than easier. Of course, it is not impossible to develop a cognitive neuroscience of idiolectal variation. Just as we recognise minor biological differences between individuals, so we may argue for similar individual differences in cognitive structures. To ignore cognitive neuroscience in discussions of idiolect would be reckless, but it is extremely difficult to use this body of work to explain actual individual differences between texts written by the same or different authors. By contrast stylistic theories of idiolect can and indeed do explain individual differences between authors.

Stylistic Theories of Idiolect

Forensic stylistics is sometimes seen as being in opposition to more cognitivist approaches to idiolect. From the cognitivist perspective, it has been suggested that those who take a more stylistic approach to authorship analysis have a weaker theory of idiolect and that the variables used are not on as solid a foundation in terms of linguistic theory (Howald 2009). Proponents of the more stylistic approaches naturally take issue with such an evaluation arguing that theories of stylistic variation are essential to understanding differences which occur between individuals (McMenamin 2002). My argument is that understanding language variation stylistically, as the interaction between habit and context, does not imply a lack of linguistic theory so much as an alternative linguistic theory. Stylistic and variationist theories of language are less focused on providing species-wide explanations of language production than on developing explanations as to how and why language varies and/or remains constant across sociolinguistic contexts. Such an approach may in fact be able to provide a better explanation of variation between individuals than cognitivist approaches. Individuals will have different linguistic experiences and these will be revealed in their language production. This is not idiolect free authorship analysis, but rather authorship analysis which has a different conception of the nature of idiolect.

Johnstone (1996, 2009) studying the language of Barbara Jordan, and Kredens (2002, 2003) studying the language of Morrissey, separately describe the consistency of individual linguistic stance across texts, contexts and indeed across a lifetime of textual production. In these detailed descriptions, it is possible to draw some individual historical and social explanations for consistent features of language use. For example, Johnstone (1996: 155) concludes of some low-level aspects of Barbara Jordan's style that her language reflects 'her disregard for appearances, and her lifelong refusal to adapt to social expectations about how a southern black woman should live and behave'. In other words, Johnstone is arguing that, Jordon's language draws upon her individual social history and upon a construction of herself as a participant in that history. Such case studies are invaluable in demonstrating the development and persistence of a linguistic individual across a variety of sociolinguistic contexts. Perhaps even more important for theories of idiolect and for forensic authorship analysis such insights allow us to develop explanations for the specifics in an individual's style. In this respect, one possible criticism of these studies might be their choice of interesting individuals; Johnstone's case study of Barbara Jordan, a United States political figure famous for her oratory, and Kredens' case study of singer songwriter, Morrissey, known for his imaginatively gloomy lyrics, are together somewhat elitist choices, perhaps unrepresentative of the average language user. Both individuals may in different ways be aiming to project a particular persona through their public language and have the talent and linguistic skill to achieve this. These concerns aside, the approach taken by both Johnstone and Kredens suggests that individuals taking a constant or repeated linguistic stance can create stylistic traits which in turn can be construed as the creation of a linguistic individual.

In so far as these stylistic approaches only identify consistent and distinctive features of linguistic output for an individual, they fare no better than cognitivist approaches in suggesting a strong theory of idiolect. There is, however, rather more of an attempt at explanation for the creation of a linguistic individual amongst these theorists and in particular a live debate as to whether the intersection of sociolinguistic factors *determine* a linguistic individual (as discussed by Kredens 2002) or whether an individual's history and context are *resources* which can be drawn upon, a position preferred by Johnstone (1996, 2009). One advantage of this idea that we might draw upon our individual sociolinguistic resources in the creation of a linguistic persona is that it allows for the additional possibility that we might also draw upon other language resources. In particular, it is possible to speculate that a linguistic individual might draw upon a combination of sociolinguistic resources and cognitive resources. Accepting that an idiolect may not be determined by either cognitive capacities or sociolinguistic history, but that each may provide resources and constraints in the creation of a linguistic individual suggests the possibility of a more unified theory of idiolect.

A Unified Approach to the Linguistic Individual

Coulthard (2004) demonstrated just how individual an apparently everyday utterance can be. Using a series of Google searches he shows how the apparently everyday phrase 'I asked her if I could carry her bags', is probably a unique utterance. He points out that at each stage in the construction of the phrase from a one-word utterance, to a two-, three-, four- and eventually nine-word utterance it increases in rarity to become apparently unique. He suggests 'I asked her' may be a pre-formed idiom, and so too, 'if I could' but where these appear together to form, 'I asked her if I could ... ', this showed only 7,740 Google hits in 2004. There is apparently a fairly open choice as to the verb which might follow this construction. In Coulthard's example, the word 'carry' is used and shows its rarity by scoring only seven Google hits. A range of alternative words might have replaced it. These include, 'take', 'hold', 'bring', etc. One idiolectal question is why one individual would use 'carry', whilst another individual might use 'bring'. Work on lexical priming offers one answer to such a question.

Hoey's (2005) work on lexical priming is situated firmly in a corpus-based tradition and yet aspects of lexical priming have long been researched by cognitive psychologists interested in the mental lexicon. Hoey's work concentrates on collocation, and details how one word *primes* the occurrence of its collocates. Although Hoey is not, in this work, interested in theories of idiolect he does discuss how such collocates emerge and from this one can infer how priming and collocation can spread from one individual to another and how an individual's own language can be affected by these collocational pressures. In contrast, cognitive psychologists' interest in priming has been experimental, and has described systematic patterns in reaction time as to how a word's frequency, rarity and semantic relation affects our ability to recognise or recall it (e.g. Sloboda 1986). These two perspectives on lexical priming might be seen as coming together in the developing interest of the cognitivist neuroscientists in the malleability or plasticity of the brain.

Recent work in cognitive neuroscience considers not only the cognitive structures common between individuals but also how the brain is altered by environmental stimuli. Greenfield (2008) describes the plasticity of the brain to external stimuli. At a gross level this can be illustrated by the example of how London taxi drivers, who have to memorise 'the Knowledge' of the driving geography of London before obtaining a license, develop an expanded area of the hippocampus. A more linguistic example might include evidence that bilinguals develop different parts of their brain to speak their different languages (e.g Ibrahim 2008). Using evidence such as this Greenfield elaborates a description of the mind as the 'personalisation of the brain' by individual external stimuli each making tiny incremental changes to neuronal activity and structure. Extrapolating from such a model it is possible to conceive the beginnings of a theory of idiolect as the personalisation of the language systems by exposure to differing linguistic stimuli. One potent force of such personalisation would be the statistical weight of collocation. My exposure to a certain variety of language containing one set of collocates would be different from my neighbour's and this personalisation would gradually cause individual differences in our language production. Idiolectal consistency and variation would draw on the resource of my cognitive capacity for language production and also draw on the complexity of my personal sociolinguistic history. According to this potential theory of idiolect, the cognitive capacity is itself structured but malleable and the sociolinguistic history is realised in incremental changes to that neuro-cognitive capacity.

In conclusion, theories of idiolect cannot merely notice consistent and distinctive features of the language of an individual. They should also attempt to provide explanations for these facts. We have seen that although cognitivist theories can provide convincing explanations for some aspects of language production these theories hold less power in and of themselves in explaining individual variation. Conversely, while stylistic approaches to the linguistic individual do concentrate on providing explanations for language variation between individuals they are perhaps less interested in explaining how these might be realised psychologically. I have speculatively indicated a possible future path which might help these different and sometimes competing theories of idiolect to provide complementary explanations for the construction of an individual. The question that remains is how far these theoretical discussions of idiolect can or should impact on forensic authorship analysis.

Text Messaging Authorship Analysis

In the two text messaging cases referred to at the beginning of the chapter, the problem brought to the linguist by the police was to determine which of two authors was more likely to have written a series of messages. In forensic casework, this is perhaps the most common type of problem, at least when the linguist is commissioned by the police. Typically, by the time the police approach a linguist they will have identified a suspect and are trying to build an evidential case to put to the suspect in interview. In the Danielle Jones and the Jenny Nicholl cases, the question put was whether it was more likely that the queried messages were written by the suspect or by the supposed victim. The police investigators may have, or believe they have, other non-linguistic evidence which makes the possibility of a third unknown person, already very unlikely or even impossible. It is of course possible to write a conditional opinion of the sort that, if it is known that one of the two candidate writers did write the disputed text message, then of these two X is a more likely author than Y. Clearly, however, such a conditional opinion is not ideal. In the UK system the expert works for the Court even if instructed by the police and it would be better practice ethically and methodologically to step back from the expectations of the police and truly account for the possibility of other potential authors. This raises the question of how rare one person's text messaging style might be, or even whether it could be unique.

The issue of linguistic distinctiveness between individuals has two levels which may be independent. If it can be demonstrated that the suspect exhibits a consistent style in text messaging and also that the victim has a consistent but different style then the first level of distinctiveness will have been proved. I shall refer to this as pair-wise distinctiveness and I will argue that answering this question does not depend upon a strong theory of idiolect, but only upon the degree of consistency of style within each author and the difference which is demonstrable between them. To this extent, any such analysis might be characterised as idiolect-free authorship analysis. The second possible level of distinctiveness, however, may have more profound implications for theoretical discussions of idiolect. This would occur if one person's text messaging style can be said to be distinctive, unusual or even unique against a reference population of text messages. This I shall refer to as population-level distinctiveness. As we shall see, it is possible to explore questions of consistency of style and both pair-wise and population distinctiveness using statistical methods. These methods were in fact developed in forensic psychology for the investigation of serial crime (e.g. Bennell and Canter 2002; Woodhams and Toye 2007).

The issue of consistency is also one of degree and has to be judged in the context of pair-wise as well as population-level distinctiveness. In a recent text messaging case in which I was involved, the linguistic issue involved determining which of two people was the more likely writer of a sequence of 20 text messages. For each writer I was provided with about 200 messages of known authorship. Within this known set, some features appeared to be absolutely consistent and absolutely discriminating. For example, every time Author A used the word 'don't' they spelt it 'dont', i.e. without the apostrophe. In contrast, every time Author B used the word 'don't' they used the abbreviation, 'dnt'. Other features demonstrated only degrees of consistency; Author A for example, always used the standard spelling, 'just', while Author B used 'just' about one third of the time, 'jst' two thirds of the time. The spelling 'jst' in a particular message obviously contains some authorship information but, it can be argued that, in the context of pair-wise distinctiveness, so too does the spelling 'just'. This spelling is more consistent with author A than B. Calculating the degree to which this can be used in determining an opinion, however, requires statistical sophistication (see Lucy 2005 for a good introduction on the application of Bayesian inferencing to resolving this sort of problem).

In the Jenny Nicholl murder case, Coulthard took a more traditional descriptive linguistic approach. He initially analysed a series of messages known to have been written by Nicholl and later also a series of messages known to have been written by Hodgson. From this examination, he identified nine low-level stylistic features which were seen to discriminate between the text messaging styles of the two possible authors. Some of these messages are now in the public domain and these include eleven messages known to have been written by Nicholl (reproduced in Table 6.1) and seven known to have been written by Hodgson (reproduced in Table 6.2). A further complication with Hodgson's messages was that two of the messages were produced on request in a police interview thereby giving Hodgson the opportunity to deliberately disguise his style. Finally, there were four disputed messages (reproduced in Table 6.3).

Example features used by Coulthard in this case include the abbreviation 'im' for 'I am', a lack of a space after using '2' for 'to' (both used by Nicholl and not Hodgson) and the use of

Table 6.1 Messages from the trial of David Hodgson for the murder of Jenny Nicholl: Known messages of Jenny Nicholl

Sum black+pink k swiss shoes and all the other shit like socks.We r goin2the Indian.Only16quid.What u doin x
Yeah shud b gud.i just have2get my finga out and do anotha tape.wil do it on sun.will seems keen2x
Shit is it.fuck icant2day ive already booked2go bowling.cant realy pull out.wil go2shop and get her sumet soon.thanx4tdlin me x
No reason just seing what ur up2.want2go shopping on fri and2will's on sun if ur up2it
Sorry im not out2nite havnt seen u 4a while aswel.ru free2moro at all x
No im out wiv jak sorry it took me so long ive had fone off coz havnt got much battery
Only just turned my fone.havnt lied bout anything.no it doesnt look good but ur obviously jst as judgmental than the rest.cu wen I cu&I hope its not soon
I havnt lied2u.anyway im off back2sleep
I know I waved at her we wer suppose2go at4but was a buffet on later on so waited.anyway he had a threesome it was great cu around
Im tierd of defending myself theres no point.bye
Happy bday!will b round wiv ur pressent2moz sorry i cant make it2day.cu2moz xxx

Table 6.2 Messages from the trial of David Hodgson for the murder of Jenny Nicholl: Known messages of David Hodgson

has he got his phone on him
ave dun he aint got it he will b in witherspoons she in got puddings and tissues in me pnckets.ave2 hope he rings b4 he goes up back in 30
put it on at 3.30 at 150 ok and top on at 4.45 but dont put glass lid on just the suet ok and the spuds separate
put them on at ten 2 ok thats 4.50 ok
Messages produced in police interview
HI JENN TELL JACKY I Am KEEPING My PhONE of because I am living in Scotland with my boyfriend I mite be in trouble with my dad myself. DaDs going to kill me I told him I was leaving Keswick why Does he hate me everyone hates me in RICHMOND you are the only mate I have got Have to go see you.
Hi jenn tell jacky i am keeping my phone of because i am living in Scotland with my boyfriend i might be in trouble with dad myself dads going to kill me i told him i was leaving Keswick why does he hate me everyone hates me in Richmond you are the only mate i have got have to go see you

Table 6.3 Messages from the trial of David Hodgson for the murder of Jenny Nicholl: Disputed messages

Thought u wer grassing me up.mite b in trub wiv me dad told mum i was lving didnt giv a shit.been2 kessick camping was great.ave2 go cya
Hi jen tell jak i am ok know ever 1s gona b mad tell them i am sorry.living in Scotland wiv my boyfriend. shitting meself dads gona kill me mum dont give a shite.hope nik didnt grass me up.keeping phone of.tell dad car jumps out of gear and stalls put it back in auction.tell him i am sorry
Y do u h8 me i know mum does.told her i was goin.i aint cumin back and the pigs wont find me.i am happy living up here.every1 h8s me in rich only m8 i got is jak.txt u couple wks tell pigs i am nearly 20 aint cumin back they can shite off
She got me in this shit its her fault not mine get blame 4evrything.i am sorry ok just had 2 lve shes a bitch no food in and always searching me room eating me sweets.ave2 go ok i am very sorry x

'me' and 'meself' rather than 'my' and 'myself' (used by Hodgson and not Nicholl). He judged these to be consistently used by each of the two candidate authors.

Coulthard was the only linguist to give evidence at trial and his opinion was careful and correct. He was able to say that the suspect messages were inconsistent with the described style of Jenny Nicholl. A slide demonstrating this point and used by Coulthard in presenting his analysis can be seen at http://news.bbc.co.uk/1/hi/sci/tech/7600769.stm. His conclusion with regard to Hodgson was measured. He gave the opinion that '*Linguistic features identified in Mr Hodgson's and the suspect texts are compatible with their having been produced by the same person*' and when pressed at trial he emphasised that Hodgson was one of a group of possible authors, and that the linguistic evidence could not go further than that (personal communication). The description of the consistencies in style and this pair-wise distinctiveness contributed to the case which convinced the jury to convict David Hodgson of Jenny Nicholl's murder and an appeal on the grounds that the linguistic evidence was unsound failed.

One challenge for forensic authorship analysts when considering text messages is to adopt something like the approach demonstrated in Coulthard's method and expression of opinion and to develop this approach further. In particular, comparisons between authors could be enhanced if the descriptive methods used by Coulthard can be developed to enable the quantified comparison of degrees of consistency and distinctiveness. Fortunately, forensic linguistics can borrow from its sister discipline of forensic psychology to achieve this aim.

Forensic Psychology and Case Linkage Work

Forensic psychologists have been involved in developing methods to determine whether a particular crime is an independent event, or alternatively, whether it is in fact part of a series of linked crimes committed by the same offender. This work, known as case linkage, typically relies on the statistical or computational analysis of offenders' behaviours in databases of offences and depends upon the twin principles of behavioural consistency and behavioural distinctiveness. The parallels with authorship analysis as described are clear. These case linkage principles have been investigated and demonstrated across a series of types of crime including car crime (Tonkin *et al.* 2008), commercial burglary (e.g. Bennell and Canter 2002; Woodhams and Toye 2007), sexual crime (e.g. Santtila *et al.*, 2005b; Woodhams, Grant and Price 2007), arson (Santtila *et al.* 2005a) and murder (Salfati and Bateman 2005) and a theoretical discussion exploring the nature of behavioural consistency in forensic work is beginning to be well developed (Woodhams and Toye 2007; Woodhams, Hollin and Bull 2007). Methods taken from this body of work can be adapted and applied to text messaging authorship analysis. Instead of scoring the presence and absence of crime scene behaviours, we can score the presence and absence of stylistic features.

Statistical Consistency and Distinctiveness

Returning to the Nicholl case, these methods can be exemplified even with the relatively small number of publicly available text messages. Because of the small number of messages, it is a simple matter to code each text as having or lacking each of the features noticed by Coulthard. The presence of each feature in each text message is scored as a one and its absence is scored as a zero. This creates an array of zeros and ones for every message sent. An example is shown as Table 6.4.

Using these representations, pairs of messages can then be compared for similarity or dissimilarity using a binary correlation analysis called Jaccard's coefficient. Jaccard is a statistical tool for measuring the degree of similarity. It produces results ranging from zero

Table 6.4 Example coding of text message

Text message	im	I am	am not/ I'm not/	aint/	ive/	ave/	my/ myself/	me/ meself/	of/	off/	to=2- space/	to=2 + space/	cu/	cya/	fone/	phone	shit/	shite/
got pudding and tissues in me pnckets.ave2 hope he rings b4 he goes up back in 30	0	0	0	0	0	1	0	1	0	0	0	1	0	0	0	0	0	0

to one, with zero indicating total dissimilarity and one indicating identity. For the purposes of this worked example, I wish to follow Coulthard's analysis and this produces a slight peculiarity in results. Coulthard's method is to use reciprocal coding to create a series of contrasts, for example, Nicholl's use of 'im' with the suspect's 'I am' and this produces two coding columns which indicate the presence of 'im' in some of Nicholl's messages but none of Hodgson's whereas for 'I am' the reverse pattern is true. This choice of features, along with the small number of messages, together produces the mathematical effect of reducing some of the Jaccard scores to zero and this in turn requires the use of one-sample t-tests (with a test score of zero) to make some of the comparisons. This, however, does not affect the theoretical or practical implications of the method more generally. Calculations for both t-tests and Jaccard coefficient will be performed by most statistics programme (such as SPSS) and described in their manuals and help files and also in most introductory text books on statistics (e.g. Dancey and Reidy 1999).

One feature of Jaccard which is crucial for both the analysis of text messages and for its parallel use in criminal case linkage is the fact that the occurrence of two absence scores, two zeros, has no effect on the overall similarity metric. A writer may be consistent in their preference of 'im' over 'I am' but this consistency will not be revealed in every message. In a similar vein in crime analysis, the absence of evidence of the carrying of a weapon at a scene is not evidence of its absence from that scene and Jaccard allows for this.

Having calculated Jaccard's coefficient between pairs of messages it is very straightforward to statistically demonstrate consistency of style and pair-wise distinctiveness between authors. To demonstrate the degree of consistency in Nicholl's messages using this coding system it is possible to take all of Nicholl's eleven messages and pair each message with every other. This produces 110 pairs and subsequently 110 Jaccard scores (mean = 0.23, SD = 0.20). A similar process can be carried out with Hodgson's seven messages creating 42 Jaccard scores (mean = 0.11; SD = 0.19). Removing the messages which Hodgson produced at interview leaves 20 Jaccard scores and raises the mean Jaccard score slightly and reduces the standard deviation (mean = 0.15; SD = 0.12).

If we move to examine all the pairs of messages where each pair contains a Nicholl text and a Hodgson text the Jaccard scores fall to zero for each and every one of these possible between-author pairs. (Included in this analysis are those text messages elicited from Hodgson during police interview.) This zero score is a representation of the difference in style between Hodgson and Nicholl. It is atypical to score zero, rather than a low decimal close to zero, but as commented above this is at least in part an artefact of using Coulthard's features which result in reciprocal coding. The zero result perhaps argues for a broader description of the messages than the nine features chosen by Coulthard for their absolute discriminatory power. Nevertheless, the zero score makes the point statistically that Coulthard was making descriptively; Nicholl's and Hodgson's texts are demonstrably stylistically distinct from one another. We have demonstrated that pairwise distinctiveness exists in this case. It is possible to reinforce this assertion by statistical testing. The appropriate test is a one-sample t-test and this shows a significant reduction in similarity when messages paired between the two authors are compared with Nicholl's within-author pairs ($t_{(109)} = 12.02$, $p < 0.01$, Cohen's $d = 1.55$). There is also a significant reduction in similarity when the between-author pairs are compared with Hodgson's within-author pairs ($t_{(41)} = 3.79$, $p < 0.01$, Cohen's $d = 0.81$). Collectively these results demonstrate statistically consistency of style within the text messages of Nicholl and consistency in the style within the text messages of Hodgson and also distinctiveness between the two styles.

Thus far, only texts of known authorship have been examined. The forensic questions require consideration of the disputed messages. When these disputed messages are paired with Nicholl's messages these mixed pairs are shown to be significantly less similar than the Nicholl-only pairs of messages ($t_{(145)} = 9.38$, $p < 0.01$, Cohen's $d = 1.41$). In contrast to this result there is no significant reduction in similarity when pairs of texts known to have been written by Hodgson are compared with pairs with one Hodgson text and one disputed message ($t_{(62)} = 8.36$, $p = 0.41$, Cohen's $d = 0.14$). In summary, Nicholl's and Hodgson's styles each demonstrate a degree of internal consistency and distinctiveness from one another. Nicholl's texts can also be shown to be distinctively different from the disputed texts but Hodgson's texts cannot.

This statistical demonstration of pair-wise distinctiveness and its post hoc application to Coulthard's case supports but adds little evidential weight to Coulthard's own descriptive analysis. Being able to measure consistency and distinctiveness is a methodological advance in that it allows some quantification of stylistic distance between groups of texts and thus some quantification of probabilities that one group of texts is inconsistent with another. The method however is intended to address only pair-wise distinctiveness. This distinctiveness can be shown to exist irrespective of whether there is any strong explanation for it and in this sense the method might be said to be idiolect free.

The pair-wise approach, does, however, suggest a further method for demonstrating population-level distinctiveness. The forensic psychology studies investigate which sets of features are most discriminating at a population level (e.g. Woodhams and Toye 2007) and a similar analysis can be carried out on text messaging features. Such an analysis would help determine empirically which sorts of features are most useful in idiolectal discrimination. Such an empirical finding might then have theoretical implications. For example, it might be shown that in text messaging a tendency for abbreviation is more generally discriminating between authors than the use of grammatical ellipsis. If such a finding arose, it would provoke questions as to why one type of feature might show more between-author variation than another.

This is just one aspect of the considerable further work to be carried out on these techniques and some of it is already underway. A general description of texting language is already developing outside of the forensic field (e.g. Crystal 2008) and this is already proving useful in exploring the population-level questions. In addition the statistical techniques used in case linkage are also under rapid development not least with the creation of a taxonomic similarity measure (Woodhams *et al.* 2007a) developed in relation to sexual crime. The application of this taxonomic similarity to text messaging forensics is also being explored. In spite of the speed of development, it is already possible to reflect on the implications of methods such as these for understandings of idiolect and of the role of idiolectal theories in forensic casework.

Implications for Theories of Idiolect

As we have seen, it is possible to construct a method for authorship analysis based on stylistic variation. The steps which comprise this method can be clearly described and followed to produce replicable results on the same data set and can also be applied to different data sets. The method primarily demonstrates that different authors can be consistent and distinctive in their style of textual production. This does not mean that individuals are absolutely consistent; language is naturally variable. Neither does it mean that every author will be consistent in the same way. This method allows for and detects the fact that one author may be consistent in, for example, a form of abbreviation, whilst another author may tend to punctuate in an idiosyncratic manner. This is a strength of this method and it is a contrast with more traditional stylometric approaches. The stylometric approaches tend to carry with them the assumption that a 'good' marker or feature of authorship is one which will show between-author variation and within-author consistency across a sample of authors (e.g. Chaski 2001; Grant 2007). Examples of such stylometric markers might include measures involving word frequency distributions, frequency of use of functional words, or measures of syntactic structures. Many stylo-metric approaches are very successful in dealing with longer texts written in standard language variants but they do tend to struggle with the short and fragmentary language of text messaging.

Using the technique described here, it is possible to demonstrate not only consistency but also to show pair-wise distinctiveness between text messages by two authors. Observation of stylistic consistency and distinctiveness in this way is good evidence that idiolect exists. Observation that the writings of some, many or most authors can be discriminated using stylometric markers of authorship is also good evidence that idiolect exists. As I have argued above, however, mere observation and description of consistency and distinctiveness is not a theory of idiolect. Theories have to have explanatory power. Any investigation limiting itself to observation and description of consistency and distinctiveness in authorship style might fairly be considered idiolect free authorship analysis.

It is possible to draw separate parallel conclusions outlining the possible contribution to a theory of idiolect of both the stylistic and the cognitivist stylometric approaches to authorship analysis.

Using a more stylistic, sociolinguistic or variationist approach in observing specific features of a particular author's language we may be able to explain some of those features by appealing to that author's social and linguistic background. The use of 'me' for 'my' in a text message might, for example, be explained in terms of the dialect background and pronunciation of that writer. Such specific explanations, however, may not always be available to us. Why a second individual with a similar social and geographic background, and perhaps with a similar pronunciation, chooses to follow the more standard spelling may well seem inexplicable. At a general level, however, we can provide some explanation of stylistic variation between individuals. This explanation rests on the fact that individuals vary in their social and linguistic history, and in their lexical priming, and this produces variation in the sociolinguistic resources upon which they draw for language production.

Using a more stylometric approach in observing specific features in an individual's language may not commit one to an interest in cognitivist theories of language production but many stylometric measures will be based on insights derived from such theories. To claim that a measure is based on a cognitive or neuropsychological understanding of language production does not of itself explain between-author variation in that measure. Without relying on sociolinguistic explanations, why two individuals with similar cognitive and neurological structures vary in such a measure may well seem inexplicable. At a general level, however, we can provide some explanation of cognitive variation between individuals. This explanation rests on the fact that individuals may show some variation in their biology, but there will also be variation in sociolinguistic history and thus in lexical priming, and this produces personalisation of the neurological and cognitive resources upon which they draw for language production.

With regard to theories of idiolect, I would argue that consistency and pair-wise distinctiveness are matters of empirical observation upon which forensic authorship analysis can rely. Any such comparison must be based in sound methods which can convincingly demonstrate the degrees of consistency and distinctiveness found in a particular comparison of texts known to have been written by the authors but the results of such comparison have little to contribute to theoretical discussions of idiolect. Such matters of fact do not of themselves explain idiolect. The possibility of pair-wise distinctiveness, wider distinctiveness or even population-level distinctiveness, however, does seem to demand some explanation. To the extent that it can be shown that one individual's language is measurably unique in the population of all language users, this is, or would be, an astounding fact. Even less extreme individual linguistic distinctiveness demands a combination of cognitive and social investigation and demands a combination of cognitive and social explanations. Observable individual linguistic uniqueness demands a theory of idiolect.

Further Reading

Crystal, D. (2008) *Txtng: The Gr8 Db8*, Oxford: OUP.

Grant, T. (2007) 'Quantifying evidence for forensic authorship analysis,' *International Journal of Speech, Language and the Law*, 14: 1–25.

Greenfield, S. (2008) *ID: The Quest for Identity in the 21st Century*, London: Sceptre.

Howald, B.S. (2009) 'Authorship attribution under the rules of evidence: Empirical approaches in the layperson legal system,' *International Journal of Speech, Language and the Law*, 15: 219–47.

Johnstone, B. (2009) 'Stance, style, and the linguistic individual,' in Jaffe, A. (ed.) *Sociolinguistic Perspectives on Stance*, Oxford: Oxford University Press.

READING SEVEN

Electronic Evidence and Criminal Justice

BY UNODC REPORT

This Chapter considers the criminal justice process in cybercrime cases, starting from the need to identify, collect and analyse electronic evidence through digital forensics. It examines the admissibility and use of electronic evidence in criminal trials, and demonstrates how a range of prosecutorial challenges can impact on criminal justice system performance. It links law enforcement and criminal justice capacity needs with a view of delivered and required technical assistance activities.

Introduction to Electronic Evidence and Digital Forensics

KEY RESULTS

- Evidence is the means by which facts relevant to the guilt or innocence of an individual at trial are established. Electronic evidence is all such material that exists in electronic, or digital form
- Digital forensics is concerned with recovering—often volatile and easily contaminated—information that may have evidential value
- Forensics techniques include the creation of 'bit-for-bit' copies of stored and deleted information, 'write-blocking' in order to ensure that original information is not changed, and cryptographic file 'hashes,' or digital signatures, that can demonstrate changes in information

Electronic Evidence in Criminal Proceedings

Evidence is the means by which facts relevant to the guilt or innocence of an individual at trial are established. Electronic evidence is all such material that exists in electronic, or digital, form. As noted in Chapter One (Global connectivity), electronic evidence is central not only to the investigation and prosecution of forms of cybercrime, but increasingly to crime in general. Legal frameworks optimized for electronic evidence, together with law enforcement and criminal justice capacity to identify, collect and analyse electronic evidence, are thus central to an effective crime response.

During information gathering for the Study, countries were asked about the capacity of law enforcement authorities and prosecutors to collect and handle electronic evidence. Countries were also asked about legal frameworks for electronic evidence, including admissibility and evidentiary laws and rules that apply to electronic evidence.[1] Before consideration of country responses, this section contains a brief introduction to the nature of electronic evidence and the means through which it can be collected, including digital forensics.

Generating evidence—User interaction with computer devices produces a wealth of computer-generated digital traces (sometimes called digital fingerprints or artefacts). Computer data and electronic communications potentially relevant to a criminal act may include gigabytes of photographs, videos, emails, chat logs and system data. Locating relevant information within this data can be extremely time-consuming. The variety of possible file formats, operating systems, application software, and hardware particulars also serves to complicate the process of identifying relevant information.

Computer artefacts can be easily modified, overwritten or deleted, thus posing challenges where sources of digital information must be authenticated and verified.[2] Evidence rules vary considerably between jurisdictions, even amongst countries with similar legal traditions. In general terms, however, legal systems of the common law tradition tend to have defined rules as to the admissibility of evidence. In legal systems of the civil law tradition, in which professional judges retain a high degree of control over the court proceedings, admissibility of evidence may be flexible, although the weighing of evidence (including ascertaining its credibility and authenticity) can also obey a comprehensive set of rules.[3]

In many legal systems, the quality of procedures applied to maintain the integrity of digital information from the moment of creation to the point of introduction in court must be demonstrated by the proponent of the evidence. The integrity and authenticity of digital information has a direct bearing on the weight of evidence, in terms of its reliability and trustworthiness. The party seeking to introduce evidence must usually demonstrate evidence continuity, or 'chain-of-custody,' so that it can be proved that the evidence has not been tampered with or otherwise altered. Evidence continuity is typically a question of fact and the chain-of-custody process is the mechanism applied for maintaining and documenting the chronological history of the evidence as it moves from one place to another.[4]

In the case of digital information, evidence continuity must be maintained for both the *physical device* housing the data (when received or seized), and the *stored data* residing on the device.[5] As such, the party offering the evidence must demonstrate that: (i) the digital information obtained from the device is a true and accurate representation of the original data contained on the device (authenticity); and (ii) that the device and data sought to be introduced as evidence is the same as that which was originally discovered and subsequently taken into custody (integrity). The objective is to show that the device is what it is purported to be and that the digital information is trustworthy, and has not been tampered with or altered.[6]

The reliability of computer-generated and computer-stored information has also been challenged on the basis of security vulnerabilities in operating systems and programs that could give rise to threats to the integrity of the digital information. The susceptibility of digital information to manipulation has been considered by courts when introducing electronic evidence, with emphasis on '*the need to show the accuracy of the computer in the retention and retrieval of the information at issue*.'[7] The admissibility of computer-generated information (such as log file records) detailing the activities on a computer, network, or other device may be open to challenge when the system generating the information does not have robust security controls.[8]

Forensics scenario: Evidence of computer fraud from an Internet café

Scenario: A fraud has been attempted via email. Police gain evidence that the emails in question may have been sent from a desktop computer in a local internet café

A typical internet café setup resembles, in many ways, a home network environment. It is likely to contain multiple laptop or desktop computers connecting over a combination of wireless and wired network devices. For the purposes of billing usage of computers, a cybercafé may require user identification; in several jurisdictions this is mandatory, and provides an audit trail to link an individual to a particular computer at a given time. It may also be possible to identify an individual using a computer at a given time through footage from security cameras.

If an investigation occurs swiftly enough, or if prior knowledge of activities is given, then forensic investigators may be in a position to gain physical access to the computer and to conduct a standard investigation. This process is complicated by the public nature of the device, which consequently contains traces of many users' activity.

An internet café, regularly handling more users and traffic than a home network, is likely to have additional network devices such as proxy servers that keep copies of commonly-requested web pages in order to speed up traffic; and firewall hardware for security. These devices may be analysed for traces of network activity linked to the suspicious activities of the user.

In addition to demonstrating authenticity and integrity of evidence, challenges to the use of electronic evidence arise, in some jurisdictions, from the application of particular *evidential rules*. It may need to be demonstrated, for example, that electronic evidence falls within particular exceptions to a general prohibition on 'hearsay' evidence,[9] or that a 'print-out' of computer data satisfies requirements such as a 'best evidence' rule.[10] National approaches to such issues reported through the Study questionnaire are addressed in this Chapter.

Digital Forensics

Many forms of electronic evidence may be comparatively straightforward, such as a printout of a readily available email sent by a perpetrator, or IP connection logs reported directly by an internet service provider. Other forms, on the other hand, may require sophisticated techniques in order to recover traces of activity or data from computers and networks that can provide evidence of criminal behaviour. Digital forensics is the branch of forensic science concerned with the recovery and investigation of material found in digital and computer systems. To discover such traces, digital forensics experts take advantage of the tendency of computers to store, log and record details of almost every action that they, and hence their users, perform.

Information stored on electronic devices, including computers and mobile phones, is volatile and easily altered or corrupted in investigations. At the same time, such information is easily duplicated. A crucial first step in many digital forensics investigations is therefore to create an undisturbed forensic *image* (or 'bit-for-bit' copy) of the storage device, containing as detailed a copy of the original device as can be obtained. By operating on the image rather than the original device, the data can be examined without disturbing the original, thus providing a safeguard against any tampering or falsification. A forensic image is typically created with the aid of a special device called a *write-blocker* that prevents any alterations being made to the original data.[11]

In addition to the ability to create a 'bit-for-bit' copy of stored information, other important forensics tools include the use of 'data carving' or 'file carving' that can

Forensics scenario: Evidence from a mobile carrier of conspiracy to commit a serious crime

Scenario: An individual is investigated under suspicion of conspiring to commit homicide.

As part of the investigation, police request data from the individual's mobile phone network.

The capabilities of a mobile phone provider are similar to those of an internet service provider combined with a standard telephone provider, with the important addition of geolocation data that reveals a user's physical location.

Telephone traffic details, in most jurisdictions, will store dialled telephone numbers as well as the time and duration of the call. Wiretap capabilities function much as those of other telephony providers. This information can reveal patterns of calls to other individuals, as well as providing correlations between real-world events, such as a phone call made shortly after a crime was committed.

The most significant difference with mobile phones, however, is that the device is typically carried by the owner at all times, and constantly connects to local mobile base stations that relay the phone's signals. By tracking the base stations to which a phone connected at a given time, the location of the owner can be inferred within a given region. If actively triangulated using multiple base stations, a phone can be localized to within tens of metres.

Depending on jurisdiction and data retention policies, providers may store the geographical location of mobile phones whenever they send or receive messages or phone calls, as in the case of the European Union's Data Retention Directive. Others jurisdictions may not store this data at all, except when explicitly requested by law enforcement, at which point explicit triangulation of location may allow for accurate location of an individual via their phone.

Case example: Identifying an internet extortionist (A country in North America)

One law enforcement investigation into an alleged extortionist demonstrates some of the techniques used to track down online criminals. The accused threatened to post sexual images of his victims on their own social networking pages.

Investigators received information from the security division of the social networking site about logins to the victims' accounts, all originating from a single IP address. Someone at that IP address had accessed 176 different accounts in less than two months, mostly from the same computer. Many of the users of those accounts had disabled their accounts after being hacked. The same IP address had been used to access the suspect's own account 190 times, more than any other address. It had also been used to login 52 times to one of the victims' webmail accounts. A separate login to the suspect's account occurred from an IP address registered to a company listed as the suspect's employer on his social network profile. On this basis, a request was made to an ISP for subscriber information connected to the IP address. Within one week, the ISP responsible for the suspect's IP address provided subscriber information, including a physical address that matched other public records. Investigators executed a search warrant at this premises, seizing further evidence used to indict the suspect later the same month.

Source: http://www.justice.gov/usao/cac/Pressroom/2013/016.html and http://arstechnica.com

retrieve deleted or corrupted files from the remnants of raw data that remain on storage devices even after the original file is gone.[12] In addition, to compare files quickly and accurately, analysis tools make use of cryptographic *hashes* that correspond to a small and unique 'signature' for a given piece of data. Changing the data by even the slightest amount results in a different hash.

Different devices require different investigative and forensic techniques. Examination of mobile devices requires a different set of tools to those employed when examining a desktop computer or network server. Varying types of hardware, software and operating systems each present their own challenges associated with retrieving information.

Computer forensics focuses on analysing traditional desktop computers and laptops as found in both homes and businesses. Computers usually contain high-capacity hard drives that store a great deal of information, including photos and videos, as well as histories of web browsing, and email and instant messaging information. They typically run a small number of well-known operating systems including Windows, Mac OS, and Linux.

Mobile device forensics examines low-powered mobile devices, with smaller capacity for storage compared to computers, and with simpler software to facilitate phone calls and internet browsing. The gap between phones and computers is, however, getting smaller in terms of functionality, processing power and software. A distinguishing feature of mobile phones is their mobility—they are usually with their owner at all times—and their constant connectivity. This extends to monitoring reasonably accurate geographic location in modern systems. Mobile phones often contain both a relatively complete contact list, as well as call records. All data and information typically flows over the mobile ISP's network, enabling investigators to obtain a large range of information related to the use of the phone. Tablet devices are often simply scaled-up versions of a mobile phone, making tools designed for mobile phones also applicable.

Network forensic techniques are critical now that mobile phones and computers, and many of the actions for which they are used, are associated with online services and cloud storage. These services store data on the internet rather than the user's device, reducing the amount of information that can be gathered without the use of network analysis. Network traffic is largely transient. In order to gain detailed information about activities taking place on a network, traffic must be actively gathered and stored for subsequent analysis. This can include analysis of log files from network devices such as firewalls and intrusion detection and prevention systems, as well as analysing the content of logged network traffic, if available.[13]

In situations where an attacker may have gained electronic access to a computer system, any data on that computer may have been compromised by the attacker. In such cases, log files of that system's activity are likely to be considered unreliable, and network forensics may be the only form of data available to an analyst. The major challenge in a forensic investigation of a network lies in reconstructing the actions that have taken place across a network from the limited log data available. This may be used to identify hacking attempts, unauthorized access to systems and denial of service attempts, as well as data concerning which resources were accessed by individuals at given times.

Capacity for Digital Forensics and Electronic Evidence Handling

KEY RESULTS

- While almost all countries have some digital forensics capacity, many responding countries, across all regions, report insufficient numbers of forensic examiners, differences between capacity at federal and local level, lack of forensics tools, and backlogs due to large quantities of data for analysis
- Over half of countries report that suspects make use of encryption, rendering access to this type of evidence difficult and time-consuming without the decryption key
- All countries in Africa and one-third of countries in other regions report insufficient resources for prosecutors to handle and analyse electronic evidence
- Electronic evidence is admissible in court in more than 85 per cent of responding countries, although in small number legal obstacles such as the inadmissibility of all electronic evidence, and the inadmissibility of extraterritorial electronic evidence, present serious obstacles to the prosecution of cybercrime acts

Forensics Capacity

The ability of law enforcement to collect and analyse electronic evidence during investigations can be critical to the successful identification and prosecution of perpetrators. Responding countries to the Study questionnaire indicated a range of capacities in this regard. More than 90 per cent of countries, across all regions of the world, reported some capability to conduct digital forensics-based investigations.[14] Additional information provided by countries on access to forensic resources and levels of capability, however, reveals a more divergent picture. Less than half of countries in Africa and around two-thirds of countries in the Americas reported sufficient law enforcement resources (such as electricity, hardware, software, and internet access) for carrying out investigations and analysing electronic evidence.[15] In contrast, almost 80 per cent of countries in Europe, and Asia and Oceania, reported sufficient resources.

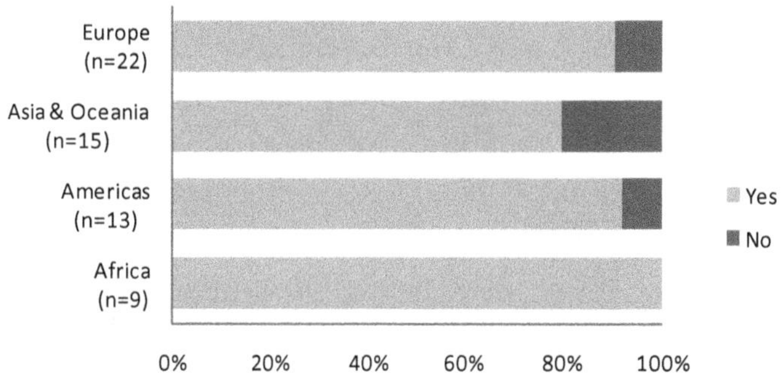

Figure 7.1 Law enforcement capabilities to conduct electronic forensics
Source: Study cybercrime questionnaire. Q110. (n=59)

However, many countries including some developed countries, reported challenges associated with processing large volumes of data and an increasing number of devices submitted for forensic analysis.[16] One country in Europe, for example, reported that *'On a national level the police are capable of performing high level computer forensics. At a district and local level there is only capacity to undertake basic computer forensic work.'* The same country noted that *'The increasing amount of electronic evidence seized during the investigation of all kinds of crimes is a challenge, especially to the local police who handle a large amount of cases.'* Similarly, one country in the Americas highlighted that *'The challenge is not in the expertise, but in the quantity of data that must be analysed,'*[17] and another noted that *'the amount of seized information and data is causing more and more problems for storing and analysis.'*[18]

While some countries reported a federal or centralized capacity of a *'central [forensics] laboratory and peripherals that are in charge of expert analysis of electronic evidence seized in police investigations'*[19] others reported using a distributed approach with *'forensic units throughout the country'*[20] that *'conduct electronic forensic examinations with specialized forensic tools...used on networks, computer systems, cellular phones, and storage devices.'*[21] Many countries, especially developing countries, highlighted a lack of resources for technical forensics equipment and challenges in recruiting personnel with sufficient skills to conduct investigations and process electronic evidence. One country in Africa, for example, stated that *'A few forensic examiners are available at the Federal level, but not enough to serve the whole country. Only one laboratory is functional.'*[22]

A number of countries reported encountering encryption of data during the course of law enforcement investigations and analysis of electronic evidence. Between around 60 and 80 per cent of countries in all regions, with the exception of Asia and Oceania, reported that electronic evidence was often encrypted by suspects.[23] Several countries reported an increase in use of encryption by perpetrators. One country observed that *'depending on the crime type, encryption is becoming much more common.'*[24] This view was not universal however. One country from Europe, for example, reported that *'collected evidence is very rarely encrypted compared to the enormous amount of seized data.'*[25] In addition, it is unclear whether the low proportion of encryption reported by countries in Asia and Oceania is due to differences in

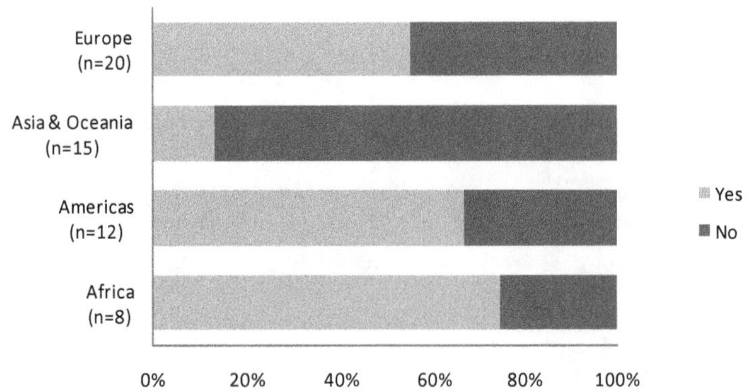

Figure 7.2 Electronic evidence encrypted by suspects
Source: Cybercrime study questionnaire. Q112. (n=55)

underlying use of encryption by suspects, or to capacities of law enforcement to detect and analyse encrypted material.

Countries noted that there was *'no simple way'* to overcome the *'daunting challenge'* of encryption *'that requires expert technical assistance and capacity.'*[26] Several countries indicated that they did not possess the means or tools to address the problem of encryption, without obtaining or seizing keys from the suspect. One country reported, for example, that: *'If the suspected is arrested or known, then the decryption keys are obtained from the suspect during investigation.'*[27] Some jurisdictions have legal remedies to compel cooperation.[28] If the suspect will not reveal decryption keys, investigators may use a variety of software programs, engage technical expertise, or refer the potential evidence to their forensics labs or specialized personnel for attempted decryption. One country mentioned using *'certified professionals and certified software'*[29] in decryption efforts. Other countries referred to the possibility of arresting a suspect *'while the machines are open, up, and running'*[30] when data may be in an unencrypted state.

In addition to the challenges presented to digital forensics by encryption technology, perpetrators may also make use of 'steganography' (information 'hiding'). This involves concealing information or communications within otherwise innocent files, such as graphic images, documents, audio samples or applications. Media files are ideal hosts for steganography as they are typically large and will not immediately arouse suspicion. From a forensic perspective, identification of hidden data may be achieved by comparing suspect files or data streams with known originals. A number of responding countries highlighted a general increase in use of obfuscation techniques and encryption. One country in the Americas reported *'criminal organizations try to make investigations difficult by storing criminal data in foreign servers or in cloud storage systems, and use cryptography and other data obfuscation techniques.'*[31]

Increasing use of cloud computing presents particular challenges for digital forensics. Information stored remotely by perpetrators in cloud services may become visible to investigators during a search or forensic examination—such as when live internet sessions are encountered on running computers, or through remote services available on seized mobile devices. In addition to legal considerations associated with direct law enforcement access to extraterritorial data (examined in Chapter Seven (International cooperation)), cloud data storage complicates the forensic process of identification, collection, and analysis of electronically stored information.[32] The possibility that one cloud user may gain access to another's data also introduces the possibility of further challenges to data authenticity.

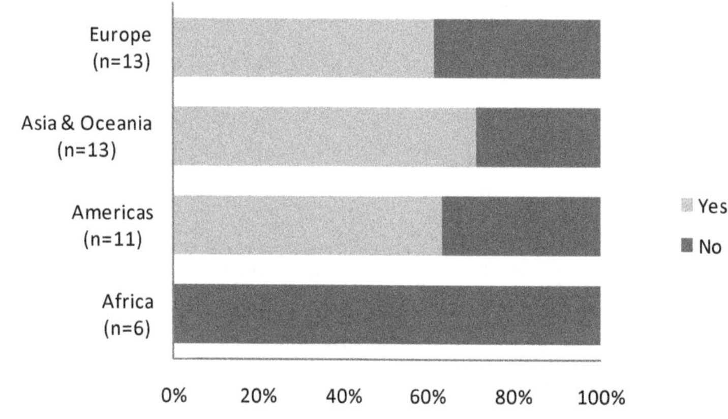

Figure 7.3 Sufficiency of resources to handle and analyse electronic evidence
Source: Study cybercrime questionnaire. Q149. (n=44)

Faced with such challenges, responding countries reported that a variety of techniques are used to ensure that the integrity of electronic evidence collected through digital forensics is maintained. Countries referred, for example, to the use of forensic imaging; the use of sworn statements attesting to the authenticity of data; forensic hash values; the use of write blockers; capture of internet data through screen shots; systematic labelling, documentation, packaging and transportation methods; and sealing of forensic images recorded on optical disk.[33] With respect to standards and guidelines for forensic investigations, a few countries referred to the Association of Chief Police Officers' Good Practice Guide for Computer-Based Electronic Evidence.[34]

Countries also reported a number of practices for storing electronic evidence in order to protect against degradation and damage. These included the use of multiple clone copies from a single master copy; storage of computer data within a designated IT-forensic network under restricted access; the use of humidity, temperature, and electromagnetic radiation controlled facilities; the use of safes; the use of anti-static devices; use of supervised evidence lockers; and use of sealed bags.[35]

In addition to law enforcement capacity for digital forensics, it is also important that *prosecutors* have sufficient resources to handle and analyse electronic evidence. Electronic evidence that is not presented at trial can play no role in helping just adjudication of the accused. Country responses show that prosecutors typically report a lower level of resources for handling electronic evidence than for law enforcement.[36] Some countries, for example, commented that prosecutors often experience difficulty in making sense of electronic evidence and require the assistance of other professionals to identify trends and give data meaning.[37] None of the African respondents reported that prosecutor resources for electronic evidence were sufficient—highlighting an urgent area for focus in technical assistance and support.

Electronic Evidence in Criminal Proceedings

More than 85 per cent of responding countries reported that electronic evidence was admissible in criminal proceedings.[38] A small number of countries—predominantly in Africa and Asia—stated, however, that electronic evidence was not admissible. One country in Africa, for example, held that electronic evidence was '*Not defined in our law and hence inadmissible*.'[39] Where this is the case, a serious obstacle to the successful prosecution of cybercrime and crimes involving electronic evidence exists. For those countries where electronic evidence is generally admissible in criminal proceedings, such admissibility is subject to conditions, such as the demonstrated integrity of the data, the discretion of the court, or authorization procedures, in around 70 per cent of countries.[40]

Despite general recognition of electronic evidence in national courts, one country reported not recognizing electronic evidence from *outside* of its jurisdiction.[41] In the case of a transnational crime such as cybercrime, such a restriction can impact upon the possibility for successful prosecutions. A number of countries reported that admissibility issues for extraterritorial electronic evidence often turn on whether mutual legal assistance procedures have been properly followed. One country, for example, emphasized that '*foreign evidence adduced in criminal proceedings must be in the form of testimony and any exhibit annexed to such a testimony...; testimony must be taken under oath or affirmation, under such caution or admonition as would be accepted by the court in the foreign country, or under an obligation to tell the truth imposed, whether expressly or by implication, by or under a law of the foreign country, and the testimony must purport to be signed or certified by a judge, magistrate or officer*.'[42] In many jurisdictions, such requirements frequently prevent extraterritorial electronic evidence obtained through *informal* police-to-police channels from being relied upon in criminal trials.

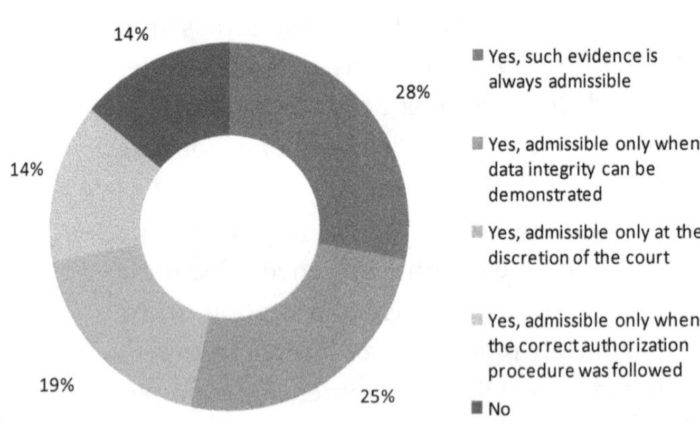

Figure 7.4 Electronic evidence admissible in criminal proceedings
Source: Study cybercrime questionnaire. Q144. (n=43)

The greater number of countries that admit electronic evidence reported that it is treated in the same way as physical evidence. Just under 40 per cent of countries, for example, reported the existence of a legal distinction between electronic and physical evidence.[43] While approaches vary, many countries considered that it was good practice not to make a distinction, as this ensures fair admissibility of electronic evidence alongside all other types of evidence. For countries without a legal distinction between electronic and physical evidence, many reported that electronic evidence, like its traditional counterpart, *'must be: admissible; authentic; accurate; complete and convincing to juries.'*[44] Admissibility of electronic evidence was also reported to be dependent on the general rules that apply to all evidence, including that the elements *'were obtained legally, respecting the principles of relevance and abundance.'*[45] In a few countries, courts have the discretion to *'to decide whether any [electronic] evidence is admissible or not.'*[46]

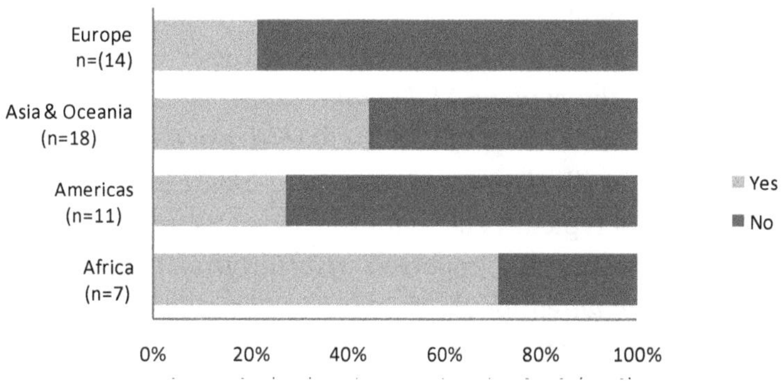

Figure 7.5 Legal distinction between electronic evidence and physical evidence
Source: Study cybercrime questionnaire. Q143. (n=50)

Electronic evidence was reported to be transferred to prosecution or judicial authorities, and used in a criminal trial, in a number of ways. Responding countries reported all of: the physical transportation of seized computers to court; the use in court of copies of computer data stored on optical disk; the use in court of printouts of electronic evidence filed in binders; and the presentation of an expert analytical report and testimony only to the court (with the computer data remaining in storage).[47] A few countries stated, for instance, that electronic documents or data *'must be printed out before it is possible to read it out in the main hearing.'*[48] Some countries also emphasized that *'only the relevant part of the collected evidence is transferred to prosecutors—irrelevant material or data is stored with the police.'*[49]

Countries also provided details on a number of forms and means by which electronic evidence might be presented in court. These included through testimony delivered by police officers; through testimony delivered by forensic practitioners, including presentation of digital information on projectors and widescreen monitors; and through printouts identifying objects, documents, photographs, logs, and screen captures.[50] One country in Asia focused on the use of expert reports, noting that *'Usually written reports are presented with explanations concerning the technical data.'* Other countries recounted the presentation of electronic evidence on computer screens: *'In a sophisticated computer crime case, the user of a projector in court, as a way of screening the evidence, has provide itself as an efficient way to pass the information from the prosecution to the court.'*[51]

Still others reported multiple means of presentation. One country in Europe, for example, noted that presentation of electronic evidence in court '*Depends on the actual state and place of the evidence. [electronic evidence may be introduced as] hardcopy prints, digital media (hard drives, CD, DVD, flash drives), laptop or desktop presentations, remote presentations and [live] access in rare cases.*' Some countries, however, highlighted that courtrooms were not typically set up for the use of technology in criminal trials. One country in the Americas, for instance, reported that '*Electronic trials are not yet common place. Not all courtrooms are wired for the purpose of allowing the [State] to present its case electronically. Currently the [State] must obtain the consent of the judge and defence counsel to use technology in the courtroom.*'[52]

Very few countries reported the existence of special evidentiary laws governing electronic evidence. For those that did, laws concerned areas such as legal assumptions concerning ownership or authorship of electronic data and documents, as well as circumstances in which electronic evidence may be considered authentic.[53] Other countries provided information on the way in which 'traditional' rules of evidence may be interpreted in the context of electronic evidence. One country from Oceania, for example, clarified how the 'hearsay' rule applied to electronic evidence in its jurisdiction: '*For electronic evidence specifically, the hearsay rule would not apply if the information contained in the electronic evidence relates to a communication which was transmitted between computers and has been admitted in order to identify the sender, receiver, date and time of the transmission.*'[54] Another country also noted that a '*general presumption*' exists that '*where evidence that has been produced by a machine or other device is tendered, if the device is one that, if properly used, ordinarily produces that outcome, it is taken that the device was working properly when it produced the evidence.*'[55]

Finally, countries reported on the *ways* in which electronic evidence could be used to establish a link between a criminal act and a specific perpetrator. The nature of cybercrime means that a *mediating* device, in the form of a computer system, is usually situated between the perpetrator and the victim—leading to challenges in *attribution* of acts to specific persons. In cases where a defendant is prosecuted, for example, for possession of illegal computer content, it must be established that the content was knowingly placed on the device by the defendant, and not by another person with access to the device. In this respect, one country commented that: '*Circumstantial evidence will often be the only means by which to establish identification of who is speaking or communicating. The following methods have proven helpful: proving possession of the communication device (seizure upon arrest or execution of a warrant), subscriber information, surveillance (pursuant to a court authorization, where required), analysis of the content of the communication, and forensic examination of the communication device.*'[56] Another country observed that 'there are often multiple different sets of electronic evidence that must be brought together to place a suspect behind an electronic device at a particular time and place.'[57]

Most countries reported that specific steps or criteria to establish this link did not exist. Rather, countries referred to a variety of traditional and cyber-specific techniques to '*associate the electronic evidence to a computer system under the control of [the] defendant, or to which [the] defendant has access. Standard proof techniques apply including motivation, opportunity, corroborative non-electronic evidence, control of evidence, state-of-mind evidence, and evidence which supports excluding others.*'[58]

Overall, responding countries reported a significant amount of accumulated knowledge in the area of identification, collection, analysis, and presentation of electronic evidence. Good practices in this area were highlighted not only by developed countries, but also by a number of developing countries—indicating increasing levels of global dialogue and dissemination of technical standards in the areas of electronic evidence. Nonetheless, many institutions in developing countries—including law enforcement and prosecution authorities—highlight a significant lack of capacity and resources to fully implement such standards. In addition, in a few countries, legal obstacles such as the inadmissibility of all electronic evidence, and the inadmissibility of extraterritorial electronic evidence, present serious obstacles to the prosecution of cybercrime acts.

Cybercrime and the Criminal Justice System in Practice

KEY RESULTS

- Prosecutors report a range of challenges to the successful prosecution of cybercrime, including sufficiency of legal frameworks, difficulties in the attribution of acts to individuals, delays due to international cooperation procedures, and evidentiary challenges
- Such challenges are reflected in available statistics on the ratio of suspects to police-recorded acts, and in 'attrition' measures that compare the number of convictions with the number of recorded acts

This section widens the discussion from forensics and electronic evidence to the performance of the criminal justice system, as a whole, in cybercrime cases. It considers challenges and good practices reported by prosecutors and courts, and identifies the possible impact of these on prosecutions and convictions of cybercrime perpetrators.

Prosecution Challenges and Good Practices

Responding countries identified prosecution good practices and challenges across the criminal justice process, from case intake to final case disposition. Once country, for example, proposed a comprehensive set of good practices in the areas of case management, evidence disclosure, and presentation of evidence at trial: '*1) Collaborate/communicate early on with investigators, IT personnel, paralegals and defence counsel. 2) Address quality control safeguards, e.g., business rules. 3) Inventory investigation and index disclosure. 4) Identify an expert witness who can testify to quality control issues such as completeness and integrity of prosecution database. 5) Ensure compatibility/interoperability of police/government computer systems. 6) Meet and confer with defence counsel early in the case. 7) Avoid mixing media. 8) Be able to defend the disclosure. 9) Think about metadata from the beginning and seek assistance/ support from experts. 10) Ensure e-documents have been properly redacted. 11) Pick the right e-tool to fit the type of evidence you will present at trial. One size does not fit all. 12) Get the judge's permission. 13) Identify trial exhibits early, test the equipment in office/courtroom, have a backup plan, and be prepared.*'[59]

Reported obstacles to successful prosecution generally related to the sufficiency of the legal framework, identification of suspects, availability and interpretation of evidence, and the proper evidence handling procedures.

With respect to legislation for procedural powers (discussed in Chapter Five (Law enforcement and investigations)), responding countries highlighted, for example, that '*lack of a legal framework*', '*lack of procedural legislation*', '*lack of proper investigatory powers which do not compromise the right to privacy and free speech in an excessive way,*' and lack of '*specific legislation on privacy protection*'[60] complicates and delays investigations.

Prosecutors also identified the challenge discussed in the previous section of this Chapter of attribution of evidence of an act to an individual. One country, for example, stated that '*In general, attribution is the hardest thing in a cybercrime investigation, so therein lies a practical obstacle to successful prosecution.*'[61] Prosecutors from responding countries further highlighted the challenges of cases with an extraterritorial dimension, including '*difficulty in obtaining evidence requiring international cooperation of other countries,*' and '*delay in the investigation and prosecution of cybercrime offences*' due to formal international cooperation processes, such as mutual legal assistance.[62]

Evidentiary issues were reported as major barriers to successful prosecution, including '*the large volume of evidence*', '*the short period of time during which service providers store information needed for investigation purposes'* and *'maintaining integrity of electronic evidence from the time of seizure to the point of completion of the case', 'failure to establish chain of custody of evidence, and lack of proper storage facilities to maintain evidence.'*[63] *'The production of cybercrime evidence is still a challenge in court'* and *'lack of integrity of evidence from improper handling thereof by law enforcement'*[64] were also identified as particularly challenging by several countries.

Countries repeatedly reinforced the importance of evidence collection and presentation. *'Close working relationships on the prosecution team between the prosecutor and investigator that result in collection of all relevant properly authenticated evidence'*[65] are essential to success in prosecution. *'Hardware, and where appropriate software, are to be seized from the accused as quickly as is lawfully possible ... followed by rapid evaluation by specially-trained highly skilled staff or external specialists.'*[66] *'Separate identification and tracking of all the relevant computer documents/images,'*[67] a *'clear chain of custody of exhibits,'*[68] and *'developing policies in relationship to evidence presentation in court based on successful previous presentations'*[69] were important components of successful prosecutions and convictions. Finally, a *'perceived lack of fluency in the legal community with respect to technological concepts and how these impact the administration of justice'*[70] and *'understanding of digital evidence by judicial officers'*[71] were reported as additional obstacles to successful prosecution and conviction in cybercrime cases.

Additional training and resources were indicated as challenges, including *'better guidance to the courts at all levels by summarizing (and sharing) judicial experience to allow identification and uniform standards in computer information system security cases.'*[72] One country highlighted that *'It is important and decisive for good management of cybercrime cases, that the national courts have adequate financial means to acquire necessary technical equipment.'*[73] The necessity for public-private partnerships with *'internet access providers, website hosting providers, and other service providers'*[74] and banking and telecommunications companies was also reported as a productive method to enhance evidence collection.

Criminal Justice System Effectiveness and Outcomes

Core aims of the criminal justice response, to any crime, are to achieve just outcomes for perpetrators and victims, alongside specific deterrence, rehabilitation and societal reintegration for convicted offenders, and a sense of general deterrence for potential perpetrators.[75] Measurement of how 'efficiently' or 'effectively' this is achieved is extremely challenging. Measures range from 'attrition' rates that provide information on the numbers of persons suspected, prosecuted, and convicted by the criminal justice system for specific crimes, to measures of 'timeliness' of case disposition, 'punitivity' and 'recidivism.'[76] While such measures are commonly reported, it should be noted that they do not represent direct indicators of the 'quality' of justice, and can be heavily influenced by differences in criminal justice system mechanisms, such as the application of suspect counting rules, thresholds applied in recording of cases, or prosecutorial involvement in the initial investigation stage.

Nonetheless, with a view to further understanding the criminal justice system response to cybercrime, the Study questionnaire asked countries to report available statistics on the number of recorded cybercrime offences, and numbers of persons suspected (or 'brought into formal contact with the police') for cybercrime offences, as well as numbers of persons prosecuted and convicted for cybercrime offences.[77]

As noted in Chapter Two (The global picture), reported police statistics were found not to represent a strong basis for cross-national comparative measurement of cybercrime trends.[78] Law enforcement and criminal justice statistics *within* individual countries may, however, allow case and suspect 'attrition' calculations for that country, where reported case numbers are not small, and year-to-year effects (such as cases carried over from one year to the next) can be accounted for.

In general, responding countries were able to provide comparatively few law enforcement, criminal justice, and court statistics. For a set of six countries, mostly in Europe, however, it was possible to calculate the average number of persons brought into formal contact with law enforcement authorities per recorded offence for the cybercrime acts of illegal access, computer-related fraud and forgery, and child pornography offences.

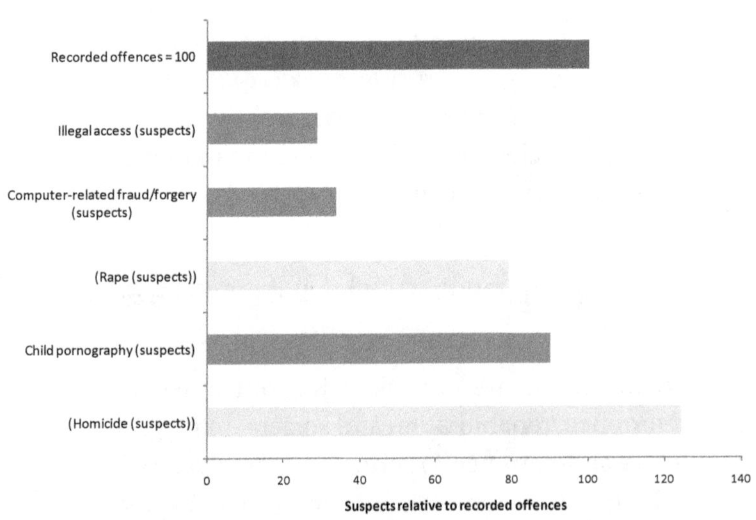

Figure 7.6 Persons brought into formal contact per recorded offence (6 countries)
Source: Study cybercrime questionnaire. Q54–70.

Figure 7.6 shows these results alongside the suspects to offence ratios for rape and homicide in the same six countries.[79] A significant difference exists between child pornography offences and the other computer offences of illegal access and fraud or forgery. Suspect to offence ratios for child pornography are similar to that for 'conventional' crimes. Those for illegal access and computer-related fraud or forgery are significantly lower—representing around 25 recorded suspects per 100 offences.

This may be indicative of a number of factors, including differences in police investigative capabilities for different cybercrime offences, differences in police investigative focus, and variations in the point at which different cybercrime acts are recorded as offences for statistical purposes. In addition, however, the pattern may reveal genuine underlying differences in the steps taken by, and capabilities of, perpetrators to conceal criminal activity and to evade detection by law enforcement investigations.

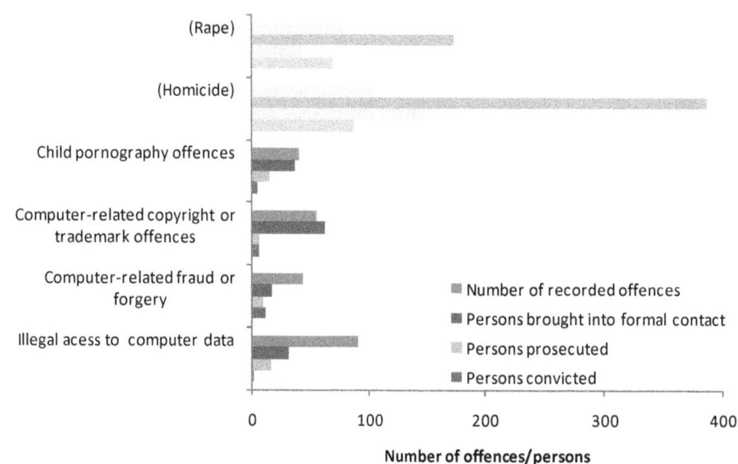

Figure 7.7 Criminal justice system attrition in cybercrime cases
Source: Cybercrime study questionnaire. Q54-70.

While suspect to offence ratios could be calculated as an average for a number of countries, sufficient statistics for calculation of a complete 'offence to conviction' attrition rate were provided by only one country in response to the Study questionnaire. Figure 7.7 shows the number of police recorded offences, persons brought into formal contact, persons prosecuted and persons convicted for four cybercrime acts in one country in Eastern Europe, alongside equivalent data for the 'conventional' crimes of rape and homicide. The data confirm the picture of a higher number of suspects per recorded offence for child pornography offences than other cybercrime acts. This pattern is repeated for another content-related offence—that of computer-related copyright or trademark offences. In general, however, all cybercrime offences show far fewer persons prosecuted or convicted than for the conventional crimes. For the reporting country, cybercrime convictions represent, on average, 10 per cent of police-recorded offences, compared to around 80 per cent for rape and homicide.

The pattern demonstrates that the large number of cybercrime prosecution challenges referred to by responding countries are borne out in the reality of lower conviction rates for cybercrime offences—at least for this one example country. As discussed in the following section of this Chapter, in many developing countries, the prosecution of cybercrime offences faces the challenge not only of transnational evidence gathering and perpetrator obfuscation, but also of prosecutorial and judicial capacity and specialization limitations.

Criminal Justice Capacity

KEY RESULTS

- Levels of prosecutorial cybercrime specialization are lower than for law enforcement authorities. Around 60 per cent of all responding countries have put in place specialized prosecutorial structures for cybercrime
- Developed countries show higher levels of prosecutorial specialization than developing countries
- Over 60 per cent of lesser developed countries reported that specialized prosecutors either had basic or no IT skills, and intermediate computer equipment or none at all
- Courts show minimal levels of specialization for cybercrime, with just 10 per cent of countries reporting specialized judicial services. The vast majority of cases are handled by non-specialized judges, who, in 40 per cent of responding countries do not receive any form of cybercrime-related training

In the same way as cybercrime and electronic evidence-based investigations require specialization within law enforcement, the prosecution and adjudication of cybercrime cases also calls for specialization within the criminal justice system. Such specialization requires personnel that have an understanding of concepts of computing and the internet, a knowledge of cybercrime legislative frameworks, and the ability to present and understand electronic evidence in court.

This section presents information reported by countries on the capacity of prosecutors and courts to prosecute and adjudicate cybercrime. As in Chapter Five (Law enforcement and investigations), institutional 'capacity' has a number of elements, including strategic and operational capabilities, technical skills of personnel, and sufficiency of personnel and resources; as well as degree of specialization. The point made in Chapter Five concerning an increasing need for *all* law enforcement officers to routinely handle and collect electronic evidence equally applies to prosecutors and judges. As the digital world advances, it may become hard to image the adjudication of *any* offence without the presentation and consideration of electronic evidence.

Organizational Specialization

Country responses to the Study questionnaire show that the degree of organizational cybercrime specialization for prosecution authorities is significantly less than that reported for law enforcement agencies. Whereas more than 90 per cent of countries reported some degree of cybercrime specialization within law enforcement, this proportion drops to around 60 per cent for prosecution authorities, across all responding countries.[80] This figure conceals, however, significant differences according to levels of country development.

Almost 80 per cent of more highly developed countries report some form of prosecutorial cybercrime specialization. Around half of these countries have a specialized unit, while the other half have either a specialized agency, another specialized unit (such as for organized crime), or specialized personnel who are not organized in a separate unit. In contrast, less than 60 per cent of less developed countries report prosecutorial cybercrime specialization. In the majority of these, the degree of specialization is at the level of a specialized unit.

For developed countries reporting organizational specialization, many indicated that a specialized division or unit exists at the federal, provincial or state level in the ministry of justice or the national prosecution agency, frequently overseeing, coordinating or supporting specialized units or generalists in field and local offices. Some countries also reported technical and investigatory support from '*a dedicated team of police investigators, computer engineers and prosecutors that both investigate and prosecute cybercrime.*'[81] '*In some cases, individual prosecution offices have special competences to deal with prominent sets of proceedings related to information and communication crime, and for cybercrime in the strict sense.*' Another developed country noted that: '*There is some variation, but [a] small number of local offices have specialized internet child exploitation teams.*'[82]

In less developed countries, arrangements are often less established. One country in Africa reported that its newly established unit was tasked with prosecution '*as well as advice on policies and legislation, provide technical assistance to other prosecutors and law enforcement agencies, [but] as a new unit, training and equipment needs are yet to be met.*'[83] In some, there is a reported '*lot of*

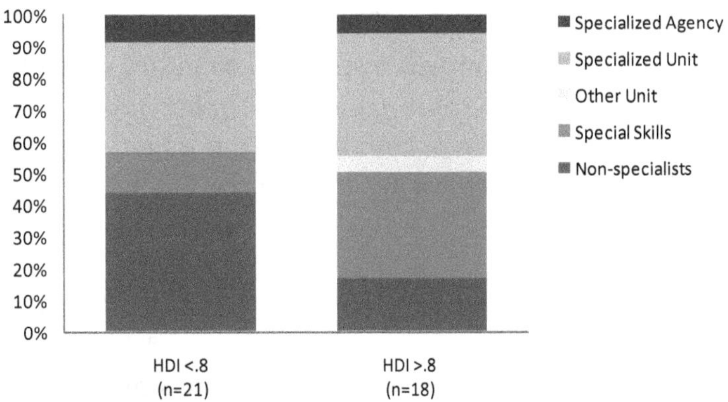

Figure 7.8 Prosecution structure for preventing and combatting cybercrime
Source: Study cybercrime questionnaire Q157. (n=41)

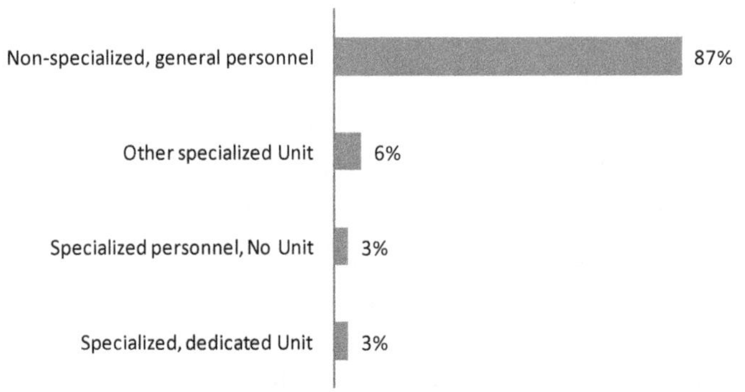

Figure 7.9 Court structure for cybercrime cases
Source: Study cybercrime questionnaire. Q186. (n=31)

space for improvement.' One country in Africa reported that *'There are no prosecutors assigned to do cybercrime cases. Any prosecutor is required to cover cybercrime even those who have not been trained on cybercrime.'*[84]

A few countries without specialized prosecution structures indicated plans to create a new prosecution structure for cybercrime. Such plans included proposals *'to create a number of specialized units'* and *'plans to create task forces in major cities that currently do not have specialized prosecution structures.'*[85] One country in Europe envisages creating *'independent units in prosecutors' offices with a great volume of activity and in the remaining offices to combine cyber specialized prosecutors with other types of specialized'*[86] units. Other countries reported no plans for a specialized unit, although some of these reported planning to integrate cyber-specialists into existing prosecutorial structures.

Court structures show the least degree of specialization, with around 10 per cent of all responding countries reporting some degree of court cybercrime specialization. Only three per cent of all responding countries reported a specialized, dedicated cybercrime judicial unit. Some six per cent reported another type of specialized judicial unit, such as a commercial crimes court. Three per cent reported the judicial oversight of cybercrime cases by specialized judicial personnel.

A few countries indicated that there are currently plans under way, either through legislation or administrative measures, to create specialized cybercrime courts or tribunals. In general, however, responding countries were of the view that they *'do not generally involve specialized courts based on thematic subject matter, although some judges at various levels do specialize in criminal cases as a matter of practice, and may tend to have criminal cases assigned to them by Chief Justices.'*[87]

Personnel Specialization

In the same way as prosecution structures show less organizational specialization for cybercrime than law enforcement, so countries also reported lower levels of technical capabilities amongst specialized prosecutors than for law enforcement officers. Figure 7.10 shows country responses concerning law enforcement and prosecutorial IT skills.[88] While very few cybercrime prosecutors reported advanced IT skills compared with law enforcement officers specialized in cybercrime, this may, in part, reflect the different functional roles of each. Although prosecutorial involvement in investigations varies across legal systems, in general, law enforcement officers may be more often required to conduct or supervise initial forensics investigations and collection of electronic evidence.

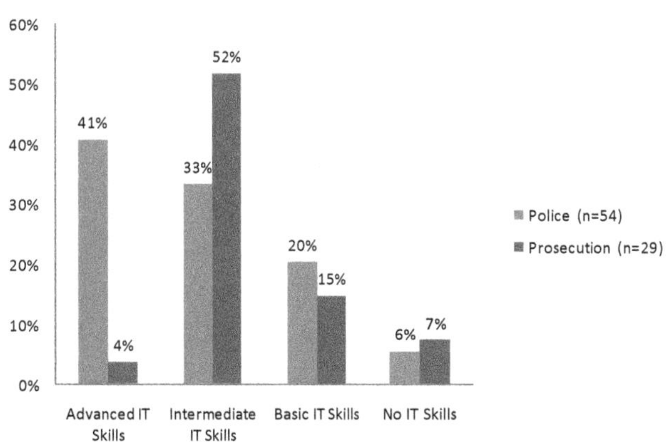

Figure 7.10 Technical capabilities of police and prosecutors
Source: Study cybercrime questionnaire. Q116 and Q160. (n=54, 29)

Technical capabilities of prosecutors vary significantly by level of country development. More developed countries reported that around 80 per cent of prosecutors had intermediate IT skills and access to sophisticated equipment. Eight per cent had advanced IT skills. None of the developed countries reported that prosecutors did not have IT skills or computer equipment.

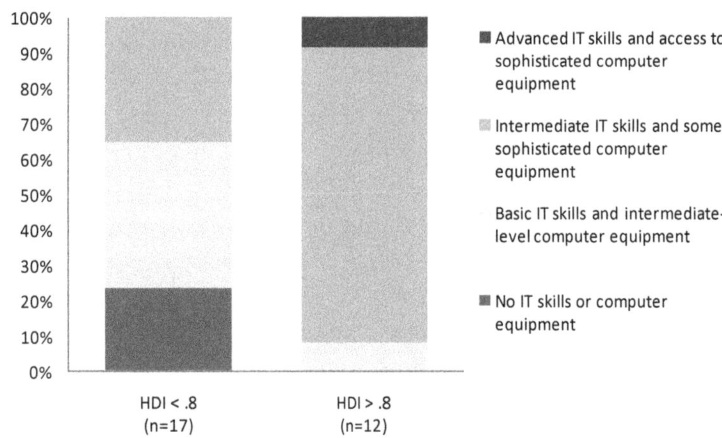

Figure 7.11 Technical capabilities of prosecutors
Source: Study cybercrime questionnaire. Q160. (n=29)

In contrast, over 60 per cent of less developed countries reported that specialized prosecutors either had basic or no IT skills, and intermediate computer equipment or none at all. These findings indicate significant gaps in capacity. In one less developed country, necessary computer equipment is '*available upon request,*'[89] although almost all countries reportedly face challenges in both training and equipment. '*Technical training is insufficient*' and more '*support in the area of training is needed to improve outcomes.*'[90] One more developed country reported '*Prosecutors have varying levels of advanced and intermediate IT skills, but have no access to sophisticated or even intermediate computer equipment.*'[91]

Personnel Development

Reported training for specialized prosecutors covered a range of topics, with half of responding countries indicating that prosecutors were trained in multiple topics. In addition to the topics identified in Figure 7.12, others include '*operation of the Internet, types of cybercrime as well as investigations and jurisprudence*,'[92] information security, and '*preservation of electronic evidence with regard to money laundering offences*.' One country noted that '*Occasionally, prosecutors participate in the training that police organizations provide to their own experts.*'[93] Subject matter for training of specialized prosecutors is not as varied as that seen for law enforcement personnel and this may be linked with differences in the roles of each within the criminal justice process. Several developing countries emphasized the need for more technical training for prosecutors. One country noted, for example, that '*Preparation in criminal law is of high quality, technical training is insufficient.*'[94] Another stated that '*We need more support in the area of training to improve outcomes.*'[95] Others emphasized that they '*require[d] more training in concepts such as information technology.*'[96]

Country responses also showed substantial variation in the frequency and duration of training for specialized prosecutors. Overall, over 40 per cent of responding countries reported that prosecutors received regular training, with just over 20 per cent reporting training more than twice a year. As with organizational specialization and technical capabilities, differences are also apparent by level of country development.

One quarter of specialized prosecutors in less developed countries do not have access to specialized training. Around 40 per cent receive regular training.

In contrast, none of the countries in the more developed cohort reported that no training was available, and over half of those countries reported that specialized prosecutors received regular training of more than once a year. Several more developed countries also detailed additional aspects related to training frequency including '*annual interdisciplinary training programs*,' '*e-learning modules*,' '*conference attendance*' and '*monthly training on specialized topics conducted by in-house and external experts*.'[97]

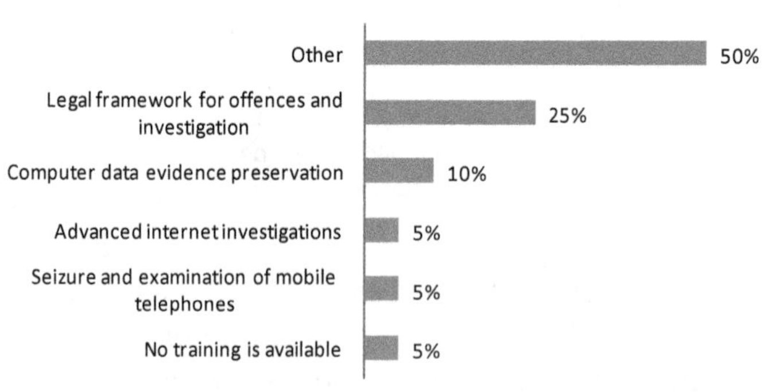

Figure 7.12 Training subject matters for specialized prosecutors
Source: Study cybercrime questionnaire. Q161. (n=20)

The most commonly reported training provider for specialized prosecutors was the training unit of the prosecution agency. Judicial academies and ministries of justice along with multiple agencies each constituted around 10 per cent of reported training providers for prosecution specialists. A very small proportion—three per cent—of specialized prosecutors was reported to have been trained by international or regional organizations. Some six per cent of countries reported that no specialized training has yet been conducted for prosecutorial personnel.

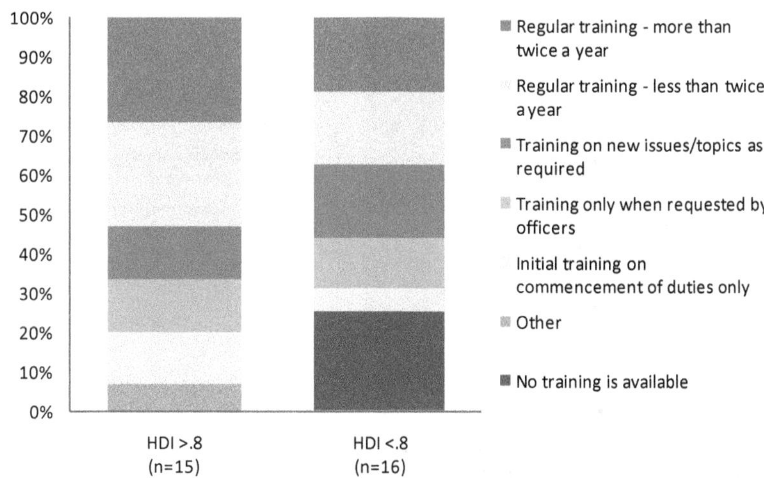

Figure 7.13 Frequency of training for specialized prosecutors
Source: Study cybercrime questionnaire. Q162. (n=31)

A number of responding countries recognized the importance of providing training on cybercrime also for *non*specialist prosecutors. One country, for example, stated that *'During the last years, we have developed several activities in order to facilitate to all prosecutors an adequate knowledge of these [cybercrime] themes, with the purpose to provide them the best skills related to new technologies.'*[98] Another country highlighted that broader training was *'intended not only to enrich knowledge of legal doctrine of these crimes, but also seeks to raise awareness about the importance of adapting the classic procedural concepts to new technologies and forensic possibilities.'*[99] Overall, around 60 per cent of countries reported the existence of cybercrime training for non-specialized prosecutors. Figure 7.15 shows, however, differences by level of country development, with almost 40 per cent of lesser developed countries reporting that non-specialized prosecutors

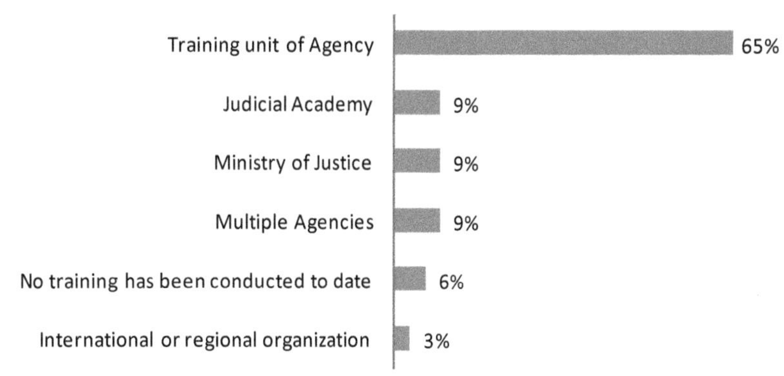

Figure 7.14 Training provider for specialized prosecutors
Source: Study cybercrime questionnaire. Q163. (n=34)

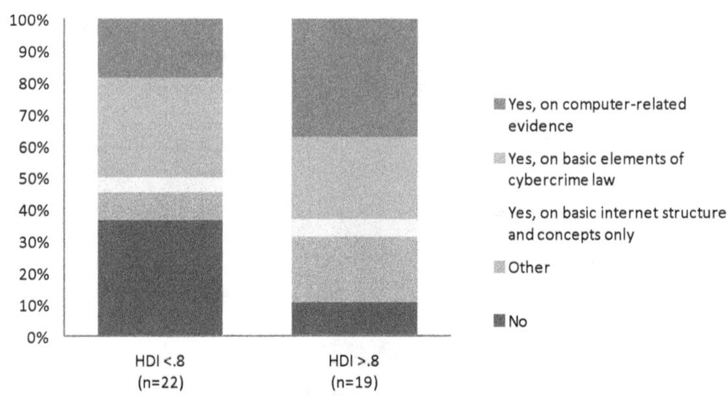

Figure 7.15 Training for non–specialized prosecutors
Source: Study cybercrime questionnaire. Q164. (n=41)

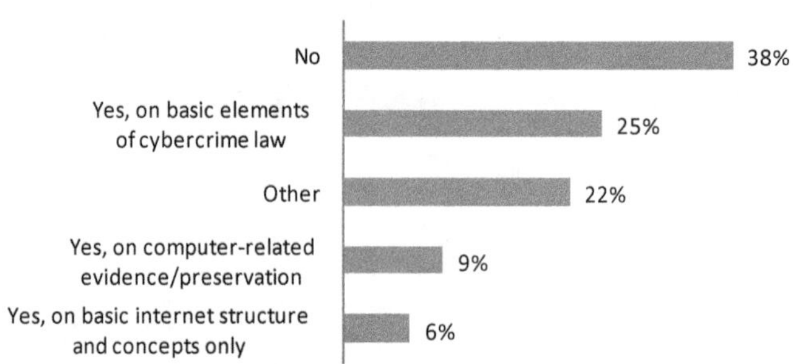

Figure 7.16 Cybercrime investigation training for non-specialized judges
Source: Study cybercrime questionnaire. Q192. (n=32)

do not receive any form of cybercrime training.

Amongst the judiciary, around 40 per cent of all responding countries reported that no cybercrime-specific training is available for judges. One-quarter of responding countries reported training on basic elements of cyber-crime law. Many countries' responses were similar to that of one Northern European country which commented that: '*Since there are no specialized judges, the training is covered by continuous training programmes organized by the magistracy which is open to all the magistrates. It is organized on an annual basis and usually has the duration of two days. This kind of training is rather of a general nature, such as an introduction to cybercrime.*'[100] One country reported judicial training '*aimed at covering cases based on national legislation on cybercrime, as well as summaries of recent cases.*'[101] In general, countries emphasized that a significant need exists for judicial training on '*cyber-crime law, evidence collection, and basic and advanced computer knowledge.*'[102]

Such training as currently takes place was reported to be conducted by judicial training boards and centres, court and judicial training units, and ministries or institutes of justice. Several countries reported that judges may '*voluntarily elect to participate in professional development programs. Programs vary in the content they address and there is no prescribed training material for judges or magistrates involved in cybercrime cases.*'[103]

Capacity Building and Technical Assistance

KEY RESULTS

- 75 per cent of responding countries, across all regions of the world, reported requiring technical assistance in the area of cybercrime
- Technical assistance to date has mostly been delivered in the area of general cybercrime investigations and computer forensics and evidence. Reported need suggests that there is scope for assistance in the areas of international cooperation and prosecution, and trial support in particular
- A range of government institutions report requiring technical assistance, highlighting the need for a multi-disciplinary, holistic approach to cybercrime technical assistance
- The dominance of technical assistance activities lasting under one month indicates a clear need for longer term, sustainable investment

As a counterpart to the questions on the capacity of law enforcement, prosecution and court authorities to prevent and combat cybercrime, the Study questionnaire also included questions on needs for, and delivery of technical assistance by countries.

Overall, 75 per cent of responding countries, across all regions of the world, reported requiring technical assistance in some thematic area linked with cybercrime. Every responding country in Africa indicated a need for technical assistance.

Over 70 per cent of all responding countries reported having provided some form of technical assistance to other countries, although less than 20 per cent of countries reported having received technical assistance. This could be indicative either of the fact that a large number of donor countries focus on a smaller number of recipient countries, or of the fact that a significant proportion of the world's least developed countries did not respond to the Study questionnaire.

For European countries, just over half reported having received technical assistance, while less than half reported requiring or providing technical assistance in the area of cybercrime. In Asia, Oceania and the Americas, over 80 per cent of countries reported that they required technical assistance. A majority of countries in Asia and Oceania reported having provided technical assistance, and slightly less than half have received technical assistance. In the

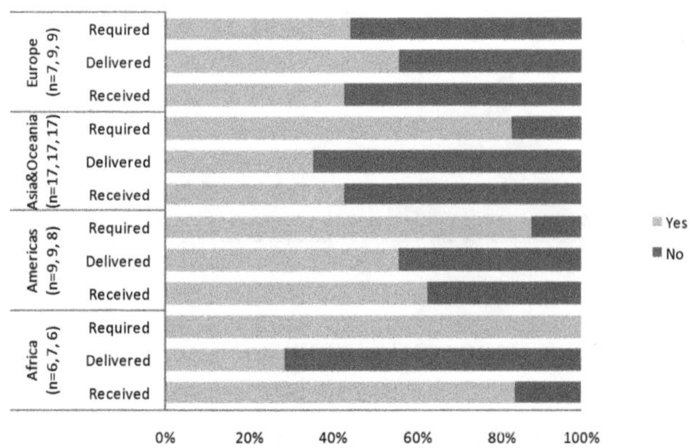

Figure 7.17 Technical assistance required, delivered, and received
Source: Study cybercrime questionnaire. Q241, Q253, Q250 (n=40, 42, 39)

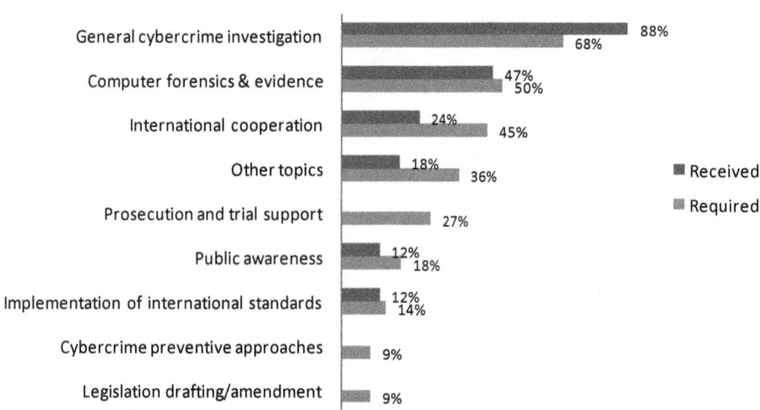

Figure 7.18 Technical assistance topics received and required
Source: Study cybercrime questionnaire. Q243 and Q251. (n=17, r=36; n=22, r=61)

Americas, less than half have provided technical assistance while more than a third have received some form of technical assistance.

Topics—'General cybercrime investigations' was the most commonly reported subject matter area for both technical assistance received and required, and the only subject matter area for which technical assistance was reported as received more often than reported as needed. This may suggest that there is scope for cybercrime technical assistance to move beyond a traditional focus on law enforcement investigations and to encompass a broader range of areas. In particular, the areas of 'international cooperation' and 'prosecution and trial support' represent fields in which assistance was reported to be required, but in which little was reported to have been delivered. One UN entity reported that '*Governments are requesting more training in these areas.*'[104]

Institutions—A large range of government authorities reported both requiring and receiving technical assistance—emphasizing the importance of a multi-disciplinary, holistic response to cybercrime. National police and law enforcement agencies reported having received technical assistance more frequently than requiring technical assistance. This may indicate the extent to which focus has been placed on strengthening capacity of law enforcement institutions as 'front line' responders to cybercrime. A higher level of reported delivery of technical assistance to law enforcement agencies may also correspond with reported higher levels of organizational and personnel specialization amongst law enforcement than for other criminal justice agencies (see Chapter Five (Law enforcement and investigations). Figure 7.19 also shows the relatively limited degree to which institutions such as prosecution offices and courts have received technical assistance, confirming the thematic picture in Figure 7.18.

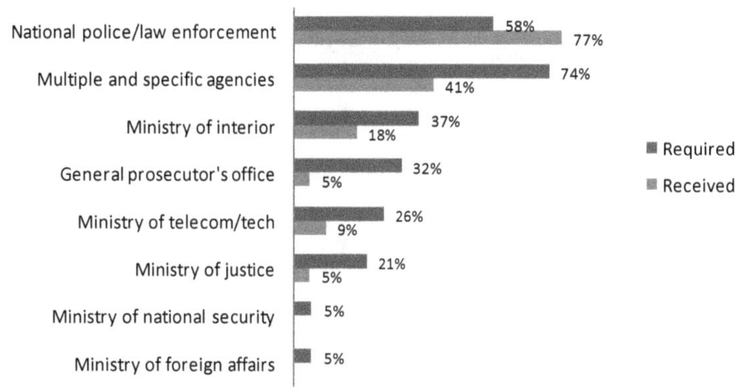

Figure 7.19 Agencies requiring and receiving technical assistance
Source: Study cybercrime questionnaire. Q244 and Q252. (n=22, r=34; n=19, r=49)

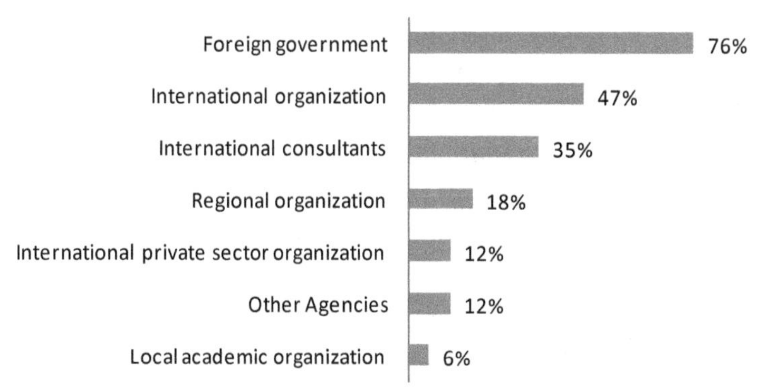

Figure 7.20 Institution delivering technical assistance
Source: Study cybercrime questionnaire. Q247. (n=17, r=35)

Delivery and donors—Governments were reported as the institution most frequently delivering technical assistance (over 75 per cent), followed by international organizations and international consultants. Regional organizations, such as the African Union, the Organization of American States, and the Council of Europe, were reported as providers of technical assistance by 20 per cent of responding countries. It should be noted, however, that 'delivery' structures for technical assistance may involve multiple modalities. The 'delivery' of a particular technical assistance programme or project, for example, may often be carried out through partnership between governments, and international or regional organizations, as well as independent consultants and academic organizations. Notably, international private sector organizations—with whom such partnerships also often exist—were reported to have delivered technical assistance to around 10 per cent of responding countries, highlighting the importance of private sector organizations as key partners in this area.

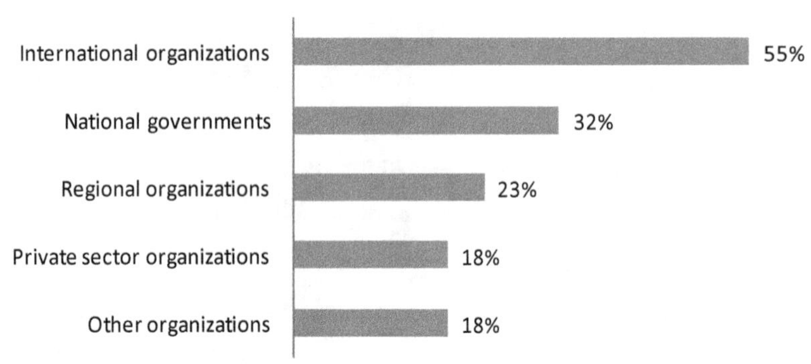

Figure 7.21 Organization or Donor supporting Technical Assistance Received
Source: Study cybercrime questionnaire. Q245. (n=22, r=32)

Responses from intergovernmental organizations to the Study questionnaire further highlighted the role that such organizations play in delivery of technical assistance. Organizations provide technical assistance on a variety of topics, from general investigation techniques, forensics and evidence preservation, to development of legislation, public-private cooperation, and international standard-setting and awareness-raising. A number of United Nations entities highlighted the importance of having a '*multilevel and holistic approach*' to technical assistance.[105] Many emphasized that it was important to build capacity in partnership, such as through '*networks of judicial training institutions*'[106] and using an approach such as '*train-the-trainer for IT crime investigators/examiners*.'[107] One organization, for example noted that it was important that '*all information and materials*' can be used by '*participants so as to provide the same training in their country domestically*.'[108] Depending on the focus of the programme, the target audience varies from the individual, such as law enforcement officers and forensic investigators, to the institutional, such as ministries of interior, justice, and communication. International organizations have provided training in every region; most reported that training programmes are ongoing and in great demand, although sometimes constrained by resource availability.

A number of intergovernmental organizations raised the important question of *standards* and *certification*. One organization referred to the used of forensic training '*accredited by [a] University ... delivered in 3 segments; a foundation level course in 2010, advanced courses in 2011, with an online Masters Degree pending for 2012*.'[109] One UN entity highlighted the challenge of identifying and knowing which professional standards should be followed and promoted during the delivery of training. The same entity reported, for example, that '*there is not yet any consensus on [forensic] curriculum requirements. As the field evolves there will likely be further course offerings and some standardization*.'[110] Other UN entities highlighted the challenge of a lack of resources and awareness concerning the problem of cybercrime as inhibiting the delivery of technical assistance. One UN entity indicated that '*We have the expertise but we don't have the resources to combat cybercrime*.'[111]

Support for technical assistance comes from a relatively small number of national governments, international, regional, and private sector organizations. The top reported support source for technical assistance was international organizations, with a majority (55 per cent) of countries indicating some form of technical assistance from this source. One UN entity indicated the importance of '*Training provided by experienced organizations in the region.*'[112] National governments were reported as the providing or supporting donor by almost one third of respondents while regional organizations accounted for almost one-quarter of support for technical assistance. Private sector and other types of organizations were reported as donors or sponsors for technical assistance by almost 20 per cent of respondents.

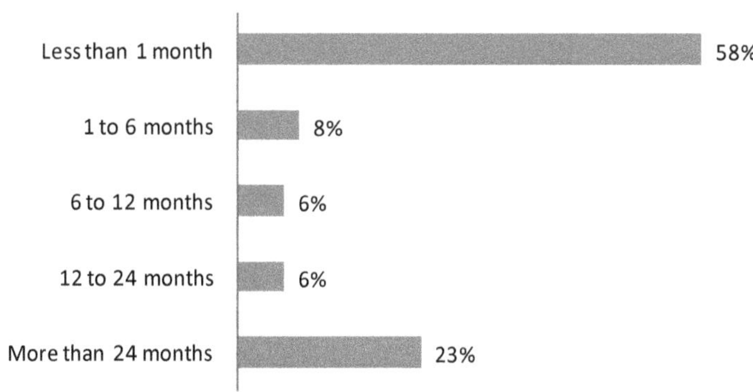

Figure 7.22 Duration of technical assistance received
Source: Study cybercrime questionnaire. Q246. (n=24, r=52)

Duration—Almost 60 per cent of reported technical assistance programs lasted for less than one month. Only one quarter lasted for over two years. While technical assistance needs related to cybercrime may be all of long-term, medium-term, and short-term, the dominance of shorter-term technical assistance activities indicates a clear need for longer term, sustainable investment, that focuses on building core structural capacity of the range of government authorities and stakeholders involved in the cybercrime response.

Notes

1. See Study cybercrime questionnaire. Q109–112, and Q143–150.
2. See for example *United States v Whitaker*, 127 F3d 595, 602 (7th Cir. 1997).
3. See Jackson, J.D., and Summers, S.J., 2012. *The Internationalisation of Criminal Evidence: Beyond the Common Law and Civil Law Traditions*. Cambridge: Cambridge University Press.
4. Casey, E., 2011. *Digital Evidence and Computer Crime: Forensic Science, Computers and the Internet*. New York: Elsevier.
5. U.S. Department of Justice, 2007. *Digital Evidence in the Courtroom: A Guide for Law Enforcement and Prosecutors*. National Institute of Justice, p.16.

6. Marcella Jr., A.J., Greenfield, R.S., (eds.), 2002. *Cyber Forensics: A Field Manual for Collecting, Examining, and Preserving Evidence of Computer Crimes*, 2nd edn. Boca Raton: CRC Press, p.136.
7. *Re Vee Vinhnee, Debtor American Express Travel Related Services Company, Inc v Vee Vinhnee* 336 BR 437 (9th Cir BAP, December 16, 2006), p.18.
8. Chaikin, D., 2006. Network investigations of cyber attacks: the limits of digital evidence. *Crime, Law and Social Change*, 46(4-5):239-256, 249.
9. Hearsay is often defined as *'evidence given of a statement made on some other occasion, when intended as evidence of the truth of what was asserted'* (*Halbury's Laws*, Vol. 17). Certain types of digital evidence may strictly constitute hearsay, but could be admitted under exceptions such as 'business records.' See Thomson, L.L., 2011. Admissibility of Electronic Documentation as Evidence in U.S. Courts. Appendix IX.B.1, Center for Research Libraries, *Human Rights Electronic Evidence Study*.
10. As a general principle, courts are entitled to the best evidence that is available. If a best evidence rule is applied, copies of an original may not be admissible as evidence unless it can be demonstrated that the original is unavailable due to destruction or other circumstances. The printout of information located on a computer or other storage device might not technically be regarded as 'original.' In some jurisdictions, however, the best evidence rule does not operate to exclude printouts, provided that the printout accurately reflects the actual data. See, for example, *Doe v United States*, 805 F. Supp. 1513, 1517 (D. Hawaii. 1992); and *Laughner v State*, 769 N.E.2d 1147, 159 (Ind. Ct. App. 2002).
11. US National Institute of Standards and Technology, 2004. *Hardware Write Blocker Device (HWB) Specification, Version 2.0.*
12. Gutmann, P., 1996. Secure Deletion of Data from Magnetic and Solid-State Memory. *Proceedings of the 6th USENIX Security Symposium.*
13. Chappell, L., 2012. *Wireshark Network Analysis (Second Edition): The Official Wireshark Certified Network Analyst Study Guide.* Laura Chappell University.
14. Study cybercrime questionnaire. Q110.
15. Study cybercrime questionnaire. Q109.
16. Study cybercrime questionnaire. Q110.
17. Study cybercrime questionnaire. Q109.
18. *Ibid.*
19. *Ibid.*
20. *Ibid.*
21. *Ibid.*
22. Study cybercrime questionnaire. Q111.
23. Study cybercrime questionnaire. Q112.
24. *Ibid.*
25. *Ibid.*
26. *Ibid.*
27. *Ibid.*

28. The *Regulation of Investigatory Powers Act 2000* in one country in Northern Europe, for example, provides the power to impose a disclosure requirement upon a suspect to divulge the key to protected information in their possession. Failure to comply with a notice to disclose can result in a term of imprisonment and/or fine upon conviction. Similarly, the *Cybercrime Act 2001* in one country in Oceania allows a magistrate to make an order requiring a specified person to provide any information or assistance that is reasonable and necessary to allow a law enforcement officer to access data held in or accessible from a computer.
29. *Ibid.*
30. *Ibid.*
31. Study cybercrime questionnaire. Q85.
32. Reilly, D., Wren, C., and Berry, T., 2011. Cloud computing: Pros and Cons for Computer Forensic Investigators. *International Journal Multimedia and Image Processing*, 1(1):26–34, 33.
33. Study cybercrime questionnaire. Q111.
34. See http://www.met.police.uk/pceu/documents/ACPOguidelinescomputerevidence.pdf
35. Study cybercrime questionnaire. Q111.
36. Study cybercrime questionnaire. Q149.
37. Study cybercrime questionnaire. Q149.
38. Study cybercrime questionnaire. Q144.
39. Study cybercrime questionnaire. Q143.
40. *Ibid.*
41. Study cybercrime questionnaire. Q145.
42. *Ibid.*
43. Study cybercrime questionnaire. Q143.
44. Study cybercrime questionnaire. Q143.
45. Study cybercrime questionnaire. Q144.
46. *Ibid.*
47. *Ibid.*
48. *Ibid.*
49. Study cybercrime questionnaire. Q143.
50. Study cybercrime questionnaire. Q150.
51. *Ibid.*
52. *Ibid.*
53. Study cybercrime questionnaire. Q147.
54. Study cybercrime questionnaire. Q146.
55. Study cybercrime questionnaire. Q143.
56. Study cybercrime questionnaire. Q148.
57. *Ibid.*
58. *Ibid.*
59. Study cybercrime questionnaire. Q142.

60. *Ibid.*
61. *Ibid.*
62. *Ibid.*
63. *Ibid.*
64. *Ibid.*
65. Study cybercrime questionnaire. Q142.
66. Study cybercrime questionnaire. Q183.
67. Study cybercrime questionnaire. Q142.
68. *Ibid.*
69. *Ibid.*
70. Study cybercrime questionnaire. Q141.
71. *Ibid.*
72. Study cybercrime questionnaire. Q142.
73. Study cybercrime questionnaire. Q183.
74. *Ibid.*
75. Albanese, J.S., 2012. *Criminal Justice*. 5th edn. Upper Saddle River: Prentice Hall.
76. See for example, Harrendorf, S., Smit, P., 2010. Attributes of criminal justice systems—resources, performance and punitivity. *In*: European Institute for Crime Prevention and Control Affiliated with the United Nations (HEUNI). 2010. *International Statistics on Crime and Justice*. Helsinki.
77. Study cybercrime questionnaire. Q54-70, Q121-137, and Q165-181.
78. See Chapter Two (The global picture), Section 2.1 Measuring cybercrime, and Section 2.3 Cybercrime perpetrators, 'Typical offender' profiles.
79. Study cybercrime questionnaire. Q54-70; and United Nations Survey of Crime Trends and Operations of Criminal Justice Systems, latest available year.
80. Study cybercrime questionnaire. Q157.
81. Study cybercrime questionnaire. Q157.
82. *Ibid.*
83. *Ibid.*
84. Study cybercrime questionnaire. Q160.
85. Study cybercrime questionnaire. Q157.
86. *Ibid.*
87. Study cybercrime questionnaire. Q187.
88. Study cybercrime questionnaire. Q116 and Q160.
89. Study cybercrime questionnaire. Q160.
90. *Ibid.*
91. *Ibid.*
92. Study cybercrime questionnaire. Q161.
93. *Ibid.*

94. Study cybercrime questionnaire. Q160.
95. *Ibid.*
96. *Ibid.*
97. Study cybercrime questionnaire. Q162.
98. Study cybercrime questionnaire. Q164
99. *Ibid.*
100. Study cybercrime questionnaire. Q189.
101. *Ibid.*
102. *Ibid.*
103. Study cybercrime questionnaire. Q192.
104. Study cybercrime questionnaire (IGO and academia). Q20.
105. Study cybercrime questionnaire (IGO and academia). Q52.
106. *Ibid.*
107. *Ibid.*
108. *Ibid.*
109. *Ibid.*
110. Study cybercrime questionnaire (IGO and academia). Q51.
111. *Ibid.*
112. Study cybercrime questionnaire (IGO and academia). Q52

CHAPTER 2

Conclusion, References, and Review

Digital evidence, both content-based and non-content-based, encompasses a sprawling breadth of possibilities. While the most common electronic devices that produce such evidence are the Internet, computers, and mobile devices, this chapter emphasized the countless other sources of digital evidence analyzed by certified digital forensic examiners, along with the steps, regulations, and procedures they must follow. Digital evidence is commonly recovered in the majority of modern-day criminal investigations, bringing to light jurisdictional concerns for law enforcement and judicial entities, but also highlighting the new role of "digital crime scenes" in modern-day policing and the absolute necessity for increased law enforcement training in digital evidence handling and recovery.

The readings in this chapter introduced the basic necessary procedural steps for collecting various forms of digital evidence from physical and digital crime scenes, as well as for transporting the materials and maintaining a proper chain of custody for each digital evidentiary piece. In addition to discussing practical and technical procedures, this chapter also introduced the concept of forensic linguistics as it pertains to criminal investigations. Behavioral analysis and forensic psychological techniques were elaborated on for the purpose of case linkage and predictive analytics. This latter discussion emphasized the broad range of key individuals central to cybercrime investigations: aside from identifying and arresting perpetrators responsible for cybercriminal acts, law enforcement officers must also rely on laboratory technicians and other software experts to help access and preserve the evidence, as well as social scientists (e.g., criminologists and forensic psychologists) to assist in analyzing behavioral patterns to distinguish between isolated events and more established patterns of criminal-related behavior. In the following chapter, the role of these important actors is discussed in the broader context of myths and realities of cyber-related police investigations.

Reference

Cohen, Charles, "Growing Challenge of Computer Forensics." *The Police Chief* 74, no. 3 (2007): 6–14.

Chapter 2 Review

SECTION A

Choose the best match from the list below. Answers are listed at the back of the book.

1. _____ Write-blocker
2. _____ Cloud computing
3. _____ Forensic wipe
4. _____ Data carving
5. _____ Bit-for-bit copy
6. _____ Digital evidence
7. _____ Hash value
8. _____ Source code
9. _____ Digital forensics
10. _____ Forensic linguistics

A. An undisturbed forensic image of the storage device retrieved during an investigation, containing as detailed a copy of the original device as can be obtained.

B. The analysis of language patterns such as word usage and syntax to distinguish between the writings of multiple parties.

C. Information and data that is of value to an investigation and is stored on, received or transmitted by an electronic device.

D. A verifiable procedure for sanitizing a defined area of digital media by overwriting each byte with a known value; this process prevents cross-contamination of data.

E. Used to query large sums of data such as databases or hard drives for specific terms; also used to substantiate the integrity of digital evidence and/or for inclusion and exclusion comparisons against known value sets.

F. A special device used to create a forensic image or bit-for-bit copy that prevents any alternation being made to the original data.

G. The branch of forensic science concerned with the recovery and investigation of material found in digital and computer systems.

H. Software, applications, and digital storage that are accessed on the Internet through a web browser or desktop or mobile app; the software and user's data are stored on servers at a remote location.

I. The instructions written in a programming language used to build a computer program.

J. A forensic tool that can retrieve detected or corrupted files from the remnants of raw data that remain on storage devices even after the original file is gone.

SECTION B

Discussion questions. Answer these questions given the context of the readings in the chapter.

1. Consider the arguments made in this chapter by Grant (2010). Do you consider forensic linguistics to be an empirically valid forensic approach that should be allowed as testimony in a criminal court case? Why or why not? Use readings from this chapter to back up your answer.

2. According to the UNODC (2013) report, law enforcement entities in most countries do not feel that they have access to adequate resources: they experience deficiencies of technical specialists, encryption complications, cloud computing difficulties, and additional legal obstacles. What can national and international governing bodies do to reduce these problems? Can these problems be solved by an international effort, or should nations be required to address these problems individually?

CHAPTER 3

Policing Cyberspace: Myths and Realities Surrounding Cyber-Related Law Enforcement Investigations

It is a well-known fact that police officers working their local beats have easy access to the latest and greatest technologies, and forensic investigators are able to assist law enforcement at a moment's notice and process digital evidence within hours—right? Wrong. As much as law enforcement agencies around the world try to keep up with technological innovations, they lag very much behind. While they might not be used much, typewriters—yes, typewriters—can still be found in plenty of local, state, and federal law enforcement offices around the United States, along with computers and related equipment from the 1990s. As budgets continue to shrink following the "great recession" of the late 2000s, purchasing new forensic laboratory equipment has become less of a top priority for smaller law enforcement agencies (as has new investigative software), and police departments are rendered less able to offer new in-service training to allow officers to keep up with ever-changing cybercrime trends. Also due to budget restraints, over recent years many police departments and other law enforcement agencies have either endured a hiring freeze or two, or have greatly reduced the number of new personnel hired; this means fewer technologically savvy investigators are being added to the ranks, and there is less room for hiring much-needed digital forensic examiners.

In large police departments and federal agencies with thicker wallets, this situation is not so dire; evidence of the digital revolution in policing is more apparent in agencies like NYPD, the FBI, and the U.S. Secret Service, all of whom do have very sophisticated laboratory equipment, computers, and forensically trained personnel. Yet, in many other cases, investigators are still using the old "pen and paper" process, and rely on traditional policing methods and in-service training for existing personnel. One punch to the gut that all law enforcement entities in the United States experience is the enormous and ever-growing backlog of digital evidence waiting to be processed. Especially in smaller, rural parts of the country, local (and sometimes even state) agencies do not have the capabilities necessary to process digital evidence, which results in the evidence being shipped out of state to regional or federal governmental laboratories. Six months may pass without so much as a status update on where the agency's evidence is in the waiting line for processing.

Countries around the world have joined the debate as to whether or not it would be beneficial to privatize forensic services to help relieve the building pressure on law enforcement (McAndrew, 2012; Tilstone, 1991). In some cases, higher educational institutions (such as the University of Rhode Island, the University of Alabama, Marshall University, and Stanford University) are even helping out law enforcement by building forensic laboratory space and operating related centers to aid in digital evidence processing, train students and officers in digital forensic procedures, and provide law enforcement with internship-related manpower. The voices debating privatization and outsourcing digital forensic services grow louder as the backlog of case-related digital evidence continues to plague the law enforcement community.

It may not come as much of a surprise, but the "digital revolution" in policing has also captured the imagination of the media. Popular "cop shows" on television portray all of the investigational technologies we believe the police *should* have at their disposal to help them catch the bad guy. Holographic, 3-D images of persons of interest or entire neighborhoods, fancy undercover police cars with more technological capabilities than we can conceive of, and the ability to search through thousands of electronic records all centrally housed—these images create the illusion of super-powered policing that defines "cop drama" TV. Perhaps most exaggerated by the media are the digital forensic tools used by investigators in these television shows. Same-day forensics processing of evidence (such as DNA, digital evidence, or lab tests on suspected drugs) is in actuality a distant dream. Since the United States operates on a decentralized model of policing, records-keeping is also decentralized. This means every police department keeps its own records housed in its respective departments, and federal agencies do not have a magic password that gives them access to each department's files; most of these files are not even in electronic format. The notion that a forensic scientist can casually sit down at a computer in the office, enter a few characteristics into the search box, and sip coffee for a few seconds while the computer searches through local, state, and federal databases simultaneously before generating "hits" that reveal every detail of the suspect's life, whereabouts, current location, and favorite color, is one "reality" constrained entirely to the television world. It is exciting, though, to imagine all of the possibilities that might, just might, eventually become future realities in the world of policing.

However, even if all of the technology in the world (real or imagined) was easily accessible to police and forensic investigators, they can still only investigate the cybercrimes they know about. As discussed in previous chapters in this book, the confusion about who to contact in the event of becoming a victim of cybercrime poses perhaps the biggest hurdle for society. Whether it's the belief that the damages weren't enough to warrant police action, the idea that "the police can't (or won't) do anything about it anyway," or simply not knowing who to call in such events, the dark figure of cybercrime (referring to the unreported number of cybercrime acts) is massive and a problem that needs to be addressed (Fafinski and Minassian, 2009; McQuade, 2006). Some countries have made great efforts to centralize reporting of cybercrimes and increase public awareness of such reporting measures. For instance, in the United States, the Federal Bureau of Investigation (together with the National White Collar Crime Center) operates the Internet Crime Complaint Center (IC3). Via their website (http://www.ic3.gov/default.aspx), victims of any form of cybercrime can report the instance(s), which then get logged and prioritized for investigation by law enforcement. According to the most recent IC3 annual report (FBI, 2014), more and more people are reporting to IC3 in the United States, but the dark figure still looms. In other countries, however, reporting cybercrimes is not nearly as simple: in some cases, such acts online are not even defined as "illegal" by the country the victim resides in (UNODC, 2013). This presents quite the difficulty for concerted efforts to reduce the dark number of reported cybercrimes, as well as a problem for police investigating international, cross-jurisdictional instances of cybercrime complaints.

The goal of this chapter is to reveal the crucial realities of investigating cyber-related crimes in the United States and around the world, from both police and forensic examiner viewpoints. The first of the two readings in this chapter stems from the UNODC (2013) report and provides a macro-level, global picture of the realities of cyber-related police investigations. According to the more than fifty countries that responded to this study's questionnaire, only an estimated *one percent* of actual cybercrime is reported, revealing a stark discrepancy between cybercrime victimization and the reporting and investigation of cybercrimes.

These statistics stand in comparison to those illustrating that, while between fifty and one hundred percent of cybercriminal activities handled by law enforcement involve a transnational component, more than *ninety percent* of cybercriminal acts are brought to the attention of law enforcement by individual or corporate victims. This reading also provides an overview of the investigative elements involved for law enforcement in regards to cybercrimes. Various challenges of investigating cybercriminal activity are presented, including lack of appropriate legal frameworks and the sufficiency of the responding countries' powers to investigate cybercrimes. Three main trends identified within this sample revealed that many countries have no specific statutes regarding cybercrimes and use broad interpretations of established legal frameworks to investigate cybercrimes, while others have either amended established statutes for specific issues or recently introduced investigative statutes specifically pertaining to cybercrime investigations. The complexity of privacy issues in regards to cybercrime is also discussed, with a particular focus on international human rights law and jurisdictional complications of cybercrime evidence. Information provided by responding private-sector organizations reveals the complicated interactions between private-sector obligations and law enforcement investigations from the private sector perspective. The reading concludes with a discussion of the capacity or capability of law enforcement agencies to handle cybercrimes by discussing the structural and personnel specialization variations between responding countries.

The second and final reading of this chapter, written by Johnny Nhan and Laura Huey (2013), directly addresses myths surrounding technologies used by police and digital forensic examiners. Despite popular media portrayals like *CSI* and *Law and Order*, this reading argues that, to the contrary, police investigations are not driven by the latest technological advancements and instead remain relatively low-tech. Investigating actual methodologies of forensic science and digital evidence (two increasingly depicted domains of police investigations), reveals the stark inconsistencies between actual policing and televised portrayals of law enforcement investigations. The first of two studies examined in this reading consisted of qualitative interviews with police investigators and Forensic Identification Officers (FIOs). The interviews were aimed at gauging how and to what extent police officials think actual policing aligns with or diverts from televised portrayals, and what their perceptions are about how televised accounts of police investigations influence public expectations. The results revealed that television depictions dramatically differed from reality in numerous ways: actual police lack many technologies or access to them, the technologies and methods presented on television often do not exist or their usage is not properly portrayed, and an emphasis in television is placed on technology that also does not exist in reality. The latter references the fact that in reality, forensics are considered by police as a set of corroborative investigative tools, and not as the crux of the investigation. The second study also consisted of qualitative interviews with various law enforcement officials to investigate the variables involved in investigating highly technologically complex cybercrimes. These results revealed that cybercrime investigations, like regular police investigations, remain virtually unchanged and still rely mainly on traditional investigatory skills despite technological advancements. These two studies together conclude that police in the United States prefer the "traditional" methodologies of police work (e.g., interviewing suspects and witnesses, experiencing a crime scene for themselves) to the high-tech alternatives, and are hesitant to adopt new methods of investigation.

KEY WORDS FOUND IN THIS PART

- Strategic policing objectives
- Tactical policing objectives
- Subscriber data
- Traffic data
- Content data
- Technopolicing
- DNA identification
- Geographical information system (GIS)
- Organizational resistance
- Internet Protocol (IP) address

READING EIGHT

Law Enforcement and Investigations

BY UNODC REPORT

This Chapter examines law enforcement cybercrime investigations from a range of perspectives, including legal powers for investigatory measures, subject privacy safeguards, investigation challenges and good practices, interactions between law enforcement and the private sector, and law enforcement training and capacity. It demonstrates the complexities of cybercrime investigations and the need for effective legal frameworks, combined with law enforcement resources and skills in practice.

Law Enforcement and Cybercrime

KEY RESULTS

- Over 90 per cent of responding countries report that cybercrime acts most frequently come to the attention of law enforcement authorities through reports by individual or corporate victims
- The proportion of actual cybercrime victimization reported to the police ranges upwards from 1 per cent. One global private sector survey suggests that 80 per cent of individual victims of cybercrime do not report to the police
- Law enforcement authorities aim to address underreporting through a range of measures including awareness raising and outreach
- An incident-driven law enforcement response to cybercrime must also be accompanied by medium and long-term strategic investigations that focus on crime markets and criminal scheme architects
- The proportion of cybercrime acts detected through proactive investigations is low, but a number of countries are focusing on undercover strategic operations

The Role of Law Enforcement

Article 1 of the United Nations Code of Conduct for Law Enforcement Officials[1] highlights that the role of law enforcement is to fulfil the duty imposed upon them by law, *'by serving the community'* and *'by protecting all persons against illegal acts.'* This duty extends to the full range of prohibitions under penal statutes.[2] As cybercrime acts become ever more prevalent,[3] law enforcement agencies increasingly face the question of what it means to 'serve' and 'protect' in the context of a crime with global dimensions.

During information gathering for the Study, more than half of countries reported that between 50 and 100 per cent of cybercrime acts encountered by the police involve a *transnational* element.[4] At the same time, responding countries indicated that the majority of cybercrime acts come to the attention of the police through individual victim reports. Cybercrime thus *occurs globally*, but is *reported locally*. The report may reach a national cybercrime hotline or specialized police unit, but can also reach a municipal or rural police office more accustomed to dealing with 'conventional' burglary, robbery, theft, or homicide. In the same way as 'conventional' crime, however, both 'cyber' victims and 'cyber' perpetrators are real individuals with real geographic locations—both of which fall within a local police jurisdiction.

Local police stations may often transfer cybercrime cases to a specialized national-level law enforcement lead. However, the growing involvement of electronic evidence in *all* crime types is likely to revolutionize policing techniques, both at central *and* local level, in the coming decades. In some countries, for example, local police stations have been routinely equipped with desktop technology for extracting mobile phone data from suspects.[5] Country responses to the Study questionnaire highlight considerable variation in the capacity of police forces to investigate cybercrime both between and within countries. As one country noted: '*The police corps of the localities differ a lot when it comes to cybercrime. Some have well organized cyber units, others barely have a few trained officers.*'[6]

An incident-driven response to cybercrime must, however, be accompanied by medium and long-term strategic investigations that focus on disrupting cybercrime markets and bringing to justice criminal scheme architects. The prevention of *any* form of crime requires a proactive and problem-oriented approach to policing, with police working alongside other multidisciplinary partners[7] towards the overall aim of the maintenance of social order and public safety.[8]

Notions of police 'community' engagement and 'public safety' require some translation in the move from the offline world to the online world. Nonetheless, country responses to the Study questionnaire suggest that this principle, as well as many other elements of police good practice in the prevention of 'conventional' crime, are equally applicable when it comes to cybercrime. These especially include the need for law enforcement agencies to work with private sector and civil society partners, and to apply 'intelligence-led' policing to pre-empt and prevent cybercrime—using problem-solving approaches based on sound information and 'horizon scanning.' As highlighted by one responding country, for example: '*attacks are becoming more and more advanced, more and more difficult to detect and in the same time the techniques quickly find their way to a broader audience.*'[9]

As discussed in this Chapter, critical elements of a consistent law enforcement response to reported acts of cybercrime thus include: (i) an effective legal framework for investigative measures that reaches an appropriate balance between respect for individual privacy and investigative powers; (ii) access to investigative tools and techniques in practice, including means of obtaining electronic evidence from third parties, such as internet service providers; and (iii) sufficient training and technical capabilities both for specialized and non-specialized officers.

What do the Police Encounter?

During information gathering for the Study, responding countries stated that more than 90 per cent of acts that come to the attention of the police do so through reports from individual and company victims.[10] The remainder of acts were reported to be detected directly by police investigators or obtained from ISP reports.

The picture of cybercrime seen by law enforcement is, as with any crime, necessarily incomplete—being constructed from a mixture of individual investigated cases and broader criminal intelligence. The transnational nature of cybercrime exacerbates the challenge, as investigative leads arrive at overseas servers or IP-addresses, creating delays while formal or informal cooperation mechanisms are engaged.

As noted by one responding country in Africa, for example, '*Most of the crimes, including the unreported ones, involve transnational dimensions. Targets are mostly outside of national boundaries.*'[11] Another country, also in Africa, reported that '*Most of the reported offences are initiated outside this country. In most cases we act as a conduit,*' while one country in Europe highlighted that '*All cybercrime investigations conducted in the last five years have had a transnational dimension. Examples are offences related to use of e-mail accounts, social media and proxy servers.*'[12]

In addition to transnational elements, significant *under*reporting of cybercrime acts in the first place can contribute to a limited picture of the underlying phenomenon. Of the 90 per cent of cybercrime acts that come to the attention of the police through victim reporting, countries estimate that the proportion of *actual* cybercrime victimization reported to the police ranges upwards from only one per cent.[13] One survey conducted by a private sector organization suggests that 80 per cent of individual victims of core cybercrime acts do not report the crime to the police.[14]

Responding countries to the Study cybercrime questionnaire attributed under-reporting of cybercrime acts to a number of factors, including a lack of public confidence in the capacity of police to address cybercrime, a lack of awareness of victimization and of reporting mechanisms, victim shame and embarrassment, and perceived reputation risks for corporations. One country, for example, stated that: '*Estimation is very difficult. Companies and banks are not interested in reporting cybercrimes due to reputational risks.*'[15]

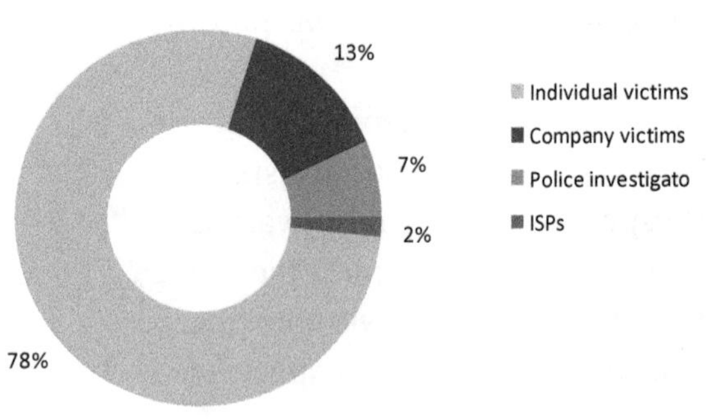

Figure 8.1 Sources of cybercrime reports to police
Source: Study cybercrime questionnaire. Q78. (n=61)

Another highlighted that '*Most victims do not even realize that [they] have become targets or the damage done is insignificant enough for them to ignore*.'[16] When cases do come to the attention of the police, subsequent investigation may reveal a much wider pool of victims and offenders than initially identified at the outset of a case. As noted by one responding country: '*Some of these [crimes] may be more common [than those reported]*.'[17]

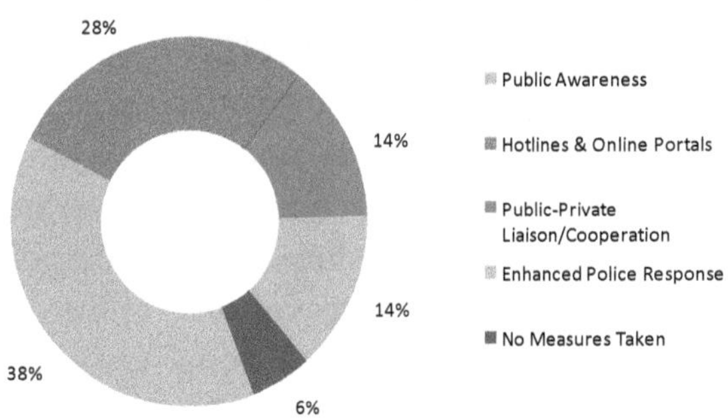

Figure 8.2 Measures taken to increase reporting of cybercrime to police
Source: Study cybercrime questionnaire. Q79. (n=57, r=107)

Many responding countries reported strategies and approaches used to increase reporting of cybercrime. As shown in Figure 8.2 these include the use of public awareness campaigns, creation of online and hotline reporting systems, liaison with private sector organizations, and enhanced police outreach and information sharing. Out of almost 60 responding countries, less than 10 per cent reported not having taken any measures aimed at increasing reporting of cybercrime acts.[18]

Country responses also showed the need for law enforcement authorities to work closely with other stakeholders, such as the private sector—in order to increase reporting and for intelligence purposes. One country, for example, highlighted that it was important to '*establish 24 hour connectivity between important website administrators, ISPs, police and a centre for coordination of security incidents*.' Another country in the Americas reported that '*The Federal Police is pursuing agreements with public and private companies so that crimes committed against those companies and their clients are informed electronically to the Federal Police*.'[19] Overall, however, the comparatively low proportion of cybercrime acts reported by company victims or internet service providers, suggests that additional outreach and development of public-private partnerships may be needed, in order to strengthen reporting of cybercrime acts from these sources. The development of public-private partnerships and service provider responsibilities is discussed further in Chapter Eight (Prevention). Interactions between law enforcement and third party service providers during police investigations are addressed below in this Chapter.

A notable feature from Figure 8.1 is the low proportion of cybercrime acts that are detected by law enforcement investigators in the absence of victim reports. Accordingly, responding countries did not, in general, refer to proactive investigations in written responses to the questionnaire. One country did, however, note that '*In some cases cybercrime acts come to the attention of the police while police [are] performing operational activities.'*[20] Another country, in Europe, also reported that '*For child pornography offences, the investigations start mostly from information coming from other police forces, and open sources,*' indicating underlying police intelligence work.

The distribution of the source of identified cybercrime acts is indicative, in part, of the challenge of addressing both *strategic* and *tactical* policing objectives. Strategic policing objectives are threat-driven and relate to longer-term law enforcement goals, with a focus on the root causes and circumstances of serious crime. Tactical policing objectives are incident-driven and time-sensitive, with an emphasis on preserving evidence and following investigative leads. In the case of cybercrime, the investment in police time and resources required for responding to individual cases is substantial. As discussed later in this Chapter, many countries highlighted the voluminous amounts of evidence associated with cybercrime investigations and the time consuming nature of investigations into reported cases. One country in the Americas, for example, stated that '*the complexity of cybercrime offences and cybercrime elements of traditional offences has increased significantly, which places additional demands for the training and maintenance of highly-skilled investigators and technical experts, and also increases the amounts of time that need to be spent on individual cases.'*[21] In many countries, law enforcement agency capacity is fully occupied with day-to-day cases. In response to questions on law enforcement capacity for forensic investigations, for example, one country in Africa reported that '*A few forensic examiners/investigators are available at the Federal level, but not enough to serve the whole country. Only one laboratory is functional.'*[22] Another country in the Americas highlighted that '*The challenge is not in the expertise, but the quantity of data that must be analysed.'*[23] The nature of forensic investigations, and law enforcement capacity in this area, is discussed in detail in Chapter Six (Electronic evidence and criminal justice).

In addition to the challenge of capacity and resources, the extent to which proactive cybercrime investigations can be undertaken by law enforcement may also be affected by underlying differences between common and civil law systems regarding prosecutorial and judicial oversight over the initial stages of an investigation,[24] as well as the extent to which intrusive investigative measures can be authorized in intelligence-based or prospective investigations. As discussed in this Chapter, cybercrime investigations often make use of tools, including interception of communications and electronic surveillance, which have the potential to infringe upon privacy-based rights. Countries with international human rights law commitments will need to ensure a proportionate balance between protection of privacy, and infringements for legitimate crime prevention and control purposes. The section below on privacy and investigations examines this area in greater depth.

Nonetheless, law enforcement authorities in developed countries, and also in a number of developing countries, are engaged in medium and long-term strategic investigations. These often involve undercover units targeting offenders on social networking sites, chat rooms, and instant messaging and P2P services. Examples include the infiltration or establishment of online 'carding' forums,[25] the forensic examination of forums used by child pornography offenders,[26] the use of law enforcement officers posing as minors online,[27] and the examination of malware command and control servers.[28] Many of these investigations involve multiple law enforcement agencies and a large range of investigative measures, including those carried out pursuant to judicial authority, such as search or interception orders. Indeed, both strategic and tactical investigations require access to a range of investigative powers, which—in accordance with rule of law principles—must be firmly grounded in legal authority. The next section of this Chapter examines typical cybercrime investigative powers found in international and regional instruments, and in national laws.

Investigative Powers Overview

KEY RESULTS

- Many countries outside of Europe perceive their national legal frameworks to be insufficient for the investigation of cybercrime
- Overall, national approaches to cybercrime investigative powers show less core commonality than for criminalization
- While legal approaches vary, key investigative powers required include search and seizure, orders for computer data, real-time collection of data, and data preservation
- Across ten investigative measures, countries most often reported the existence of general (non-cyber-specific) powers. A number of countries reported cyber-specific legislation, notably for ensuring expedited preservation of computer data and for obtaining stored subscriber data
- Many countries reported a lack of legal power for advanced investigative measures, such as remote computer forensics

Cyber-Specific and General Investigative Powers

The evidence of cybercrime acts is almost always in electronic, or digital, form. This data can be stored or transient, and can exist in the form of computer files, transmissions, logs, metadata, or network data. Obtaining such evidence requires an amalgamation of traditional and new policing techniques. Law enforcement authorities may use 'traditional' police work (interviewing victims or undercover visual surveillance of suspects) in some stages of an investigation, but require computer-specific approaches for other parts. These can include viewing, and seizing or copying, computer data from devices belonging to suspects; obtaining computer data from third parties such as internet service providers, and—where necessary—intercepting electronic communications.

While some of these investigative actions can be achieved with traditional powers, many procedural provisions do not translate well from a spatial, object-oriented approach to one involving electronic data storage and real-time data flows. In some countries, computer data can be covered by 'traditional' powers of search and seizure of 'anything' believed to be relevant to an offence. Existing 'wiretap' or 'communications interception' laws may also provide sufficient authority for some aspects of cybercrime investigations. In other countries, however, traditional procedural laws might not be capable of being interpreted to include intangible data or IP-based communications. In addition, investigative powers must be able to address challenges such as the volatile nature of electronic evidence, and use of obfuscation techniques by perpetrators—including the use of encryption, proxies, cloud computing service, 'innocent' computer systems infected with malware, and multiple (or 'onion') routing of internet connections.[29] These aspects, in particular, present particular challenges to traditional powers. Many responding countries reported that investigative powers are frequently '*out of step with new and emerging technologies*' and often '*legislation [is] designed for physical search and search, and therefore the law's instructions ... don't feed the needs, interests and constitutional procedures relevant for cybercrime investigations*.'[30]

Legal frameworks for the investigation of cybercrime—whether predominantly 'general' or 'cyber-specific' laws—thus require both: (i) a clear scope of application of the power, in order to guarantee legal certainty in its use; and (ii) sufficient legal authority for actions such as ensuring preservation of computer data, and the collection of stored and real-time data. In this respect, specialized procedural frameworks offer the possibility to clearly define relevant concepts—such as 'computer data' in the first place, as well as data 'at rest' and data 'in transit.'[31] They also allow differentiation between types of data, such as 'subscriber' data (the basic registration details of computer service users, such as name and address), 'traffic' data (data indicating the origin, destination, route, time, date, size, duration, or type of a communication made by means of a computer system), and 'content' data (the actual content of a communication).[32]

During information gathering for the Study, countries were asked about the existence of either general or cyber-specific legal powers for 10 different actions relevant to law enforcement investigations into cybercrime (and other crimes involving electronic evidence). The investigative actions asked about were: (i) law enforcement search for computer hardware or data; (ii) seizure of computer hardware or data; (iii) order to a person for supply to law enforcement of subscriber information; (iv) order to a person for supply of stored traffic data; (v) order to a person for supply for stored content data; (vi) real time collection of traffic data; (vii) real-time collection of content data; (viii) order to a person to preserve and maintain the integrity of computer data under their control for a specified period of time ('expedited preservation' of data); (ix) use of remote computer forensics tools; and (x) direct law enforcement access to extraterritorial computer data ('trans-border' access to computer data).[33]

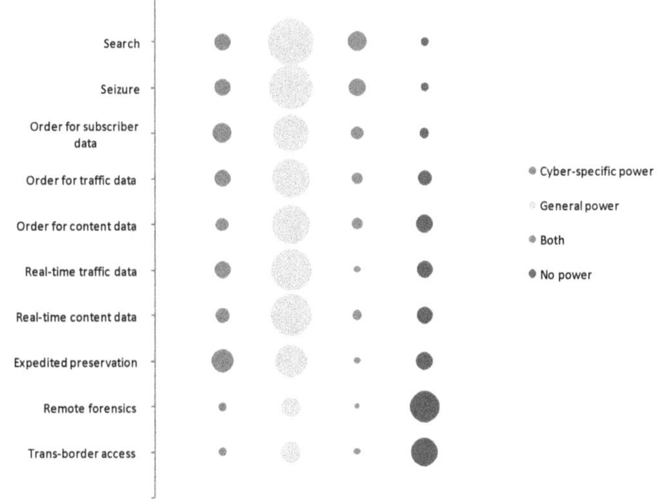

Figure 8.3 National approaches to investigative measures for cybercrime
Source: Study cybercrime questionnaire. Q42–51. (n=55)

Figure 8.3 provides a broad overview of the existence of legal provisions covering the ten investigative actions, as reported by over 50 country responses to the Study questionnaire. Responses demonstrate that the majority of countries rely on *general* legal powers for the investigation of cybercrime. This is the case across a range of investigative actions, including search, seizure, orders for data addressed to third parties, real-time collection of data, and orders for preservation of data. For more intrusive, complex, investigative measures such as remote computer forensics, almost half of responding countries indicated that such measures were not authorized by law. Around 20 per cent of countries reported that no legal power existed for real-time collection of computer data, or for ordering expedited preservation of computer data. Even for basic search and seizure of computer hardware or data, 10 per cent of countries reported that no legal power existed.

Countries that reported the existence of cyber-specific powers showed broad geographic distribution throughout Europe, North and South America, the Caribbean, Western and South-Eastern Asia, the Caribbean, and Northern and Western Africa. Investigative actions most often covered by cyber-specific provisions were orders for subscriber data and for expedited preservation of data—with around 25 to 30 per cent of responding countries reporting the existence of cyber-specific provisions in these areas. The actions of search and seizure for computer hardware and data are most often covered by *both* cyber-specific and general provisions—a situation reported by around 20 per cent of responding countries.

Sufficiency of Investigative Powers for Cybercrime

With respect to the perceived sufficiency of investigative powers, country responses to the Study questionnaire showed a similar pattern to that for criminalization laws. Around 70 per cent of responding countries from Europe reported that investigative powers were sufficient. The remainder viewed investigative powers as sufficient 'in part,' with only one country indicating that powers were insufficient. In other regions of the world, between 20 and 65 per cent of countries reported that investigative powers were insufficient.

When asked about the main *gaps* in investigative powers, many countries referred to a lack of power to 'enter' electronic networks in order to search for evidence, as well as a lack of power for preservation of computer data. Countries from Oceania and Europe reported that there was a need for a '*mechanism to expeditiously preserve computer data to support existing search powers,*' and one country in South America highlighted that there was a '*lack of regulation on access to data and connection logs [as well as a] lack of regulation on virtual search possibilities.*'[34]

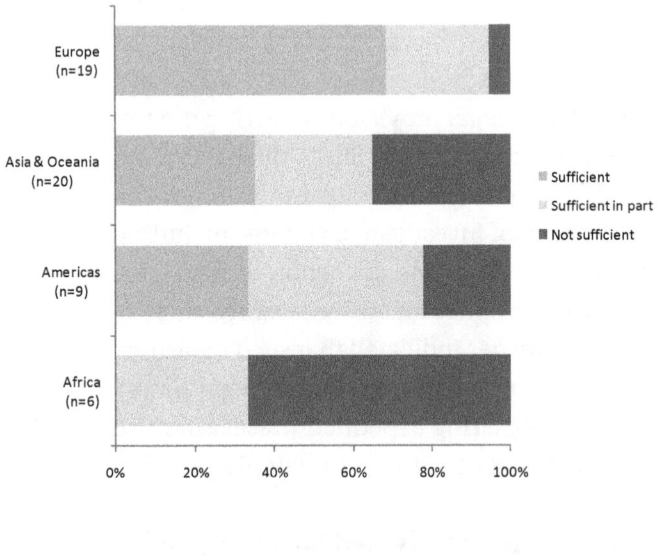

Figure 8.4 Sufficiency of national law for cybercrime investigations
Source: Study cybercrime questionnaire. Q53. (n=54)

On the other hand, while many countries reported a complete lack of legal framework specific to cybercrime, a few countries also cited the successful extension of general powers. One country in Southern Africa, for example, reported that '*the Criminal Procedure Act allows the State to seize anything ... [even though] the Act does not provide specifically for cybercrime.*'[35] Some countries also reported that it was good practice for powers of investigation relating to computers and other devices to '*extend to all crimes and not just traditional computer crimes*' and that relevant procedural laws should be both '*comprehensive*' and '*precise*.'[36]

Overall, three main approaches were apparent from country responses to the Study questionnaire: Some countries have no specific laws for cybercrime investigations and apply traditional procedural powers as far as possible under a broad interpretation. Other countries have amended general investigatory powers in respect of some specific issues and, through use of general and cyber-specific powers, are able to apply a range of measures such as orders for data, search and seizure of data, and preservation of data. Finally, some countries have introduced a comprehensive range of new investigative powers specifically designed for obtaining electronic evidence. Legislative provisions in one country in Southern Europe, for example, specify four different ways in which data may be considered '*seized*'—(i) seizing the medium itself; (ii) making a copy; (iii) maintaining the integrity of data without removal or copying; and (iv) removing the data or blocking access to the data. Such provisions assist in removing legal uncertainty surrounding the application of 'traditional' investigative powers.

Comprehensive investigative powers for cybercrime: National example from a country in Southern Europe

Seizure of computer data

Seizure of computer data, depending on what is deemed to be most appropriate or proportional, taking into account the interests of the case, may take the following forms: a) Seizing the computer system support equipment or the computer-data storage medium, as well as devices required to read data;

a. Making a copy of those computer data, in an autonomous means of support, which shall be attached to the file;
b. Maintaining by technological means the integrity of data, without copying or removing them; or
c. Removing the computer data or blocking access thereto.

Examination of the relationship between existence of specialized legislative powers, and the perceived sufficiency of cybercrime investigation frameworks, shows some degree of correspondence for countries that responded to the questionnaire. For those countries that reported investigative frameworks to be 'sufficient' or sufficient 'in part,' around 40 per cent of all investigative actions asked about were covered by cyber-specific powers. In contrast, for those countries that reported investigative frameworks to be 'insufficient,' only 20 per cent of all investigative actions were covered by cyber-specific powers.[37] This finding highlights the importance of the development of specialized investigative powers—at a minimum, for measures where the extension of traditional powers is in doubt. Chapter Seven (International cooperation) of this Study highlights that the global nature of cybercrime means that a lack of investigative powers in one country can have an impact on other countries where they request international cooperation in the gathering of extraterritorial evidence.

As discussed in Chapter Three (Legislation and frameworks), a number of international and regional instruments provide for comprehensive investigative power frameworks.[38] The table in Annex Three summarizes the powers, by article, in a number of these frameworks. The next section of this Chapter continues to examine, in detail, the nature of investigative power provisions, both as found in multilateral instruments and as reported at the national level through the Study questionnaire. It does so for the powers of: (i) search and seizure; (ii) preservation of computer data; (iii) orders for computer data; (iv) real-time collection of computer data; (v) use of remote forensic tools; and (vi) direct law enforcement access to extra-territorial data.

Search and Seizure

As noted above, countries may face a range of challenges to the extension of 'traditional' search and seizure powers to intangible data.[39] For this reason, seven international or regional cybercrime instruments[40] contain provisions with specific powers to search, or similarly access, computer systems or computer-data storage media. Six of these instruments also provide for an extension of the search to another computer system within the territory of the country, if it is discovered that the information sought after is not in the original system or media searched.[41] A number of multilateral instruments also clarify ways in which computer data can be 'seized.' The Commonwealth Model Law, for example, states that the term 'seized' includes '*taking a printout of output of computer data.*'

At the national level, responses to the Study questionnaire showed that search and seizure of computer hardware or data are authorized by *general* criminal procedure laws for the majority of countries (around 50 per cent), rather than by cyber-specific powers.[42] As regards the application of general

Search and seizure warrant: National example from a country in the Americas

2. A warrant issued under this section may authorize a police officer to:
   a. seize any computer, data, programme, information, document or thing if he reasonably believes that it is evidence that an offence under this Act has been or is about to be committed;
   b. inspect and check the operation of any computer referred to in paragraph *(a)*;

c. use or cause to be used any computer referred to in paragraph *(a)* to search any programme or data held in or available to such computer;
d. have access to any information, code or technology which has the capability of transforming or converting an encrypted programme or data held in or available to the computer into readable and comprehensible format or text, for the purpose of investigating any offence under this Act;
e. convert an encrypted programme or data held in another computer system at the place specified in the warrant, where there are reasonable grounds for believing that computer data connected with the commission of the offence may be stored in that other system;
f. make and retain a copy of any programme or data held in the computer referred to in paragraph *(a)* or *(e)* and any other programme or data held in the computers.

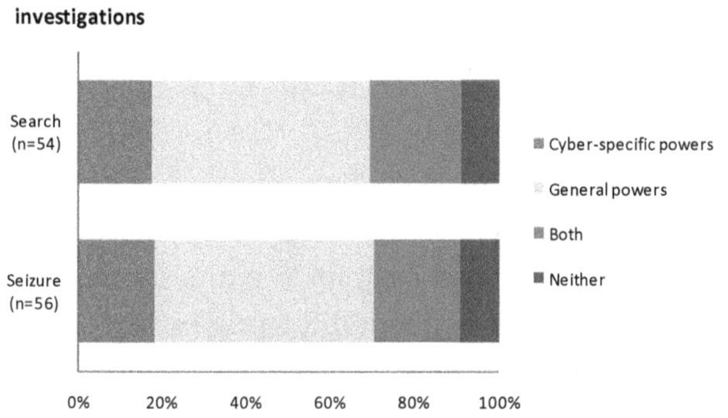

Figure 8.5 Search and seizure instruments used in cybercrime investigations
Source: Study cybercrime questionnaire. Q42 and Q43. (n=54, 56)

search powers, one country in Eastern Asia clarified that traditional provisions on searches could also be applied to '*computer searches*', but that the provision only allowed searches for hardware and not of computer data.[43] Less than 20 per cent of responding countries indicated the existence of cyber-specific powers for search or seizure.

Just under 10 per cent of countries reported that there was *no* power at all for search and seizure—at least for computer data. One country from Western Asia, for example, stated that '*In relation to accessing equipment and hardware, the Criminal Procedure Code deals with the case of physical access by members of the judicial police to homes, but does not address electronic crime ... These texts do not allow members of the judicial police to enter electronic networks and email on the grounds of suspicion of commission of an offence.*'[44] The same country noted that law reform would be required in order to provide such powers and currently '*If such entry [were to] take place in the absence of a legal provision, that would violate the provisions of the Constitution and the law.*'

Preservation of Computer Data

Storing computer data requires resources and money. As a result, computer data is typically stored only for the amount of time for which it is needed for processing. In the case, for example, of 'chat' or VOIP content that passes through a service provider's service, this might only be for the amount of time needed for operational purposes, such as the identification of system faults, or customer billing. This could range from a few seconds, to hours, or a few days, or weeks. In addition to the pragmatic cost implications of data storage, many countries also have data protection frameworks that specify that data must not be retained for periods longer than that required by the purposes for which the data are processed.[45] Due legal process requirements, or—in transnational cases—international cooperation requests, may easily take a longer time than the lifespan of the data, before the relevant search warrant or order for supply of stored data can be obtained.[46]

Expedited preservation of data: National example from a country in Southern Africa

Preservation order

1. Any investigatory authority may apply to the Judge in Chambers for an order for the expeditious preservation of data that has been stored or processed by means of a computer system or any other information and communication technologies, where there are reasonable grounds to believe that such data is vulnerable to loss or modification.
2. For the purposes of subsection (1), data includes traffic data and subscriber information.
3. An order made under subsection (1) shall remain in force
   a. until such time as may reasonably be required for the investigation of an offence;
   b. where prosecution is instituted, until the final determination of the case; or
   c. until such time as the Judge in Chambers deems fit.

As a result, seven international and regional cybercrime instruments contain provisions aimed at establishing mechanisms for preventing the deletion of computer data important to cybercrime investigations.[47] Such actions may be given effect to by an order to a person in control of computer data to preserve and maintain the integrity of the data for a specified period of time, or by expedited procedures for otherwise securing the data, such as through a search and seizure warrant. Key features of typical 'expedited' preservation provisions may include application of a more limited set of conditions and safeguards than for disclosure of the data, due to an arguably less prejudicial nature of the preservation measure (before the point of any disclosure). In this respect, however, it should be noted that international human rights mechanisms have held that mere storage of information about an individual amounts to an interference with rights to private life.[48] Exercise of preservation orders therefore still requires an assessment of the proportionality of the measure—in particular where compliance with the order would require specific data to be held for longer than the time period envisaged by data protection legislation.

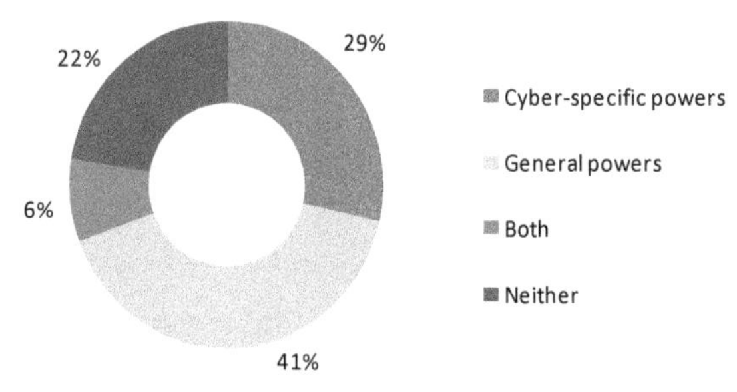

Figure 8.6 Expedited preservation of computer data
Source: Study cybercrime questionnaire. Q49. (n=49)

Nonetheless, preservation of data represents an important measure for maintaining vital evidence prior to a full order for disclosure—in particular in the context of transnational investigations. Indeed, the separation of the two obligations, 'preservation' and 'disclosure' is a key element of the measure.[49]

At the national level—perhaps due to the influence of international and regional cybercrime instruments—expedited preservation of data is the measure in respect of which the highest proportion of countries report a cyber-specific power. Nonetheless, country responses also indicated that general provisions could cover the measure in various ways. One country in Western Asia, for example, stated that provisions on search and seizure were interpreted as providing for expedited preservation. Another country in Southern Africa also explained that computer data can be preserved according to its legislation by means of computer seizure, and one country in Western Europe noted that it uses general provisions on seizure of correspondence and other information.[50] In addition, however, over 20 per cent of responding countries indicated that national law did not include a power to ensure expedited preservation of data. The absence of legal authority for such a fundamental investigative tool presents a significant challenge—not only for those particular countries, but also for any other country wishing to seek investigative assistance.

Orders for Computer Data

As discussed in Chapter One (Connectivity and cybercrime), a large part of the infrastructure and computer systems used for internet communications are owned and operated by the private sector. Internet service providers, as well as electronic communication providers and

Order for computer data: National example from a country in the Americas

If a magistrate is satisfied on the basis of an application by a police officer that specified computer data, or a printout or other information, is reasonably required for the purpose of a criminal investigation or criminal proceedings, the magistrate may order that-

a. a person in the territory of <country> in control of a computer produce from the computer specified data or a printout or other intelligible output of that data;
b. an Internet service provider in <country> produce information about persons who subscribe to or otherwise use the service; or
c. a person in the territory of <country> who has access to a specified computer process and compile specified computer data from the computer and give it to a specified person

web-service providers, therefore route, store, and control a significant amount of computer data related to internet connections, transactions, and content. The use of coercive measures, such as search and seizure, by law enforcement for obtaining these data are unfeasible in the majority of circumstances—due both to the volume of individual cases investigated, and disruption to legitimate business activity. Orders to such third parties to the investigation for computer data thus provide a due legal process route to obtaining electronic evidence.

In many countries, such orders may be possible under existing investigative powers, such as general production orders, or document disclosure orders. Nonetheless, procedural challenges can also arise. These could include in respect of 'traditional' requirements for *identifying information* about a suspect before orders for evidence can be made. In cybercrime investigations, at the time of request to an internet service provider, the only known information may be an IP-address or similar connection-based information.

Accordingly, five international or regional cybercrime instruments contain specific provisions regarding orders for obtaining stored data.[51] In doing so, instruments typically refer to the distinction made earlier in this Chapter—between 'subscriber,' 'traffic,' and 'content' data. Such provisions usually concern information that are in the '*possession or control*' of the person or service provider. The order only applies therefore, to the extent that the data are in existence at the time of the order, and can be retrieved by the subject of the order. The existence of such investigative powers alone does not in itself oblige service providers to collect or retain information they would not otherwise so process. In respect of *traffic* data, some multilateral instruments[52] also include a mechanism for 'partial' expeditious disclosure of sufficient traffic data to enable law authorities to identify the service providers and the path through which the communication was transmitted. This can be important where multiple service providers are involved in processing computer data or electronic communications.

Figure 8.7 shows that at the national level, general powers are again predominant amongst countries for the authorization of orders for subscriber, traffic, and content data.[53] The proportion of countries that employ cyber-specific orders for obtaining subscriber data is slightly higher than for the other two data categories. In addition to the influence of international and regional cybercrime instruments, this may also reflect a common need for this type of data, and a requirement on behalf of service providers for clear legal powers and procedures in requesting such information.

This is supported by comments from responding countries. One country in the Americas, for example, stated that, although providers often cooperate with law enforcement agencies voluntarily, the application of existing general procedural provisions to orders for supply of data was too onerous and impractical. The country had therefore initiated the process of adopting a cyber-specific provision for subscriber data orders.[54] On the other hand, a few countries reported successful use of general provisions. One country in South-Eastern Asia, for instance, highlighted the possibility of extension of a general investigative power to order *'any document or other thing.'* One country in South America also reported that the power of a judge to *'examine sealed correspondence'* had been extended to stored data.[55]

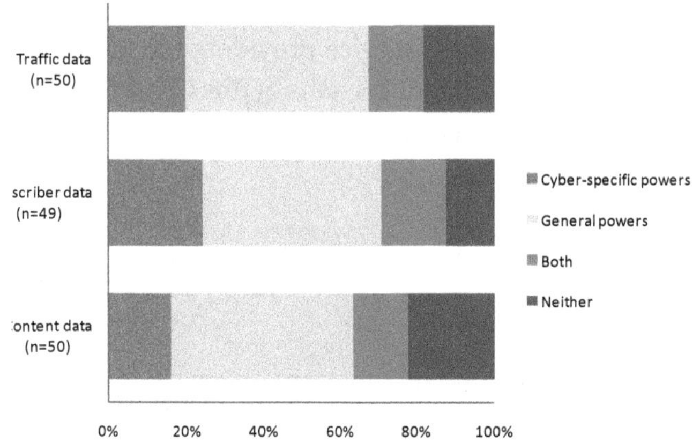

Figure 8.7 Order for stored traffic, subcriber and content data
Source: Study cybercrime questionnaire. Q44, Q45, and Q46. (n=50, 49, 50)

Order for traffic data: National example from a country in Oceania

Disclosure of traffic data

Where a magistrate is satisfied on the basis of an application by any police officer that specified data stored in a computer system is reasonably required for the purpose of a criminal investigation or criminal proceedings, the magistrate may order that a person in control of the computer system disclose sufficient traffic data about a specified communication to identify:

a. the service providers; and
b. the path through which the communication was transmitted

Aside from the legal form of investigative powers, the interplay between law enforcement and internet service providers for the obtaining of electronic evidence can be particularly complex. Later sections of this Chapter examine the use of powers *in practice*, as well as challenges faced by, and good practice used by, law enforcement in obtaining data from service providers.

Real-time Collection of Data

Orders for data represent an investigative measure for obtaining *stored* computer data. Crucial electronic evidence may also, however, never be stored at all (existing only in transient communications), or require 'real-time' collection, due to the urgency, sensitivity, or complexity of a law enforcement investigation.

Accordingly, six international or regional cybercrime instruments include provisions on real-time collection of computer data. In doing so, instruments typically make a distinction between real-time collection of traffic data[56] and of content data.[57] This distinction relates, not least, to differences in the level of intrusiveness into the private life of persons subject to each of the measures.[58] The section on privacy and investigations in this Chapter examines further possible safeguards that can be required by international human rights law. In this respect, one international instrument, the Council of Europe Cybercrime Convention explicitly refers to interception of content data in relation *'to a range of serious offences to be determined by domestic law.'*[59] From a practical perspective, multilateral instruments often envisage that real-time collection of data can be carried out either directly by law enforcement authorities through the application of their own technical means, or by compelling a service provider, within its existing technical capability, to collect or record computer data, or to

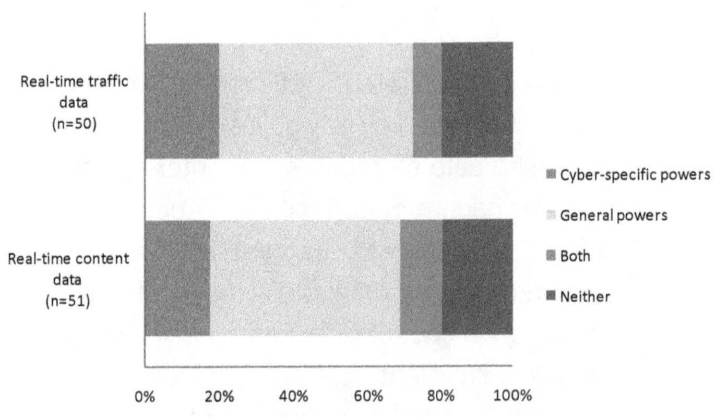

Figure 8.8 Order for real-time traffic and content data
Source: Study cybercrime questionnaire. Q47 and Q48. (n=50, 51).

co-operate and assist authorities to do so.

At the national level, around 40 per cent of responding countries reported that a general investigative power was used to authorize real-time interception of traffic and content data. A number of countries referred, for example, to the extension of general 'Telecommunications intercept acts' or 'Eavesdropping laws' to the real-time collection of computer data.[60] Overall, more than 60 per cent of responding countries reported the existence of a legal power for real-time collection of data—either through a general or cyber-specific power. Some countries highlighted the application of safeguards to such powers, including the limitation of real-time collection of content data only to serious crimes.[61]

As regards the practicalities of data interception, a distinction is often made between private and public service providers. National legislation in one country in Western Europe, for example, specifies that interception of computer data carried by public providers shall be intercepted with the cooperation of the service provider, unless such cooperation is not possible or is contrary to the interests of the investigation. For nonpublic service providers, the national legislation providers that the service provider will be '*offered*' the opportunity to cooperate in the interception, unless this is impossible or undesirable.[62]

Real-time collection of data: National example from a country in Western Asia

Real-time collection of traffic data

1. If there is a probable cause that a person commits a crime though a computer system, a prosecutor is authorized to file a motion with a court having jurisdiction over the investigation place, to issue an order requesting real-time collection of traffic data, thereby a service provider is obliged to cooperate with and assist an investigative body in real-time collection or recording of traffic data which are associated with specified communications made and transmitted by means of a computer system within the territory ...
2. Motions provided by paragraph 1 of the present Article shall consider technical capability for real-time collection and recording of traffic data of the service provider. The term for real time collection and recording of traffic data shall not exceed the term necessary for collecting evidence in criminal case.
3. Motions provided by paragraph 1 and 2 of this Article, shall be considered by the court in accordance with the procedure established by Article < ... > of the present Code.

Remote forensic software: National example from a country in Oceania

Remote access search of thing authorized by warrant

Every person executing a search warrant authorising a remote access search may—

a. use reasonable measures to gain access to the thing to be searched; and
b. if any intangible material in the thing is the subject of the search or may otherwise be lawfully seized, copy that material (including by means of previewing, cloning, or other forensic methods).

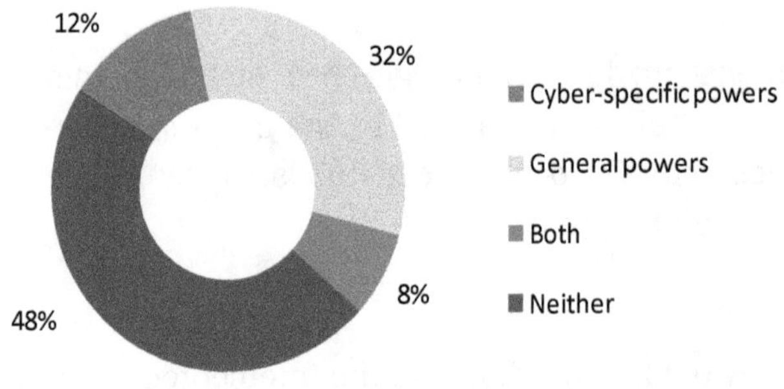

Figure 8.9 Use of remote forensics tools
Source: Study cybercrime questionnaire. Q50. (n=40)

Remote Forensic Tools

A range of technological tools offer possibilities to law enforcement agencies both for the direct remote collection of evidence from computer systems, and for the collection of intelligence or investigation-related information more generally. Tools such as key-loggers and remote-administration software, when placed on the device of a suspect, can remotely supply information about keyboard activity and computer data stored on, or transmitted or received, by the device.[63] Due to the range of personal information stored on computer devices, the use of such tools represents a significant intrusion into the private life of investigation subjects. From an evidential perspective, evidence obtained by the use of remote tools on 'live' computer systems may also be open to challenge. It must be demonstrated, for example, that the operations performed by the examiner did not themselves alter the state of the system under investigation.[64]

Only one (non-binding) international or regional instrument refers to the use of remote forensic tools as an investigative measure. The ITU/CARICOM/CTU Model Legislative Text (Art. 27) provides that a judge may authorize a police officer to utilize '*remote forensic software*' for a specific task required for an investigation. More generally, the Council of Europe Child Protection Convention (Art 30(5)) also refers to the obligation to take necessary legislative and other measures in order to allow, where appropriate, for the possibility of '*covert operations*.'

More than one-third of country respondents to the Study questionnaire did not provide an answer regarding the existence of legislation authorizing the use of remote forensic tools in law enforcement investigations. Of those that did, almost half reported that no such power existed. For the other half of respondents that indicated such powers were included in legislation, the majority referred to a general power, rather than a cyber-specific power. Comments provided by countries ranged from explicitly stating that '*there are no legislative provisions for ... use of remote forensic tools*', to confirming that national law '*permits the installation of a data surveillance device*.'[65] Other countries commented more generally that procedural frameworks provided, in certain circumstances, for the use of '*technical or scientific expertise*' in order to obtain information required during an investigation.[66]

Direct Law Enforcement Access to Extra-territorial Data

Global connectivity means that computer data relevant to law enforcement investigations—both for cybercrime and crime in general—is increasingly found extraterritorially to the investigating jurisdiction. As discussed in Chapter Seven (International cooperation), traditional formal means of international cooperation may not be sufficiently timely to ensure access to extraterritorial volatile data. In recognition of this challenge, three international or regional instruments contain provisions on 'trans-border' access to computer data.[67] Such provisions typically envisage that law enforcement authorities may access or receive, through a computer system in the national territory, stored computer data located in another country, with the lawful and voluntary consent of a person who has lawful authority to disclose the data.[68]

As with remote forensic tools, over one-third of responding countries did not respond to the question in the Study questionnaire on existence of powers for 'trans-border' access. Of those that did, slightly more than half indicated that such a power existed. Countries interpreted the term widely, however, to

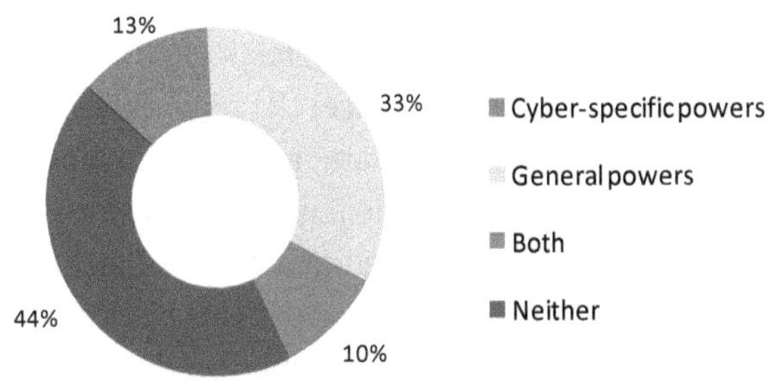

Figure 8.10 Trans-border access to a computer system or data
Source: Study cybercrime questionnaire. Q51. (n=39)

also include the situation where consent to the measure is obtained from the authorities of the country in which the measure is implemented. One country, for example, reported that legislation allows for the issue of a warrant permitting the installation of surveillance devices in '*overseas premises/objects*.' However, this can only be done where a '*judge ... issuing the warrant is satisfied that the surveillance has been agreed to by an 'appropriate consenting official' of the foreign country*.'[69] Some countries that indicated 'trans-border' access powers in national law, referred in written comments to the use of mutual legal assistance instruments. Thus, the overall proportion of countries reporting legislative authority for 'trans-border' access through the Study questionnaire, may be larger than the group of countries with the power to authorize 'trans-border' access in the stricter sense (ie. without authorization from national authorities) envisaged by some international and regional instruments.

Chapter Seven (International cooperation) examines issues of direct law enforcement access to extraterritorial data in greater depth—including with reference to police use of such measures in practice.

Discussion

Examination of the legal basis for investigative powers used in cybercrime (and, indeed, for any crime involving electronic evidence) reveals considerable diversity in approach at national level. This includes regarding the extent to which 'traditional' powers can be interpreted to apply to non-tangible data, as well as the extent to which legal authority exists for particularly intrusive measures, such as remote forensic investigations. Overall, national approaches to cybercrime investigative powers show less core commonality than for criminalization of many cybercrime acts. Nonetheless, while legal powers vary, a good degree of consensus appears to exist on the *types* of investigative measure that *should* be available. These are comparatively straight forward and correspond to those found in many multilateral instruments—(i) powers for search and seizure; (ii) powers for obtaining stored computer data; (iii) powers for real-time collection of data; and (iv) powers for ensuring expedited preservation of data.

In addition to the legal basis of such powers, two further issues require consideration—(a) the limits and safeguards that should be applied to such powers; and (b) the use of investigative powers in practice. The next section of this Chapter examines limits and safeguards through the lens of international human rights standards on privacy. Subsequent sections of the Chapter consider use of investigative measures in practice.

Privacy and Investigative Measures

KEY RESULTS

- Almost all responding countries report that privacy-based protections are applicable in the context of computer data and electronic communications
- Countries report the existence of a wide range of safeguards for the protection of privacy during law enforcement investigations, including restrictions on data that can be accessed, time limits, 'probable cause' requirements, and prosecutorial and judicial oversight
- International human rights law sets out clear protections for the privacy rights of persons subject to law enforcement investigations. Core principles include that investigative powers must give a clear indication of the conditions and circumstances under which measures may be used, together with effective guarantees against abuse
- The development of cloud computing introduces a high degree of uncertainty for users concerning the privacy regime that will apply to their data, and the circumstances under which privacy may legitimately be infringed for the purposes of law enforcement investigations or security surveillance

Human Rights and Law Enforcement Investigations

International human rights law has a specific concern for the *manner* in which the state achieves its crime prevention and criminal justice goals.[70] All aspects of the investigation and prosecution of crime have the potential to engage human rights standards, and criminal *procedure* law and practice therefore come under particular scrutiny from international human rights law.[71]

A range of rights potentially apply to law enforcement investigations—including rights to liberty and security of person, and rights to fair trial.[72] Often, however, challenges in this area are founded on *privacy*-based protections within international and national law. All of the ICCPR, ECHR and ACHR contain prohibitions on arbitrary interference with privacy, family, home and correspondence.[73] The scope of 'privacy' under international law is broad[74] and case law is clear that the intrusive nature of criminal investigations will engage privacy-based rights[75]—including where a suspect is unaware that information is being collected,[76] and even where the mere existence of legislation providing for investigative powers entails such a threat.[77]

As with a number of other rights, privacy rights in international law are not absolute and are subject to limitations—including, in the case of the ECHR, specifically for '*the prevention of disorder or crime*.'[78] In this respect, safeguards in criminal procedure law such as the definition of the conditions and circumstances under which investigative powers can be used; the identity of authorizing officials; the manner of authorization; and the length of time investigative measures may be applied, are critical to the human rights assessment of whether criminal investigations that infringe privacy are acceptable as lawful and necessary.[79]

When it comes to the investigation of cybercrime, each investigative measure must be assessed in its own legal and practical context, in order to determine whether its interference with the privacy, family, home or correspondence of its subject is justified. While the often covert and/or electronic surveillance nature of cybercrime investigative techniques may raise particular privacy challenges,[80] it is important to remember that the proportionality requirements of privacy rights apply equally to 'simple' search and seizure measures.[81] Procedural law limits and safeguards must therefore reflect the varying intrusiveness of investigative measures—ensuring that each measure is only used as necessary in a democratic society.

Existence of Privacy Protections and Procedural Safeguards

During information gathering for the Study, countries responded to questions about the legal protection of privacy in the context of computer data or electronic communication and about how privacy rights function as safeguards during law enforcement investigations. Countries were also asked under what circumstances privacy rights may be restricted for the purposes of detecting and investigating cybercrime, and about extra-jurisdictional and international cooperation-related elements of privacy rights.

Almost all responding countries indicated that privacy protections applied in the context of computer data and electronic communications. The way in which such protections are enshrined in law, however, showed considerable differences. Many countries referred to generic constitutional privacy rights which were also applied to computer data. A few countries even highlighted the 'technologically neutral' approach of privacy rights in their national law. Others cited specific legislation, including 'privacy' acts; 'privacy protection' laws; 'telecommunications regulatory' acts; 'protection of privacy in electronic communications' acts; 'criminal code' offences on invasion of privacy; 'search and surveillance' acts; 'confidentiality of correspondence' laws; and 'communications secrets acts.'[82] Some countries referenced international instruments, such as the ECHR, as sources of national privacy protections. A few countries stated explicitly that they had no 'general' privacy law. Nonetheless, computer data and electronic communications in these countries was reported to benefit from protections such as confidentiality and legal professional privilege laws.[83]

A number of countries confirmed that privacy protections were applicable in the context of law enforcement investigations, but highlighted that privacy had to be balanced against the need to prevent and investigate crime. While some countries described how this balance was achieved, the majority of countries referred only to the requirements for warrants or judicial or prosecutorial authority for intrusive searches or monitoring. One country highlighted that national law specified that '*due care shall be exercised [during search and seizure] in order to prevent the disclosure of private circumstances not connected with the criminal proceedings*.'[84] Another noted that wiretapping of communications must be used only as a '*supplementary*' means of facilitating a criminal investigation. Some countries highlighted, in particular, that data protection laws (which function as an important means of protecting privacy in the context of personal data controlled and processed by third parties) contained exclusions allowing, for example, third parties to disclose information to a law enforcement agency where 'reasonably necessary' for the enforcement of criminal law.[85]

Further detail about the nature of procedural safeguards that help secure human rights and respect for privacy during the investigative process was also requested by the Study questionnaire from law enforcement officials. In response to this question, the majority of states (85 per cent) specified that national limits and safeguards existed for law enforcement investigative cybercrime measures.[86] Surprisingly, therefore, a few countries stated that safeguards did *not* exist—a situation which may lead to incompatibility with international human rights law.

Reported safeguards included restrictions on the types of computer data that may be accessed by law enforcement, as well as supervision of investigative measures by the court or prosecutor. Some states also referred to time limits placed on the use of investigative measures.[87] Other countries cited protective regimes including limitations on access to computer data once acquired by law enforcement, limitations on its use, destruction requirements, and internal

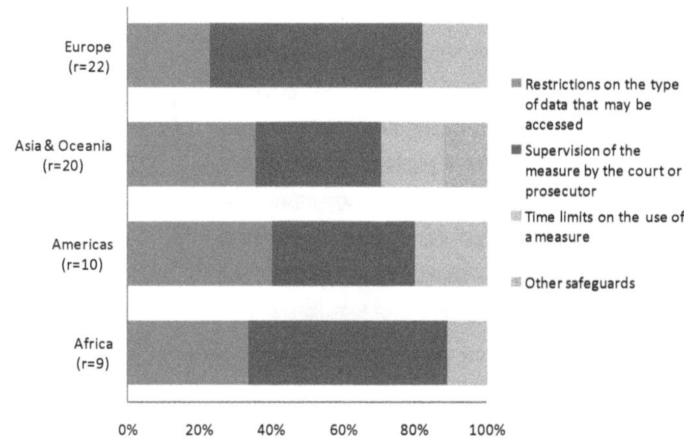

Figure 8.11 Limits and safeguards on investigations
Source: Study cybercrime questionnaire Q100. (n=45, r=61)

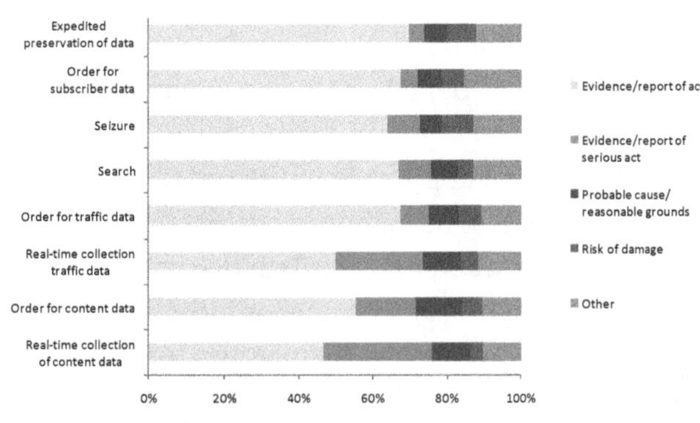

Figure 8.12 Lega requirements for use of investigative measures
Source: Study cybercrime questionnaire. Q87-96. (n=51)

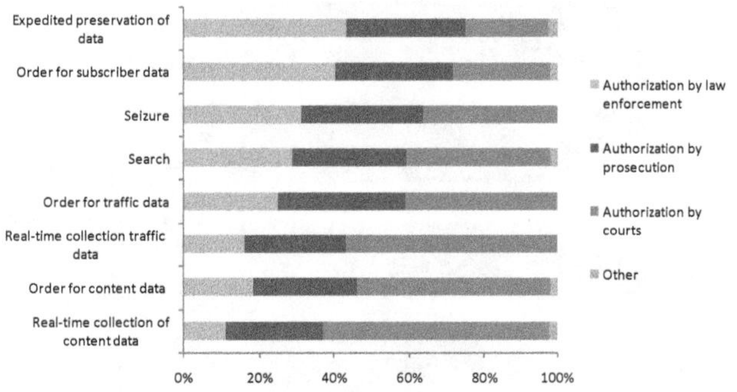

Figure 8.13 Authorization of investigative measures
Source: Study cybercrime questionnaire. Q87-96. (n=51)

and independent oversight mechanisms.[88] One country reported that *'A wide variety of limits and safeguards apply, with different limitations and safeguard regimes being applied to each access power (telecommunications data, stored content and live content). These regimes include requirements that must be met before access is granted, limitations on access once granted, limitations of the use of material once accessed, destruction requirements, internal and independent oversight regimes, and public reporting requirements.'*[89]

The majority of countries (over 75 per cent), said that safeguards were build into primary legislation. The remainder of countries reported that safeguards derived from secondary legislation, executive decree, court decisions or law enforcement of prosecution policies.[90] While safeguards might legitimately derive from sources other than primary legislation, they must still—as discussed below—be enshrined in 'law' that provides adequate and effective guarantees against abuse of the investigative measure itself.

Countries were also asked further detail about specific procedural safeguards. These included the nature of legal requirements to be met before a particular investigative measure could be used, as well as the identity of authorizing authorities. With respect to procedural requirements, the majority of countries reported that a large range of investigative measures could be initiated on the basis of *'evidence or report of a [cybercrime] act.'*[91] For measures with a higher degree of intrusiveness, such as real-time collection of data, or collection of content data, countries more often required evidence or report of a '*serious*' cybercrime, or procedural requirements such as demonstration of '*probable cause*' or '*reasonable grounds*' of suspicion of an offence.[92]

A similar pattern was observed with respect to the identity of the authorizing authority for different investigative measures. Countries frequently reported that comparatively less intrusive measures, such as expedited preservation of data, or orders for subscriber data, could be ordered by law enforcement authorities, as compared with more intrusive measures.[93] Over 80 per cent of responding countries, for example, stated that intrusive measures such as orders for content data or real-time collection of data, required authorization by a prosecutor or by the courts, rather than directly by law enforcement officers. Nonetheless, a small number of countries reported that law enforcement authorities were able to authorize such investigations—raising potential concerns over the sufficiency of safeguards for these measures. One country in the Americas, for example, reported that an article of its procedural law, which had provided for interception in exceptional circumstances without a warrant, had been declared unconstitutional by the Supreme Court.[94]

Assessing Safeguards Through a Human Rights Lens

Case law from international human rights courts and tribunals emphasizes that procedural protections are critical to respecting privacy in the context of law enforcement investigations. The table shows the core international right to privacy provisions, as well as human rights decisions related to issues such as the absence of authorizing legislation for investigative measures; legislative safeguards; and the use of investigative measures in practice. To date, few international human rights decisions have directly addressed law enforcement cybercrime investigations.[95]

One important judgement of the ECtHR has, however, considered the balance of privacy and law enforcement investigations. In the context of an online content offence involving a minor, law enforcement agencies were unable to obtain subscriber data from an ISP due to confidentiality protections contained in the telecommunications law. The Court found that this prevented effective steps from being taken to identify and prosecute the perpetrator.[96]

Although freedom of expression and confidentiality of communications are primary considerations and users of telecommunications and Internet services must have a guarantee that their own privacy and freedom of expression will be respected, such guarantee cannot be absolute and must yield on occasion to other legitimate imperatives, such as the prevention of disorder or crime ... It is the task of the legislator to provide the framework for reconciling the various claims which compete for protection in this context.

ECtHR Application No. 2872/02

A number of other decisions are also particularly relevant to the cybercrime

International human rights law provisions

ICCPR, Article 17, ECHR Article 8, ACHR Article 11

[No one shall be subjected to arbitrary or unlawful interference with his privacy, family, home or correspondence (ICCPR)] [Everyone has the right to respect for his private and family life, his home and his correspondence (ECHR)] [No one may be the object of arbitrary or abusive interference with his private life, his family, his home, or his correspondence (ACHR)]

Absence of authorizing legislation for investigative measures

ECtHR Application No. 8691/79

In the absence of legal rules, the practice of voluntary supply by a telecommunications service provider of records of telephone numbers dialled and call duration, upon request, to police when 'essential for police enquiries and in relation to serious crime' was found to be incompatible with the right to privacy. The Court highlighted the absence of legal rules concerning the scope and manner of exercise of the discretion.

ECtHR Application No. 47114/99

The interception of pager messages by law enforcement using a 'clone' of a suspect's personal pager in the absence of laws

investigative context. In the European system, the voluntary supply of telephone records by a telecommunications service provider to law enforcement, for example, has been found to be incompatible with the right to privacy in the absence of specific legal rules.[97] Similarly, in the Americas, the recording of telephone conversations authorized by mere judicial annotation and not linked with an established investigation has been found to violate the right to privacy.[98]

It is very likely that existing principles from such cases will be applied in future cybercrime cases. The search of a computer system for files, or the covert monitoring of emails or IP traffic, for example, shows close parallels with traditional physical search and wiretaps. The actions of ISPs in delivering data to law enforcement authorities (whether under an informal cooperation agreement, or pursuant to a warrant, subpoena or other legal order) are equivalent to those of telecommunication providers. In particular, the potential for cybercrime investigations to access a wide range of personal information—including emails, VOIP calls, internet browsing histories, and photographs—presents a particularly high level of potential intrusiveness. In many cases, such as when records are requested from an ISP or real-time data collection is authorized, the subject of the investigation will likely be unaware of the fact of the investigation and of the nature and extent of data gathered, thus engaging human rights jurisprudence on secret surveillance.[99] In such circumstances—due, not least, to resultant vulnerabilities to misuse—regional human rights tribunals have urged particular caution.[100]

The range of privacy and safeguard approaches reported by countries through the Study questionnaire—and, indeed, the range of situations brought before international human rights tribunals—demonstrates a considerable diversity in privacy protection during law enforcement investigations. Examination of relevant *national* privacy decisions further highlights this point. National decisions on the procedure for law enforcement access to ISP subscriber information, for example, range from those which hold that police requests to ISPs for subscriber information *without* judicial authorization are *compatible* with customer privacy expectations, to those which hold that proper judicial process is *required* by privacy rights.[101]

As with a human rights assessment of criminalization, international human rights law is, to some extent, able to accommodate such differences through doctrine such as the margin of appreciation.[102] Nonetheless, it is clear that divergent national privacy approaches will become an increasing challenge in the context of trans-national law enforcement investigations and developments such as cloud computing.

regulating the interception of page messages was found to be incompatible with the right to privacy. The Court noted that domestic law must provide protection against arbitrary interference with the right to privacy.

Legislative safeguards for investigative measures

UN-HRC Communication CCPR/C/82/D/903/1999

The interception and recording of data traffic on the written authorization of an investigating judge, in the context of a preliminary judicial investigation into the involvement of an individual in a criminal organization, was found not to violate the right to privacy. The Committee highlighted that authorizing legislation detailed the precise circumstances in which interference may be permitted and that the interference was proportionate and necessary to achieve the legitimate purpose of combating crime.

ECtHR Application No. 2872/02

The lack of an effective criminal investigation due to the absence of an explicit legal provision authorizing the disclosure of telecommunications data in the case of an online content offence was found to be incompatible with the positive obligations of the right to privacy. The Court highlighted that the victim had not been afforded effective protection.

ECtHR Application No. 62540/00

The provisions of a national law regulating secret surveillance measures were found to be incompatible with the right to privacy. The Court emphasized that the law did not provide for any review of implementation of measures by an external body or official; that it did not set out procedures for preservation of the integrity and confidentiality of evidence obtained, or procedures for its destruction; and that overall control of surveillance rested with a member of the executive, rather than an independent body.

Investigative measures in practice

IACtHR *Escher* Judgment of 6 July 2009

The recording of telephone conversations by the state and their subsequent dissemination without full respect for national legal requirements was found to be incompatible with the right to privacy. The Court emphasized that the monitoring petition was not linked to an established police investigation or criminal proceeding. The Court also highlighted that the interception was authorized by a mere judicial annotation that did not demonstrate reasoning, procedural requirements, or duration of the measure.

ECtHR Application No. 13710/88

A search impinging on the profession secrecy of a lawyer's office under a broad warrant authorizing search for and seizure of 'documents' was found to be incompatible with the right to privacy. The Court held that the measure was not proportionate to its aims.

Privacy, Jurisdiction and the Cloud

Cloud data processing involves multiple data locales or data centres, distributed across different national jurisdictions, and with different private data controllers and processors.[103] Under present conditions, although data location may be technically knowable, cloud computing users are not always informed exactly 'where' their data is held. In turn, jurisdictional approaches both to the *data protection* regime governing data held by cloud service providers, and *criminal procedure law* governing national law enforcement investigations are complex.[104]

This introduces a high degree of uncertainty for users concerning the privacy regime that will apply to their data and the circumstances under which privacy may be infringed for the purposes of law enforcement investigations or security surveillance. Legislation in some countries, for example, contains extensive surveillance powers that could apply, without judicial authorization, to the data of non-nationals which is 'at rest' in cloud servers located within the national jurisdiction.[105] Where national privacy guarantees differentiate between nationals and non-nationals,[106] users may have (i) no knowledge of such actions; and (ii) no legal recourse, either under the law of the state applying such investigative measures, or—depending upon the jurisdictional application of their home laws (and the legal incorporation structure of the cloud service provider)—within their own countries.

Divergences in privacy law jurisdiction are suggested by country responses to the Study questionnaire. Responding countries reported a range of legal positions regarding the extra-territorial application of national privacy protections. A few countries noted that privacy protections do have extra-territorial effect, including under conditions such as where the act or practice falling outside of the territory nonetheless has an '*organisational link*' with the country. Other countries confirmed that national privacy laws do not apply to computer data or electronic communications, either in real-time or stored outside of the territory. One country stated that it was an '*open question, whether computer material located abroad would enjoy the same [privacy] protection as computer material located in a server [within the territory].*'[107] The majority of responding countries were nonetheless clear that national privacy protections would apply to investigative actions carried out within the territory at the request of foreign law enforcement. One country noted, for example that '*when a request for mutual legal assistance by a foreign country intrudes upon the domestic law which protects privacy, such request can be set aside.*'[108]

Recent work by the European Parliament finds that '*in the field of cybercrime, the challenge of privacy in a cloud context is underestimated, if not ignored.*'[109] While countries may have developed a range of privacy safeguards for law enforcement action within a national context, these are diverse and may not be easily reconciled in trans-national cybercrime investigation situations—potentially leading to conflicts of laws or jurisdictional gaps. As countries work to promulgate laws that address the delicate balance between individual privacy and the prevention and control of crime, it is critical that national laws reflect common rule of law and human rights principles for law enforcement investigative actions.

One strong starting point can be found in the human rights jurisprudence discussed above and summarized in the box below—which sets out clear rule of law principles for surveillance laws. Even such principles, however, have yet to grapple with the challenging questions of cross-territorial data transfers. In this respect, while harmonization of privacy standards will help to increase the predictability of law enforcement access to user data, including by foreign authorities, countries will also increasingly need to address the jurisdictional reach of national privacy protections. This may entail both: (i) ensuring that support to foreign law enforcement investigations is fully subject to national privacy standards; and (ii) that causes of action are available to persons outside of national jurisdictions that are affected by the actions of the law enforcement authorities of that country.

Rule of law principles for surveillance laws

- Law must be sufficiently clear to give an adequate indication of conditions and circumstances in which authorities are empowered to use an investigative measure, including:
  - The nature of the offences which may give rise to use of the measure
  - A definition of the categories of people liable to the measure
  - A limit on the duration of the measure
  - The procedure to be followed for examining, using and storing the data obtained
  - Precautions to be taken when communicating the data to other parties
  - The circumstances in which data obtained may or must be erased or destroyed
- Adequate and effective guarantees must exist against abuse, taking into account:
  - The nature, scope and duration of the possible measures
  - The grounds required for ordering them
  - The authorities competent to permit, carry out and supervise them
  - Remedies provided in national law
- Laws should provide for review or oversight of implementation of measures by a body or official that is either external to the services deploying the measure or having certain qualifications ensuring its independence
- Laws should provide that as soon as notification can be made without jeopardising the purpose of the measure after its termination, information should be provided to the persons concerned

ECtHR Application No. 62540/00

Use of Investigative Measures in Practice

KEY RESULTS

- Irrespective of the legal form of investigative powers, all responding countries use search and seizure for the physical appropriation of computer equipment and the capture of computer data
- The majority of countries also use orders for obtaining computer data from internet service providers, real-time collection of data, and expedited preservation of data
- Law enforcement authorities encounter a range of challenges in practice, including perpetrator techniques for hiding or deletion of computer data related to an offence

Irrespective of the legal form of powers, law enforcement respondents to the Study questionnaire indicated that a range of investigative measures—from search and seizure, to expedited preservation of data—are widely used in practice. Almost all countries, for example, reported using search and seizure for the physical appropriation of computer equipment and the capture of computer data. Responses from law enforcement officers also suggested that more than 90 per cent of countries made use of orders for obtaining stored computer data. Around 80 per cent of respondents reported making use of expedited preservation of data.[110] Corresponding with the low proportion of countries reporting relevant legal powers, less than 40 per cent of countries reported making use of remote forensic tools or 'trans-border' access.[111]

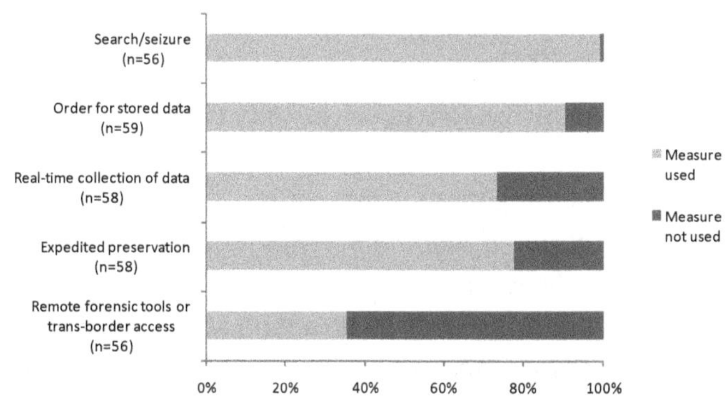

Figure 8.14 Use of investigative measures by law enforcement
Source: Study cybercrime questionnaire. Q87-97. (n= 56, 59, 58)

While these responses fit broadly with the reported existence of legal powers, expedited preservation was reported to be

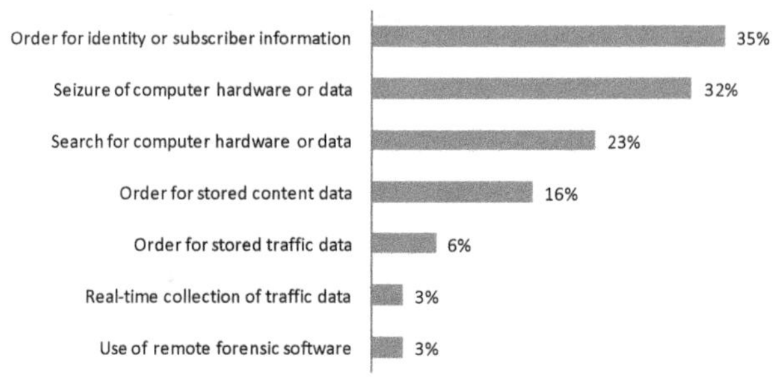

Figure 8.15 Most commonly used investigative measures
Source: Study cybercrime questionnaire. Q98. (n=31, r=37)

used *in practice* somewhat more frequently than responses on the existence of *legal powers* suggested.[112] This may be indicative of expedited preservation of data in practice through *informal* working relationships between law enforcement and service providers.

Country responses regarding the *most commonly* used investigative powers also highlighted the importance of search and seizure, as well as the use of orders to obtain subscriber data from service providers. As more and more devices become connected to the internet, computer data that may previously have been stored only on a local computer device is increasingly processed by private sector service providers, including in cloud services. The importance for law enforcement officers of obtaining electronic evidence from service providers is reflected in the fact that orders for subscriber information are reported to be the most commonly used investigative measure. The section below on investigations and the private sector examines law enforcement and service provider interactions in detail.

Investigative Challenges and Good Practice

Responding countries identified a number of challenges and good practices related to the use of investigative measures and cybercrime investigations in general. Good practices reported by countries frequently highlighted the importance of careful organization and ordering of investigations. One country, for example, reported that '*Preservation of data, and seizure of stored data and computer data in a forensically sound manner is a baseline for successful cybercrime investigations*.'[113] Another stated that '*All actions should be recorded and leave an auditable trail. Each action, URL, e-mail address, etc., should be timed and dated, information sources and contacts recorded*.'[114] In addition, a number of countries noted that the starting point for successful investigations is frequently information such as an IP address. As a result, it was considered good practice to focus on ensuring the capability for timely obtaining of subscriber information.[115]

With respect to investigative challenges encountered, many responding countries opened their remarks on law enforcement cybercrime investigations by highlighting an increasing level of criminal sophistication, and the need for law enforcement investigations to 'keep up' with cybercrime perpetrators. One country from Europe, for example, noted that '*attacks are becoming more and more advanced, more and more difficult to detect, and at the same time the techniques quickly find their way to a broader audience ... we've also seen that digital components (as means, crime scene or target) become of more and more importance in basically every crime.*'[116] Another country emphasized that '*increases in the incidence of cybercrime offences are being driven by the advancement of technical and programmatic tools available to attackers underpinned by an illicit market for the commercialization of tools for committing cybercrime.*'[117]

Increasing levels of sophistication bring increased challenges in areas such as locating electronic evidence; use of obfuscation techniques by perpetrators; challenges with large volumes of data for analysis; and challenges with obtaining data from service providers. At a basic investigative level, for example, digital storage and connectivity are increasingly integrated into common household and personal items, such as pens, cameras, watches with flash storage and USB jewellery flash drives. In addition, wireless storage devices may be hidden in wall cavities, ceilings and floor spaces. As noted by one country, such physical (and electronic) '*ease of concealment*' of computer data can present difficulties for investigations.[118] Countries also highlighted problems of '*deletion of data storage devices.*' Where perpetrators use online communication services, such as VOIP, computer data may flow directly from user to user (and not through service provider servers),[119] meaning that only local copies of certain data are available—and vulnerable to subsequent deletion. In addition, perpetrators may make use of 'dead-dropping' of messages in draft folders of webmail accounts (allowing communication without a 'sent' email), combined with use of free public Wifi access points, or pre-paid mobile and credit cards. One country, for example, highlighted challenges in '*pinpointing location*' due to '*availability of numerous free access points.*'[120] Many countries also reported the use of encryption and obfuscation techniques by perpetrators. This area is address in detail in Chapter Six (Electronic evidence and criminal justice).

Finally, many countries noted that significant challenges were faced in obtaining information from service providers. One country in the Americas, for example, reported that the supply of subscriber information by internet service providers on a voluntary basis led to inconsistent practice across the country.[121] Other countries reported that service providers did not store computer data for '*long enough*', and that it '*takes too much time for the subscriber to provide the data to the police.*'[122] A country in Asia further reported the challenge of '*inaccurate registration details*' stored by service providers.[123] The interactions—both formal and informal—between law enforcement and service providers are examined in the next section of this Chapter.

Investigations and the Private Sector

KEY RESULTS

- The interplay between law enforcement and internet service providers is particularly complex. Service providers can hold subscriber information, billing invoices, some connection logs, location information, and communication content
- National legal obligations and private sector data retention and disclosure polices vary widely by country, industry and type of data. Some countries report challenges in obtaining data from service providers
- Service providers most commonly report requiring due legal process for disclosure of customer data. Accordingly, countries most often report using court orders to obtain electronic evidence from service providers
- In some cases, however, law enforcement may be able to obtain data directly. This can be facilitated by informal partnerships between law enforcement authorities and service providers

Obtaining Data from Service Providers

Country and private sector responses to the Study questionnaire represent a mixed and complex picture concerning interactions between law enforcement and the private sector. This picture is characterized by: (i) differences between countries in legal powers to order release of computer data by service providers; (ii) challenges where service providers are located extraterritorially; and (iii) differences in private sector policies and degrees of formal and informal cooperation with law enforcement authorities.

Electronic service providers hold subscriber information, billing invoices, some connection logs, location information (such as cell tower data for mobile providers), and communication content, all of which can represent critical electronic evidence of an offence. Electronic service providers are generally not, however, obliged to affirmatively report criminal activity on their networks to law enforcement, (although in several countries, the identification of child pornography engages a mandatory reporting obligation). As a result, responding countries make use of legal powers to obtain computer data from service providers that is required in the course of a criminal investigation. As discussed above, the majority of responding countries reported the existence of general or cyber-specific powers for ordering supply of data from third parties such as service providers.

Responding countries stated, for example, that '*According to Criminal Procedure Law, a person directing proceedings authorized by prosecutor ... can demand necessary retained data that could be related to the crime committed.*'[124] Countries also noted that '*police can ask persons and companies to testify as witnesses, hand over data or do anything else that could help the case.*'[125] Nonetheless, responding country comments indicated that a number of countries either still do not have sufficient legislative powers, or experience challenges in *practice* in obtaining data.[126] A common reported issue was that internet service providers are frequently not under any obligation to retain computer data, and that by the time necessary orders had been authorized, connection logs were no longer available.[127] A number of countries also highlighted challenges in resolving privacy issues related to the supply of data by service providers.[128]

Such challenges were more frequently reported in countries outside of Europe. This pattern is also confirmed by law enforcement responses to a question on the ability to compel non-targets of an investigation to provide information. Figure 8.16 shows that only around 60 per cent of countries in Africa, Asia and Oceania, and the Americas reported that this was possible. Almost all countries in Europe, on the other hand, report the ability to compel the production of information from third parties. This information represents the law enforcement 'practical' perspective, in contrast to the earlier data presented in this Chapter on existence of 'legal' power in principle.

In practice, law enforcement officers most often reported using formal court orders in order to obtain computer data from service providers. Figure 8.17 shows the relative distribution of responses for methods used to obtain subscriber data, stored traffic and content data, and real-time traffic and content data. As might be expected from its least intrusive nature, methods used to obtain subscriber data were most diverse—including all of orders issued by courts, prosecution, and police.

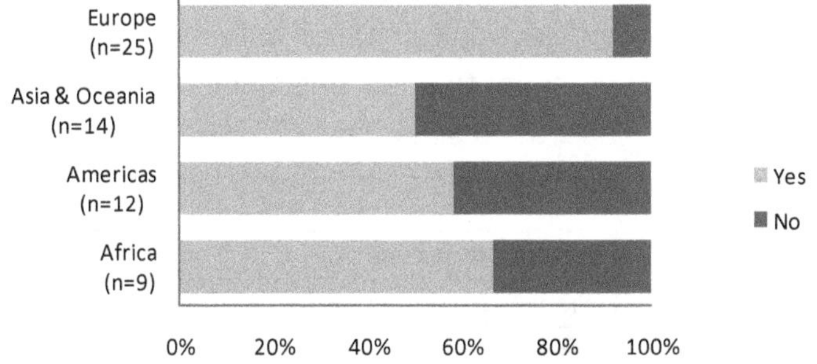

Figure 8.16 Law enforcement compel non-targets to provide information
Source: Study cybercrime questionnaire. Q101. (n=60)

A number of countries reported that multiple means of obtaining data were available, depending upon a number of factors, including the stage of investigation or proceedings, and the urgency of the

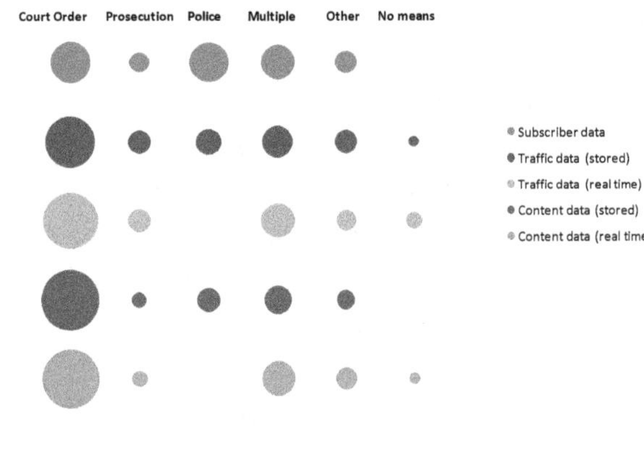

Figure 8.17 Practical and legal procedures to obtain information and evidence from service providers
Source: Cybercrime study questionnaire. Q102. (n=58)

request. One country in Western Asia, for example reported that stored content data could be obtained from a service provider '*Based on the order of the public prosecutor during the process of investigation ... or on the order of the court during the trial process.*'[129] Another country noted that subscriber data could be obtained on the basis of a '*Prosecutor order, or in case of emergency, a police letter with formal agreement of the prosecutor.*'[130] 'Other' means for obtaining data were also referred to. One country, for example, highlighted simplified means of obtaining subscriber data, through '*accessing the Integrated Public Number Database which is a database of subscriber information*

Obtaining data from service providers: National example from a country in the Americas

Federal legislation from one country in the Americas provides that a government entity may require the disclosure by a provider of an electronic communication service of the contents of a wire or electronic communication that is in electronic storage in an electronic communications system for one hundred and eight days or less, only pursuant to a warrant. Under this legislation, domestic law enforcement may obtain access to some types of data through a subpoena (issued usually by a prosecutor), but require a court-issued warrant in order to obtain other forms of data.

Email communication	Authorization procedure
In remote storage, opened	Subpoena
In remote storage, unopened and stored for more than 180 days	
In transit	
In storage on home computer	Warrant
In remote storage, unopened and stored for 180 days or less	

The national legislation also contains provisions compelling an ISP to disclose customer communications in '*exigent circumstances*.' Several national laws also permit the disclosure of communications content and non-content to a governmental entity, if the provider, in good faith believes that an emergency involving danger of death or serious physical injury to any person requires disclosure without delay of communications relating to the emergency.

Law enforcement officials may also issue a letter to a service provider to order preservation of records and other evidence in its possession pending the issuance of a court order or other process for up to 90 days. Non-compliance with such an order is generally confined to civil remedies and fines against the company.

managed by a large carrier pursuant to legislation.'[131] Overall, responses showed significant diversity in means employed by States, including police requests, 'formal' requests, legal notices, warrants, judicial orders, and subpoenas.

Private Sector Perspectives

Information gathering for the Study also included the collection of information from private sector organizations regarding perspectives on, and experience of, cooperation with law enforcement authorities. Private sector organizations that completed the Study questionnaire reported a range of internal polices and external obligations concerning domestic and foreign law enforcement data requests. In addition, many private sector polices are publicly available in the form of 'law enforcement handbooks' that provide guidance on data retention polices and frameworks for law enforcement requests.[132]

In response to the Study questionnaire, many law enforcement authorities highlighted challenges regarding short data retention times by private sector organizations and service providers.[133] With a view to providing information on retention practice, the table below provides information from a sample of private sector retention and law enforcement access policies. The table demonstrates that a range of data are generated and stored during the provision of computing and electronic communication services. It also shows divergent data retention policies for these different types of data—giving a strong indication of the challenges faced by law enforcement and private sector organizations in identifying and securing appropriate information for use in evidence. None of the service providers reviewed, for example, retained identical information for identical time periods. Publicly available retention periods ranged from as little as one day to indefinitely. Some information appeared to only be retained during the period in which the subscriber account remained active. A number of private sector organizations indicated that responding to law enforcement requests can be time-consuming and not always easily accomplished due to storage and records retention protocols and policies. The availability of sufficient personnel to respond requests may also hamper compliance or its timeliness. For smaller organizations, compliance with law enforcement requests appears to be more burdensome in terms of expenditures of personnel and resources.[134]

Private sector organization data storage and retention

Company	Types of data produced	Data retention period	Requirement of a formal request for disclosure
Communication and Information Services Provider #1	Chat room dialogue Instant messenger conversations Member directory logs Email IP/connection access logs Group IP logs Internet connection access logs TV phone (ANI) connection logs	None 60 days	Yes
Communication and Information Services Provider #2	IP connection history records Transactional data Email account registration records Game account ID records	60 days 90 days (Private)/60 days (Groups) As long as account exists	Yes
Communication and Information Services #3	Web mail account information IP address log files Account records Call detail records	Different retention periods 180 days Minimum 2 years	Yes
Communication Services Provider	Instant messaging Video message content Voicemail Financial transactions Registration data Service and account information	30–90 days As long as necessary	Yes
Game Developer and Network Provider	Private user communications Account information IP logs	Different retention periods (up to 180 days) Indefinitely	Yes

Information and Services Provider #1	Domains Email Proxy IP connection logs Member IP connection logs Source IP connection logs Session logs	Different retention periods (1 day to indefinite) 5-7 days 90 days 6 months	Yes
Information and Services Provider #2	Domains/web-hosting activity logs and content Group content and activity log Chat/Instant messenger logs Email Subscriber information Account content Profiles Account log-in IP addresses	Minimum of 30 days after termination of Group/ website/domain 45-60 days 4 or more months of inactivity 18 months after inactivity 90 days after deletion of account Up to one year	Yes
Messaging Service Provider	Subscriber information Account content Links, cookies Location information Log data Widget data	Different retention periods Up to 37 days after account deletion	Yes
Social Network Provider #1	Registration data (User Basic Subscriber Information) Transactional data (IP Logs)	Up to 90 days after account deletion	Yes
Social Network Provider #2	Private user communications Basic user identity information, general records IP address logs	Different retention periods As long as account exists/10 days after account deletion 90 days	Yes

The overriding concern of corporations with respect to law enforcement requests appeared to be that of being able to supply data where requested, but '*without infringing on the scope of other legislative or regulatory requirements*.'[135] Private sector organizations referred frequently to customer terms of service use, and to privacy considerations. Nonetheless, private sector organizations highlighted, in particular, that they should respond rapidly and positively where '*life is at risk*,' but also noted that '*is very, very rare*.'[136] Responding private sector organizations, including service providers, drew a clear distinction between formal legal requirements to provide data, and informal requests. Almost all responding corporations reported that they '*must*' and '*do*' respond to formal domestic court orders to produce information '*according to applicable laws*'[137] and '*in accordance with our legal responsibilities*.'[138] Upon receiving a request, for example, one private sector organization reported that the first step is to identify '*if there is an underlying statutory right to request the information or there is a statutory disclosure obligation to provide information and to seek to ensure we do not violate any other laws or company's contractual obligations to clients' and customer privacy*.'[139]

The majority of private sector organizations reported that they did not consider themselves to be under any obligation to provide data in response to an 'informal' request—such as a telephone call—from law enforcement authorities. Although a number of organizations reported that they may choose to provide data voluntary to informal requests in accordance with their own internal polices. One international corporation noted, for example that it could respond to such requests '*if the data is available and providing it is in accordance with company legal and human resource regulations*.'[140] A larger number of organizations reported that they could provide data in response to a 'formal' law enforcement request—such as an official letter. Almost all, however, indicated that this was not an absolute obligation and data could only be provided under certain conditions, such as where '*there is a statutory obligation to provide information and the disclosure does not violate other laws or company contractual obligations*.'[141]

International corporations and national service providers frequently reported the appointment of law enforcement focal points in order to facilitate cooperation with law enforcement authorities. These included in-house CSIRT, IT security, legal, risk management, or security departments. Other companies have cross-disciplinary teams or task forces to manage relationships with law enforcement. Some private sector organizations reported that mechanisms for strengthening cooperation and information exchange with law enforcement were still in the course of development.[142] Such mechanisms were viewed as important in light of an increasing number of law enforcement requests for data from service providers. One multinational telecommunications operator, for example, reported a 50-fold increase in the number of formal requests for computer data received between the years 2008 and 2010.[143]

Private sector organizations also highlighted the fact that they often received both *domestic* and *foreign* law enforcement requests. Many corporations reported that they only considered *foreign* law enforcement requests where made through *formal national* channels.[144] Some corporations, stated, for example, that foreign law enforcement authorities are required to obtain an order for data from a national court, through a mutual legal assistance request. Corporations with offices in multiple countries reported that different national operations would always need to take into account local laws and regulations. However, multinational private sector organizations generally identified a primary 'seat' jurisdiction for the receipt of law enforcement requests globally.[145]

In addition to a general requirement for due legal process in the jurisdiction of the 'seat' of a corporation, a number of private sector organizations noted that informal foreign law enforcement requests may also be complied with on a *discretionary* basis.[146] Publically available information for global service providers such as Google, for example, states both that: '*Using Mutual Legal Assistance Treaties and other diplomatic and cooperative arrangements, [foreign] agencies can work through ['seat' national authorities] to gather evidence for legitimate investigations*', and that: '*On a voluntary basis, we may provide user data in response to valid legal process from [foreign] agencies, if those requests are consistent with international norms, ['seat' national] law, Google's polices and the law of the requesting country*.'[147]

This adds up to a picture of a default requirement for foreign law enforcement authorities to obtain requisite subpoenas, warrants or orders in the 'seat' jurisdiction of a service provider, combined with a certain discretion to supply data to law enforcement within the limits of national laws and customer terms of use. Such discretionary relationships between the private sector and law enforcement are largely built on trust and are not considered legally binding—they usually exist therefore within limited geographic or socio-political areas. One company from Central America, for example, stated that it accepted obligations derived from informal law enforcement requests, but limited compliance exclusively to those issued by local authorities.[148] One European company specified that it treated informal requests from foreign law enforcement authorities in the same way as requests by national authorities, but did not consider itself legally bound to comply in either scenario.[149] As publically noted by one leading online services provider: '*we are operating in good faith with ... authorities, but we have no obligation to do so ... If that good faith is abused, we would have to think much more carefully about that cooperation*.'[150] In other words, within the constraints of data protection laws and customer terms and conditions, service providers have a significant amount of latitude over data disclosed, including to foreign law enforcement agencies. These decisions are often based on existing working relationships and perceptions of trust. One global provider of network equipment, for example, stated that all requests would '*undergo review, in order to ensure technical feasibility and alignment with country-specific [...] legal and [...] human rights regulations*.'[151]

A combination of: (i) varying capacity of foreign law enforcement authorities to ensure due legal process in the 'seat' jurisdiction through mutual legal assistance; and (ii) the existence of networks of informal trust, results in variation in the extent of compliance with foreign requests for information by global service providers. Figure 8.18 shows the number of requests received and complied with from different countries (scaled per 100,000 internet users in the requesting country) as reported by Google Transparency Report.[152] The highest proportion of requests complied with are in the 'seat' jurisdiction. Requests from other countries vary from zero per cent of requests complied with, to almost 80 per cent, with an average of around 50 per cent complied with. This pattern likely derives from a number of factors, including: the extent to which foreign law enforcement requests are made informally or directly, rather than through mutual legal assistance; corporate policies towards informal requests from different

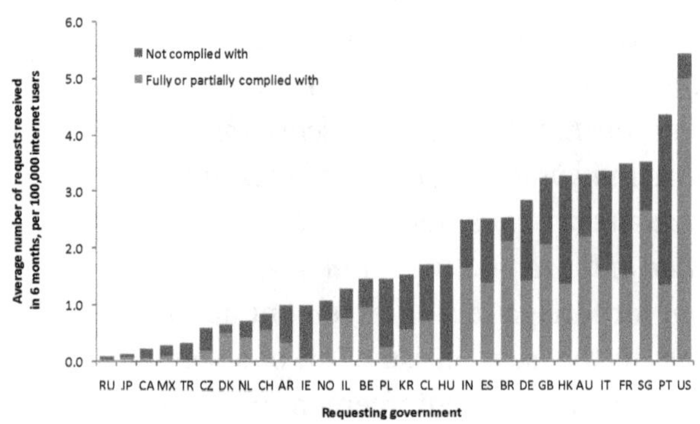

Figure 8.18 User data requests received by Google from governments (1 Jan 2011–30 Jun 2012)
Source:UNODC presentation of Google Transparency Report data.

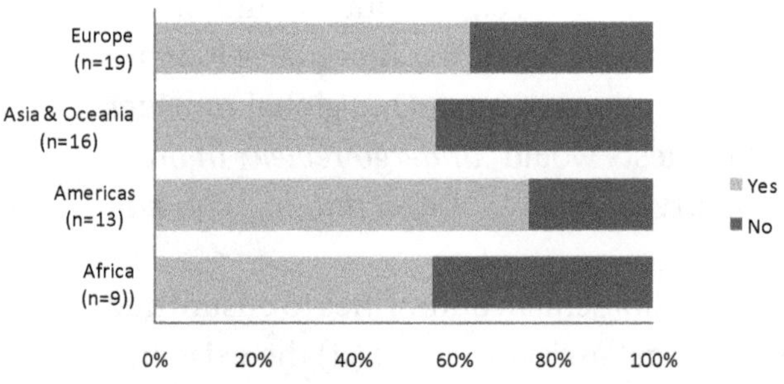

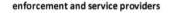

Figure 8.19 Informal relationships between law enforcement and service providers
Source: Study cybercrime questionnaire. Q103. (n=56)

countries; and the capacity of foreign authorities for the preparation of mutual legal assistance requests.

Informal relationships between law enforcement and private sector organizations can extend more broadly than the supply of computer data for investigations. During information gathering for the Study, both countries and private sector organizations reported a wide range of areas of cooperation. One country in Northern Europe, for example, reported that '*Law enforcement has an informal working relationship with the major service providers to update contact information and to develop procedures for the formal exchange of data.*'[153] Other countries noted that '*There are voluntary codes of practice that allow sharing of information, alongside formal legislation.*'[154]

Several countries reported particular emphasis on relationships with telecommunications and service provider companies. One country, for instance, highlighted that: '*Agencies maintain close relationships with the telecommunications industry—particularly large industry participants. These relationships are used primarily for discussing practical measures (such as the best procedures for serving warrants, deploying capabilities and delivering lawfully intercepted information), technical issues (such as the operation of the telecommunications networks), and policy issues.*'[155] Information provided by private sector organizations also indicates that many corporations—and not just electronic service providers—engage in partnerships with law enforcement. These include for the purposes of sharing general information on cybercrime threats and trends, and with a view to facilitating reporting of suspected cybercrime cases.[156] Public-private partnerships concerning cybercrime are discussed in broader terms in Chapter Eight (Prevention).

Responses from countries to the Study questionnaire suggest that informal relationships between law enforcement and service providers are equally common across different regions. Figure 8.19 shows that between 50 per cent and 60 per cent of countries in all regions reported the existence of such relationships.[157]

A number of countries were careful to point out that informal relationships between law enforcement and service providers involved information sharing *'not implicating private customer data.'*[158] Others, however, seemed to indicate that individual customer data could be supplied to law enforcement authorities through such arrangements.[159] While durable and efficient relationships between law enforcement and service providers can greatly assist effective cybercrime investigations, it is critical that such arrangements also meet rule of law and international human rights standards. As discussed in this Chapter, these include sufficient clarity on the conditions and circumstances in which law enforcement authorities are empowered to obtain computer data, and adequate and effective guarantees against abuse.[160] Arrangements similar, for example, to unfettered law enforcement 'terminal' access to subscriber, traffic or content data stored by service providers may be subject to particular levels of human rights scrutiny.[161]

Law Enforcement Capacity

KEY RESULTS

- Over 90 per cent of responding countries have begun to put in place specialized structures for the investigation of cybercrime and crimes involving electronic evidence
- In developing countries, however, these are not well resourced and suffer from a capacity shortage
- Countries with lower levels of development have significantly fewer specialized police, with around 0.2 per 100,000 national internet users. The rates is two to five times higher in more developed countries
- Some 70 per cent of specialized law enforcement officers in less developed countries were reported to lack computer skills and equipment

This section presents information gathered on the *capacity* of law enforcement authorities to prevent and combat cybercrime. Institutional 'capacity' in the context of policing has a number of elements, including strategic and operational capabilities, technical skills of personnel, and sufficiency of officers and resources.[162] Another important element of capacity is the degree of 'specialization.' Crimes that require a 'specialized' response are typically those that present specific challenges in terms of offence definitions, applicability of laws, or evidence gathering and analysis.[163] Cybercrime shows all of these characteristics, and a degree of law enforcement specialization is critical to an effective crime prevention and criminal justice response. Law enforcement specialization can occur at both the *organizational* and *personnel* levels—both of which often overlap. While specialization will likely always be required in the area of cybercrime and electronic evidence, it is also the case that—as the world advances towards hyperconnectivity—*all* law enforcement officers will increasingly be expected to routinely handle and collect electronic evidence.

Organizational Specialization

The majority of countries that responded to the Study questionnaire reported the existence of specialized law enforcement structures for cybercrime. More than 75 per cent of countries reported a specialized dedicated *unit* within existing enforcement organizations. Around 15 per cent reported a specialized dedicated *agency* for cyber or cybercrime related issues.[164]

Notably, both more highly developed countries (HDI>0.8) and less developed countries (HDI<0.8) reported significant degrees of specialization. Nonetheless, lesser developed countries showed a wider range of structures, with some countries reporting no specialized personnel, and some reporting the existence of specialized personnel, but not organized within a dedicated unit. With a single exception (in Africa), countries that reported a lack of specialized agency or unit indicated plans to establish one in the near future.[165]

Responding countries also showed variation across development levels regarding the way in which specialized units are integrated into federal, regional, state, and municipal law enforcement departments and agencies. In some countries, '*all federal investigative agencies have dedicated units on cybercrime.*'[166] Others reported federal level units with '*variable law enforcement arrangements at the State and Territory between the different jurisdictions.*'[167] There was also considerable variation reported within countries in terms of the geographic coverage and consistency of units within enforcement organizations or agencies.[168] Several countries reported the establishment of a national specialized unit or agency with additional plans to add personnel and units incrementally in field office locations.

Developed countries frequently reported *'a wide range of'* or *'sufficient resources',* although several indicated that *'Resources are basically adequate to conduct investigations with a view to upgrade capabilities to a higher level'* and *'All the resources are sufficient to the point that they help us get the job done. But for improved, more efficient and faster results, we would need new and updated hardware and software resources.'*[169] Other more developed countries indicated also indicated specific personnel development needs, including *'not enough human resources* and differences between federal and state resource levels of police *'some state [level] police have adequate capabilities, some don't.'*[170] Developing countries in Africa and Asia indicated needs for *'tools for forensics'* and emphasized that *'forensic computers and computer forensic application are outdated.'*[171]

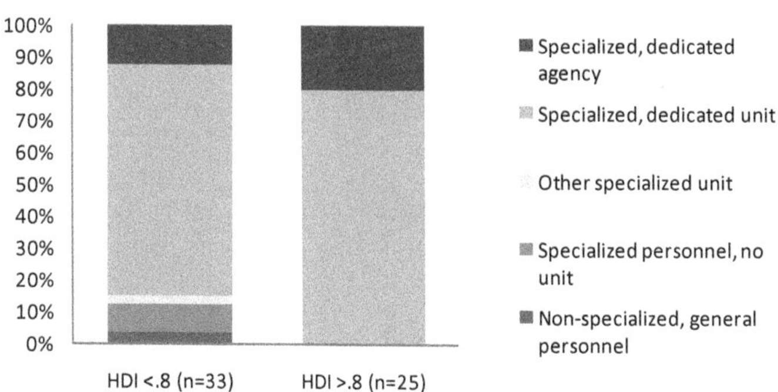

Figure 8.20 Law enforcement structure for preventing and combatting cybercrime
Source: Study cybercrime questionnaire. Q113. (n=58)

Personnel Specialization

Many countries reported the existence of law enforcement officers specialized in cybercrime.[172] Countries with lower levels of development, however, have significantly fewer specialized police, with around 0.2 specialized officers per 100,000 national internet users. The rate is two to five times higher in more developed countries. For all countries, the proportion of police specialized in cybercrime was less than one per cent of total police.[173]

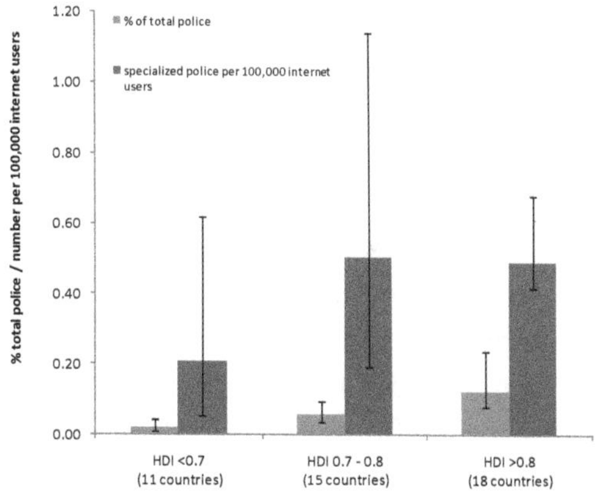

Figure 8.21 Number of specialized police, by level of country development
Source: Study cybercrime questionnaire. Q115 and Q61. (n=44)

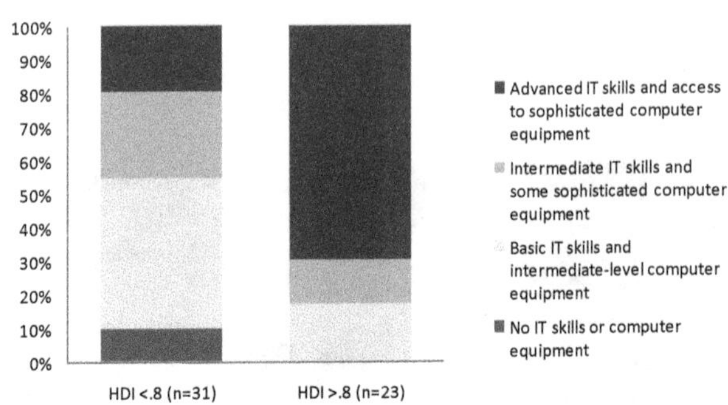

Figure 8.22 Reported technical capabilities of law enforcement
Source: Study cybercrime questionnaire. Q116. (n=54)

Overall, around 40 per cent of responding countries reported that officers specialized in cybercrime possessed 'advanced' IT skills. Just over 30 per cent of countries reported that specialized officers reported 'intermediate' skills. Twenty per cent of countries indicated that specialized officers possessed 'basic' IT skills, and six per cent reported that specialized officers did not possess any IT skills.

This overall picture masks significant differences by country development level however. In more highly developed countries around 70 per cent of specialized officers were reported to possess advanced IT skills and to have access to sophisticated computer equipment This proportion was around 20 per cent for lesser developed countries. In contrast, in lesser developed countries, some 45 per cent of countries reported that specialized cybercrime officers possessed only basic IT skills and access to intermediate-level computer equipment.

Within a country, however, the picture may also vary significantly. One country, for example, reported that '*no general statement is possible as the whole spectrum is represented*.'[174] Some units have appropriate '*equipment and software, but the level of skill (of employees) is insufficient to address a lot of issues*.' Other units '*have advanced specialized officers, but lack sophisticated resources*.'[175]

Personnel Development

Most countries reported providing some cyber-related training to both specialized and non-specialized law enforcement personnel. Specialized law enforcement officers received training that spanned a range of topics, from technology-orientation and basic investigations, to evidence and forensics issues. Multiple training topics (35 per cent), computer evidence preservation (around 20 per cent) and online child exploitation (around 15 per cent) training were the most commonly reported subject matter for specialized officer training. Other topics included advanced internet investigations, digital forensics, use of special forensic software, and malware analysis.

The extent and coverage of training programs provided to specialized officers varied widely. In some countries, all specialized officers received cybercrime training, either in person or online. In other countries, training was provided at the national level to officers in selected units on basic cybercrime terminology or basic investigative methodology. Some countries reported providing additional training on topics such as basic IT awareness, technology enabled crime awareness, data evidence preservation and remote forensics software. Training was reported as either integrated into specialized officer training or available as needed or on demand by officers.

Regular training is an important component of law enforcement capacity as it enables specialized officers to remain up-to-date with the latest techniques and developments. In both more highly developed countries and lesser developed countries, regular training (more than once a year) was reported in around 50 per cent to 60 per cent of countries. Some lesser developed countries reported, however, that training was either *'rare'* or that no training at all was available.[176]

Training for specialized officers was most often provided directly by a training unit of the law enforcement agency itself. International or regional organizations were mentioned by around 15 per cent of countries as a training provider for specialized cybercrime

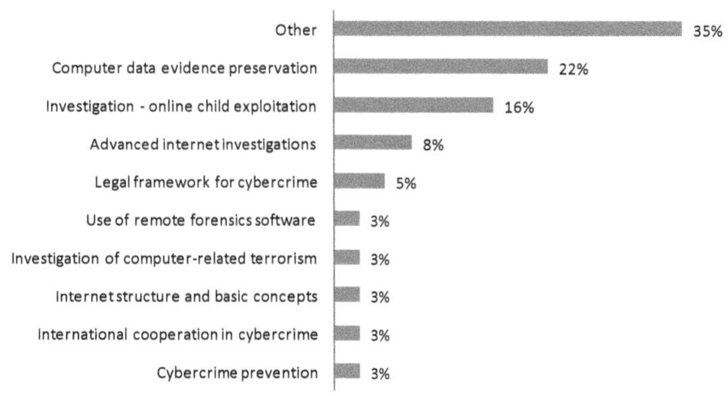

Figure 8.23 Training subject matters for specialized law enforcement officers
Source: Study cybercrime questionnaire. Q117. (n=37)

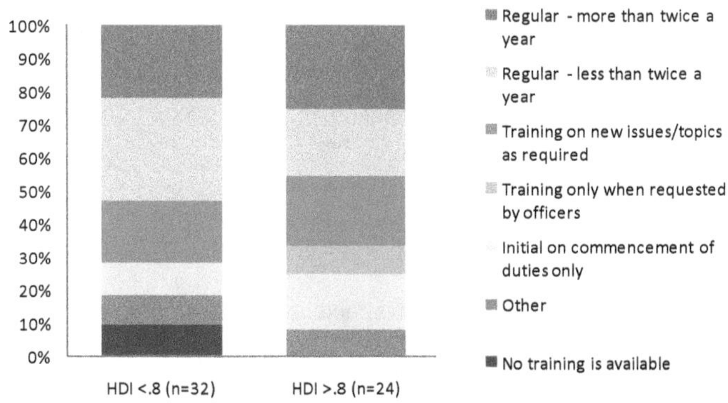

Figure 8.24 Frequency of training for specialized law enforcement officers
Source: Study cybercrime questionnaire. Q118. (n=56)

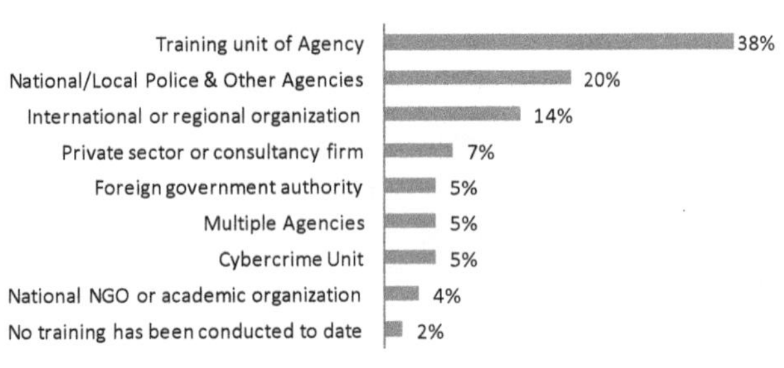

Figure 8.25 Training provider for specialized law enforcement officers
Source: Study cybercrime questionnaire. Q119. (n=56)

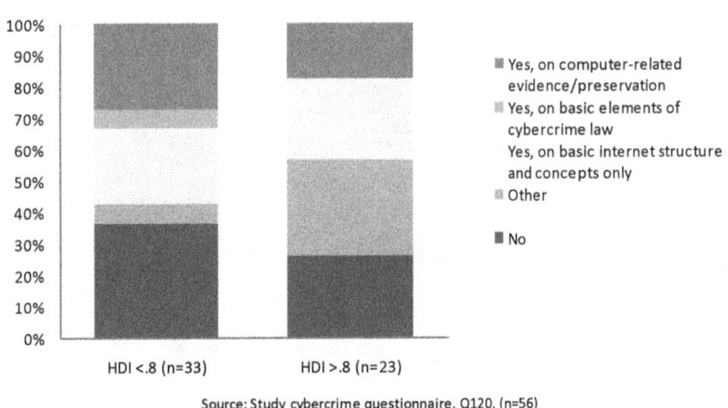

Figure 8.26 Training for non-specialized law enforcement personnel
Source: Study cybercrime questionnaire. Q120. (n=56)

law enforcement officers—indicating a significant role for technical assistance delivered by these organizations. Chapter Six (Electronic evidence and criminal justice) examines needs for, and delivery of, technical assistance in greater detail.

As electronic evidence becomes an important component in the investigation of all crime types, 'non-specialized' law enforcement officers will increasingly be required to conduct basic computer-related investigations. Responses to the Study questionnaire showed marked differences between countries concerning the delivery of cybercrime-related training to non-specialized law enforcement officers. Around 25 per cent of countries, both more highly developed and lesser developed, reported delivery of basic training on internet structure and concepts to non-specialized officers. Some 40 per cent of lesser developed countries reported, however, that non-specialized officers do not receive any training concerning cybercrime or electronic evidence. Nonetheless, a number of countries highlighted initiatives to improve cybercrime-related training for non-specialized officers. One country, for example, reported '*embarking on a 'mainstreaming' programme to give all officers a basic understanding of cyber crime and the relevant investigation techniques and legislation.*'[177] Another indicated that '*regular officers receive training on computer-related evidence preservation as part of some general investigation courses.*'[178] Others noted that cybercrime topics are '*being incorporated in the regular police education*'[179] and officer initiated training is '*available through online courses in our technology training platform.*'[180]

Notes

1. *Code of Conduct for Law Enforcement Officials*, Art.1. Annex to General Assembly Resolution 34/169, 17 December 1979.
2. *Ibid.*, Commentary to Art. 1, at (d).
3. See Chapter Two (The global picture)
4. Study cybercrime questionnaire. Q83. Some countries which could not provide exact numbers estimated the percentage to be 'very high.'
5. See http://www.bbc.co.uk/news/technology-18102793
6. Study cybercrime questionnaire. Q113.
7. UNODC. 2010. *Handbook on the Crime Prevention Guidelines: Making them work.*
8. Bowling, B., and Foster, J., 2002. Policing and the Police. *In*: Maguire, M., Morgan, R., Reiner, R. (eds.). *The Oxford Handbook of Criminology*. 3rd edn. Oxford: Oxford University Press.
9. Study cybercrime questionnaire. Q85.
10. Study cybercrime questionnaire. Q78.
11. Study cybercrime questionnaire. Q83.
12. *Ibid.*
13. Study cybercrime questionnaire. Q82.
14. Symantec. 2012. *Norton Cybercrime Report 2012.*
15. Study cybercrime questionnaire. Q82.
16. *Ibid.*
17. Study cybercrime questionnaire. Q80.
18. Study cybercrime questionnaire. Q79.
19. Study cybercrime questionnaire. Q79.
20. Study cybercrime questionnaire. Q78.
21. Study cybercrime questionnaire. Q84.
22. Study cybercrime questionnaire. Q110.
23. *Ibid.*
24. See, for example, INPROL. 2012. *Practitioner's Guide: Common Law and Civil Law Traditions.*
25. Seehttp://www.fbi.gov/news/stories/2008/october/darkmarket_102008andhttp://www.fbi.gov/newyork/press-releases/2012/manhattan-u.s.-attorney-and-fbi-assistant-director-in-charge-announce-24-arrests-in-eight-countries-as-part-of-international-cyber-crime-takedown
26. See https://www.europol.europa.eu/sites/default/files/publications/2csefactsheet2012_0.pdf
27. See http://cdrc.jhpolice.gov.in/cyber-crime/
28. See http://www.justice.gov/usao/nys/pressreleases/January13/GoziVirusDocuments/Kuzmin,%20Nikita%20Complaint.pdf
29. See, for example, Feigenbaum *et al.*, 2007. A Model of Onion Routing with Provable Anonymity. *Financial Cryptography and Data Security Lecture Notes in Computer Science*, 4886:57–71; and Schwerha, J.J., 2010.

Law Enforcement Challenges in Transborder Acquisition of Electronic Evidence from "Cloud Computing Providers," Council of Europe Discussion paper, pp. 9–10; Walden, I., 2013. Accessing Data in the Cloud: The Long Arm of the Law Enforcement Agent. *Privacy and Security for Cloud Computing. Computer Communications and Networks 2013*, pp. 45–71.

30. Study cybercrime questionnaire. Q53.
31. Walden, I., 2003. Addressing the Data Problem. *Information Security Technical Report*, 8(2); Nieman, A., 2009. Cyberforensics: Bridging the Law/Technology Divide. *JILT*, 2009(1).
32. Sieber, U., 2008. Mastering complexity in the global cyberspace: The harmonization of computer-related criminal law. *In*: Delmas-Marty, M., Pieth, M., Sieber, U. (eds.). *Les chemins de l'HarmonisationPénale/ Harmonising Criminal Law*. Collection de L'UMR de Droit Comparé de Paris. Paris: Société de législation comparée.
33. See Study cybercrime questionnaire. Q42–51.
34. *Ibid.*
35. *Ibid.*
36. *Ibid.*
37. Study cybercrime questionnaire. Q42–51 and Q53.
38. See Chapter Three (Legislation and frameworks), Section 3.1 Introduction—The role of law, Relevant categories of law.
39. See, for instance, Brenner, S. W., Frederiksen, B.A., 2002. Computer Searches and Seizures: Some Unresolved Issues. *Mich. Telecomm. Tech. L. Rev.* 39(8); Kerr, O.S., 2005. Search Warrants in an Era of Digital Evidence. *Mississippi Law Journal*, 75:85.
40. Draft African Union Convention, Arts. 3-50, 3-51; COMESA Draft Model Bill, Arts. 37, 33; Commonwealth Model Law, Arts.12, 14; Council of Europe Cybercrime Convention, Art. 19; ECOWAS Draft Directive, Art. 33; ITU/CARICOM/CTU Model Legislative Texts, Art. 20; League of Arab States Convention, Arts. 26, 27.
41. Draft African Union Convention; COMESA Draft Model Bill; Commonwealth Model Law; Council of Europe Cybercrime Convention; ITU/CARICOM/CTU Model Legislative Texts; League of Arab States Convention.
42. Study cybercrime questionnaire. Q42 and Q43.
43. *Ibid*
44. Study cybercrime questionnaire. Q53.
45. See Chapter Eight (Prevention), Section 8.3 Cybercrime prevention, the private sector and academia, Cybercrime prevention by internet service and hosting providers.
46. James Tetteh, A.-N., Williams, P., 2008. *Digital forensics and the legal system: A dilemma of our times*. Available at: http://ro.ecu.edu.au/adf/41/
47. Draft African Union Convention, Art. 3-53; COMESA Draft Model Bill, Arts. 33–35; Commonwealth Model Law, Art.17; Council of Europe Cybercrime Convention, Art. 16; ECOWAS Draft Directive, Art. 33; ITU/ CARICOM/CTU Model Legislative Texts, Art.23; League of Arab States Convention, Art. 23.
48. See, for example, ECtHR. Application No. 9248/81.

49. See Brown, I., 2010. Communications Data Retention in an Evolving Internet. *International Journal of Law and Information Technology*, 19(2):107.
50. Study cybercrime questionnaire. Q42-51.
51. COMESA Draft Model Bill, Art. 36(a); Commonwealth Model Law, Art.15; Council of Europe Cybercrime Convention, Art. 18(1)(a); ITU/CARICOM/CTU Model Legislative Texts, Art.22(a); League of Arab States Convention, Art. 25(1).
52. COMESA Draft Model Bill, Art. 34(a)(ii); Commonwealth Model Law, Art.16; Council of Europe Cybercrime Convention, Art. 17(1)(b); ITU/CARICOM/CTU Model Legislative Texts, Art.24; League of Arab States Convention, Art. 24.
53. Study cybercrime questionnaire. Q45-47.
54. Study cybercrime questionnaire. Q42-51.
55. Study cybercrime questionnaire. Q42-51.
56. COMESA Draft Model Bill, Art. 38; Commonwealth Model Law, Art. 19; Council of Europe Cybercrime Convention, Art. 20; ITU/CARICOM/CTU Model Legislative Texts, Art. 25; League of Arab States Convention, Art. 28.
57. Draft African Union Convention, Art. 3-55; COMESA Draft Model Bill, Art. 39; Commonwealth Model Law, Art. 18; Council of Europe Cybercrime Convention, Art. 21; ITU/CARICOM/CTU Model Legislative Texts, Art.26; League of Arab States Convention, Art. 29.
58. See Walden, I. *Addressing* the Data Problem: The Legal Framework Governing Forensics in an Online Environment. *Second International Conference iTrust 2004*, Proceedings. Oxford, 29 March-1 April 2004.
59. Council of Europe Cybercrime Convention, Art. 20.
60. Study cybercrime questionnaire. Q47 and Q48.
61. *Ibid.*
62. Koops, B-J. 2010. Cybercrime legislation. *Electronic Journal of Comparative Law*, 14(3).
63. See, for example, Gartner. 2012. *Remote Forensics Report 2012.*
64. Hay, B., Nance, K., Bishop, M. 2009. Live Analysis: Progress and Challenges. *IEEE Security and Privacy*, 7(2):32.
65. Study cybercrime questionnaire. Q42-51.
66. *Ibid.*
67. See COMESA Draft Model Bill, Art. 49b; Council of Europe Cybercrime Convention, Art. 32b; League of Arab States Convention, Art. 40(2).
68. 'Trans-border' access provisons typically distinguish between access to publicly available (open source) material and other material. Access to open source material for criminal justice purposes has become generally accepted practice (See Council of Europe. 2012. *Transborder access and jurisdiction: what are the options? Report of the Transborder Group Adopted by the T-CY on 6 December 2012*). Use of the term 'Trans-border' access in this Study therefore concerns access to non-open source material.
69. Study cybercrime questionnaire. Q42-51.

70. United Nations Commission on Narcotic Drugs and Commission on Crime Prevention and Criminal Justice. 2010. *Drug control, crime prevention and criminal justice: A Human Rights perspective*. Note by the Executive Director. E/CN.7/2010/CRP.6—E/CN.15/2010/CRP.1., 3 March 2010.
71. Colvin, M., and Cooper, J. (eds.) 2009. *Human Rights in the Investigation and Prosecution of Crime*. Oxford: Oxford University Press.
72. ICCPR, Arts. 9 and 14.
73. ICCPR, Art. 17; ECHR, Art. 8; ACHR, Art. 11.
74. See for example, United Nations Human Rights Committee. 1988. *General Comment No. 16: The right to respect of privacy, family, home and correspondence, and protection of honour and reputation*, 8 April 1998.
75. See for example, United Nations Human Rights Committee. *Communication CCPR/C/82/D/903/1999*; IACtHR *Tristán Donoso*. Judgement of 27 January 2009; and ECtHR Application No's 35394/97 and 13710/88.
76. See ECtHR Application No. 8691/79.
77. See ECtHR Application No. 54934/00.
78. See, for example, EHCR Article 8(2) which provides that '*There shall be no interference by a public authority with the exercise of this right except such as in accordance with the law and is necessary in a democratic society in the interests of national security, public safety or the economic well-being of the country, for the prevention of disorder or crime, for the protection of health or morals, or for the protection of the rights and freedoms of others.*'
79. The general approach adopted by the United Nations Human Rights Committee is to ask whether an interference with privacy is provided for by law, is in accordance with the provisions, aims and objectives of the Covenant and is reasonable in the particular circumstances of the case (See United Nations Human Rights Committee. *Communication CCPR/C/82/D/903/1999* and Human Rights Committee. *General Comment No. 16*.) The approach of the ECtHR in law enforcement investigations cases is to ask (i) whether there was an interference with the privacy rights protected by Article 8 ECHR; (ii) whether the interference was in accordance with law—including not only the basis in domestic law but also the 'quality' of the law, in terms of its accessibility, foreseeability and compatibility with the rule of law; and (iii) whether the interference was necessary in a democratic society (See ECtHR Application No. 62540/00).
80. See for example, UNODC. 2009. *Current practices in electronic surveillance in the investigation of serious and organized crime*.
81. See for example, ECtHR Application No. 13710/88.
82. Study cybercrime questionnaire. Q21.
83. *Ibid.*
84. *Ibid.*
85. *Ibid.*
86. Study cybercrime questionnaire. Q100.
87. *Ibid.*
88. *Ibid.* It should be noted, in addition, that countries in the European Union are subject to Council Framework Decision 2008/977/JHA of 27 November 2008 on the protection of personal data processed

in the framework of police and judicial cooperation in criminal matters, which regulates the processing of personal data by such authorities.

89. Study cybercrime questionnaire. Q100.
90. *Ibid.*
91. Study cybercrime questionnaire. Q87-96.
92. *Ibid.*
93. *Ibid.*
94. *Ibid.*
95. Although the ECtHR, for example, has considered the monitoring of email and internet usage in an employment context. See ECtHR Application No. 62617/00. In this case, the Court applied the tests of identifying whether there was an interference with privacy and (finding so), whether the interference was in accordance with the law.
96. ECtHR Application No. 2872/02.
97. ECtHR Application No. 8691/79
98. IACtHR *Escher* Judgement of 6 July 2009.
99. In addition to cases in the table, see also ECtHR Application No. 54934/00.
100. The ECtHR holds, for instance, that '*Powers of secret surveillance of citizens, characterising as they do the police state, are tolerable under the Convention only in so far as strictly necessary for safeguarding the democratic institutions.*' ECtHR Application No. 28341/95.
101. See for example, *R v Ward*, 2012 ONCA 660 and *State v. Reid*, 194 N.J. 376 (2008).
102. Legg, A., 2012. *The Margin of Appreciation in International Human Rights Law*. Oxford: Oxford Monographs in International Law.
103. On the concepts of data 'controllers' and 'processors,' see Directive 95/46/EC of the European Parliament and of the Council of 24 October 1995 on the protection of individuals with regard to the processing of personal data and on the free movement of such data (as amended by Regulation (EC) No. 1882/2003 of the European Parliament and of the Council of 29 September 2003).
104. See, for example European Parliament Directorate General for Internal Polices, Citizens' Rights and Constitutional Affairs. 2012. *Fighting cybercrime and protecting privacy in the cloud.*
105. *Ibid.*
106. See for example, *Verdugo-Urquidez* 494 U.S. 259 (1990) and USFISCR No. 08-01.
107. Study cybercrime questionnaire. Q21.
108. *Ibid.*
109. European Parliament Directorate General for Internal Policies, Citizens' Rights and Constitutional Affairs. 2012. *Fighting cybercrime and protecting privacy in the cloud.*
110. Study cybercrime questionnaire. Q87-96.
111. Study cybercrime questionnaire. Q87-96.
112. See above, Section 5.2 Investigative powers overview.
113. Study cybercrime questionnaire. Q99.

114. *Ibid.*
115. *Ibid.*
116. Study cybercrime questionnaire. Q85.
117. Study cybercrime questionnaire. Q84.
118. Study cybercrime questionnaire. Q87-96.
119. See, for example, http://blogs.skype.com/en/2012/07/what_does_skypes_architecture_do.html
120. Study cybercrime questionnaire. Q87-96
121. *Ibid.*
122. *Ibid.*
123. *Ibid.*
124. Study cybercrime questionnaire. Q101.
125. *Ibid.*
126. Study cybercrime questionnaire. Q89-91.
127. *Ibid.*
128. *Ibid.*
129. Study cybercrime questionnaire. Q102.
130. *Ibid.*
131. *Ibid.*
132. See, for example, https://www.facebook.com/safety/groups/law/guidelines/ ; http://pages.ebay.com/securitycenter/LawEnforcementCenter.html;http://support.twitter.com/articles/41949-guidelines-for-law-enforcement# ; and http://myspace.desk.com/customer/portal/articles/526170-law-enforcement-support
133. See Chapter Eight (Prevention), Section 8.3 Cybercrime prevention, the private sector and academia, Cybercrime prevention by internet service and hosting providers.
134. Study cybercrime interviews (private sector).
135. Study cybercrime questionnaire (private sector). Q24.
136. Study cybercrime questionnaire (private sector). Q26.
137. Study cybercrime questionnaire (private sector). Q24-27.
138. Study cybercrime questionnaire (private sector). Q24.
139. Study cybercrime questionnaire (private sector). Q24-27.
140. *Ibid.*
141. *Ibid.*
142. Study cybercrime questionnaire (private sector). Q30.
143. Study cybercrime questionnaire (private sector). Q35.
144. Study cybercrime questionnaire (private sector). Q28.
145. Study cybercrime interviews (private sector). Q28.
146. *Ibid.*
147. See, for example, http://www.google.com/transparencyreport/userdatarequests/legalprocess/
148. Study cybercrime questionnaire (private sector). Q28.

149. *Ibid.*
150. House of Lords and House of Commoners. *Draft Communications Data Bill Joint Committee—First Report.* Section 6 (Jurisdictional issues—Requests addressed to overseas CSPs), 28 November 2012.
151. Study cybercrime questionnaire (private sector). Q28.
152. See http://www.google.com/transparencyreport/userdatarequests/
153. Study cybercrime questionnaire. Q103.
154. *Ibid.*
155. *Ibid.*
156. Study cybercrime questionnaire (private sector). Q40–45.
157. Study cybercrime questionnaire. Q103.
158. Study cybercrime questionnaire. Q103.
159. *Ibid.*
160. See above, Section 8.3 Privacy and investigative measures, Existence of privacy protections and procedural safeguards.
161. See, for example, http://www.edri.org/edri-gram/number6.24/bulgarian-administrative-case-data-retention
162. Katz, C.M., Maguire, E.R., Roncek, D.W., 2002. The Creation of Specialized Police Gang Units. *Policing,* 25(3):472–506.
163. Mace, R.R., 1999. *Prosecution Organizations and the Network of Computer Crime Control.* (Doctoral dissertation). AAT 9920188.
164. Study cybercrime questionnaire. Q113.
165. *Ibid.*
166. Study cybercrime questionnaire. Q113.
167. *Ibid.*
168. *Ibid.*
169. Study cybercrime questionnaire. Q109.
170. *Ibid.*
171. *Ibid.*
172. Study cybercrime questionnaire. Q115.
173. Calculations based on Study cybercrime questionnaire. Q115; and United Nations Survey of Crime Trends and Operations of Criminal Justice Systems, latest available year.
174. Study cybercrime questionnaire. Q116.
175. *Ibid.*
176. Study cybercrime questionnaire. Q118.
177. Study cybercrime questionnaire. Q120.
178. Ibid.
179. Ibid.
180. Ibid.

'We Don't have These Laser Beams and Stuff Like That'

Police Investigations as Low-Tech Work in a High-Tech World

BY JOHNNY NHAN AND LAURA HUEY

Introduction

In recent years, law enforcement has increasingly adopted advanced technologies—such as DNA identification, geographic information systems (GIS) and digital forensics—into their crime control repertoire. These cutting-edge technologies have enhanced the perception of police as twenty-first-century high-tech crime fighters. Popular police investigative television shows, such as *CSI: Crime Scene Investigation* and *Law and Order*, have perpetuated this positive image. In these representations of technopolicing, technologies are the main, if not the only, force shaping police work and its outcomes. They increase the speed, the effectiveness and, through the authority of science, the legitimacy of police investigations—they produce incontrovertible evidence and make cases defence-proof.

Johnny Nhan and Laura Huey, "Chapter 6: We Don't Have These Laser Beams and Stuff Like That': Police Investigations as Low-Tech Work in a High-Tech World," *Technocrime, Policing, and Surveillance*, pp. 79-90.

Despite the plethora of media images depicting police investigational work as increasingly reliant on technological advances, previous research into both front-line and investigative policing suggests that the reality of this work is signifi-cantly different from the technology-driven images of policing frequently seen (Brodeur, 2008; Manning, 2003). Within this chapter we argue that, despite the adoption of seemingly sophisticated technologies and methodologies, police investigational work remains relatively *low-tech*. To illustrate our point, we examine two areas of police investigation that have drawn considerable popular attention: forensic science and digital evidence. What our research reveals is that the police is a slow-moving institution that continues to favour more traditional approaches to policing. Indeed, law enforcement is shown to be—for cultural, resource and other related reasons discussed—reluctant to undertake complex and expensive investigations that require the forensic and digital techniques commonly performed in popular television shows and movies—often viewing such efforts as largely unnecessary and, at best, merely corroborative. The factors identified, singly and combined, suggest that regardless of the high-tech nature of crime and crime control instruments adopted by police, investigations remain relatively low-tech work.

This chapter is presented as follows. First, we briefly offer an overview of the methods used to acquire the data which informs our work. Then we turn our attention to the use of forensic techniques, drawing upon interview data with police investigators to show that their work remains relatively grounded in traditional modes of evidence gathering. This discussion is followed by an examination of data drawn from a study on cyber-policing that demonstrates the extent to which this form of 'high-tech policing' remains low-tech work. The chapter concludes with some final remarks.

Method of Inquiry

This chapter is informed by data drawn from two studies. The first study, carried out by Huey in 2007 (published in 2010), resulted in the collection of data from in-depth qualitative interviews conducted with 31 police officers from seven Canadian municipal and regional police departments (Huey, 2010). Interviewees were police personnel from one of two occupational groups: investigators (from homicide, sex crimes, major crimes and robbery units) and Forensic Identification officers.[1] Interviews ranged in length from one to two hours and each interviewee was asked a series of questions based on two research questions:

1. To what extent do television portrayals of police investigative work cohere with actual police roles and functions?

2. Do police officers perceive television programmes, in particular *CSI*, as influencing public expectations in the field in relation to their investigative role and work duties?

To analyse the data collected, interview transcripts were printed, read and then manually coded according to themes identified during interviews. To ensure reliability, as well as to identify emergent sub-themes, transcripts were re-read and manually re-coded two further times.

The second study, conducted by Nhan from 2005 to 2007, examines high-tech and cyber-policing efforts in California (Nhan and Huey, 2008; Nhan, 2010), where 52 participants were drawn using convenience and snowball sampling. In-depth face-to-face and telephone interviews were conducted with: federal, state, and local law enforcement investigators and prosecutors (n = 22); California state representatives (n = 2); and private industry security professionals from the film industry (n = 10) and the technology sector (n = 18). Police investigators were members of a network of five regional high-tech crimes task forces located throughout the state. Some private industry representatives participated as members of the state-run High-Tech Crimes Advisory Committee (HTCAC). These task forces are part of the High Technology Theft Apprehension and Prosecution Program that handles a majority of California's high-tech and cybercrime needs. Several industry security professionals in the technology sector that were handling security duties in Califor-nia were interviewed in Washington and Arizona. In addition, several steering committee meetings were observed in order to gain additional insight into the interactions and structural frictions that occur within the security mesh of cyber security practitioners, law enforcement and the state.

This second study explored how cyber investigations are conducted in order to identify structural, cultural and legal variables that affect policing high-tech and cybercrimes. Subjects were asked semi-structured questions relating to the nature of their work and collaborative relationships. These questions ranged from, 'Do you work with law enforcement and what is the nature of your relationship?' to 'What forms of technologies are you employing during investigations?' answers were then coded into major themes in order to assemble a holistic view of policing cybercrime. This grounded approach allowed for thematic patterns to emerge from in-depth answers, consistent with qualitative inquiry (Lofland and Lofland, 1995). Follow-up interviews were conducted with some subjects to ensure validity.

'I Can't Get a Fingerprint off a Couch': Forensics in Police Work

> There's a lot of stuff, a lot of things that we can do, but let's face it, I'm not gonna pull out the laser for a $200 break and enter.
>
> (Ident officer)

Following the rise in popularity of the *CSI* and *Law and Order* television franchises and media concern over a purported '*CSI* effect',[2] police investigators in seven Canadian agencies were asked a series of questions concerning the extent to which these shows mirror policing realities. The major finding was that none of the 31 officers interviewed felt that these programmes accurately depict any element of the actual investigative process. While the officers raised a number of issues in relation to how these programmes depict their work, when forensic science and the use of technology to aid investigations was discussed, their comments boiled down to three major areas. In essence, reality diverged from television fantasy on the following points: (1) police agencies often lack either the technology depicted or ready access to it; (2) television programmes—*CSI* in particular—present technology and techniques that often do not exist, or do not work in the fashion depicted;[3] and (3) whereas television often depicts science and technology as providing the key to solving a case, police rely on non-technological investigational techniques in most situations and deem scientific solutions as either unnecessary or as only playing a supporting role in the investigational process.

High-tech crime-fighting tools readily available in television shows are often a rarity among police departments. When Huey (2010) conducted fieldwork for a study that looked at policing in San Francisco, she encountered a number of officers, including those in the San Francisco Police Department's (SFPD) investigational section, who decried the lack of available technology to assist them in performing even some of the most basic of work tasks. Some frontline officers complained about receiving phone messages on antiquated 'pink slips', and others noted that in place of computerised geographic information systems (GIS) to track crime hot spots, personnel used pushpins on maps. While the lack of access to GIS or automatic messaging systems was not found to be the case with the police agencies that participated in the present study, interviewees routinely complained about discrepancies between what television programmes depict as routine crime-fighting tools and the resources to which the police actually have access. For example, one of the most prominent myths that police officers consistently referenced was the false belief that DNA testing can quickly and easily provide solutions to even the most complex of cases. On *CSI* and similar television shows, the results of a DNA test appear on a computerised screen in a matter of moments. As the following extract from an interview with the head of a general investigation unit reveals, the speed with which results are produced on television is misleading and, even with the introduction of automated technology to speed the process, investigators must contend with laboratory backlogs:

R: Purely scientifically, my understanding from the lab experts is that it would take three days. If you gave them a known sample, currently brought them a DNA sample for comparison, by the time that it 'cooks up' and they're able to achieve results, it's three days.
Q: But realistically?
R: Months.

It is worth noting that this result is not unusual in Canada. The laboratory which the respondent was referencing was the Royal Canadian Mounted Police (RCMP) E-division laboratory in British Columbia. In his own study of 'scientific policing' in Quebec, Jean-Paul Brodeur (2008) notes similar results in relation to the provincial police laboratory operated by the *Sûreté du Québec*.

The instantaneous forensic results depicted on several television programmes are the product of computerised databases that permit fingerprint or DNA profile matching. Forensic Identification personnel, who lift and analyse fingerprints from crime scenes in Canada, laughed at the depiction of their work as computerised. Officers were clear to state that while databases may be of some use in identifying and narrowing the field of possible matches, the bulk of their work is based on manual labour performed in the Identification offices: 'There's certain aspects, they identify on the TV with a computer, when it sometimes takes us days to compare and identify a fingerprint.' In relation to DNA screening, while such database technology exists in Canada and the United States, lack of funding to get DNA profiles onto the database is an issue. This funding gap is a source of frustration for Forensic Identification personnel:

> Do you know about the funding for the DNA B&E databank? Okay, the federal government said each province gets x numbers of dollars per year to send profiles to Ottawa, and then Ottawa will look at the DNA for B&E's (break and enters) and compare it to the databank. We were given two hundred profiles. Well, the first two months, we had twenty-four hundred B&Es.

Further, while it is the case that larger police forces have more readily available access to forensic technologies, regional and municipal disparities in access are an issue as not every police agency is equipped to comparable levels. As one senior Identification officer noted:

> We look at this section and say: 'hey, we could use a lot more', but there are some there who don't even have a forensic light source. They have to call in the OPP [Ontario Provincial Police] to get a light source or the RCMP to bring in the light source or the chemicals or something into a scene.

Investigators interviewed were also critical of the depiction of technology or forensic techniques that either do not exist or do not function in the ways shown on television. As one frustrated Identification officer explained of *CSI*, 'They get it done in half an hour with their equipment, which doesn't even exist yet.' Another Identification officer laughed over some of the techniques portrayed in relation to the photographing of crime scenes: 'Their photography [on *CSI*] kills me, just kills me. How could you take that photograph from there?' Others were amused by the elaborate crime scene re-enactment scenarios their television counterparts engage in:

> Well the very first episode I saw was one where they were trying to track the path of some bullets or some projectile that had bounced around, and they had lasers set up and little mirrors all around the room and you could see the laser light everywhere you looked along its path. In real life you can't see it until it strikes the surface at ninety degrees; it doesn't illuminate the mirrors. So I kind of imagined them going around with—you know, this was digitally produced—but I kind of imagined them going around with chalkboard erasers, just to make dust, so you could see the path of this stuff.

From an interview with another Identification officer:

R: It's entertaining to watch it, though. It doesn't take very long for the episode to get so bizarre that it's funny. And then we can joke about it the next time we see each other at work, about some of the amazing things that they can do.

Q: Like what?

R: There was the famous episode where they identified the bad guy from the reflection from someone's eyeball at a bank machine.

R: Oh I hadn't heard about that.

R: They could see because they had the person at the bank machine on tape—who was later found dead—but they could tell that they kept looking off to the side and they zoomed in on the pupils and they saw the reflection of the killer. They folded it over double, profiled it and identified somebody right away. That one, and fingerprints off the eyelids from when they closed their eyes ... [*groans*].

In relation to the depiction of police investigative work on television generally, each of the interviewees agreed that a central problem with how their work is portrayed is that there is an increasing trend towards depicting forensic science as providing the ultimate solution to even the most complex of cases. In reality, investigations are multi-disciplinary efforts that rely, in large part, on the various skill sets of the investigative team, including the inter-personal skills of the investigators. As one homicide investigator explained, 'Policing is a people job ... from the rookie on the street to what we're doing here. You have to be able to get people to tell you what happened.' A senior homicide investigator in the same unit noted,

> The concept that a homicide investigation or a major crime investigation can be done almost exclusive of anything else, but forensics, is ridiculous. That seems to be what permeates these shows ... but it doesn't work that way. Very few cases are ever solved based on one discipline. It's done, put together, through multiple disciplines. Forensics tends to be corroborative, not the silver bullet that puts the case away.

Police interviewees were also quick to dispel the belief perpetuated through mass media that forensics—DNA analysis in particular—conclusively solve crimes irrespective of the efforts of police investigators:

> DNA's a powerful tool and because of all the publicity around DNA there's these expectations that it's the be-all, end-all ... . It doesn't speak to motive. It doesn't speak to opportunity always. It's often not conclusive in itself. It's corroborative in nature. In other words, if I get blood off a victim in a suspect's car, that only proves that the suspect probably transferred some of that blood from the scene to the suspect's car. It doesn't say what he did. It doesn't say if he was the only participant. It doesn't speak to any of those questions. We have to determine that through other means of investigation. You'll rarely see those types of issues addressed in those shows. The fact that they link two people is enough to charge them with these crimes on these shows and it's not realistic. There's different elements to offences. There's murder. There's manslaughter. Second degree, first degree murder. People's motives and their intent, which has to be proven as part of those offences, is critical to those prosecutions. Forensics doesn't give us that, often.

Indeed, the respondents in the present study tended to support the view, as expressed by some of the UK officers sampled by Carole McCartney (2006) for her own study of the role of forensics in criminal investigation, that the ability of forensics to 'solve crimes' has been overstated in the media and elsewhere.

The present study reveals that police investigators continue to depend on traditional investigative techniques rather than relying on forensics to assist in clearing cases. For example, investigators frequently rely on their own 'reading' of a crime scene based on experience, interviewing victims and witnesses, searching through police occurrence reports and so on. Thus, the real work of the police investigator often bears little resemblance to his or her fictional counterpart. While such a finding flies in the face of a plethora of mass media accounts of the purportedly increasing use of technology to solve criminal cases, we note that it does accord with similar results obtained by Brodeur (2008) in his study of police investigational records in Quebec (see also Manning, 2003). As Brodeur states of his own research, 'scientific policing and forensics played no immediate role in identifying and locating suspects' (Brodeur, 2008: 184). Whereas Brodeur finds that investigational technology is employed in relation to 'cold cases' (as do we), the respondents in the present study noted a slightly more significant use of forensic science in relation to their work: once a suspect has been identified through traditional means, forensic evidence can serve to corroborate other evidence gathered through traditional investigative techniques.

Our findings are also consistent with other current research, which shows that DNA evidence is used very sparingly by police departments. Schroeder and White (2009) examined 593 New York City Police Department (NYPD) homicide case files from 1996 to 2003 to show the extent of the use of DNA evidence in homicide cases and the likelihood of its effect on case clearance. They found that more than half the cases (54.5 per cent) did not require DNA collection and only in a handful (6.7 per cent) of cases was DNA evidence collected, analysed and made available for the investigation. They concluded that 'DNA evidence was largely irrelevant to pre-arrest homicide investigations conducted by the NYPD during the study period' (ibid.: 326).

One possible explanatory framework is 'organisational resistance', where 'detectives would resist the infusion of new techniques into their investigative repertoire, choosing instead to rely on more "tried and true" traditional methods such as interviewing witnesses and following investigative leads' (ibid.: 323). Our findings are further supported by work from Pratt *et al.* (2006), who examined over 96,000 national unsolved cases in the United States and found that over 50 per cent had potentially viable DNA evidence that was never tested due to lack of expertise, cost and processing time. In short, the present study adds to a growing body of research that points to the continued use of low-tech policing solutions in police work, as well as towards both cultural and structural explanations as to why police investigational work remains largely low-tech.

Perhaps, then, cybercrime—crimes that are inherently high-tech in nature—would require a technological approach that would necessitate fundamental changes to police investigations.

The second study in this chapter, however, suggests that even in cyber cases, police investigations remain fundamentally unchanged.

'The Easiest Way to Solve a Crime is not Technical': Cyber Investigations

In the field of cybercrime, crime scene investigations entail translating ubiquitous digital information into an actual transaction in physical space. Law enforcement's primary role in cybercrime is therefore to reconstruct a decentralised virtual crime scene into more simple categories that can be understood legally. This reconstruction is the only high-tech part of an investigation in that it requires technical knowledge in order to transform the technical language of internet protocol (IP) addresses—the internet equivalent of a telephone number—to physical locations. Before this crucial step, cybercrime remains in an abstract form, foreign to the law. After this transformation, it is capable of being processed like any other type of case in terms of investigations and legal sanctions.

In California, the general public can report a cybercrime to their local police department, who will then refer the case to the task force. The task-force investigator reconstructs a digital trail of IP addresses from the victim's computer back to the perpetrator. The officer then must present a warrant to the internet service provider (ISP) to release the physical address and owner of the internet account. In effect, they need to use traditional investigative skills to create evidentiary links between specific individuals and criminal acts. During an interview, a special prosecutor assigned to a task force underscored the importance of traditional police experience for 'preserving the chain of proof':

> While it is possible to trace IP addresses back to the origin, it is difficult to prove who was actually on the keyboard at the time of the incident. This part takes a lot of traditional police work … . This can only be obtained via experience from street patrol and detective work.

As Maguire (2005: 368) suggests, ultimately the goal of a criminal investigation is to be able to translate ' "social reality" into a "legal reality" that can be dealt with by prosecutors and the courts.' This is no less the case with respect to the investigation and prosecution of cybercrimes.

Even sophisticated hacking cases are handled using the transformative formula which deciphers abstract spaces into physical 'entities' and 'places' for legal purposes. Indeed, this process was observed during fieldwork conducted with a federal agency that specialises in unauthorised network intrusion cases. Hacking cases are often perceived as extremely difficult because victims and perpetrators are widely dispersed and the crimes committed usually span across many national and international jurisdictions. To solve a case, federal agents begin by mapping transactions in cyberspace to actual physical locales through IP tracing. The investigators then visually map the crime scene using a low-tech solution: onto a dry-erase board, drawing links geographically (location of networks, servers, victim locations and sources of emails). Electronic activity logs obtained from ISPs identify additional victim locations. From this information, a second map is created to plot connections to victim computer systems and networks. These victims are then contacted to obtain further information to assist in assembling the virtual crime scene. A third 'relational' map is constructed from chat-room conversations between hackers and undercover agents. This map identifies a network of individual relations, motives and additional attack patterns. A timeline is plotted against these maps to create a complete legal framework. The end product is a case that links perpetrators with victims within a familiar prosecutorial structure (*actus reus, mens rea*, concurrence, causation and harm) that can be understood by non-technical legal actors and lay jurors.

Another area that highlights the relatively low-tech institution of police work, even within high-tech crimes task forces, is in relation to unsuccessful efforts to establish a centralised database of internet-based criminal activity. The High Tech Crime Intelligence Database Project was conceived for two main objectives: an internet-based portal for storing information such as documents and photos, and a secure information-sharing component.[4] Unfortunately, the project has stalled despite funding, prompting one task-force supervisor to write it off entirely, stating: 'One of the written goals of the task forces is "maintain a database"; this part is obsolete.'

When cyber-investigators are asked about the types of factors that variously aid or impede their work, what they frequently point to is not the desire for newer or greater technologies, but a need for strengthened social relations within and across law enforcement, the private sector and the public. The network infrastructures that the investigators desire to expand and improve are not computer-based, but are human social networks. Indeed, one investigator summed up the importance of collaborative arrangements for cyber cases when he stated that 'building networks is key; set up trusted network of individuals. All investigations are based on trust.' Another investigator underscored the importance of partnerships—'everyone will incorporate civilians. You have to'—while downplaying the use of a computer database as the means to achieve this end—'It hasn't reached the *CSI* level yet ... the easiest way to solve a crime is not technical.'

Conversely, cultural and structural frictions between policing agencies—lack of trust—limits the ability and willingness of agencies to jointly invest and share in potential technological solutions to investigational problems. In speaking of the possibility of a fully operational centralised cybercrime database, a supervising task-force prosecutor pointed out that inter-agency friction and competition represents a significant barrier:

> The database they had was supposed to unify the task forces, which is not practical because we work in the realm of *all* the jurisdictions of the crime, and if all you have is the information that the other taskforces have, then chances are you're going to miss something.

Moreover, turf issues in relation to control over the technology and its use create further tensions. A state emergency services coordinator explained, 'there's a whole thing about control. I know counties don't like other counties messing with their business, but it's a growing problem. It's just getting worse and worse.'

Structural and cultural frictions that prevent the creation of a shared database at the local level can also be seen to extend to local agencies' relations with federal law enforcement. For example, one task-force investigator dismissed technological impediments as the main reason in failing to establish a database by pointing to a longstanding conflict between federal and state/local agencies:[5]

> The disconnect is with the federal government. Hoover's FBI agent would be a college graduate. He did that for a reason; he didn't want agents to have connections with local law enforcement. Some agencies are better, but FBI agents can be promoted off a good case. The incentive to share information is not there. There's an ego and attitude associated with crime. They're trained that way and that's the way they work. It's a very one way street.

Another significant factor in cyber-policing is that high-tech and cyber crimes are often marginalised within the law enforcement community, where such work is seen as competing with traditional crimes for prioritisation and funding. Perhaps not surprisingly then, complex cybercrimes often draw apathy from the vast majority of the policing community. Marc Goodman (1997) cites several reasons why police are apathetic towards computer crime. 'Real' police work has a potential for danger. Even ranking officers who no longer perform dangerous duties are given derogatory stigma, such as 'desk jockey' and 'station queen' (Goodman, 1997; Herbert, 2001). It was found that police recruits that are drawn to police work cite the desire to 'arrest bad guys' or 'help people' (Herbert, 2001: 478). Moreover, police are generally technophobic (Goodman, 1997; Huey, 2002). A task-force investigator explains: 'Cops don't like doing this. Cops want to go out and find the drug dealer and dope dealer. White-collar and cybercrime, a lot of cops back away because they don't know.' One supervisor voiced his frustration at the lack of attention his division was receiving:

Q: Why does your department, consisting of thousands of members, only have a small division handling cybercrime?
R: You hit the nail on the head. Less than one per cent of the force deals with such a growing problem of high technology. To underutilize such resources doesn't make sense.

As the present study makes evident, despite their specialisation and technical training, cybercrime task force investigators remain bounded by cultural and structural constraints of policing. Task forces generally prefer crimes that are online manifestations of street crimes that fit with existing police investigative methods. Indeed, echoing Huey's homicide investigators, a cybercrime investigator described his work as fundamentally low-tech police work: 'The problem is tracking the person,' he explained, 'that's where good old-fashioned detective skills come in place.'

Conclusion

Studies of police investigative work have led scholars to conceptualise the investigative process variously as a form of 'sense-making' (Innes, 2005), ate an alleged offender's journey through the maze of American criminal justice' by a process by which the investigator converts information gathered about a crime into an account of what happened that has both legal and social meanings (Alpert and Dunham, 1997: 11; Maguire, 2005). A significant component of the investigation process in most cases is the analysis of the crime scene. The use of technologies and procedures to 'interpret and process' a crime scene provides information 'that contributes in some way to the investigators' understanding of the incident, how it happened, and who was involved' (Alpert and Dunham, 1997: 175). This role, despite the seemingly high-tech nature of any crime or advanced technologies used during investigations, remains fundamental to police work and has not changed.

What this chapter—based on two different studies of the role of technology in policing—reveals is that despite technological advances in crime control technologies, such as DNA matching and new high-tech environments for crime, much of police investigational work remains fundamentally low-tech in nature. In contrast to popular media depictions, not only do police not necessarily embrace cutting-edge crime-control technologies, but in many instances officers tend to avoid high technologies or downplay their utility, preferring instead to rely on those skills that are seen as part of the repertoire involved in 'good old-fashioned detective work.' Such views are reinforced through structural limiters in technology use, such as DNA forensics (see Pratt *et al.*, 2006), and through cultural *habitus* (Huey, 2002).

The evidence presented in this chapter does not contradict the argument that the adoption of new crime-control technologies has transformed many aspects of policing. It does, however, show that despite advanced technologies, the vast majority of policing remains fundamentally unchanged at its core. Yet technopo-licing remains a central theme in contemporary media reports and in fictional accounts—as well as in the public image of expertise, leadership and innovation that most police organisations try to project.

Notes

1. In various jurisdictions in the United States, Ident personnel would be known by the term 'crime scene investigator.'
2. This is the phenomenon of elevated expectations of police forensic science created by television crime programmes. For a discussion of this topic, see Cole and Dioso-Villa (2007) and Shelton (2008).
3. We issue a caveat here: although we have found similar circumstances while examining police jurisdictions in the United States (Huey, 2010), we note that some police agencies may not face the same issues as the Canadian investigators interviewed for this study, or may utilise forensic technology in their work to a greater extent than the officers studied.
4. High Tech Crime Intelligence Database Project Request for Application. See www.oes. ca.gov.
5. For discussion of this subject, see Geller and Morris (1992) and Baker (1999).

References

Alpert, G. P. and Dunham, R. G. (1997). *Policing Urban America* (3rd edn). Prospect Heights, IL: Waveland Press.

Baker, Jr, J. S. (1999). 'State police powers and the federalization of local crime.' *Temple Law Review*, 72, 684–687.

Brodeur, J.-P. (2008). 'Scientific policing and criminal investigation.' In Leman-Langlois,

S. (ed.), *Technocrime: Technology, Crime and Social Control* (pp. 169–193). Portland, OR: Willan.

Cole, S. A. and Dioso-Villa, R. (2007). 'CSI and its effects: media, juries and the burden of proof.' *New England Law Review*, 41(3), 435–470.

Ericson, R. (1982). *Making Crime: A Study of Detective Work.* Toronto: University of Toronto Press.

Geller, W. A. and Morris, N. (1992). 'Relations between federal and local police.' *Crime and Justice*, 15, 231–348.

Goodman, M. (1997). 'Why the police don't care about computer crime.' *Harvard Journal of Law and Technology*, 10(3), 466–495.

Herbert, S. (2001). ' "Hard charger" or "station queen?" Policing and the masculinist state.' *Gender, Place & Culture: A Journal of Feminist Geography*, 8(1), 55–72.

Huey, L. (2002). 'Policing the abstract: some observations on policing cyberspace.' *Canadian Journal of Criminology*, July, 243–254.

Huey, L. (2010). ' "I've seen this on *CSI*": criminal investigators and the management of public expectations in the field.' *Crime, Media, and Culture*, 6(1), 49–68.

Innes, M. (2005). *Investigating Murder: Detective Work and the Police Response to Criminal Homicide.* Oxford: Oxford University Press.

Lofland, J. and Lofland, L. H. (1995). *Analyzing Social Settings: A Guide to Qualitative Observation and Analysis* (3rd edn). Belmont, CA: Wadsworth Publishing.

McCartney, C. (2006). *Forensic Identification and Criminal Justice: Forensic Science, Justice and Risk.* Cullompton: Willan Publishing.

Maguire, M. (2005). 'Criminal investigation and crime control.' In Newburn, T. (ed.), *Handbook of Policing* (pp. 363–393). Portland, OR: Willan.

Manning, P. K. (2003). *Policing Contingencies.* Chicago: University of Chicago Press.

Nhan, J. (2010). *Policing Cyberspace: A Structural and Cultural Analysis.* New York: LFB Publishing.

Nhan, J. and Huey, L. (2008). 'Policing through nodes, clusters and bandwidth.' In Leman-Langlois, S. (ed.), *Techno-crime: Technology, Crime, and Social Control* (pp. 66–87). Portland, OR: Willan.

Pratt, T. C., Gaffney, M. J., Lovrich, N. P. and Johnson, C. L. (2006). 'This isn't *CSI*: estimating the backlog of forensic DNA cases and the barriers associated with case processing.' *Criminal Justice Policy Review*, 17, 32–47.

Schroeder, D. A. and White, M. D. (2009). 'Exploring the use of DNA evidence in homicide investigations: implications for detective work and case clearance.' *Police Quarterly*, 12(3), 319–342.

Shelton, D. E. (2008). 'The "CSI effect": does it really exist?' *NIJ Journal*, 259. Available at www.ojp.usdoj.gov/nij/journals/259/csi-effect.htm (accessed 15 January 2010).

CHAPTER 3

Conclusion, References, and Review

The dark figure of cybercrime is a problem that needs to be addressed by law enforcement officials, policymakers, and researchers alike. Public awareness of cybersecurity measures and reporting incidences of cybercrimes have increased over the past decade, and citizens around the world are indeed less naïve now than they were ten years ago about cyber-related risks; however, the cybercrimes currently reported to police are just the tip of the iceberg. The UNODC (2013) estimates that only one percent of all actual cybercrimes are reported to authorities, which means we really do not have an accurate picture or understanding of the global scope of cybercrime. But how would police be impacted if this dark figure were to significantly decrease, by, say, twenty-five percent over the next two years (meaning the reporting of cybercrimes increased by this amount)? What if the dark figure even decreased by five percent? Would police be able to handle the new flood of cyber-related cases? The readings in this chapter revealed that the answer is more complicated than a simple "no," but one would be remiss to say it wouldn't put even greater pressure on already strained budgets and personnel.

The readings in this chapter also highlighted the realities of the digital revolution in policing. Large-budgeted police departments and federal agencies do have more access to much of the world's latest and greatest investigational technologies than smaller-budgeted agencies; however, the reading from Nhan and Huey (2013) revealed that the majority of police investigations are not driven by the latest technological advancements and instead remain relatively low-tech. These realities of cyber-related police investigations stand in stark contrast to television's fictional depictions of police work that center entire investigations around digital forensic procedures and methods. In reality, forensics are considered by the police to be corroborative tools that assist the officer in the investigative process. Indeed, if digital forensics really were the crux of police investigations, a single case would remain unsolved for years as officers waited for the digital evidence to eventually be processed before proceeding with the investigation. This reality, though, does not make for very exciting television. The final chapter discussed these case-related realities through a legal lens, highlighting the implications of a legal system that lags behind technological advancements, Fourth Amendment concerns regarding electronic searches and seizures, and the expectations of privacy related to digital case evidence.

References

Fafinski, Stefan and N. Minassian. (2009). *UK Cybercrime Report 2009*. Invenio Research Publication, 2009. Retrieved from: https://www.garlik.com/file/cybercrime_report_attachement.

Federal Bureau of Investigation (FBI). *2013 Internet Crime Report*. Report Produced by the FBI and the National White Collar Crime Center. Washington, DC: DOJ Publication, 2014.

McAndrew, William,. (2012). "Is privatization inevitable for forensic science laboratories?" *Forensic Science Policy & Management: An International Journal*. 3, no. 1 (2012): 42-52.

McQuade, Samuel C., III. *Understanding and managing cybercrime*. Boston: Allyn and Bacon Publishing, 2006.

Tilstone, WJ. (1991). "Privatization of forensic science laboratories—six years experience in South Australia." *Journal of Forensic Science Society* 31, no.2 (1991): 187-189.

United Nations Office on Drugs and Crime (UNODC). *Comprehensive Study on Cybercrime*. New York: United Nations Publication, 2013.

Chapter 3 Review

SECTION A

Choose the best match from the list below. Answers are listed at the back of the book.

1. _____ Subscriber data
2. _____ Organizational resistance
3. _____ DNA identification
4. _____ Technopolicing
5. _____ Traffic data
6. _____ Content data
7. _____ Strategic policing objectives
8. _____ Internet Protocol (IP) address
9. _____ Geographical information system (GIS)
10. _____ Tactical policing objectives

A. The basic registration details of computer service users, such as name and address.

B. A high-tech representation of policing promoted by popular police investigative television shows that perpetuates the idea that technologies are the main force shaping police work and its outcomes.

C. Incident-driven objectives that are time sensitive, with an emphasis on preserving evidence and following investigative leads in the short term.

D. The cultural movement whereby law enforcement personnel resist the use of new techniques in their investigative repertoire, choosing instead to rely on traditional policing methods.

E. Threat-driven objectives that relate to longer-term enforcement goals, with a focus on the root causes and circumstances of serious crime

F. The actual content of a communication.

G. Data indicating the origin, destinations, route, time, date, size, duration, or type of a communication made by means of a computer system.

H. The Internet equivalent of a telephone number used by police to transform technical language into a physical location in order to track criminal activity and locate Internet users.

I. A technological investigative tool used to geographically map crime or offender trends.

J. A corroborative forensic technique used to match a suspect's DNA, recovered from fingerprints, blood, and other human organic matter, to a crime scene.

SECTION B

Discussion questions. Answer these questions given the context of the readings in the chapter.

1. Prior to reading this chapter, what were your perceptions of actual police investigations? In light of what this chapter identified as "the CSI effect," have your perceptions of police investigations altered since reading the article? Why or why not?

2. Why do you think that only one percent of actual cybercrimes are reported? What factors do you believe produce this dramatic "dark figure" of cybercrime? Use the readings from this chapter to support your answer.

CHAPTER 4

Cyber Forensics, Policing, and the Law

As previously discussed, laws governing online behaviors lag significantly behind technological innovations. Without a unified definition of "cyberspace" or what constitutes "cybercrimes," these concepts have remained open for legal interpretation on a case-by-case basis in the United States and around the world; however, evidence of this is beginning to change. In recent years, lawmakers have begun to devise more broad legislation to directly address deviant behaviors occurring via the Internet. It may seem unbelievable, but many deviant online acts that we may immediately assume are illegal may or may not have been formally defined as such by the courts. The range of cyber behaviors considered to be against the law varies greatly based on which country you reside in; in many cases, mere unauthorized access to a computer system is not considered illegal (UNODC, 2013). According to the UNODC (2013), sixty percent of countries outside of Europe reported that criminalization of cyber acts was insufficient. In the majority of countries around the world, spam is not considered to be against the law; many more countries outlaw possession of computer-related child pornography than they do computer-based identity theft. In the Americas, more than fifty percent of police departments reported that national laws for criminalization of cyber acts were inadequate—roughly the same percentage as law enforcement agencies in Africa (UNODC, 2013). This underlines the point that the legal struggle with cybercrime is *not* a problem unique to the United States, nor is it a problem unique to specific parts of the world. To further illustrate the fragmented nature of cyber-related legislation, in 2013 it was determined that, among a survey of ninety-seven countries:

- While consensus exists regarding broad areas of criminalization, detailed analysis of the provisions in source legislation revealed divergent approaches (in both national and international cases);
- Offenses involving illegal access to computer systems and data differ with respect

to the object of the offense (data, system, or information) and regarding the criminalization of "mere" access or the requirement for the circumvention of security measures or further intent, such as to cause loss or damage;

- Criminalization of illegal interception differs by virtue of whether the offence is restricted to non-public data transmissions or not, and concerning whether crime is restricted to interception "by technical means" (UNODC, 2013).

To give an example from the United States, consider that prior to 2008, it was *not* illegal to purchase prescription drugs online without a valid prescription (DEA, 2009). Since the passing of the Ryan Haight Act of 2008, however, US pharmacies operating online now have new regulations requiring them to post truthful information as to their physical location, list the US Drug Enforcement Administration (DEA) license numbers of their pharmacists, and get an additional endorsement from the DEA in order to conduct a business over the Internet. The new law also requires online pharmacy customers to have valid prescriptions from a licensed medical doctor; if the prescription is a new prescription (e.g., not a refill), the physician must examine the patient in person before the prescription can be written and subsequently filled online. Finally, the Ryan Haight Act also criminalized the use of the Internet to advertise the illegal sale of a controlled substance. Prior to 2008, it was not specifically illegal to do so.

This discussion brings to light the underlying larger debate behind regulating and legislating online behavior: how do we balance the right to personal privacy with the right to be secure while we surf the web? If the police suspect an individual of stealing online identities through phishing methods, how do searches and seizures (both with and without a warrant) apply to police collecting the electronic evidence? What are our expectations of privacy in terms of e-mails, social media websites, and other daily online activities? The state and federal courts in the United States have begun answering these questions, and are discussed in this chapter in greater detail.

This legal debate also impacts the forensic investigation of evidence related to cybercrimes and how such information is stored and used by law enforcement. Throughout this book, the procedures for collecting, transporting, and preserving digital evidence have been discussed. However, what needs further defining by the courts relates to the life of the stored digital evidence. Storing electronic documents is infinitely easier than storing the same information in hard copy: just picture rooms containing wall-to-wall, floor-to-ceiling, overstuffed file cabinets filled with items like case files, cassette tapes (what are those?!?) containing voice recordings, and personnel files. As an example of the immense electronic storage capacity cheaply available to law enforcement agencies today, consider that in 1996, a two-gigabyte (two billion bytes) hard drive cost approximately $440; in 2006, one could purchase a one-terabyte (one *trillion* bytes) hard drive for the same $440 (Cohen, 2007). Today, in 2014, $440 won't buy you a single hard drive because none are that expensive (aside from high performance enterprise level drives); now, for $440 one could purchase approximately eleven terabytes (*eleven* trillion bytes) of hard drive space. That is 5,500 times more space to house digital evidence in 2014 than we had in 1996, which is a very impressive amount of space for very little money. Think of all the things we could electronically store! But does that mean we should? Because, remember, it also means that now there is more than 5,500 times as much material (i.e., stored evidence) for forensic examiners, attorneys, and police officers to sift through and try to make sense of *per department* (or really, per $440). In addition to investigative issues, the long-term storage of digital evidence housed in databases raises issues of personal privacy. How much information on you should the government be allowed to store, just because they now have cost-effective capabilities of doing so, and for how long can they keep it on electronic file? These are valid questions that are currently being hotly debated and addressed on a case-by-case basis by the courts in the United States, and are discussed in the following readings.

The final chapter in this book elaborates on these various legal topics concerning cyber forensics and policing, to include search and seizure issues, electronic surveillance, and privacy concerns. The majority of the focus in this chapter is on legal matters in the United States; however, the final reading in this chapter takes an international approach. The first reading in this chapter comes from a National Institute of Justice (NIJ) report produced in 2007 that outlines and reviews the various federal US statutes related to search and seizure concerns that are included in the Electronic Communications Privacy Act, and which contain the following components: the Wiretap Act, the Pen Register and Trap and Trace Statute, the Stored Wire and Electronic Communications Act, and the Privacy Protection Act. This reading also addresses

US constitutional issues involved in the collection and use of digital evidence in criminal court procedures and rulings. For each statute, information is provided about what content is included and excluded in the statute, as well as information pertaining to the necessary steps to take in order to procure the sought-after evidence (e.g., through the use of a subpoena, court order, or search warrant). After discussing the general procedural guidelines, applicable provisions, and exceptions for each of the statutes stated previously, the chapter summarizes the general guidelines and options for proceeding when dealing with privileged or proprietary information and the obtaining of records from out-of-state entities. This reading provides a brief introduction to the intricacies of properly obtaining and handling digital evidence by evaluating various legal statutes that monitor, prohibit, and govern the collection of numerous types of evidentiary material.

The second reading in this chapter, by Mark D. Young (2011), discusses how the evolving development of, and dependence on, digital technology affects matters of national security and surveillance policies in the United States. By first providing a brief review and history of US electronic surveillance law—from the first electronic surveillance case (*Olmstead v. United States*) in 1928 to the 2001 Patriot Act revisions to the Foreign Intelligence Security Act of 1978—the inconsistencies become apparent between the rapid evolution of digital technology and the lacking evolution of policy amendments to combat the growing threats of digital-age security risks and to assist in law enforcement investigations. After outlining the development of surveillance law, the reading then discusses legal insufficiencies and the impact of those insufficiencies on national cybersecurity investigations. Matters such as dual citizenship issues, varying definitions of what the term "cyberspace" entails, covert action concerns, and the conception of online privacy are all discussed as issues that must be addressed by the legal community and policymakers if our intelligence agencies are to appropriately and effectively combat cyber security threats. This reading further highlights the insufficiencies of three specific statutes (Electronic Communications Privacy Act, Stored Communications Privacy Act, and the Foreign Intelligence Surveillance Act), while also arguing for necessary amendments to each, to prevent the continuing adverse effects on national security and the hindrance of counterterrorism surveillance efforts.

The third reading, written by Jesika Wehunt (2013), discusses privacy-related legal concerns surrounding the government's ability to store large amounts of data for varying lengths of time. The reading focuses on one type of physical evidence, which currently reigns as the highest standard for forensic analysis in the courts (and its popularity and usage only increases with technological advancements): DNA evidence. While DNA evidence itself is not digital, the forensic processing and storing of test results are housed electronically, and in some cases are stored in large, centralized databases. This reading strives to point out the constitutional issues involved in DNA collection and retention of arrested individuals. Although previously, convicted individuals were required to provide DNA samples for collection and storage, today, in many states, individuals who have simply been arrested are also required to provide DNA samples; if exonerated, those individuals must face a lengthy and legally complex process if they want their samples expunged (i.e., destroyed and deleted from electronic records). First, this reading provides a brief account outlining the history of DNA discovery, forensic usage, and the statutory development regarding the collection, storage, and expunging of DNA samples. Next, Fourth Amendment reasonable expectation of privacy and probable cause issues are addressed, including the "special needs test" and the "totality of the circumstances test," along with the 2011 case of *United States v. Buza*. This was a case, discussed in length in this reading, in which an arrested individual was subjected to DNA collection based on the arresting officer's determination of probable cause rather than a judicial determination. After explaining the potential systematic abusive nature of allowing DNA collection upon arrest and the exacerbation of the problem by current expungement statutes, two statutory amendments—concerning when DNA sampling can be done during an investigation, along with the transition from individual responsibility to state responsibility in expunging DNA samples—are proposed to combat the constitutional deficiencies of current DNA collection and storage policies.

The final reading in this chapter, written by Pauline Reich (2012), brings an international perspective to the discussion of privacy concerns, freedoms, and governmental actions in the digital age. She analyzes various concerns and developments regarding the intricate complexity of finding a suitable and acceptable balance between personal privacy and national security as it pertains to the surveillance of private citizens' online communications. Issues such as constitutional ambiguities related to the domain of cyberspace, specific legal cases associated with privacy and security concerns, current statutes and recent amendments to privacy laws, and comparative evaluations of other countries regarding their privacy and surveillance laws are discussed. Questions and concerns regarding how the Fourth Amendment applies to the protection of online privacy in the United States are presented; to highlight the challenge of this issue and the evolving nature of privacy in an increasingly electronic world, Reich discusses several legal cases and numerous governmental policies related to cyber security measures. From the international perspective, this reading addresses the problem of balancing privacy and security as it pertains to the legal statutes of numerous countries, including Germany, France, Canada, Australia, and the United Kingdom. How these various governments are balancing the defense of their citizens' right to privacy with the protection of their countries' national security through online surveillance are scrutinized, compared, and contrasted. The reading concludes with policy proposals aimed at finding an answer to this complicated situation, but the solution is ultimately left unanswered, with no resolution in sight.

KEY WORDS FOUND IN THIS PART

- Sniffer software
- Internet Service Providers (ISP)
- Network
- Server
- Electronic evidence
- Privilege teams
- DNA Index System (NDIS)
- Combined DNA Index System (CODIS)
- Special master
- EINSTEIN
- Malware Lab Network
- 24/7 Incident Handling and Response Center

Important Court Cases and Statutes in This Part:

- *Olmstead v. United States* (1928)
- *Katz v. United States* (1967)
- *Berger v. New York* (1967)
- *United States v. United States District Court* (1972)
- Foreign Intelligence Surveillance Act of 1978 (FISA)
- PATRIOT Act
- *United States v. Buza* (2011)

Search and Seizure Issues

BY NIJ REPORT

Background

The collection of digital evidence in criminal cases is governed at the Federal and State levels by numerous constitutional and statutory provisions, including statutes that regulate the communications and computer industries and that directly govern the gathering and use of digital evidence. Court decisions and procedural rules also need to be considered.

This chapter discusses several Federal statutes that govern access to and disclosure of certain types of information deemed deserving of special treatment by Congress: the Electronic Communications Privacy Act (which includes the Wiretap Act, the Pen Register and Trap and Trace Statute, and the Stored Wire and Electronic Communications Act) and the Privacy Protection Act. Also reviewed are principles applicable under the Fourth Amendment to the U.S. Constitution. Investigators, examiners, and prosecutors should be familiar with these statutes because their breach may result in evidentiary challenge or civil suit. (Other Federal provisions and State laws are beyond the scope of this guide.)

"Search and Seizure Issues," *Digital Evidence in the Courtroom: A Guide for Law Enforcement and Prosecutors*, National Institute of Justice, pp. 1-15.

Wiretap Act

The Wiretap Act (18 U.S.C. § 2510 et seq.) focuses on the interception of the content of communications while they are in transit. Examples of such interceptions include wiretapping a telephone, placing a listening device or "bug" in a room to pick up conversations, and installing "*sniffer*" software that captures a hacker's instant messages. The Wiretap Act also governs the disclosure of intercepted communications.

The Wiretap Act generally and broadly prohibits anyone in the United States from intercepting the contents of wire, oral, or electronic communications. As a basic rule, the Wiretap Act prohibits anyone who is not a participating party to a private communication from intercepting the communication between or among the participating parties using an "electronic, mechanical, or other device," unless one of several statutory exceptions applies.

One exception is the issuance of an order by a court of competent jurisdiction that authorizes interception. The requirements to obtain such an order are substantial. Violation of the Wiretap Act can lead to criminal and civil liability. In the case of wire and oral communications, a violation by government officials may result in the suppression of evidence. To ensure compliance, an initial determination should be made about whether:

- The communication to be monitored is one of the protected communications defined in the statute.
- The proposed surveillance constitutes an "interception" of the communication.

If both conditions are present, an evaluation should be conducted to determine whether a statutory exception applies that permits the interception.

NOTE: A comprehensive analysis of Federal search and seizure issues can be found in *Searching and Seizing Computers and Obtaining Electronic Evidence in Criminal Investigations* (www.cybercrime.gov/s&smanual2002.htm).

Pen/Trap Statute

The Pen Register and Trap and Trace Statute (18 U.S.C. § 3121 et seq.), known as the *Pen/Trap statute,* governs the real-time acquisition of dialing, routing, addressing, and signaling information relating to communications. Unlike the Wiretap Act, the Pen/Trap statute does not cover acquisition of the content of communications. Rather, it covers the information about communications. The term "pen register" refers to a device that records outgoing connection information. A "trap and trace" device records incoming connection information. For example, a pen register captures the telephone number dialed by an individual under surveillance, while a trap-and-trace device captures the telephone number of the party who is calling the individual under surveillance.

The Pen/Trap statute applies to telephone and Internet communications. For example, every e-mail communication contains "to" and "from" information. A pen/trap device captures such information in real time.

The statute generally forbids the nonconsensual real-time acquisition of noncontent information by any person about a wire or electronic communication unless a statutory exception applies. When no exception to this prohibition applies, law enforcement must obtain a pen/trap order from the court before acquiring noncontent information covered by the statute.

NOTE: Some States have versions of the Wiretap Act that are more restrictive than the Federal act. The Federal act does *not* preempt State laws unless Federal officers are conducting the investigation. State and local law enforcement must comply with any such State act, even if no violation of the Federal Wiretap Act occurs.

In *U.S. v. Councilman*, 418 F.3d 67 (1st Cir. 2005)(en banc), involving the use of delivery software to copy e-mails while those messages existed in the provider's RAM or hard drive pending delivery to the customer, the court ruled that "the term 'electronic communication' includes transient electronic storage that is intrinsic to the communication process, and hence that interception of an e-mail in such storage is an offense under the Wiretap Act." *Id.* at 85.

Stored Communications Provisions of the Electronic Communications Privacy Act

The stored communications chapter of the Electronic Communications Privacy Act (***ECPA***) (18 U.S.C. § 2701 et seq.) provides privacy protections to customers of and subscribers to certain communications services providers. This statute protects records held (e.g., billing) as well as files stored (e.g., e-mail, uploaded files) by providers for customers and subscribers. Depending on the type of provider, ECPA may dictate what type of legal process is necessary

NOTE: Examples of requests for Federal pen/trap orders may be found at *Searching and Seizing Computers and Obtaining Electronic Evidence in Criminal Investigations* (www.cybercrime.gov/s&smanual2002.htm). Some States have versions of the Pen/Trap statute that are more restrictive than the Federal act. The Federal act does not preempt these laws unless Federal ***agents*** conduct the investigation. State and local law enforcement must comply with any such State act, even if no violation of the Federal Pen/Trap statute occurs.

to compel a provider to disclose specific types of customer and subscriber information to law enforcement. ECPA also limits what a provider may and may not voluntarily disclose to others, including Federal, State, or local governments. (For a quick-reference guide to ECPA's disclosure rules, see appendix B.)

ECPA applies when law enforcement seeks to obtain records about a customer or subscriber from a communications services provider (e.g., an ***Internet service provider*** (***ISP***) or cellular phone provider). For example, ECPA may apply when law enforcement seeks to obtain copies of a customer's e-mails from an ISP. ECPA does not apply when law enforcement seeks to obtain the same e-mails from the customer's computer.

Under ECPA, the production of some information may be compelled by subpoena, some by court order under section 2703(d) (discussed below), and some by search warrant. Generally speaking, the more sensitive the information (from basic subscriber information to transactional information to content of certain kinds of stored communications), the higher the level of legal process required to compel disclosure (from subpoena to court order under 2703(d) to search warrant).

As the level of government process escalates from subpoena to 2703(d) order to search warrant, the information available under the less exacting standard is included at the higher level (e.g., a search warrant grants access to basic subscriber information, transactional information, and content of stored communications).

A. Subpoena: Subscriber and Session Information

Under ECPA, law enforcement may use a subpoena to compel a service provider to disclose the following information about the identity of a customer or subscriber, that person's relationship with the service provider, and basic session connection records:

1. Name.
2. Address.
3. Local and long distance telephone connection records, or records of session times and durations.
4. Length of service (including start date) and types of service used.
5. Telephone or instrument number or other subscriber number or identity, including any temporarily assigned ***network*** address.
6. The means and source of payment for such service (including credit card and bank account numbers).

NOTE: Because providers may use different terms to describe the types of data they hold, it is advisable to consult with each provider on its preferred language to make obtaining the information as easy as possible.

Notably, this list does not include extensive transaction-related records, such as logging information that reveals the e-mail addresses of persons with whom a customer corresponded during prior sessions, or "***buddy lists.***"

Court Order Under 2703(D): Other Noncontent Subscriber and Session Information

Law enforcement must obtain a court order under 18 U.S.C. § 2703(d) to compel a provider to disclose more detailed records about a customer's or subscriber's use of services, such as the following:

1. Account activity logs that reflect what Internet protocol (IP) addresses the subscriber visited over time.
2. Addresses of others from and to whom the subscriber exchanged e-mail.
3. Buddy lists.

Law enforcement can also use a 2703(d) order to compel a cellular telephone service provider to turn over, in real time, records showing the cell-site location information for calls made from a subscriber's cellular phone. These records provide more information about a subscriber's use of the system than those available by subpoena, but they do not include the content of the communications.

A Federal magistrate or district court with jurisdiction over the offense under investigation may issue a 2703(d) order. State court judges authorized by the law of the State to enter orders authorizing the use of a pen/trap device may also issue 2703(d) orders. The application must offer "specific and articulable facts showing that there are reasonable grounds to believe that ... the records or other information sought are relevant and material to an ongoing criminal investigation."

Content of Stored Communications

ECPA distinguishes between communications in storage that have already been retrieved by the customer or subscriber and those that have not. In addition, the act distinguishes between retrieved communications that are held by a private provider (e.g., an employer who offers e-mail services to employees and contractors only) and those held by a provider that offers its services to the public generally.

NOTE: In general, ECPA provides more privacy protection for the contents of communications and files stored with a provider than for records detailing the use of a service or a subscriber's identity. Refer to *Searching and Seizing Computers and Obtaining Electronic Evidence in Criminal Investigations* (www.cybercrime.gov/s&smanual2002.htm) for examples of applications for an order under 2703(d).

1. Subpoena: retrieved communications held by private provider.

ECPA applies only to stored communications that a customer or subscriber has retrieved but left on a public service provider's ***server***, if the service provider offers those services to the public (see section IV.C.2). If a provider does not offer such services to the public, no constraints are imposed by ECPA on the provider's right to disclose such information voluntarily.

ECPA does not require any heightened or particular legal process to compel disclosure of such records. For example, ECPA does not apply to a government request to compel an employer to produce the retrieved e-mail of a particular employee if the employer offers e-mail services and accounts to its employees but not to the public generally. Where ECPA does not apply, such information may be available through traditional legal processes.

2. Subpoena or 2703(d), with notice: retrieved communications, unretrieved communications older than 180 days, and other files stored with a public provider.

ECPA applies to stored communications that a customer or subscriber has retrieved but left on the server of a communications services provider if the provider offers those services to the public. Such communications include text files, pictures, and programs that a customer may have stored on the public provider's system. Under the statute, such a provider is considered a "remote computing service" and is not permitted to disclose voluntarily such content to the government.

Law enforcement may use either a subpoena or a 2703(d) court order to compel a public service provider to disclose the contents of stored communications retrieved by a customer or subscriber. In either case, however, law enforcement *must give prior notice of the request to the customer or subscriber.*

NOTE: ECPA may apply if the e-mail being sought resides on the employer's server and has not yet been retrieved by the employee. In this instance, the rules discussed under section IV.C.3 (below) apply.

Another ECPA provision allows law enforcement to delay giving notice to the customer or subscriber when it would jeopardize a pending investigation or endanger the life or physical safety of an individual. If using a subpoena to compel the disclosure of stored, retrieved communications from a public service provider, law enforcement may seek to delay notice for 90 days "upon the execution of a written certification of a supervisory agent that there is reason to believe that notification of the existence of the subpoena may have an adverse result." If using a 2703(d) order, law enforcement may seek permission from the court to delay notice as part of the application for the order.

At the end of the delayed notice period, law enforcement must send a copy of the request or process to the customer or subscriber, along with a letter explaining the delay.

Law enforcement may also use a subpoena or a 2703(d) order with prior notice to compel a service provider to disclose communications that are unretrieved but have been on the server more than 180 days. As a practical matter, most providers will not allow unretrieved messages to stay on a server unaccessed for such a long period.

If law enforcement is using a search warrant or seeking noncontent information, no notice is required.

NOTE: In *Theofel v. Farey-Jones*, 359 F.3d 1066 (9th Cir. 2004), the court ruled that copies of e-mails remaining on an ISP's server after delivery to the customer receive the same protection under ECPA as e-mails stored pending delivery.

3. Search warrant: unretrieved communications.

Unretrieved communications, including voice mail,* held by a provider for up to 180 days have the highest level of protection available under ECPA. ECPA covers such communications whether the service provider is private or public. The service provider is generally not permitted to voluntarily disclose unretrieved communications to the government.

For example, under ECPA an e-mail sent to a customer is considered unretrieved if it resides on the server of the customer's provider (i.e., an ISP or the customer's employer), but the customer has not yet logged on and accessed the message. Once the customer accesses the e-mail (but a copy remains on the server of the provider), the e-mail is deemed retrieved. (Refer to chapter 1, section IV.C.1, of this guide for more details about retrieved communications.)

Law enforcement may seek a search warrant, such as a warrant provided by 2703(a), to compel a service provider to produce unretrieved communications in storage. No prior notice to the customer or subscriber is required.

NOTE: Nonpublic providers may voluntarily disclose subscriber and session information, transactional information, and stored communications and files to the government and others without violating ECPA. Under certain circumstances, public providers may also voluntarily disclose information without violating ECPA. Some States may have applicable laws that are more restrictive than the Federal act. The Federal act does *not* preempt these laws unless Federal agents are conducting the investigation. State and local law enforcement must comply with any such State act, even if no violation of the Federal statute occurs.

Remedy: Civil Damages

Civil damages are the exclusive remedy for nonconstitutional violations of ECPA. Evidence seized in violation of ECPA alone should not be suppressed.

Privacy Protection Act

The Privacy Protection Act (PPA) (42 U.S.C. § 2000aa et seq.) limits law enforcement's use of a search warrant to search for or seize certain materials possessed for the purpose of public dissemination. The protected materials may be either "work products" (i.e., materials created by the author or publisher) or "documentary materials" (i.e., any materials that document or support the work product).

For example, a person who is creating an online newsletter may possess interview notes that could be considered "documentary materials"; the text of the newsletter to be published could be considered a "work product."

If the material is covered by PPA, law enforcement cannot use a search warrant to obtain it. PPA's prohibition on the use of a search warrant may *not* apply when:

- Materials searched for or seized are "fruits" or instrumentalities of the crime or are contraband.
- There is reason to believe that the immediate seizure of such materials is necessary to prevent death or serious bodily injury.
- There is probable cause to believe that the person possessing the materials has committed or is committing a criminal offense to which the materials relate. (Except for the possession of child pornography and certain government information, this exception does not apply where the mere possession of the materials constitutes the offense.)

NOTE: For further information on the Privacy Protection Act, see *Searching and Seizing Computers and Obtaining Electronic Evidence in Criminal Investigations* (www.cybercrime.gov/s&smanual2002.htm).

If evidence of a crime is commingled on a computer with PPA-protected materials, issues concerning proper scope and execution of a search warrant will arise. Recent cases indicate that the courts are limiting the scope of PPA protection to people who are not suspected of committing a crime. Evidence seized in violation of PPA alone will not be suppressed.

Civil damages are the exclusive remedy for violation of PPA.

Constitutional Issues

Searches for digital evidence, like searches for other forms of evidence, are subject to the constraints of Federal and State constitutional search and seizure laws and court rules. Traditional Fourth Amendment principles, such as those governing closed containers, apply to digital evidence.

A. Applying the Fourth Amendment

The Fourth Amendment protects individuals from unreasonable searches and seizures. Two primary requirements are necessary for Fourth Amendment protections to apply:

- Is government action involved?
- Does the person affected have a reasonable expectation of privacy in the place to be searched or thing to be seized?

1. Government action.
   In most circumstances, government action is implicated when a government official conducts a search. Generally speaking, the Fourth Amendment's limitations do not apply to searches by private parties unless those searches are conducted at the direction of the government. Private parties who independently acquire evidence of a crime may turn it over to law enforcement. (Law enforcement may replicate a private search, but may not exceed the scope of that search without a warrant or exception to the warrant requirement.)

For example, if an employee discovers contraband files on a computer that is being repaired in a shop, the employee's subsequent release of information to law enforcement does not violate the Fourth Amendment. In such a case, law enforcement may examine anything that the employee observed.

2. Reasonable expectation of privacy.
   The Fourth Amendment applies when the searched party has an actual expectation of privacy in the place to be searched or thing to be seized, and then only if it is an expectation that society is prepared to recognize as reasonable. Some courts treat a computer as a "closed container" for Fourth Amendment purposes. In some jurisdictions, looking at a computer's subdirectories and files is akin to opening a closed container.

B. Satisfying Fourth Amendment Requirements

If the Fourth Amendment is implicated in the search at issue, then generally law enforcement must obtain a warrant unless an exception to the warrant requirement applies.

1. Warrantless searches.
   There are several well-recognized exceptions to securing a warrant. Although the following is not an exhaustive list, the examples provide an idea of how the common exceptions apply to the search and seizure of digital evidence.
   a. Consent.
      Consent is a valuable tool for an investigator. It can come from many sources, including a log-in banner, terms-of-use agreement, or company policy. Some considerations include:
      i. Like a shared apartment, a computer can have multiple users. Consent by one user is always sufficient to authorize a search of that person's private area of the computer, and in most instances is sufficient to authorize a search of the common areas as well. Additional consent may be needed if an investigator encounters password-protected files. Also, a parent in most cases can consent to a search of a minor child's computer.
      ii. Consent can be limited by subject matter, duration, and other parameters. Consent can be withdrawn at any time (see appendix C for a sample consent form).
      iii. The general rule is that a private-sector employer can consent to a search of an employee's workplace computer. The rules are more complicated when the employer is the government.

NOTE: For further information on consent rules, refer to Searching and *Seizing Computers and Obtaining Electronic Evidence in Criminal Investigations* (www.cybercrime.gov/s&smanual2002.htm).

b. Exigent circumstances.
To prevent the destruction of evidence, law enforcement can seize an electronic storage device. In certain cases in which there is an immediate danger of losing data, law enforcement may perform a limited search to preserve the data in its current state. Once the exigent circumstances end, so does the exception.

c. Search incident to arrest.
The need to protect the safety of law enforcement or to preserve evidence can justify a full search of an arrestee and a limited search of the arrest scene. This search incident to arrest can include a search of an electronic storage device, such as a cell phone or pager, held by the subject.

NOTE: Although a search incident to arrest may allow the search of electronic storage devices found on the suspect, the arresting law enforcement officer should take care to maintain the integrity of the evidence.

d. Inventory search.
The inventory search exception is intended to protect the property of a person in custody and guard against claims of damage or loss. This exception is untested in the courts, so it is uncertain whether the inventory search exception will allow law enforcement to access digital evidence without a warrant.

e. Plain view doctrine.
The *plain view* doctrine may apply in some instances to the search for and seizure of ***electronic evidence***. For plain view to apply, law enforcement must legitimately be in the position to observe evidence, the incriminating character of which must be immediately apparent. Law enforcement officials should exercise caution when relying on the plain view doctrine in connection with digital media, as rules concerning the application of the doctrine vary among jurisdictions.

2. Searches and seizures pursuant to warrants.
If the Fourth Amendment is implicated in a search and none of the search warrant exceptions applies, law enforcement should obtain a search warrant. Generally, the same warrant rules apply when preparing and executing a search warrant for digital evidence as in other investigations. Law enforcement should consider the following when preparing and executing a search warrant for electronic evidence:

   a. Describing property.
   If the evidence sought is the computer itself (and the hardware is an instrumentality, a fruit of the crime, or contraband), then the warrant should describe the computer as the target of the search.

   If the evidence sought is information that may be stored on digital media, then the warrant should describe what that evidence is and request the authority to seize it in whatever form (including digital) it may be stored. This includes requesting authority to search for evidence of ownership and control of the relevant data on the media. Avoid drafting warrants that would unnecessarily restrict the scope of the search.

NOTE: For sample language, see *Searching and Seizing Computers and Obtaining Electronic Evidence in Criminal Investigations* (www.cybercrime.gov/ s&smanual2002.htm).

   b. Conducting a search.
   In some cases, a search of an electronic storage device can require significant technical knowledge and should be conducted by appropriate personnel who are supplied with a copy of the search warrant to ensure that the search is within its scope.

   In the course of conducting a search, law enforcement may discover passwords and keys that could facilitate access to the system and data. Law enforcement may also find evidence of a crime that is outside the scope of the search warrant. In such an event, consider securing another warrant to expand the scope of the search.

   See chapter 2 for more indepth discussion.

NOTE: For a discussion of some of the issues concerning evidence collection, see *Electronic Crime Scene Investigation: A Guide for* ***First Responders*** (www.ojp.usdoj.gov/ nij/pubs-sum/187736.htm).

c. Reasonable accommodations.

In some cases, it might be impractical to search the device onsite. If a device is to be searched offsite, law enforcement should consider adding language to the warrant affidavit that justifies its removal.

If a device is removed for an off-scene search, the search should be completed in a timely manner. Law enforcement may consider returning copies of noncontraband seized data, even if they are commingled with evidence of a crime, to accommodate a reasonable request from suspects or third parties.

See chapter 2 for more indepth discussion.

Privileged or Proprietary Information

In some instances, law enforcement may have reason to believe that the place to be searched will contain information that is considered "privileged" under statute or common law (e.g., the office of a lawyer, health professional, or member of the clergy). Before drafting a warrant and conducting the search, law enforcement should take care to identify and comply with the legal limitations that the jurisdiction may impose. Law enforcement also may wish to:

- Consider the use of ***taint teams*** (also known as ***privilege teams***), ***special masters***, or another process, as approved by the court.
- Consider in advance whether the media to be seized contain privileged or proprietary information.
- Consider obtaining a stipulation before seizing information from the target to avoid confiscating potentially privileged or proprietary information. (See appendix D, "Stipulation Regarding Evidence Returned to the Defendant," for an example.)
- To avoid tainting the acquisition of evidence, ensure that the prosecution team addresses the issue of privileged or proprietary information when drafting the search warrant.

Obtaining Out-of-State Records

A. The Problem

Often the ISP from which State or local law enforcement wishes to obtain records is located outside their State. Of course, for out-of-State entities with a physical presence in the seeking State, service of process on an appropriate local business representative or on a designated agent may be sufficient to acquire jurisdiction over the records. For out-of-State entities who have no physical presence in a State but who are registered as a foreign (out-of-State) business entity or corporation, service on a designated agent may be sufficient.

In other circumstances, the need to obtain records from out-of-State third-party recordholders presents two problems:

1. The seeking State's law may limit the jurisdictional reach of compulsory process, such as subpoenas, orders under 18 U.S.C. 2703(d) ("D-orders"), or search warrants, to its own territorial jurisdiction. Even if there is no explicit law limiting the jurisdictional scope, judges may refuse to issue extraterritorial process.
2. The out-of-State recordholders may refuse to honor process issued from outside the State in which the records are located. Only a few States explicitly require entities located within their territorial jurisdiction to comply with the out-of-State process as if it had been issued in the State. Thus, even if process can be obtained, the out-of-State entity often believes (sometimes correctly) that it is under no legal obligation to comply. Usually this refusal to comply is based on a fear of liability under the ECPA (or, in the case of banks, Federal and State bank privacy laws), i.e., if the warrant is not legally binding then it cannot protect a company from liability for disclosure. In other instances, however, this appears to be more of a "we don't have to so we're not going to" attitude.

NOTE: A few States do require entities within their State to comply with the out-of-State process as if it had been issued in State.

B. Current Options

In the following discussion of current options for obtaining out-of-State records, keep in mind that even if the use of State procedures to obtain out-of-State records is held invalid, there is no suppression remedy under the U.S. Constitution. The only Federal remedy for improperly seized ISP records is statutory under the ECPA, which does not include a suppression remedy for nonconstitutional violations. State constitutional or statutory provisions, however, may provide a State suppression remedy. Current options are discussed below.

1. Persuade the court.
   Unless the seeking State has specific prohibitions against extraterritorial process, the prosecution may attempt to persuade the court to issue such process on the grounds that:

a. There is no specific prohibition on the issuance of such process.
b. There may be State case law recognizing that search warrants can legitimately be served like a subpoena.
c. If the warrant is viewed like a subpoena supported by probable cause, then the issue of whether a domestic (in-State) court can direct peace officers of another State does not arise as the foreign State's peace officers are not involved.
d. As some commentators have argued, local courts have jurisdiction to compel production of evidence located in other States at least to the same extent they have jurisdiction to compel the attendance to trial of out-of-State witnesses.

   The justification for a court's authority to issue warrants for out-of-State records is that the judge is ordering law enforcement to execute the search by faxing or otherwise serving the warrant from the home State on the out-of-State recordholder.

2. Persuade the recordholder.
   Officers from the seeking State who have a validly issued extraterritorial search warrant may be able to persuade an otherwise reluctant out-of-State recordholder to comply. By using some of the same arguments law enforcement used to convince the judge to issue the warrant, law enforcement can attempt to convince the recordholder that (a) the ECPA requires the production of records in response to a lawful search warrant, and (b) the officer has a lawful search warrant. Officers may explain that an entity with a good-faith reliance on process enjoys a complete defense to any civil or criminal action brought under ECPA.
3. Consider other options.
   If a presiding judge refuses to issue an extraterritorial search warrant or a recipient refuses to comply, law enforcement will have to consider other options, such as:

   a. Trial subpoena (if charges have been filed).
   b. Grand jury or other investigative subpoena (prefiling), which does not have territorial limitations.
   c. Trial or grand jury subpoena, used together with the Uniform Act to Secure the Attendance of Witnesses From Without a State in Criminal Proceedings (hereafter referred to as "the Uniform Act").

A subpoena may succeed when a warrant does not. Most States do not have laws directly limiting the jurisdictional reach of subpoenas (and in the case of the Uniform Act, States that have adopted the Act have implicitly or explicitly asserted jurisdiction to issue subpoenas [including subpoenae duces tecum] to residents of other States).

The successful use of a subpoena, however, depends on whether the records sought are obtainable under the ECPA by subpoena as opposed to D-order or search warrant.

The first two subpoenas (trial subpoena or grand jury subpoena) may present the same problem as a search warrant does—the recipient may choose not to comply.

The Uniform Act offers the advantage of the full force of law. Judges have authority to issue subpoenas under the Act, and the recipient must comply. The procedure, however, is cumbersome and time consuming and can only be used to obtain documents when a court hearing is scheduled.

4. "Domesticate" the warrant.

An effective method of getting a valid, enforceable warrant is to prepare an affidavit, send it to law enforcement in the foreign State, and request that that State's law enforcement use the seeking State's affidavit to obtain its own search warrant.

There are several disadvantages to using this process:

- It depends on cooperation from law enforcement in the foreign State.
- It is cumbersome, in that it requires two law enforcement agencies to be involved.
- The seeking State is dependent upon the foreign law enforcement agency's agreement that probable cause for a search exists.

C. Proposed Federal legislation

Federal legislation has been proposed that would require each State to give full faith and credit to the production orders issued by State courts in criminal cases. If enacted, this legislation could be a starting point for a nationwide system allowing States to issue fully enforceable production orders to recordholders in other States. To obtain information on this and other legislation, go to www.ecpi-us.org.

In the meantime, some States have adopted the approach of requiring out-of-State companies registered in State to designate an in-State agent to accept service of in-State process, and requiring companies incorporated in State to accept out-of-State process as if it were issued in State.

Note

1. The USA PATRIOT Improvement and Reauthorization Act of 2005 (P.L. 109-177) made permanent section 209 of the USA PATRIOT Act, which allows retrieval of voice mail with a search warrant rather than an intercept order.

READING ELEVEN

Electronic Surveillance in an Era of Modern Technology and Evolving Threats to National Security

BY MARK D. YOUNG*

The world isn't run by weapons anymore, or energy, or money. It's run by little ones and zeroes, little bits of data. It's all just electrons.[1]

Introduction

Linking hundreds of individual computer networks has created a virtual space on which much of the world's commerce and communication now depends. Electronic mail, peer-to-peer data sharing, Voice-over-Internet Protocol (VoIP), and wireless networks are examples of the technology that enables almost unlimited access to information. This access comes with significant risk. Criminals, terrorists, hostile nation-states, and foreign industrial competitors share this ubiquitous access to information. In the industrial age, we protected ourselves with high walls and long-range weapons; in the digital age, the availability and rapid development of cyber weapons requires layers of defenses and improved awareness of adversarial capabilities and intentions.

Since the first Internet transmission on October 29, 1969 we have been deepening our dependence on digital communications.[2] There are almost two billion users of the Internet.[3] The United States economy depends on it; our critical infrastructure is controlled by it; and our national security is empowered by it, yet vulnerable because of it. Despite our digital dependence, our policy framework, our legal authorities, and our judicial precedent remain underdeveloped.

The cyber security legal landscape is a patchwork of federal and state statutes, federal regulation, and executive branch policy that evolved to address technologies that may no longer exist. Federal government "capabilities and responsibilities are misaligned within the U.S. government."[4] There is no shortage of threats to our information infrastructure. The media has reported that computer-controlled electric power grids are "plagued with security holes that could allow intruders to redirect power delivery and steal data ... ."[5] Other reports claim that the Chinese military is responsible for the highly sophisticated January 2010 attack against Google's corporate network that sought to access the company's source code.[6] According to the Congressional Research Service, "[t]hreats to the U.S. cyber and telecommunications infrastructure are constantly increasing and evolving as are the entities that show interest in using a cyber-based capability to harm the nation's security interests."[7]

This Article will review the history of electronic surveillance authorities, explain how these authorities are relevant to today's cyber security issues, identify the insufficiencies of the three specific laws on this topic, and recommend discrete amendments to these statutes. The text highlights the deficiencies in the authorities governing U.S. government action in cyberspace and argues that specific sections must be amended to enhance cyber security and enable information sharing between the public and private sector. This Article does not address the federal statutes that govern cybercrime. It focuses on cyber security authorities in the national security context, but the legislative changes recommended here will also benefit law enforcement operations.

Evolution of Electronic Surveillance Authorities

The use of computer technology to gain intelligence or as a vector to deny, degrade, or disrupt an adversary's capabilities presents new questions for the laws of electronic surveillance, intelligence collection, and war.[8] In the context of the Fourth Amendment, Professor Orin Kerr of George Washington University Law School notes, "Courts have only recently begun to address these questions, and the existing legal scholarship is surprisingly sparse."[9] What is true of the scholarship in the Fourth Amendment criminal context is doubly true in the national security realm. Current scholarship is either "highly abstract or else focuses only on discrete doctrinal questions."[10]

Since computers and networks are by nature electronic devices, electronic surveillance authorities play an important role in state surveillance for both law enforcement and national security investigations. The history of electronic surveillance law is relevant to understanding how specific statutes are inconsistent with privacy and state investigations. Although there are numerous statutes that regulate government electronic surveillance,[11] this analysis focuses on the Electronic Communications Privacy Act, the Stored Communications Act, and the Foreign Intelligence Surveillance Act:

> Electronic surveillance law in the United States is comprised primarily of two statutory regimes: (1) the Electronic Communications Privacy Act ("ECPA"), which is designed to regulate domestic surveillance; and (2) the Foreign Intelligence Surveillance Act of 1978 ("FISA"), which is designed to regulate foreign intelligence gathering. While other statutes provide additional protection, ECPA and FISA are the heart of electronic surveillance law.'[12]

The Fourth Amendment requires a particularized description of the places to be searched and the things to be seized.'[13] Reasonableness is "the ultimate touchstone of Fourth Amendment legitimacy."[14] Because electronic surveillance authority is such a comprehensive investigatory power, the government's surveillance authority must be tightly controlled. Electronic surveillance records on-line behavior, social contacts, interests, and other activities that may extend beyond intended investigatory matters and for longer than is necessary for the investigatory purpose. The objective of electronic surveillance law is to limit government access to the electronic lives of U.S. citizens, while providing reasonable access for proper investigations. The law seeks to provide "oversight of government surveillance, accountability for abuses and errors, and limits against generalized forms of surveillance."[15]

Eavesdropping has existed since before the founding of the United States.'[16] Electronic communication resulted in the birth of a new form of eavesdropping: electronic surveillance. The U.S. Civil War saw extensive wiretapping of Union and Confederate telegraph wires.[17] On the first day of World War I, the British cable ship *Telconia* severed German transatlantic cables in the North Sea forcing Germany to communicate in ways that the United Kingdom could monitor.

Germany was now forced to communicate with the world beyond the encircling nations of the United Kingdom, France, and Russia by radio or over cables controlled by enemies. Germany thus delivered into the hands of her foes her most secret and confidential plans, provided only that they could remove the jacket of code and cipher in which Germany had encased them.[18]

It was during World War I that the U.S. Congress enacted the first temporary federal wiretap law to prohibit the tapping or disclosure of the contents of telegraph or telephone messages.'[19] After the War, the Radio Act of 1927 prohibited the interception or disclosure of private radio messages.[20]

In 1928, the first electronic surveillance case reached the U.S. Supreme Court. In *Olmstead v. United States,*[21] the Court held that the tapping of telephone wires by federal agents did not violate the Fourth Amendment since there was no "entry of the houses or offices of the defendants," and the agents only obtained the content of their conversations. In other words, no place was searched and no property was seized. Justice Brandeis was prescient in his dissent in *Olmstead,* noting:

> [t]he progress of science in furnishing the Government with means of espionage is not likely to stop with wire-tapping. Ways may someday be developed by which the Government, without removing papers from secret drawers, can reproduce them in court, and by which it will be enabled to expose to a jury the most intimate occurrences of the home.[22]

In the wake of the *Olmstead* opinion, Congress expanded the protections in the Radio Act. With the Federal Communications Act of 1934, wire communications were now also protected.[23] It said nothing, however, about the use of mechanical devices to record in-person conversations. Without this prohibition, Fourth Amendment challenges to electronic surveillance greatly increased and the increasing inventory of court opinions began to erode the trespass reasoning in *Olmstead.*[24]

In 1967, the trespass doctrine in *Olmstead* was replaced by the reasonable expectation of privacy doctrine from *Katz v. United States.25* It was then clear that "wiretapping and electronic eavesdropping are subject to the limitations of the Fourth Amendment."[26] A consequence of this decision is the attachment of the warrant requirement in investigations involving electronic surveillance. "To avoid constitutional problems and at the same time preserve wiretapping and other forms of electronic eavesdropping as a law enforcement tool, some of the states established a statutory system under which law enforcement officials could obtain a warrant, or equivalent court order, authorizing wiretapping or electronic eavesdropping."[27]

However, in the same year, the New York Code of Criminal Procedure, which included detailed electronic surveillance warrant requirements, was struck down by the Supreme Court in *Berger v. New York.*[28] The Court found the statute unconstitutional because it failed to require a description of the place to be searched, the crime to which the search related, and a description of the conversation to be seized. Both *Katz and Berger* persuaded Congress to pass the Omnibus Crime Control and Safe Streets Act of 1968.[29] Title III of the Act generally prohibited wiretapping and electronic eavesdropping, but provided federal and state law enforcement authorities some authority for electronic surveillance, albeit under strict limitations.

There was a national security exception in Title III, however. Section 2511 stated that nothing in the title

> shall limit the constitutional power of the President to take such measures as he deems necessary to protect the Nation against actual or potential attack or other hostile acts of a foreign power, to obtain foreign intelligence information deemed essential to the security of the United States, or to protect the United States against the overthrow of the government by force or other unlawful means.[30]

Congress recognized that law enforcement wiretaps were not the same as the collection of foreign intelligence and that no warrant was required for national security investigations. A decade later, the Supreme Court would invite Congress to more carefully legislate the President's surveillance powers in national security cases.

In 1972, the President's authority to conduct warrantless wiretaps was the issue in *United States v. United States District Court,*[31] where the government monitored a "domestic radical group engaged in a conspiracy to destroy federal government property" without a warrant.[32] The Court acknowledged the government's strong investigative duty in national security matters, but also noted that "Fourth Amendment protections become more necessary when the targets of official surveillance may be suspected of unorthodoxy in their political beliefs."[33] The opinion stated, "Congress may wish to consider protective standards for [domestic security surveillance] which differ from those already prescribed for specified crimes in Title III."[34]

After the Court rejected the claim of inherent presidential electronic surveillance authority in domestic national security cases, Congress amended the President's authority to collect foreign intelligence with the Foreign Intelligence Security Act of 1978 (FISA).[35] "FISA provides a procedure for judicial review and authorization or denial of wiretapping and other forms of electronic eavesdropping for purposes of foreign intelligence gathering."[36] It also created the Foreign Intelligence Surveillance Court as a judicial venue to adjudicate executive surveillance applications, with emergency authority provided to the Attorney General.

After the September 11, 2001 terrorist attacks, FISA was criticized for excessively limiting law enforcement personnel's access to FISA surveillance data.[37] These restrictions became known as the FISA "wall." "[This] wall addressed the concern that law enforcement and prosecutorial personnel might use the FISA instrument, or infornation obtained from FISA surveillance, to either negate the necessity of a Title III order or to develop the probable cause to get one."[38]

Within their response to the September 11 terrorist attacks, known as the PATRIOT Act, Congress sought to remove the wall by changing the FISA certification requirement.[39]

Previous interpretation of FISA meant that the sole-purpose of the surveillance must be to obtain foreign intelligence. "As a result, guidelines since the 1980s and across administrations had limited the extent to which the [Department of Justice] criminal division could direct and receive foreign intelligence surveillance."[40] The PATRIOT Act changed the certification requirement of foreign intelligence collection from a "sole-purpose test"[41] to a "significant-purpose test."AI With this amendment, government officers could now use FISA for electronic surveillance that had both an intelligence and law enforcement objective.

FISA was amended twice more, once in 2007 by the Protect America Act[42] and again in 2008 with the Foreign Intelligence Surveillance Act of 1978 Amendments Act.[43] The 2008 legislation repealed the Protect America Act and remains in effect. It provides authority to collect foreign intelligence on overseas targets,[44] it reaffirms that FISA and Title III are the exclusive authorities for electronic surveillance,[45] and it protects from civil liability commercial entities that assist with government surveillance.[46]

For law enforcement electronic surveillance, Congress amended Title III with the Electronic Communications Privacy Act (ECPA) in 1986.[47] The amended law attempted to balance privacy interests and law enforcement needs, but it also showed Congress's support of the expanding communications technology industry.[48] The statute included "new protection and law enforcement access provisions for stored wire and electronic communications and transactional records access (e-mail and phone records), and for pen registers as well as trap and trace devices (devices for recording the calls placed to or from a particular telephone)."[49] The ECPA enhanced Title III to incorporate new forms of electronic communication, such as e-mail. It also provided protection beyond message transmission to those communications stored in computer systems.[50]

Title II of the ECPA is known as the Stored Communications Act.[51] This section regulates law enforcement access to electronically stored communications[52] and to "subscriber records of various communications service providers, such as [Internet Service Providers (ISPs)]."[53] The law defines electronic storage as "any temporary, intermediate storage" that is "incidental" to the communication and "any storage of such communication by an electronic communications service for purpose of backup protection of such communication."[54] This definition means that e-mail that is on the ISP's computers but has yet to be accessed by the recipient is considered to be in "electronic storage." Once accessed, the recipient may still maintain copies of the e-mail on the ISP's server.

The Stored Communications Act distinguishes communications that have been stored for more than six months. "Government officials may gain access to wire or electronic communications in electronic storage for less than six months under a search warrant issued upon probable cause to believe a crime has been committed and the search will produce evidence of the offense."[55] A warrant is required if the ISP customer or subscriber is not to be notified of the government access to the communications, or government accesses communications older than six months, or communications stored on remote computers.[56]

Electronic Surveillance and Cyberspace

The electronic surveillance authorities discussed above are relevant to national security investigations because computer servers and ISPs are provided privacy protections under U.S. law and there is an expanding possibility that terrorists will hold dual citizenship. An example of the unique circumstances under which federal law enforcement and the American intelligence community must now operate is the status of Anwar al-Awlaki. This radical Muslim cleric was born in New Mexico in 1971. As an illustration of the significance of the dual citizenship issue, there has been recent debate about the Obama administration's authorization for the targeting and killing of al-Awlaki.[57]

These statutes are also relevant to U.S. cyber activities because of the definition of electronic surveillance:

> The acquisition by an *electronic, mechanical, or other surveillance device of the contents of any wire or radio communication* sent by or intended to be received by a particular, known United States person who is in the United States, if the contents are acquired by intentionally targeting that United States person, under circumstances in which a person has a reasonable expectation of privacy and a warrant would be required for law enforcement purposes.[58]

The definition also includes the collection of communications content if it occurs *within* the United States.[59] Thus, if the government wanted to see the content of an e-mail sent from al-Awlaki to a recipient in Saudi Arabia, but collected the e-mail from somewhere within the United States, the collection is electronic surveillance and subject to the limitations of electronic surveillance law. The definition means that national security and law enforcement investigations, which include online monitoring, are subject to the Fourth Amendment and the regulations that have evolved with electronic surveillance authorities.

The final parts of the electronic surveillance definition accommodate the decision in *Katz* incorporating the acquisition of the contents of any communication *"in which a person has a reasonable expectation of privacy and a warrant would be required for law enforcement purposes,* and if both the sender and all intended recipients are located within the United States."[60]

According to a National Defense University International Cyber Security Conference:

> The first requirement when seeking to coalesce cyberspace governance is the recognition that spoken and written words form the foundation of our understanding of cyberspace and its governance. As such we need to come up with clear definitions if effective governance is to exist. We also need a common lexicon and broader understanding of criminal threats, governance tools and what constitutes cyber security.[61]

The cyber lexicon remains confusing. The Department of Defense's *Dictionary of Military and Associated Terms* originally defined cyberspace as "the notional environment in which digitized information is communicated over computer networks."[62] The definition was amended in 2008 to a "global domain within the information environment consisting of the interdependent network of information technology infrastructures, including the Internet, telecommunications networks, computer systems, and embedded processors and controllers."[63]

A new definition of cyber space has been published by the Vice Chairman of the Joint Chiefs of Staff: "[A] [d]omain characterized by the use of electrons and the electromagnetic spectrum to store, modify, and exchange data via network[ed] systems and associated physical infrastructures."[64] There are myriad definitions of cyberspace-and associated terms-that confuse the issues within the federal government.[65]

According to a cyber security workshop hosted by the American Bar Association's Standing Committee on National Security, the National Strategy Forum, and the McCormick Foundation, "the laws of intelligence collection have applicability to our cyber activities in two contexts: as rules of authorization and limitation within the domestic sphere and as rules of public disclosure."[66] The workshop report acknowledges the intelligence community's concerns about cyber vulnerabilities that may enable adversarial cyber intrusions. The intelligence community may share cyber vulnerability information within the U.S. government, but current law prohibits the government from disclosing the same information to the private sector. In the cyber domain-most of which is owned by the private sector-information sharing between the government and private sector is largely prohibited. "This is one legal area that clearly requires work."[67]

The definitions of cyber space are illustrative of the different understandings held by different parts of the government. It is difficult to discuss the privacy, policy, and legal issues surrounding the national security sector's cyber activities if no one agrees on what cyber space is. The inconsistent understanding compounds the challenge of discussing how electronic surveillance should be regulated. Cyber investigations are a significant instrument for monitoring terrorist and adversarial state activity, but without at least a general understanding of cyber space and how much government activity is appropriate in cyber space, we are less secure and may be providing criminals and terrorist an online sanctuary.

Legal Insufficiencies

The government is attempting to protect national interests from myriad cyberspace threats and shift its organizational structures to better manage its limited cyberspace resources. It is doing this, however, without adjusting one of the biggest cyber vulnerabilities facing the country: insufficient legal authorities to allow federal action in the cyber domain. According to the Quadrennial Defense Review (QDR) Independent Panel, established by Congress "to review the QDR, assess the long term threats facing America, and produce recommendations regarding the capabilities which will be necessary to meet those threats,"[68] national security planners must use a comprehensive approach to address current threats. The panel recommended a review and restructure of the laws governing the armed forces and national defense. To better address cyber threats aligning against U.S. interests, criminal statutes must be included in any analysis that seeks to improve interagency coordination and clarification of departmental and agency authorities and responsibilities.

The first and most significant cyber policy issue in the national security arena concerns covert action. There is ongoing debate among government lawyers about the Pentagon's legal authority to disrupt a foreign network during peacetime operations. "The CIA has argued that doing so constitutes a 'covert' action that only it has the authority to carry out, and only with a presidential order."[69] Others argue that the Defense Department can conduct traditional military activities online.[70]

The extant legal authorities governing cyber activities within the Department of Defense provide insufficient statutory authority for military cyber operations. According to General Keith Alexander, the Commander of U.S. Cyber Command and the Director of the National Security Agency, "offensive [cyber] capabilities must be based on 'the rule of law.' [71]

The Department of Defense believes its current authority provides significant intelligence authority to the Secretary of Defense. Title 10 is vague about the intelligence responsibilities of the Secretary of Defense.[72] Title 50 acknowledges that the Defense Department conducts intelligence operations in support of military operations. It also mandates that the Secretary of Defense ensure that "the tactical intelligence activities of the Department of Defense complement and are compatible with the intelligence activities under the National Intelligence Program."[73] The lack of clarity in the authorities of the Department of Defense exacerbates the challenges of cyber operations. If it is unclear whether the clandestine collection of information from a foreign computer network is "defense-related intelligence," then it will be unclear whether it is within the Defense Department's authority to collect that information. It also remains to be decided if computer network operations should be classified as covert action.

Covert action is "an activity or activities of the United States Government to influence political, economic, or military conditions abroad, where it is intended that the role of the United States Government will not be apparent or acknowledged publicly."[74] It does not include "activities the primary purpose of which is to acquire intelligence" or "traditional diplomatic or military activities or routine support to such activities."[75] The term *traditional military activity* is not defined by statute or military doctrine. The inherent anonymity of actions in cyberspace does not mean the operation is a covert action, merely because the Defense Department fails to acknowledge its involvement publicly. As a policy matter, we must decide into which category the online activities of our military and intelligence agencies belong. Without this policy decision, our ability to use cyberspace to protect American interests is significantly burdened. We must decide if everything each of the elements of our national security community does on computer networks is subject to electronic surveillance law.

Second, we must reconsider our concept of online privacy. Within a relatively short period of time, there have been significant shifts in what different age groups consider private.

Younger "Digital Natives" have a culture of sharing built though forwarded e-mails and social-networking site posts. Their idea of privacy is different from older "digital immigrants." Digital natives have:

> [O]ver 10,000 hours playing videogames, over 200,000 emails and instant messages sent and received; over 10,000 hours talking on digital cell phones; over 20,000 hours watching TV (a high percentage fast speed MTV), over 500,000 commercials seen-all before the kids leave college. And, maybe, *at the very most,* 5,000 hours of book reading.[76]

Cyber security presents novel issues that cut across areas of law that have successfully represented our national values, but now may not be appropriate for current technology. We may have to review how much Fourth Amendment protection we provide to online activity. The legal regimes governing electronic surveillance have unsuccessfully tried to remain current with modern technology. The Supreme Court's opinion in *Katz v. United States* notwithstanding, some argue that the Fourth Amendment should not protect some forms of online communications. Professor Orin Kerr argues that the "contents of online communications ordinarily should receive Fourth Amendment protection but that non-content communications should not be protected.[77] "Online, non-content surveillance is usually surveillance related to identity, location, and time; content surveillance is surveillance of private thoughts and speech."[78]

The distinction between government surveillance of activities within enclosed spaces and government surveillance in public space is applicable to government surveillance online. "So long as conduct is out in the open, it is not protected by the Fourth Amendment."[79] In contrast, "entering enclosed spaces ordinarily constitutes a search that triggers the Fourth

Amendment."[80] The inside/outside distinction in the physical domain should be applied as a content/non-content distinction in the cyber domain.

Internet surveillance of non-content information should not trigger the Fourth Amendment just like surveillance of public spaces does not trigger the Fourth Amendment. Surveillance of content should presumptively trigger the Fourth Amendment in the Internet setting just like surveillance of inside spaces presumptively triggers the Fourth Amendment in the physical world.[81]

Kerr does acknowledge that the difference between content and non-content information can be difficult to determine.[82] Adopting the content/non-content distinction, however, would be useful in evolving electronic surveillance laws that are critical to ensure the national security community has both adequate legal authorities with which to apply its evolving cyber capabilities. It would put the military and intelligence agencies on firmer foundations to conduct cyberspace activities.

Some critics of the content/non-content paradigm argue that Internet surveillance is less-expensive, easier to conduct, and much more invasive than conventional surveillance. While this may be true in some circumstances, "online surveillance varies greatly in its ease, cost, and invasiveness: it can be cheap, easy and highly invasive, or it can be expensive, difficult, and much less invasive than physical surveillance."[83] The expanding use of commercially available encryption, anonymizers, and proxy servers makes Internet surveillance much more difficult, expensive, and time consuming.

Electronic Surveillance Insufficiencies Hinder U.S. Cyber Security Efforts

Laws that set the boundaries of government cyber activity include the Electronic Communications Privacy Act, the Stored Communications Act, the Foreign Intelligence Surveillance Act, the Computer Fraud and Abuse Act, the Federal Information Security Management Act, the Communications Assistance for Law Enforcement Act, and the laws governing intelligence collection. None of these laws provide adequate guidance, flexibility, or privacy protections for the national security community charged with protecting the nation and its critical infrastructure from cyber exploitation or attack. The President's National Security Telecommunications Advisory Committee recognizes the significant legal impediments that may exist to appropriate cyber security information sharing.[84]

Although each of these statutes should be amended to enhance U.S. cyber security, the priority should be amendments to the Electronic Communications Privacy Act (ECPA), the Stored Communications Act (SCA), and the Foreign Intelligence Surveillance Act (FISA). Elements of the ECPA encumber information sharing between the government and the private sector. The SCA restricts the disclosure of data before it is accessed by the recipient or if it is left in storage by the recipient.[85] Like the ECPA, the SCA may prevent ISPs from sharing metadata or content from the draft folder of a terrorist's e-mail account with the national security community for fear of criminal or civil liability.[86] Amended in 2008, FISA's provisions created an unintentional gap in the government's cyber capabilities. Congress amended FISA in a way that may require the loss of collection by intelligence agencies at the exact instant when the need for intelligence on the intentions of a target is highest.

Electronic Communications Privacy Act

The National Security Strategy prioritizes the prevention of nuclear weapons proliferation to violent extremists.[87] Counterterrorism operations have been an obvious priority since September 11, 2001. The United States has a clear interest in deterring terrorism; in order to do that, the national security elements of the federal govemment must have adequate authority to investigate terrorists and act once they are discovered.

Modem technologies provide a means of coordination for terrorists, just as they make communication and commerce more convenient. The technology provides anonymity, convenience, and rapid communication. E-mail, peer-to-peer connections, voice over intemet protocol (VoIP), and social networks such as Facebook and MySpace provide forums for extremists to share their ideologies and their techniques and procedures for conducting illicit activities.

With the enactment of the ECPA,[88] Congress sought to adapt privacy protections to technologies that were new in 1986.[89] The statute was effective in protecting communications privacy until technology and network structures developed in such a way as to hinder reasonable law enforcement and national security investigations. Modem technology has made ECPA "unwieldy and unreliable ... immensely difficult for judges and investigators to apply, confusing, costly, and full of legal uncertainty for communications and other technology tools and service providers, and an unpredictable guardian of our country's long cherished privacy values."[90] The confusion with ECPA also has an impact on national security investigations. Under ECPA, government access to an e-mail from a potential terrorist is subject to different legal standards depending on when the recipient accessed the e-mail.[91] If the e-mail is stored and has not yet been accessed by its recipient, ECPA requires a warrant for the government to see its contents.[92] Once the same e-mail is opened, the government may access the content with a subpoena.[93] Although there is disagreement among circuit courts on this "open and unopened" communications distinction, according to the Department of Justice, the government may subpoena the e-mail contents if they are more than 180 days old.[94] "The different standards are the unanticipated byproduct of technology changes, and not a careful balancing of the needs of law enforcement and the privacy rights of individuals."[95] Issuance of a wiretap warrant requires probable cause, but ECPA requirements "prohibit[] law enforcement from using wiretaps in the early stages of an investigation and make it one of the hardest warrants to obtain."[96] The needs of the national security community are similarly impacted by these ambiguous standards.

The ECPA applies to all online communications. It includes VolP communications.[97] The "by the aid of wire, cable, or other like connection" requirement includes wireless connections such as mobile phones, satellites, and fiber-optic cables.[98] The law also protects communications that are "furnished or operated by any person engaged in providing or operating such facilities" for communications.[99] In the computer context, "software installed on two computers may be the 'facility' for communication."[100]

Any federal law enforcement or intelligence activity online will implicate ECPA. However, sections of ECPA are clearly inconsistent with U.S. national security. Most agree that federal cyber security efforts must include better partnering between the federal and private sectors.[101] According to Melissa Hathaway, former Acting Senior Director for Cyberspace at the National Security Council, "the ISPs want to provide threat data, but the government either can't take it or won't."[102] Lawyers for the major data providers interpret the ECPA to prohibit the voluntary provision of customer data. In some cases, "the government won't take the [threat] information because they have no technical way to receive it."[103] Hathaway explained that various providers format their information differently and that the national security sector cannot receive, store, or analyze the large volumes of information even if the ISPs did make it available to the government.

It is understandable why the private sector is concerned about breaking this law. Criminal violations of ECPA may make an offender liable for fines or up to five years in prison, or both.[104] Civil liability includes injunctive or declaratory relief, and damages of at least $10,000.[105]

Under § 2702 of ECPA, civil liability attaches for the unlawful disclosure of communications data by service providers.[106] Notwithstanding the extensive list of exceptions and defenses to this liability,[107] service providers are less willing to provide data to the government after the controversy and legal suits that followed the December 2005 disclosure of the Terrorist Surveillance Program at the National Security Agency.[108] Litigation against the service providers for allegedly unlawfully providing customer data to the government continues today.[109] The legal issue with the TSP arose "because the data NSA tapped reportedly came in by fiber-optic cable, so FISA applied unless the physical tap took place outside the sovereign territory of the United States–a few miles offshore for example."[110]

The statute prohibits wiretapping and electronic surveillance in certain circumstances. "An interception can only be a violation of ECPA if the conversation or other form of communication intercepted is among those kinds which the statute protects, in oversimplified terms–telephone (wire), face-to-face (oral), and computer (electronic)."[111] "Surreptitious 'access' is at least as great a threat as surreptitious 'interception' to the patrons of electronic mail (email), electronic bulletin boards, voice mail, pagers, and remote computer storage."[112]

These sections that limit the interception of, access to, and disclosure of data in transmission require amendments in order to better protect the privacy of American citizens while allowing the national security community to remain current with the online activities of adversaries. Amendments to § 2702 allowing more flexibility for the ISPs would reduce their reluctance to share threat data with the government. As previously noted, "while a failure to follow the ECPA in obtaining e-mail information may not result in suppression of the evidence, it may result in civil liability for ECPA violators."[113]

The Department of Justice's Office of Legal Counsel has opined that an ISP may not even disclose its relationship with a customer without a national security letter.[114] According to this opinion, "when the FBI identifies a subscriber by name, section 2702(a)(3) [of the ECPA] forbids a provider from divulging the existence of that person's or entity's subscription with the provider."[115] ECPA also prohibits ISPs from identifying a customer if the FBI provides a phone number instead of a name. Without consent from a customer, ECPA prohibits the voluntary provision of information by the ISPs. In some cases, it even limits what can be provided by the ISPs with a national security letter.

Section 2709(b)(1) limits what the FBI can request and what an ISP may provide under a national security letter to the name, address, length of service, and local and long distance toll billing records of a person or entity.[116] The structure of the statute also supports these limitations on the sharing of subscriber information: "Section 2709 is an exception to the background rule of privacy established by 18 U.S.C. § 2702(a), which bars a provider from giving the Government a record or other information pertaining to a subscriber or customer."[117] Private defendant suits are still being litigated against telecommunications companies after the disclosure of the TSP.[118] Despite the outcome of past and pending TSP litigation, private sector companies are less likely to assist the government in law enforcement or national security investigations if their cooperation risks a civil suit.

Any amendments permitting a less burdensome regime for government access to information, for which the public believes it has an expectation of privacy, may cause civil liberties concerns, but these may be mitigated through a statutory definition of the types of data the ISPs could share and the setting of guidelines under which the data could be shared. For example, the Communications Assistance for Law Enforcement Act (CALEA) was created to ensure that telecommunications companies had the capabilities "to assist law enforcement in conducting digital electronic surveillance regardless of the specific telecommunications systems or services deployed."[119]

A similar approach should be used to allow the ISPs to share either metadata or content data with the government. An amended ECPA could include a provision that allows the disclosure of customer information, describing imminent acts dangerous to human life that are violations of the criminal laws of the United States, and not protected by the First Amendment to the U.S. Constitution. If the information describes imminent activity to "intimidate or coerce a civilian population; to influence the policy of a government by intimidation or coercion; [or] to affect the conduct of a government by mass destruction, assassination or kidnapping" ISPs should not be held liable for disclosing this information without a court order.[120] Such an amendment could outline the process by which the government should work with the ISPs to enhance their ability to detect threats to national security.

Stored Communications Privacy Act

Title II of the ECPA regulates access to stored communications and records.[121] It distinguishes between data in transit and data at rest. These distinctions are artificial, however, in light of the development of technology such as cloud computing[122] and remote computing services. "Today, the distinctions between and among data in transit, data in electronic storage, data stored by a remote computing service, and data more [than] 180 days old no longer conform to the reasonable expectations of Americans, nor do these distinctions serve the public interest."[123] These distinctions are irrelevant in the context of national security operations. "The SCA prohibits the unauthorized access to an electronic communication service or facility 'and thereby obtain[ing], alter[ing], or prevent[ing] authorized access to a wire or electronic communications while it is in electronic storage.' "[124] Thus, "when a communication is in transmission between the source and the destination, the ECPA governs.[125] However, when a communication reaches its destination, the SCA governs.[126]

Arguing against an "automobile-exception"[127] to the Fourth Amendment warrant requirement for computer information, Orin Kerr argues that "computer data moves in a very different sense than automobiles or ships move."[128] In contrast to what occurs when law enforcement officers lose track of a vehicle in the process of getting a warrant, computer data is copied, rather than being physically moved. "When a file is transferred from one place to another, a new copy is generated and that new copy is sent to the new place. The old copy is ordinarily left behind. Further, when a copy is made, that copy can be controlled and protected from interference." Kerr concludes that, since the data remains on a computer, the government "can copy the data-or order a copy to be made by the server that hosts the data-and then access the copy at a later time."[129] Because the data is not destroyed and is still accessible, "there is no general exigency that justifies a rule that the government can access Internet communications without a warrant."[130]

However, Professor Kerr underestimates the operational security practices of terrorists and criminals. Commercially available encryption, proxy-servers, unknown e-mail accounts, and small, highly concealable storage media negate Kerr's argument. Data can disappear, or be made inaccessible in seconds. Computer hard drives can be destroyed in five seconds,[131] and small storage media can hold eight gigabits of data on a device no larger than a quarter.[132] Because data can quickly be made inaccessible, there should be an exigency exception for the warrant requirement for computer data. In the national security context, warrants are inappropriate in cases where a U.S. citizen is not the target of the investigation. If the investigation does involve an entity protected by the Fourth Amendment, then there should be a legal accommodation to access fleeting data without an *a priori* warrant application.

The distinction between stored and transit data may not be as relevant today as it was when the SCA was passed, but the statute also distinguished between electronic communications service providers and remote computing service providers.[133] Each is subject to distinct exceptions for consent disclosures. Communications content may be disclosed with consent from only one party to the communication. In contrast, remote computing service providers ... may also disclose with the consent of a subscriber to the service.[134] In 2008, the Ninth Circuit held that the provider of a text messaging service was an electronic communications service provider rather than a remote computing service provider, and consequently, it was in violation of the Section 2702 when it disclosed to the city-subscriber the content of messages sent to and from a city employee's pager.[135]

There is little judicial consensus concerning how SCA should be applied to contemporary communications. The difficulty flows from the fact that the definitions used for terms in section 2703 were crafted for the technology of an earlier day. Application becomes an issue because under one construction the content of electronic communications can only be secured under a warrant; under another, a subpoena will suffice; and under a third, the required disclosure provisions of section 2703 do not apply at all.

A warrant is required for disclosure to authorities by a provider of "electronic storage" of the contents of a communication "in electronic storage" in a wire or "electronic communications system" for less than 181 days.[136] A subpoena or court order will suffice after 180 days or when authorities seek content disclosure from a provider of "remote computing service" of a communication "held or maintained on that service—(A) on behalf of, and received by means of electronic transmission from (or created by means of computer processing of communications received by means of electronic transmission), a subscriber or customer of such remote computing service; and (B) solely for the purpose of providing storage or computer processing services to such subscriber or customer, if the provider is not authorized to access the contents of any such communications for purposes of providing any services other than storage or computer processing."[137]

One court has concluded that a web-based e-mail provider must comply with a criminal trial subpoena for the contents of a subscriber's opened e-mail even though it had been stored with the provider for less than 181 days.[138] The district court determined that the e-mail was not in the type of "electronic storage" that would have triggered the application of section

2703(a)'s warrant requirement. The court reasoned that the e-mail of web-based users is not in electronic storage because it does not fit the "backup" requirements of 2510(17)(B). From the court's perspective, the backup reflects the practice of non web-based e-mail users who download their e-mail to their own computers and only leave their e-mail with their service provider as backup. Web-based email users may store their e-mail with their providers, but since they ordinarily do not download them such storage cannot be considered backup.[139]

The SCA makes it more difficult for the federal government to access Facebook and MySpace communications. Private litigants were unsuccessful when they sought to acquire webmail and private messaging from Facebook and MySpace in *Crispin v. Christian Audigier, Inc.*[140] The litigants argued that the subscribers whose communications were at issue had no standing.[141] Nor could they convince the court that section 2703(e), which immunizes providers from compliance with court orders and subpoenas, contemplated private party access to provider-held customer communications.[142]

Federal officials may secure electronic communications service or remote computing service customer-related transaction information (name, address, means of payment, etc.) under an administrative subpoena without the necessity of notifying the customer.[143] If an ISP is served a search warrant for electronic communications content, pursuant to 18 U.S.C. § 2703(a) the service provider must comply with Rule 41 of the Federal Rules of Criminal Procedure, which includes providing a copy of the warrant and receipt for any property seized to the service provider as required by Rule 41(f)(1)(C).[144] Neither SCA nor the Fourth Amendment, however, requires them to notify the person to whose communication they have access.[145]

Like the ECPA, the SCA should contain additional provisions that permit more information sharing between the private sector and the government in context of national security. The need for severe sanctions for abusing this information sharing should be balanced as to not chill the relationship between the government and private sector in the information sharing arena. "Lack of statutory clarity [may cause] judicial uncertainty,"[146] but it may also prevent the national security community from accessing threat information that could interrupt an attack against Americans or American interests. Because courts are increasingly denying government requests for retrospective geolocation data without a warrant (citing the SCA), [147] statutory amendments must include the authority for the national security community to access this information.

The Gaps in the Foreign Intelligence Surveillance Act

The Foreign Intelligence Surveillance Act of 1978148 established a "statutory procedure authorizing the use of electronic surveillance in the United States for foreign intelligence purposes."[149] Amended many times since passage, FISA governs most national security electronic surveillance. Its threshold requirement is "probable cause to believe that 'the target of the electronic surveillance is a foreign power or agent of a foreign power."[150] Even in its amended form, FISA hinders national security investigations.

FISA has been outpaced by technology. According to Benjamin Wittes, "the communications and data infrastructure FISA sought to regulate no longer exists ... .[151] Current cyber security threats require access to data from cyberspace with appropriate executive, legislative, and judicial oversight mechanisms. Electronic surveillance law must recognize that in the world of social networking, instant messages, and packetized data streams, state boundaries are meaningless. Rather than being geographically focused, surveillance law needs to be at least as concerned with how data is used as it is about "how easily [the] government can collect it in the first place."[152]

FISA's standards for access by the government to electronic communications are much more demanding than those under the SCA.[153] The few publicly available FISA decisions indicate that litigation may arise under sections 1806(f) and 1825(g) that allow for limited challenges to the exercise of FISA authority in the context of electronic surveillance and physical searches.[154]

After the Terrorist Surveillance Program was disclosed in 2006, the Electronic Frontier Foundation sued AT&T for assisting NSA with the surveillance of AT&T customers.[155] There was strong debate in the U.S. Senate about new FISA legislation that granted "retroactive immunity to telecommunications companies that assisted the NSA in warrantless surveillance of Americans."[156] Some senators argued that "telecommunications companies should not be punished for assisting the government in its fight against terrorism."[157] Others argued that the bill rewarded telecommunications companies for violating the law and betraying the privacy of their customers. Despite dissent, the bill passed and President Bush signed the FISA Amendments Act of 2008 into law on July 10, 2008."[158]

The FISA, even in its amended form, has already hindered counterterrorism network surveillance.[159] An important addition to FISA under this Act was its expansion of FISA's coverage to include surveillance of Americans living overseas. Under § 702(b) of FISA, the government may not "intentionally target a United States person reasonably believed to be located outside the United States."[160] Previously there was no procedure for obtaining a warrant for surveillance of Americans overseas because magistrate judges had no extraterritorial jurisdiction under the Federal Rules of Criminal Procedure.[161] "By placing Americans overseas under

FISA, Congress created a procedure for protecting the privacy of all Americans subject to foreign intelligence surveillance."[162] In addition, Section 702 outlines the procedures for targeting non-U.S. citizens outside the United States.[163] It includes a provision that prohibits the intentional electronic surveillance of "any person known at the time of acquisition to be located in the United States."[164] This means that the collection of a terrorist target must stop when and if the government discovers that the target of surveillance has landed in the United States.

Section 703 outlines the Foreign Intelligence Surveillance Court's authority for approving the surveillance of U.S. persons outside the United States.[165] It states:

> The Foreign Intelligence Surveillance Court shall have jurisdiction to review an application and to enter an order approving the targeting of a United States person reasonably believed to be located outside the United States to acquire foreign intelligence information, if the acquisition constitutes electronic surveillance or the acquisition of stored electronic communications or stored electronic data that requires an order under this Act, and such acquisition is conducted within the United States.
>
> *If a United States person targeted under this subsection is reasonably believed to be located in the United States during the effective period of an order issued pursuant to subsection (c), an acquisition targeting such United States person under this section shall cease unless the targeted United States person is again reasonably believed to be located outside the United States while an order issued pursuant to subsection (c) is in effect.* Nothing in this section shall be construed to limit the authority of the Government to seek an order or authorization under, or otherwise engage in any activity that is authorized under, any other title of this Act.[166]

This section emphasizes that electronic surveillance must stop when the government recognized that the target is inside the United States.

Until recently, these protections seemed reasonable in accordance with the Fourth Amendment and to have little effect on the electronic surveillance of terrorist targets. The growing number of U.S. citizens or dual citizenship terrorists has changed this calculus. With U.S. persons now recognized as potential terrorists, electronic surveillance laws such as the FISA must adapt to allow the access of computer network communications such as e-mails and instant messages to be collected. Under the current regime, electronic surveillance of any target must stop once the government recognizes the target is in the United States. Furthermore, if the target is recognized as a U.S. citizen that collection must stop until the intelligence community obtains approval from the Foreign Intelligence Surveillance Court.

The FISA must be adjusted to accommodate for the U.S. citizen terrorist and to close the gap between section 702 and FISA Title I collection. There must be amended FISA language that accommodates the transfer of collection from authorities found under section 702 and those under FISA Title I.

In 2000, future Director of National Intelligence Mike McConnell said that "New thinking is required ... to harness [signals intelligence] capabilities to control vulnerabilities of the information age."[167] McConnell was prescient in describing the challenges now shared between the National Security Agency and U.S. Cyber Command:

> No other government agency, now or in the foreseeable future, will match NSA's ability to detect and react to an information attack. This point is controversial because today cyber penetrations are no longer hindered by traditional borders, and it is increasingly difficult to distinguish between foreign and domestic threats; yet, NSA's capabilities are limited to use against only foreign targets. Now that telecommunications and networking have eliminated many of the traditional boundaries that protected the United States from foreign influence and activity, we need to think differently about how to use and develop NSA's capabilities.[168]

The FISA is an important capability used by the national security community. Malicious activity in cyberspace is difficult to classify as a "foreign nation state [attack]—an intelligence and defense or national security event, a domestic attack-a law enforcement concern-or an attack by a terrorist group—a law enforcement concern as well as an intelligence and defense or national security event."[169] Modem electronic surveillance authorities must incorporate this reality and enable the power of the national security community to be applied in a manner that is effective and effectively overseen.

Conclusion

Laws intended to govern domestic electronic surveillance now have an adverse impact on national security activities because they influence how cooperative the information service providers can be with the national security community. Laws such as the Electronic Communications Privacy Act and the stored Communications Act may create criminal and civil liabilities for the private sector that eliminate their motivation to assist in issues of national security. These laws provide needed protections for the privacy of ISP customers, but amendments must be made to allow the sharing of network security and threat information with the government.

The FISA attempts to govern electronic surveillance in the national security context, but the law has been outpaced by technology and compromised by terrorists who are also U.S. citizens. The law must be amended to permit seamless collection against threats to homeland security. The law can be amended in accordance with the content/non-content regime advocated by Professor Orin Kerr:

> The same principles should allow particularity for Internet searches that specify a particular individual rather than a specific Internet account. In the Internet setting, there are two different kinds of evidence collection: real-time wiretapping, which would be done under the Wiretap Act, and access to stored materials, done pursuant to the Stored Communications Act.[170]

Electronic surveillance law has evolved at a slower pace than electronic communications technology. In the digital age, given our digital dependence, we must amend the regulation of government electronic surveillance to better defend against current cyber threats.

Notes

* Special Counsel for Defense Intelligence, House Permanent Select Committee on Intelligence. The views expressed in this article are those of the author and do not reflect the official policy or position of any members or staff of the House Permanent Select Committee on Intelligence or any part of the **U. S.** government. This article is derived entirely from open source material and contains no classified information.

1. SNEAKERS (Universal Pictures 1992).
2. *See* Melissa Hathaway, Digital Dependence: Cybersecurity in the 21st Century, *Orkand Chair Distinguished Lecture Series*, UNIVERSITY OF MARYLAND UNIVERSITY COLLEGE, http://www.umuc.edulorkandlecture/pastlectures.shtml (last visited Feb. 5, 2010); *see also* Stuart H. Starr, *Toward* A *Preliminary Theory of Cyberpower,* CYBERPOWER AND NATIONAL SECURITY 43 (Franklin D. Kramer, Stuart H. Starr & Larry K. Wentz eds., 2009).
3. INTERNET WORLD STATS (June 30, 2010), http://www.intemetworldstats.com/stats.htm.
4. QUADRENNIAL DEFENSE REVIEW INDEPENDENT PANEL, THE QDR IN PERSPECTIVE: MEETING AMERICA'S NATIONAL SECURITY NEEDS IN THE 21ST CENTURY 61 (United States Institute of Peace 2010) [hereinafter QDR Independent Panel], *available at* http://www.usip.org/files/qdr/qdrreport.pdf.
5. Siobhan Gorman, *Grid is Vulnerable to Cyber-Attacks,* WALL ST. J., Aug. 3, 2010, at A3, *available* at http://online.wsj.com/article/SB10001424052748704905004575405741051458382.html.

6. Bill Gertz, *Inside the Ring: PLA Hack on Google?,* WASH. TIMES, July 8, 2010, at A7. *See generally* Kim Zetter, *Google Hack was Ultra Sophisticated, New Details Show,* WIRED (Jan. 14, 2010), http://www.wired.com/threatlevel/201 0/01/operation-aurora.
7. John Rollins & Anna Henning, Cong. Research Serv., R40427, Comprehensive National Cybersecurity Initiative: Legal Authorities and Policy Considerations 2 (2009).
8. *See generally* K.A. Taipale, Deconstructing Information Warfare, Presentation to Committee on Policy Consequences and Legal/Ethical Implications of Offensive Information Warfare, The National Academies (Oct. 30, 2006), *available at* http://www.information-retrieval.info/PIW/deconstructing/Taipale-IW-1 03006.pdf.
9. Orin Kerr, Applying the Fourth Amendment to the Internet: A General Approach, 62 STAN. L. REV. 1005, 1006 (2010).
10. *Id. See generally* Lawrence Lessig, Code and other Laws of Cyberspace 109–10 (1999) (advocating the translation of constitutional principles to the Internet); Patricia L. Bellia & Susan Freiwald, *Law in a Networked World: Fourth Amendment Protection for Stored E-mail,* 2008 U. Chi. Legal F. 121, 125 (2008); Max Guirguis, *Electronic Mail Surveillance and the Reasonable Expectation Of Privacy,* 8 J. TECH. L. & POL'Y 135, 135 (2003).
11. *See* Gina Marie Stevens & Charles Doyle, Cong. Research Serv., 98–326, *Privacy: An Overview of Federal Statutes Governing Wiretapping and Electronic Eavesdropping* (2009).
12. Daniel J. Solove, *Reconstructing Electronic Surveillance Law,* 73 Geo. Wash. L. Rev. 1264, 1266 (2004).
13. U.S. CONST. amend. IV; *Maryland v. Garrison,* 480 U.S. 79 (1987) (describing the particularity required in a warrant for the places to be searched); *Andresen v. Maryland, 427* U.S. 463 (1976) (describing the permissible breadth of warranted seizures).
14. Benjamin Wittes, Law and the Long War: The Future of Justice in the Age of Terror 233 (2008).
15. Solove, *supra* note 12, at 1270.
16. 4 William Blackstone, Commentaries on the Laws of England 169 (1769) (defining eavesdropping as a common law offense).
17. For an extensive description of wiretapping and the use of ciphers to protect from wiretapping, see David Kahn, the Code-breakers: The Comprehensive History of Secret Communication From Ancient Times to the Internet 214–229 (Scribner 1996).
18. *Id.* at 266.
19. *See* Stevens & Doyle, *supra note* 11, at 2.
20. Radio Act of 1927, Pub. L. No. 632, ch. 169, 44 Stat. 1172.
21. 277 U.S. 438 (1928); *see also* Wayne R. LaFave, Jerold H. Israel, & Nancy J. King, Criminal Procedure 259 (3rd ed. 2000) (It made no difference that the conduct was in violation of a state law making it a misdemeanor to "intercept" telegraphic or telephonic messages, as the statute did not declare evidence so obtained was inadmissible and, in any event, a state statue "can not affect the rules of evidence applicable in courts of the United States.").
22. *Olmstead,* 277 U.S. at 474 (Brandeis, J., dissenting).

23. 48 Stat. 1103–1104 (1934).
24. 24. STEVENS & DOYLE, *supra* note 11, at 3. Initially the Court applied *Olmstead's* principles to the electronic eavesdropping cases. Thus, the use of a dictaphone to secretly overhear a private conversation in an adjacent office offended no Fourth Amendment [precepts] because no physical trespass into the office in which the conversation took place had occurred. Goldman v. United States, 316 U.S. 129 (1942). Similarly, the absence of a physical trespass precluded Fourth Amendment coverage of the situation where a federal agent secretly recorded his conversation with a defendant held in a commercial laundry in an area open to the public. On Lee v. United States, 343 U.S. 747 (1952). On the other hand, the Fourth Amendment did reach the government's physical intrusion upon private property during an investigation, as for example when they drove a "spike mike" into the common wall of a row house until it made contact with a heating duct for the home in which the conversation occurred. Silverman v. United States, 365 U.S. 505 (1961).
25. 389 U.S. 347 (1967).
26. LAFAVE, ISRAEL & KING, *supra* note 21, at 261.
27. STEVENS & DOYLE, *supra* note 11, at 4.
28. 28. 388 U.S. 41 (1967).
29. Pub. L. No. 90-351, 82 Stat. 197 (1968) (then codified at 18 U.S.C. §§ 2510-2522 (2006)) [hereinafter Crime Control Act].
30. Crime Control Act, 18 U.S.C. § 2511(3) (1970).
31. 407 U.S. 297 (1972).
32. LAFAVE, ISRAEL & KING, *supra* note 21, at 276.
33. 407 U.S. at 314; *see also* LAFAVE, ISRAEL & KING, *supra* note 21, at 276. The Court also noted that Executive Officers of the government do not qualify under the Fourth Amendment as neutral magistrates, that internal security matters are not too subtle and complex for judicial evaluation and that prior judicial approval will not fracture the secrecy essential to official intelligence gathering.
34. 407 U.S. at 322.
35. 50 U.S.C. §§ 1801–1862 (2006).
36. STEVENS & DOYLE, *supra* note 11, at 5.
37. JAMES E. BAKER, IN THE COMMON DEFENSE: NATIONAL SECURITY LAW FOR PERILOUS TIMES 84–85 (2007).
38. *Id.* at 85.
39. Uniting and Strengthening America by Providing Appropriate Tools Required to Intercept and Obstruct Terrorism (USA Patriot) Act of 2001, Pub. L. No. 107-56, 115 Stat. 272 [hereinafter USA Patriot Act] (codified in scattered titles of the U.S. Code).
40. *Id.*; *see also In re* Sealed Case, 310 F.3d 717 (FISA Ct. Rev. 2002).
41. USA Patriot Act, 50 U.S.C. § 1804(a)(7)(b) (2002).
42. Pub. L. No. 110-55, 121 Stat. 552.
43. Pub. L. No. 110-261, 122 Stat. 2436 (2008).
44. 50 U.S.C. §§ 1881–1881g (2006).

45. *See* STEVENS & DOYLE, *supra note* 11, at 49, n.241 (quoting 50 U.S.C. § 1812: "(a) Except as provided in subsection (b), the procedures of chapters 119, 121, and 206 of title 18, United States Code, and this Act shall be the exclusive means by which electronic surveillance and the interception of domestic wire, oral, or electronic communications may be conducted. (b) Only an express statutory authorization for electronic surveillance or the interception of domestic wire, oral, or electronic communications, other than as an amendment to this Act or chapters 119, 121, or 206 of title 18, United States Code, shall constitute an additional exclusive means for the purpose of subsection (a)").
46. 50 U.S.C. § 1885-1885c (2006).
47. Electronic Communications Privacy Act of 1986, Pub. L. No. 99-508, 100 Stat. 1848 (codified at 50 U.S.C. §§ 1801-1862 (2006)) [hereinafter ECPA].
48. STEVENS & DOYLE, *supra note* 11, at 5 (Senate Report *541* mentioned that threats to privacy in these new communications media "may unnecessarily discourage potential customers from using innovative communications systems") (internal citation omitted).
49. *Id.* at 5-6.
50. Solove, *supra* note 12, at 1716.
51. 18 U.S.C. §§ 2701-2712 (2006).
52. 18 U.S.C. § 2510(17) (2006).
53. Solove, *supra* note 12, at 1722 (citing 18 U.S.C. § 2510(17)(B) (2006)).
54. *Id.* (citing 18 U.S.C. § 2510(17) (2006)).
55. 55. STEVENS & DOYLE, *supra note* 11, at 39.
56. 18 U.S.C. § 2703(a), (b)(1)(A), (b)(2) (2006).
57. Scott Shane, U.S. *Approves Targeted Killing ofAmerican Cleric,* N.Y. TIMES, Apr. 6, 2010, at A12, *available at* http://www.nytimes.com/2010/04/07/world/middleeast/ 07yemen.html?_r-1.
58. ECPA, 50 U.S.C. § 1801(f)(1) (2006) (emphasis added).
59. *Id.*; 18 § U.S.C. 2511(2)(i) (2006) ("It shall not be unlawful under this chapter for a person acting under color of law to intercept the wire or electronic communications of a computer trespasser transmitted to, through, or from the protected computer, if—(I) the owner or operator of the protected computer authorizes the interception of the computer trespasser's communications on the protected computer; (II) the person acting under color of law is lawfully engaged in an investigation; (Ill) the person acting under color of law has reasonable grounds to believe that the contents of the computer trespasser's communications will be relevant to the investigation; and (IV) such interception does not acquire communications other than those transmitted to or from the computer trespasser.").
60. ECPA, 50 U.S.C. § 1801(f)(1) (2006) (emphasis added).
61. Chuck Barry, Lauren Lee & Marek Rewers, INTERNATIONAL CYBER SECURITY CONFERENCE FINAL REPORT *4* (2009), *available at* http://www.ndu.edu/CTNSP/docUploaded/Cyber/o20International%20 Cyber/20Security%20Conf/20Final%20Report.pdf.
62. JOINT CHIEFS OF STAFF, JOINT PUB. 1-02: DEPARTMENT OF DEFENSE DICTIONARY OF MILITARY AND ASSOCIATED TERMS 110 (2001), *available at* http://www.bits.de/NRANEU/others/jp-doctrine/jpl_02(01).pdf.

63. JOINT CHIEFS OF STAFF, JOINT PUB. 1-02: DEPARTMENT OF DEFENSE DICTIONARY OF MILITARY AND ASSOCIATED TERMS 140 (2008), *available at* http://www.militarynewsnetwork.com/publications/military-terms.pdf.
64. Memorandum from the Vice Chairman of the Joint Chiefs of Staff to the Chiefs of the Military Services, Commanders of the Combatant Commands, and Directors of the Joint Staff Directors, Joint Terminology for Cyberspace Operations 7 (undated).
65. *See* DANIEL T. KEUHL, *From Cyberspace to Cyberpower: Defining the Problem, in* CYBERPOWER AND NATIONAL SECURITY 24-31 (Franklin D. Kramer, Stuart H. Starr & Larry K. Wentz eds., 2009).
66. ABA STANDING COMMON LAW AND NAT'L SEC. AND NAT'L STRATEGY FORUM, NATIONAL SECURITY THREATS IN CYBERSPACE 16 (SEPT. 2009), *available at* http://nationalstrategy.com/Portals// National%2Security%2Threats% 2 0in%2 Cyberspac e%20%20FINAL%2009-15-09.pdf.
67. *Id.* at 17. The Economic Espionage Act of 1996 is available for domestic purposes, but it has been an underutilized tool of law enforcement. *See* Harvey Rishikof, *Economic and Industrial Espionage, in* VAULTS, MIRRORS & MASKS (Jennifer E. Simms & Burton Gerber eds., 2009).
68. QDR Independent Panel, *supra* note 4, at iv.
69. Ellen Nakashima, *Pentagon Considers Preemptive Strikes as Part of Cyber-Defense Strategy,* WASH. POST, Aug. 28, 2010, at Al, *available at* http://www.washingtonpost.com/wp-dyn/content/article/2010/08/28/AR2010082803849.html.
70. *See generally* Chairman of the Joint Chiefs of Staff, NATIONAL MILITARY STRATEGY FOR CYBERSPACE OPERATIONS 1, 2 (December 2006), *available at* http://www.dod.mil/pubs/foi/ojcs/07-F-2105docl.pdf (stating the Department of Defense will "execute the full range of military operations (ROMO) in and through cyberspace to defeat, dissuade, and deter threats against US interests.").
71. Nakashima, *supra* note 69.
72. *See* Exec. Order No. 13,470, 3 C.F.R. 218, 232-33 (2008) (§ 1.10(a)-(k)). Exec. Order 12333 (now Exec. Order 13,470) does specify some intelligence responsibilities of the Secretary of Defense, such as "[clollect (including through clandestine means), analyze, produce, and disseminate information and intelligence and be responsive to collection tasking and advisory tasking by the Director," *id.* at 232 (§ 1.10(a)); and "[clollect (including through clandestine means), analyze, produce, and disseminate defense and defense-related intelligence and counterintelligence, as required for execution of the Secretary's responsibilities. Id (§ 1.10(b)).
73. 50 U.S.C. § 403-5(3) (2006).
74. *Id.*
75. 50 U.S.C. § 413b(e) (2006).
76. Marc Prensky, *Digital Natives, Digital Immigrants, Part II: Do They Really* Think *Differently?,* ON THE HORIZON, Oct. 2001, at 1.
77. *Kerr, supra* note 9, at 1007-08.
78. Id at 1018.
79. *Id* at 1010.

80. *Id.*
81. *Id.* at 1018.
82. Kerr notes that the subject line, the body of the message, and any attachments of an electronic mail are contents of the communication, while the *"to/from"* address and the size of the e-mail are non-content information. *Id.* at 1023.
83. *Id.* at 1032.
84. *See* THE PRESIDENT'S NATIONAL SECURITY TELECOMMUNICATIONS ADVISORY COMTRTEE, CYBERSECURITY COLLABORATION REPORT: STRENGTHENING GOVERNMENT AND PRIVATE SECTOR COLLABORATION THROUGH A CYBER INCIDENT DETECTION, PREVENTION, MITIGATION, AND RESPONSE CAPABILITY I, 15 (2009), http://www.ncs.gov/nstac/reports/2009/NSTAC CCTF Report.pdf.
85. Electronic storage is "any temporary, intermediate storage of a wire or electronic communication incidental to the electronic transmission" and "any storage of such communication by an electronic communication service for purposes of backup protection of such communication." 18 U.S.C. § 2510(17)(a)-(b).
86. Nicholas Matlach, *Who Let the Katz Out? How the* ECPA *and the* SCA *Fail to* Apply *to Modern Digital Communications and How Returning to the Principles in* Katz v. United States *Will Fix It,* 18 COMMLAW CONSPECTUS 421, 449 (2010).
87. EXECUTIVE OFFICE OF THE PRESIDENT, NATIONAL SECURITY STRATEGY 4 (2010), http://www.whitehouse.gov/sites/default/files/rssviewer/national_security_strategy.pdf.
88. ECPA, 50 U.S.C. §§ 1801-1862 (2006); *see also* S. REP. No. 99-541, at 1 (1986).
89. Matlach, *supra* note 86, at 442; *see also* S. REP. No. 99-541, at 1.
90. J. Beckwith Burr, The Electronic Communications Privacy Act of 1986: Principles of Reform 3 (WilmerHale, Memorandum), http://digitaldueprocess.org/files/DDPBurrMemo.pdf.
91. *See* Robert Gellman, Privacy in the Clouds: Risks to Privacy and Confidentiality from the Cloud Computing 12-13 (2009), *available at* http://www.scribd.com/doc/I2805751/Privacy-in-Cloud-Computing-World-Privacy-Council-Feb-2009 (describing the struggle courts have had applying ECPA to situations not contemplated by the law's drafters).
92. 18 U.S.C. § 2703(a) (2006).
93. 93. 18 U.S.C. § 2703(b)(1)(B) (2006).
94. Burr, *supra* note 90 at 8.
95. *id.*
96. Matlach, *supra* note 86 at 443.
97. 18 U.S.C. § 2510(18) (2006); *see also* S. REP. No. 99-541, at 16 (1986).
98. S. REP. No. 99-541 at 12.
99. 18 U.S.C. § 2510(1) (2006).
100. Matlach, *supra* note 86, at 445.
101. *See, e.g.,* NATIONAL SECURITY THREATS IN CYBERSPACE, *supra* note 66, at 23; INTELLIGENCE AND NATIONAL SECURITY ALLIANCE, ADDRESSING CYBER SECURITY THROUGH PUBLIC-PRIVATE PARTNERSHIP: AN ANALYSIS OF EXISTING MODELS (2009), http://insaonline.org/assets/files/CyberPaperNov09R3.pdf.

102. Interview with Melissa Hathaway, Former Acting Senior Dir. for Cyberspace, Nat'l Sec. Council, in D.C. (Sept. 8, 2010).
103. *Id.*
104. 18 U.S.C. § 2511(4)(a) (2006).
105. 18 U.S.C. § 2520(b)-(c) (2006).
106. Stevens & *Doyle, supra* note 11, at 29; *see also* 18 U.S.C. § 2702(a) (2006).
107. Section § 2702(b) requires that [a] provider described in subsection (a) may divulge the contents of a communication-(1) to an addressee or intended recipient of such communication or an agent of such addressee or intended recipient; (2) as otherwise authorized in section 2517, 2511(2)(a), or 2703 of this title; (3) with the lawful consent of the originator or an addressee or intended recipient of such communication, *or the subscriber in the case of remote computing service*; (4) to a person employed or authorized or whose facilities are used to forward such communication to its destination; (5) as may be necessarily incident to the rendition of the service or to the protection of the rights or property of the provider of that service; (6) to the National Center for Missing and Exploited Children, in connection with a report submitted thereto under section 227 of the Victims of Child Abuse Act of 1990; (7) to a law enforcement agency—(A) if the contents—(1) were inadvertently obtained by the service provider; and (ii) appear to pertain to the commission of a crime; (8) to a Federal, State, or local government entity, if the provider, in good faith, believes that an emergency involving danger of death or serious physical injury to any person requires disclosure without delay of communications relating to the emergency.

    18 U.S.C. § 2702(b) (2006). The Ninth Circuit recently explained that while a remote computer service provider may disclose to a subscriber (as noted in italics above), an electronic service provider, such as one who provides text messaging services, may not, even when the material disclosed resides in storage. Quon v. Arch Wireless Operating Co. Inc., 529 F.3d 892, 900-01 (9th Cir. 2008).
108. James Risen & Eric Lichtblau, *Bush Lets* U.S. Spy *on Callers Without Courts,* N.Y. TIMEs, Dec. 16, 2005, at Al, *available at,* http://www.nytimes.com/2005/12/16/politics/i6program.html.
109. *See generally* Charlie Savage & James Risen, *Federal Judge Finds* N.S.A. *Wiretaps Were Illegal,* N.Y. TIMEs, Mar. 10, 2010, at Al, *available at,* http://www.nytimes.com/2010/04/01/us/01nsa.html.
110. *Wittes, supra* note 14, at 235.
111. Stevens & Doyle, *supra note* 11, at 11.
112. *Id.* at 28. *See also* 18 U.S.C. §§ 2701-2711 (2006).
113. Am. Prosecutors Research Inst., The ECPA, ISPs, and Obtaining Email: A Primer for (July 2005), http://www.ndaa.org/pdf/ecp_aisps_obtaining_email_05.pdf.
114. *See* Office of Legal Counsel, Requests for Information Under the Electronic Communications Privacy Act Memorandum Opinion for the General Counsel Federal Bureau of Investigation (Nov. 5, 2008), *available* http://www.justice.gov/olc/2008/fbi-ecpa-opinion.pdf.
115. *Id.* at 11.

116. 18 U.S.C. § 2709(b)(1) (2006).
117. Office of Legal Counsel, *supra* note 114, at 3.
118. Robert M. Chesney, Nat'l Security Admin., *Litigation, and the State Secrets Privilege, in* LEGAL ISSUES IN THE STRUGGLE AGAINST TERROR 123 (John Norton Moore & Robert Turner eds., 2010).
119. PATRICIA MOLONEY FIGLIOLA, CONG. RESEARCH SERV., RL 30677, DIGITAL SURVEILLANCE: THE COMMUNICATIONS ASSISTANCE FOR LAW ENFORCEMENT ACT 2 (2007), *available at* http://www.law.umaryland.edu/marshall/crsreports/crsdocuments/RL30677_06082007.pdf.
120. USA Patriot Act § 802 (codified at 18 U.S.C. 2331 (2006)).
121. 18 U.S.C. §§ 2701-2711 (2006).
122. PATRICIA MALONEY FIGLIOLA, ANGELE A. GILROY & LENNARD G. KRUGER, CONG. RESEARCH SERV., RL 40230, THE EVOLVING BROADBAND INFRASTRUCTURE: EXPANSION, APPLICATIONS, AND REGULATION 9 (2009), *available at* http://assets.opencrs.com/rpts/R40230_20090219.pdf.
123. Burr, *supra* note 90, at 9.
124. Matlach, *supra* note 86, at 448.
125. *See* United States v. Rodriguez, 968 F.2d 130, 136 (2d Cir. 1992) (noting "when the contents of a wire communication are captured or redirected in any way, an interception occurs at that time").
126. *See* Theofel v. Farey-Jones, 359 F.3d 1066, 1072–73 (9th Cir. 2004) (noting that the SCA "reflects Congress's judgment that users have a legitimate interest in the confidentiality of communications in electronic storage at a (continued) communications facility. Just as trespass protects those who rent space from a commercial storage facility to hold sensitive documents ... the Act protects users whose electronic communications are in electronic storage with an ISP or other electronic communications facility").
127. States may allow the warrantless search of an automobile, except for the trunk, if the police officer reasonably believes that the vehicle holds evidence of a crime. The U.S. Supreme Court has determined that this exception is not a violation of the Fourth Amendment because drivers have a "reduced expectation of privacy" and because a vehicle is inherently mobile. This reduced expectation of privacy also allows police officers with probable cause to search a car to inspect drivers' and passengers' belongings that are capable of concealing the object of the search, even if there is no proof that the driver and passenger were engaged in a common enterprise. Wyoming v. Houghton, 526 U.S. 295 (1999).
128. Kerr, *supra* note 9, at 1041.
129. *Id.* at 153. This occurred in United States v. Gorshkov, No. CR00-550C, 2001 WL 1024026 (W.D. Wash. May 23, 2001), where the target had left his hacker tools on a server in Russia. FBI agents in the United States remotely accessed the account, copied the folder containing the tools, and downloaded it to a file in the United States. However, the agents did not actually open the file until they had obtained a warrant.
130. Kerr, *supra* note 9, at 1041.
131. *See* Ryan DeBeasi, *How to Destroy a Hard Drive in Five Seconds,* NETWORKWORLD.COM, June 27, 2006, *available at* http://www.networkworld.com/news/2006/062706-guard-dog.html.
132. *See generally* DT's Flash Drive Blog (Apr. 24, 2009), http://www.usbmemorysticks.net/smallest-nano-flash-drives.

133. *See* 18 U.S.C. § 2702(a)(1)-(2) (2006).
134. 18 U.S.C. § 2702(b)(3) (2006).
135. Quon v. Arch Wireless Operating Co., Inc., 529 F.3d 892, 900 (9th Cir. 2008), *rev'd on other grounds sub nom.,* City of Ontario v. Quon, 130 S.Ct. 2619 (2010). On the other hand, the Ninth Circuit has since concluded that opened messages on the Facebook and MySpace messaging services are held in remote computer service. Crispin v. Christian Audigier, Inc., 717 F. Supp. 2d 965, 991 (C.D. Cal. 2010).
136. 18 U.S.C. § 2703(a) (2006).
137. 18 U.S.C. § 2703(b) (2006).
138. United States v. Weaver, 636 F. Supp. 2d 769, 770 (C.D. Ill. 2009).
139. *Id.* at 772 ("Thus, unless a Hotmail user varies from default use, the remote computing service is the only place he or she stores messages, and Microsoft is not storing that user's opened messages for backup purposes. Instead Microsoft is maintaining the messages 'solely for the purpose of providing storage ... services to such subscriber or customer.' 18 U.S.C. §2703(b)(2)").
140. *Crispin,* 717 F. Supp. 2d, at 965.
141. *Id.* (citing J.T. Shannon Lumber Co. v. Gilco Lumber, Inc., No. 2:07-CV- 119, 2008 WL 3833216 (N.D. Miss. Aug. 14, 2008)).
142. *Crispin,* 717 F. Supp. 2d, at 965.
143. 18 U.S.C. § 2703(c)(2)-(3) (2006); United States v. Cray, 673 F. Supp. 2d 1368, 1378–79 (S.D. Ga. 2009) (citing United States v. Bobb, 577 F.3d 1366, 1368 n.l (1lth Cir. 2009)).
144. *In re* Application of the U.S., 665 F. Supp. 2d 1210, 1215–21 (D. Or. 2009) (citing *In re* Search of Yahoo, Inc., No. 07-3194-MB, 2007 WL 1539971, *6 (D. Ariz. May 21, 2007)); United States v. Berkos, 543 F.3d 392, 398 (7th Cir. 2008); *In re* Search Warrant, No. 6:05-MC-168-Orl-31JGG, 2005 WL 3844032, *5 (M.D. Fla. Feb. 13, 2006). *But see* United States v. Kemell, No. 3:08-CR-142, 2010 WL 1408437 (E.D. Tenn. Apr. 2, 2010) (holding that search warrants issued for provider-held evidence under section 2703 enjoy extraterritorial vitality notwithstanding apparent language to the contrary in Rule 41(b)).
145. *In re* Application of the U.S., 665 F. Supp. 2d at 1221–24.
146. 146. Burr, *supra* note 90, at 11.
147. *Id.* at n.64 (citing *In re* the Application of the U.S. for an Order Directing the Provider of Elec. Commc'ns Serv. to Disclose Records to the Gov't, 534 F. Supp. 2d 585 (W.D. Pa. 2008), *vacated,* 620 F.3d 304 (3d Cir. 2010) ("Government's requests for Court Orders mandating a cell phone service provider's covert disclosure of individual subscribers' (and possibly others') physical location information must be accompanied by a showing of probable cause.").
148. 50 U.S.C. §§ 1801–1862 (2006).
149. H.R. Rep. No. 95–1283, at 22 (1978).
150. Baker, supra note 36, at 80 (quoting 50 U.S.C. § 1804(a)(4)(A)).
151. WITTES, *supra* note 14, at 222. These technology changes are outlined in LTG Keith Alexander's responses to questions posed at a Senate hearing FISA for the 21st Century available at http://www.fas.org/irp/congress/2006_hr/alexander-qfr.pdf ("When FISA was enacted into law in 1978, almost all transoceanic

communications into and out of the United States were carried by satellite and those communications were, for the most part, intentionally omitted from the scope of FISA, consistent with FISA's focus upon regulating the collection of foreign intelligence from domestic communications of United States persons. Congress could not have anticipated the revolution in telecommunications technology that would establish global, high-speed, fiber-optic networks that would fundamentally alter how communications are transmitted. Nor could Congress have anticipated the stunning innovations in wireless technology, or the explosion of the volume of communications, that have occurred in recent decades. Unpredicted advances in the development and deployment of new technologies, rather than a considered judgment by Congress, has resulted in the considerable expansion of the reach of FISA to additional technologies and communications beyond the statute's original focus on domestic communications.").

152. *Id.* at 231.

153. *See generally* 50 U.S.C. § 1812 (2006).

154. Two of the recent decisions, concerning challenges to the National Security Agency's purported Terrorist Screening Program, group section 1845 with sections 1806 and 1825 in their rejection of the defendant's sovereign immunity argument. *In re* Nat'l Sec. Agency Telecomm. Records Litig., 700 F. Supp. 2d 1182, 1192 (N.D. Cal. 2010) ("But FISA directs its prohibitions to 'Federal officers and employees' (see, eg, 50 U.S.C. §§1806, 1825, 1845) and it is only such officers and employees acting in their official capacities that would engage in surveillance of the type contemplated by FISA.") (quoting *In re* Nat'l Sec. Agency Telecomm. Records Litig., 564 F. Supp. 2d 1109, 1125 (N.D. Cal. 2008)).

155. John Markoff & Scott Shane, *Documents Show Link Between AT&T and Agency in Eavesdropping Case,* N.Y. TIMES, Apr. 13, 2006, at A17.

156. Jonathan D. Forgang, *"The Right of the People": The* NSA, *The* FISA *Amendments Act of* 2008, *and Foreign Intelligence Surveillance ofAmericans Overseas,* 237 FORDHAM L. REv. 78, 237 (2009).

157. *Id.*

158. Eric Lichtblau, *Senate Approves Bill to Broaden Wiretap Powers,* N.Y. TIMES, July 10, 2008, at Al.

159. *Surveillance and Shahzad: Are Wiretap Limits Making it Harder to Discover and Pre-empt Jihadists?* WALL ST. J., May 13, 2010, at A13.

160. 50 U.S.C. § 1881a(b)(3) (2006).

161. FED. R. CRIM. P. 41(b); *see also* United States v. Bin Laden, 126 F. Supp. 2d 264, 275–76 n.13 (S.D.N.Y. 2000) (stating that there is not a statutory provision for searches conducted overseas), *aff'd sub nom. In re* Terrorist Bombings of U.S. Embassies in E. Afr. (Fourth Amendment Challenges), 552 F.3d 157 (2d Cir. 2008).

162. Forgang, *supra* note 156, at 238.

163. 50 U.S.C. § 1881a.

164. 50 U.S.C. § 188la(b)(1) (2006).

165. In 1990, the Supreme Court held in *United States v. Verdugo-Urquidez,* 494 U.S. 259 (1990) that non-U.S. citizens living in another country and searched by the American government are not entitled to the protections of the U.S. Constitution.

166. 50 U.S.C. § 1881b(a)(1)-(2) (2006) (emphasis added).

167. J.M. McConnell, *The Future of SIGINT: Opportunities and Challenges in the Information Age,* DEF. INTELLIGENCE J., Summer 2000, at 40.

168. Id.

169. *Id. at 46.*

170. 18 U.S.C. §§ 2701–2711 (2006).

Drawing the Line: DNA Databasing at Arrest and Sample Expungement

BY JESIKA WEHUNT*

> *New technologies test the judicial conscience. On the one hand, they hold out the promise of more effective law enforcement, and the hope that we will be delivered from the scourge of crime. On the other hand, they often achieve these ends by intruding, in ways never before imaginable, into the realms protected by the Fourth Amendment.*
>
> —Judge Kozinski, United States Court of Appeals, Ninth Circuit1 Circuit[1]

Introduction

In recent years, news headlines across the country have been splashed with stories of cases considered cold for decades until a new sample of DNA revealed who committed the crime.[2] Not only is DNA increasingly used to identify the culprit responsible for a crime; many innocent people have been exonerated thanks to new advances in DNA

Jesika Wehunt, "Drawing the Line: DNA Databasing at Arrest and Sample Expungement," *Georgia State University Law Review*, vol. 29, no, 4, pp. 1063-1091.

evidence.[3] As technology advances, it promises to reveal even more information about individuals from their DNA in the future.[4] Given the growing number of real-world, high-profile cases solved with DNA evidence, fictional television increasingly features shows that depict the use of DNA to solve crimes.[5] Consequently, the public has greater awareness of how DNA works, and juries demand DNA evidence from prosecutors in exchange for a conviction.[6]

In response to this demand for DNA evidence, all fifty states and the federal government allow, by statute, both collection of DNA from select individuals and storage of DNA in databases.[7] Traditionally, those *convicted* of felonies were required to submit DNA samples; however, more recently, the federal statute and some state statutes have been amended so that those who have been *arrested* are also required to submit samples.[8] In the majority of states that take DNA samples upon arrest, DNA samples and profiles of individuals who are not ultimately convicted are not automatically destroyed; rather, the exonerated individuals must go through a lengthy process of requesting an expungement.[9]

While opponents have brought many constitutional challenges to the collection and storage of DNA under the Fourth Amendment, most courts that have reviewed the state statutes requiring DNA samples from convicted persons have found them constitutional.[10] In August 2011, however, the California Court of Appeals reviewed the jurisprudence surrounding the constitutionality of DNA collection at arrest in *People v. Buza* and found the California statute for DNA collection at arrest, Proposition 69, unconstitutional.[11]

This Note addresses the constitutionality of the collection and retention of DNA samples from individuals at arrest and proposes a statutory scheme for utilizing DNA evidence while protecting arrestees' privacy rights by requiring judicial probable cause and placing the burden of expungement on the state. First, Part I provides a brief history of the use of DNA and the statutory schemes that mandate the sampling and retention of DNA.[12] Next, Part II analyzes the constitutionality of DNA sampling at arrest—as well as the subsequent retention of DNA samples and profiles of citizens who are not convicted—under the Fourth Amendment and in light of the 2011 California Court of Appeals decision, *People v. Buza*.[13] Finally, based on the analysis used by the California Court of Appeals in *Buza*, Part III proposes that DNA profiles and samples should be collected upon arrest of a suspect only with a judicial finding of probable cause. If collected, the sample should be destroyed upon immediate acquittal—instead of the current popular scheme used by most states and the federal government that requires the individual to request expungement and does not differentiate the type of probable cause required for sample collection.[14]

DNA Collection and Databasing

A. The Foundations of DNA Use

The fathers of DNA, James Watson and Francis Crick, declared on February 28, 1953, that they "had found the secret of life."[15] In fact, they had uncovered the double-helix structure of deoxyribonucleic acid (DNA) and subsequently made their research public, continuing to research and publish their findings.[16]

DNA is the foundation on which an individual's entire genetic makeup stands.[17] A person's DNA is like a genetic fingerprint; the DNA that is found in a person's blood is identical to the DNA found in his skin cells.[18] In fact, DNA is identical in every cell of a person's body and is unique to each individual.[19] The four "bases" of DNA are Cytosine (C), Guanine (G), Thymine (T), and Adenine (A), and the sequencing and order of these "bases" are what make a person's unique DNA pattern.[20] "More than ninety-seven percent of DNA is identical between all people," but the remaining base sequences, called polymorphic loci or "junk DNA," are what make each individual unique.[21] These junk DNA are analyzed to identify suspects in DNA sampling.[22]

DNA sampling for forensic identification purposes first occurred in Great Britain in the 1980s, more than thirty years after the discovery of DNA.[23] Soon after this discovery of "DNA fingerprinting,"[24] the United States had its first conviction based on DNA technology in 1987.[25] DNA provided an immediate way to identify offenders and quickly link them to a crime more efficiently than other typical methods, such as fingerprinting and mugshots.[26] DNA technology became the method of choice for forensic examination for many reasons: it has "high discrimination power";[27] the DNA of an individual remains the same for his entire lifetime;[28] it is inherited from his parents;[29] DNA samples remain stable over time;[30] and it is easily obtained from the smallest of samples of biological materials.[31] Today, DNA fingerprinting has become the "gold standard" of forensic analysis and is widely accepted by courts.[32]

The DNA Sampling and Matching Process

Collecting the DNA Samples

In an investigation, DNA must first be collected at the crime scene.[33] "Blood, semen, saliva and other types of bodily fluid or tissue are the most common types of biological evidence collected at crime scenes."[34] The unique DNA sequences from the collected evidence samples are isolated and prepared to be cross-referenced with the DNA of potential suspects by lab technicians.[35]

Potential suspects may voluntarily provide a comparison sample, or the collection of a comparison sample may be mandated by statute.[36] Samples can be taken voluntarily from a mass population of potential suspects in a process that is referred to as "DNA dragnets."[37] State or federal statutes can also require the submission of a DNA sample under certain conditions.[38] When DNA collection was in its earliest stages, "only people ... convicted of serious sexual crimes" were required to submit DNA samples.[39] As the popularity of DNA testing grew, "many states began collecting DNA from murderers, then other violent felons, and, most recently, all felons and even some misdemeanants."[40] Since a 2006 amendment to the DNA Analysis Backlog Elimination Act, the federal government has allowed collection of arrestee DNA samples merely upon arrest, prior to any conviction.[41] Statutes in twenty-five states also require suspects to provide DNA samples upon arrest.[42]

The sampling, whether voluntary or mandated by statute, is usually a non-invasive procedure, such as buccal swabbing.[43] Once the DNA sample is taken, a unique DNA "fingerprint" or "profile" of the individual is created and used only for identification purposes.[44] A DNA profile is not the sample, which is the actual physical specimen originally taken from the individual, but rather a simple series of numbers that represent the DNA sequence and do not share any information about a person's individual traits.[45]

Storage and Maintenance of DNA Profiles

Once the DNA profile is created from a collected sample, it is of little value unless it can be catalogued and compared with other profiles from crime scenes. As the amount of DNA used in criminal cases has grown, the "need to house, maintain, and recall the DNA profiles of offenders for use in solving other crimes" on a larger scale has also grown exponentially.[46] "All fifty states have passed legislative provisions authorizing the use of DNA databases to store the genetic profiles of convicted criminals."[47] Additionally, recognizing the need for an overarching profile organization system, the Federal Bureau of Investigation (FBI) created the Combined DNA Index System (CODIS).[48]

CODIS "coordinate[s] the various national, state, and local DNA databases in a centralized system" that allows for the exchange of DNA information nationwide.[49] Following the creation of CODIS in 1994, "the DNA Identification Act ('DNA Act') authorized the FBI to create the National DNA Index System ('NDIS')," which allows sharing profile information between federal and state DNA databases, and provides states with financial support to create or improve their existing state DNA databases.[50] As of March 2013, this multi-tiered system of local, state, and national databases contains more than ten million offender profiles, more than 1.3 million arrestee profiles, and almost half a million forensic profiles.[51]

"As soon as a DNA profile is uploaded, it is compared to crime scene samples in CODIS; new crime scene samples are searched against the uploaded profile, and a search of the entire system is performed once each week."[52] If there is a match, known as a "hit," between a suspect profile in the database and a sample from a crime scene, "it is confirmed with a new analysis of the profile," and the "submitting laboratory is notified and can notify the appropriate law enforcement agency."[53] The number of crimes assisted by CODIS is staggering—"[a]s of March 2013, CODIS has produced over 205,700 hits assisting in more than 197,400 investigations."[54]

Expungement and Removal of DNA Profiles from Databases

Once a profile is in CODIS, it is permanently housed in the system unless the individual seeks expungement by obtaining a court order expunging the profile from either the state or federal government.[55] State laws governing expungement of a DNA profile and sample from the state and federal system differ, with eighteen states expunging upon request[56] and only seven states expunging the profile and sample automatically upon non-conviction.[57] For example, under California's DNA Act, an individual may have his sample and DNA profile destroyed if he has "no past or present offense or pending charge which qualifies that person for inclusion within the state's DNA and Forensic Identification Database and Data Bank Program and there otherwise is no legal basis for retaining the specimen or sample or searchable profile."[58] In other words, the arrestee may not have any crimes that qualify for inclusion in the database, but it is ultimately up to the court to decide if there is a legal basis for retaining the sample and profile.

The expungement process in California is also drawn out: an arrestee has to show that "no accusatory pleading has been filed within the applicable period allowed by law charging the person with a qualifying offense" or that the charges of the qualifying offense that led to the arrest "have been dismissed prior to adjudication,"[59] and before it can grant the request."[60] Even after the statute of limitations has passed, a prosecutor can object to the individual's request, and the court's order allowing or preventing expungement is "not reviewable by appeal or by writ."[61] Furthermore, if a person had the right to have his DNA records expunged but failed to do so—either by his own delay or that of the state—and is subsequently convicted using that DNA evidence, he cannot appeal the arrest or conviction based on the delay.[62]

DNA Collection under the Fourth Amendment

DNA collection and databasing have most frequently been challenged under the Fourth Amendment's "judicially created doctrine of privacy."[63] The Fourth Amendment's Search and Seizure clause provides that "[t]he right of the people to be secure in their persons ... against unreasonable searches and seizures, shall not be violated, and no Warrants shall issue, but upon probable cause."[64] It is clear under the Fourth Amendment that collection of samples for DNA databasing constitutes a search.[65] Yet, courts have concluded that the collection of the DNA sample is merely the first search in DNA collection; the actual creation of the DNA profile from the sample and cross-referencing of that profile in the database constitutes a second search.[66] While probable cause is required to justify the first search (the sample collection), in evaluating the second search (the cross-referencing of that sample in a DNA database), the measure of the constitutionality is "reasonableness."[67] The reasonable standard requires an analysis of the individual's "subjective privacy interest" and the public's consideration of what is reasonable, and it is a lower standard than probable cause.[68]

Constitutionality of DNA Sampling from Convicted Individuals

Before the 2006 amendment to the DNA Fingerprinting Act to include sampling of arrestees, courts had settled the debate over the constitutionality of DNA sampling and databasing of convicts under the Fourth Amendment.[69] To uphold convict sampling statutes, the circuits use one of two Fourth Amendment analyses: (1) the "special needs test" or (2) the "totality of the circumstances" test.[70]

The Special Needs Test

Generally, "a warrant supported by probable cause is required" before a search.[71] The special needs test allows exceptions to this rule, permitting suspicionless searches if they are conducted for non-law enforcement purposes when the situation makes "the warrant and probable-cause requirement impractical ... ."[72] Courts that have upheld DNA collection and databasing under the special needs test have focused on the purpose of DNA collection: "to obtain a reliable record of an offender's identity that can then be used to help solve crimes."[73] The Second Circuit explained in *Nicholas v. Goord*:

Although the DNA samples may eventually help law enforcement identify the perpetrator of a crime, at the time of collection, the samples "in fact provide no evidence in and of themselves of criminal wrongdoing," and are not sought "for the investigation of a specific crime." Because the state's purpose in conducting DNA indexing is distinct from the ordinary "crime detection" activities associated with normal law-enforcement concerns, it meets the special-needs threshold.[74]

The Totality of the Circumstances Test

The "totality of the circumstances privacy interests and the "government's interest in conducting a search without a warrant supported by probable cause."[75] Therefore, in a DNA sampling challenge, a court applying this test weighs the governmental interest in maintaining DNA databases against an individual's right to the privacy of his DNA.[76] In circuits that have upheld DNA databasing of convicts, the courts have taken the individual's conviction into consideration of both the individual's interest and the government's interest.[77] In *Samson v. California*, the Supreme Court recognized a "continuum of liberty interests."[78] The court examined punishments for probationers, parolees, and convicts and concluded that probationers have more freedom than parolees, who have more freedom than convicts.[79] Convicted offenders are subject to a broad range of restrictions that are "severely constricted expectations of privacy relative to the general citizenry."[80] This diminished expectation of privacy of convicted individuals is weighed against the governmental interest in solving crimes, reducing recidivism, and exonerating the innocent.[81] Weighing the privacy interests of the convicted individual and the government's interests, courts have consistently upheld DNA statutes requiring samples from convicted individuals without a warrant, even when there is no suspicion that they may have committed additional crimes.[82]

Constitutionality of DNA Sampling from Arrestees

Arrestees with Grand Jury or Judicial Probable Cause

While the constitutionality of DNA sampling from convicted individuals appears to be settled among the circuits, the constitutionality of sampling from *arrested* individuals under the 2005 amendment to the DNA Act is less clear.[83] In 2010, the Ninth Circuit affirmed the Eastern District of California's decision upholding the statutory requirement[84] that certain arrestees are required to provide a DNA sample as part of their release conditions before trial.[85] Using the totality of the circumstances test, the Eastern District of California limited its finding to "DNA testing after a judicial finding or grand jury determination of probable cause."[86] In a similar case involving an indicted defendant who refused to provide a DNA sample, the Third Circuit found the DNA Act constitutional under the totality of the circumstances test by analogizing DNA profiles and fingerprints, finding that a DNA profile "is used solely as an accurate, unique, identifying marker."[87] The court reasoned that arrestees have "a diminished expectation of privacy" because enough probable cause existed to justify their arrest and concluded that this amount of probable cause has been used historically to collect fingerprints and photographs of arrestees.[88] While these two cases may seem to conclude DNA collection at arrest is constitutional, they both based their analyses on probable cause determined by a *grand jury or judge* prior to arrest and leave unanswered whether probable cause determined by an *officer* alone is sufficient.[89]

United States v. Buza: Arrestees with an Absence of Judicial Probable Cause

In August of 2011, the California Court of Appeals in *People v. Buza* addressed the collection of DNA based on the probable cause determination of the arresting officer and found the California statute for DNA collection from arrestees, Proposition 69, unconstitutional.[90] The analysis and reasoning of the court in *Buza,* examining the constitutionality of taking DNA samples from non-convicted persons at arrest under the Fourth Amendment, asserted that the emerging practice of DNA collection at arrest should be reconsidered.[91] In *Buza,* the court began by looking at *Haskell v. Brown,* the only case to date to examine DNA collection for "arrestees who have not been subjected to a judicial probable cause determination."[92] In *Haskell,* the Northern District of California upheld the California statute requiring arrestees to submit DNA samples, basing its decision on two grounds: (1) lessened arrestee privacy expectations and the DNA-fingerprint analogy; and (2) the strong governmental interest in identifying arrestees.[93] The *Buza* court's analysis of the totality of the circumstances test, as applied in *Haskell,* set forth several arguments against the constitutionality of DNA sampling at arrest under both Fourth Amendment tests.[94]

In *Haskell,* the court asserted that requiring the accused to submit fingerprints for identification purposes is no different than a requirement that the arrestee submit to DNA sampling upon arrest for identification purposes.[95] The *Haskell* court focused on the DNA profile containing only "junk" DNA, instead of the DNA sample itself containing all of the arrestee's genetic makeup.[96] In *Mitchell,* the court emphasized that CODIS only makes the DNA profile, not the actual sample, available and that strong protections within the Federal DNA Act limit the cross-referencing of DNA to junk DNA exclusively for identification purposes.[97]

As the *Buza* court suggested, this analogy between DNA and fingerprints is flawed for several reasons.[98] First, DNA is more valuable evidence than fingerprints because it tells investigators more about a suspect than a fingerprint and is more frequently found at crime scenes.[99] Scholars dispute whether junk DNA contains only non-genetic identifying characteristics.[100] Perhaps more troubling than the doubt among scientists of what DNA can reveal *today* is the possibility of what DNA can reveal *tomorrow* as technology advances; there is no comparable fear of privacy invasion for fingerprints in the future.[101] DNA sampling also differs from fingerprinting regarding the negative social stigma it carries.[102] Furthermore, the practice of fingerprinting has become routine without being analyzed under current Fourth Amendment jurisprudence, leaving an unstable foundation for the analogy to stand on.[103] As the court in *Buza* noted, the historical basis for allowing fingerprinting is not entirely clear and thus cannot be used as the sole foundation for allowing so-called DNA "fingerprinting" at arrest.[104]

To support the argument that DNA sampling is only for identification, the *Haskell* court defined "identification" as "both who that person is (the person's name, date of birth, etc.) and what that person has done (whether the individual has a criminal record, whether he is the same person who committed an as-yet unsolved crime across town, etc.)."[105] The "who the person is" use of DNA sampling is less effective and slower than fingerprinting; it takes thirty-one days for a DNA sample to be converted into a DNA profile and uploaded into a database, while it only takes about ten minutes for a fingerprint to be cross-referenced to identify an arrestee.[106] Also, DNA samples are not taken until *after* police identify the individual, and then samples are taken only from individuals who have not already been arrested or convicted and, thus, previously added to the database.[107] Therefore, the primary purpose of DNA sampling cannot be to identify the arrested individual.

Because DNA is less efficient than fingerprints in identifying arrestees, the second definition of identification used by *Haskell*, the "what the person has done" definition, must be the real purpose behind DNA sampling of arrestees. The court in *Buza* considered *Haskell*'s definition and concluded that the real purpose of DNA sampling is to determine if the individual has committed *a different* crime "unrelated to the crime for which they were arrested."[108] A closer examination of the intent of California's DNA Act shows the ultimate purposes of the Act are the use of DNA for crime-solving and the need to expand the database to include more potential leads for law enforcement.[109] The *Buza* court concluded that the only limitations imposed on DNA samples are that they be used for law enforcement and may not be used to identify characteristics such as gender or race for "non-law enforcement purposes."[110] "By merging the ordinarily distinct concepts of verification of identity and criminal investigation," the *Buza* court held, "the DNA Act authorizes suspicionless criminal investigation of arrestees in the name of 'identification,' absent any true need or ability to use the material collected to verify identity at the time of arrest."[111]

The government's interest in investigating crime through DNA sampling of arrestees must still be weighed against the arrested individual's reasonable expectation of privacy. While a convict or parolee's expectation of privacy is diminished enough to be outweighed by the governmental interest in collecting DNA samples, the arrestee inherently can expect a higher level of privacy.[112] The treatment of arrestees vastly differs from the treatment of convicts or parolees, as arrestees are not subject to mandatory searches, are less likely to reoffend, and thus must have a greater expectation of privacy.[113] An arrestee has not been found guilty, and unless a judge has found probable cause, the current DNA regime allows sampling based only on the probable cause of the arresting officer.[114] This creates a welcoming temptation for officers to arrest possible suspects of a crime on other grounds to obtain a sample of their DNA to prove their investigative theory.[115]

The expungement process exacerbates the problem of potential officer abuse. The federal DNA statute allows DNA sampling at arrest, while some state statutes require DNA sampling immediately after arrest.[116] This immediate sampling at arrest means that even if the arrest is later determined to be without cause, the DNA sample will remain in the database until the individual applies for expungement and will be continually cross-referenced with new samples from crime scenes, creating additional, reoccurring privacy violations with each search.[117]

Modifying Sampling Submission and Expedition of Expungement

The current statutory scheme used by most states and the federal government allowing DNA sampling at arrest fails to meet the special needs or the totality of the circumstances tests. Accordingly, should the Supreme Court have the opportunity to hear a case challenging the DNA Act or any of the similarly modeled state statutes, the Court should follow the rationale of the *Buza* court and hold that these statutes violate the Fourth Amendment. Although the possibility of review and judicial remedy by the Supreme Court[118] remains uncertain, the constitutional conflicts that DNA databasing presents may quickly and easily be remedied by modifying federal and state statutes.

While each state law could be modified individually, a nationwide statutory remedy would be more easily effectuated by Congress. Using its power to fund state DNA programs, Congress could add a requirement that mandates consistent DNA databasing and retention standards at the state level.[119] Because all state samples are eventually submitted into CODIS, the federal DNA database, Congress can also create uniform conditions for acceptance of DNA profiles into CODIS and require expedition of the expungement process.

Limiting When to Sample and Submit

The first solution to the constitutional dilemma of DNA sampling is the modification of *when*, in the judicial process, the sampling of an individual takes place. The current federal statute allows the collection of "DNA samples from individuals who are arrested, facing charges, or convicted," and many state statutes require DNA sampling immediately following arrest.[120] Reviewing the limited case law on DNA collection at arrest, courts have upheld the statutes in situations where probable cause has been determined by a *grand jury or judge* prior to arrest but have held them unconstitutional in situations where an *officer alone* determined probable cause.[121] Because of the imprecise language of the statute, the line is blurred and outcomes vary under the same statutory language. Drawing a statutory line—requiring an adequate amount of probable cause at arrest to meet the totality of the circumstances test—remedies this inconsistency.[122] While an arrestee can expect a diminished amount of privacy upon arrest, there is a clear difference between the privacy expected by an arrestee—who has the evidence against him reviewed by a grand jury of his peers or by a judge—and one who has been arrested on the conclusion of a single officer's (sometimes instant) determination of probable cause for arrest.[123]

North Carolina's DNA database statute recognizes this differentiation between the kinds of probable cause:

> The arresting law enforcement officer shall obtain, or cause to be obtained, a DNA sample from an arrested person at the time of arrest, or when fingerprinted. However, if the person is arrested without a warrant, then the DNA sample shall not be taken until a probable cause determination has been made pursuant to G.S. 15A-511(c)(1).[124]

Under this statutory scheme, "[t]he magistrate must determine whether there is probable cause to believe that a crime has been committed and that the person arrested committed [the crime] ... ."[125] Waiting to collect the DNA sample of an arrestee until after the *judicial* determination of probable cause solves the problem of arrestee privacy issues raised in *Buza* and also meets the purpose of expanding CODIS.[126]

On the federal level, Congress can require states to implement the probable cause threshold before granting any money to state DNA databases and accepting any DNA sample to be included in CODIS. In Virginia, when a DNA sample is taken and sent to the state DNA database, a copy of the warrant establishing probable cause has to be attached to the sample.[127] If Congress required a similar showing of probable cause before a sample may be admitted into CODIS and made it a condition for a state database to receive federal grants under the Debbie

Smith DNA Backlog Grant Program,[128] states would be encouraged to ensure the privacy of arrestees as mandated by the Fourth Amendment.[129]

Expediting the Expungement Process

The second remedy needed to ensure the constitutionality of DNA databasing is expediting the expungement of DNA samples and profiles and shifting the burden of responsibility in the expungement process. Under the current federal statutory scheme, the Director of the FBI as well as the individual states must expunge any DNA sample and profile from the database upon receipt of

> a certified copy of a final court order establishing that [the qualifying offense] conviction has been overturned; or ... a certified copy of a final court order establishing that [the qualifying offense] charge has been dismissed or has resulted in an acquittal or that no charge was filed within the applicable time period.[130]

The federal statute makes it clear that the DNA samples and profiles of those certified not guilty are to be promptly expunged from the database, yet, with varying state law, it remains unclear as to *who* has to request the expungement. Some states require the arrestee to apply for expungement, which can be a lengthy and complicated process.[131] Furthermore, some states will not invalidate DNA database matches obtained due to a failure to expunge or a delay in expungement by the state.[132] Under this statutory uncertainty, not only does the arrestee carry the burden of requesting expungement, but he also has no recourse if the state fails to expunge his DNA profile even after he meets this burden. The state, therefore, has no incentive to promptly comply with the court order to expunge, as it has nothing to lose.

North Carolina's newly adopted statutory scheme, which went into effect in June 2012, shifts the expungement burden to the prosecutor by requiring her, within thirty days of acquittal or dismissal of the case, to submit an official "verification form" to the State Bureau of Investigations (SBI) including verification of the facts, the arrestee's last known address, and the signature of a judge validating the acquittal or dismissal of the case.[133] Within thirty days of receiving the form, the SBI must determine if there is another legal provision requiring the arrestee's DNA sample to remain in the state database and if not, must "remove the [arrestee's] DNA record and samples" from the database.[134] This statutory scheme places the burden not only on the prosecutor but also the SBI—as the administrator of the state's database—to ensure expungement of DNA samples.

The North Carolina statute also provides that within thirty days of receiving the verification form from the prosecutor, the SBI must mail the arrestee a notice documenting the removal and destruction of the DNA sample and profile from the database or notice that the "sample d[id] not qualify for expunction."[135] If this expungement process is not enacted by the prosecuting attorney or the SBI within the prescribed time period, the arrestee may file a motion to review, and any "identification, warrant, probable cause to arrest, or arrest based upon a database match of the defendant's DNA sample which occurs after the expiration of the statutory periods prescribed for expunction" is "invalid and inadmissible in the prosecution of the [arrestee] for any criminal offense."[136]

If a statutory scheme similar to North Carolina's were adopted on a federal level, it would vastly reduce the burden on the arrestee in the expungement process. Granting the arrestee statutory standing to enforce the automatic expungement of DNA samples and profiles would cure many of the *Buza* court's concerns with continual cross-referencing of DNA samples in CODIS and lessen the fear of "dirty cop" techniques to collect DNA samples.[137] Congress could also enact this scheme by placing the burden of automatic expunction of DNA profiles and samples on the state as another requirement for a state database to receive federal grants under the Debbie Smith DNA Backlog Grant Program[138] to ensure a uniform and constitutional scheme nationwide.

Conclusion

DNA has forever changed the way crime is investigated, and many of its intricacies remain to be discovered.[139] With the expansion of DNA sampling from convicts to parolees to arrestees, a line must be drawn to prevent "encroachment on Fourth Amendment privacy rights"[140]—a line to prevent the "Orwellian prospect" of population-wide DNA sampling.[141] Using the two tests for constitutionality under current Fourth Amendment search jurisprudence—the totality of the circumstances test and the special needs test—the *Buza* court found California's all-arrestees DNA databasing statute unconstitutional.[142]

An examination of the scale of expected privacy rights reveals that there is a difference in the probable cause determinations of judicial officials versus the probable cause determinations of arresting officers.[143] Given this difference, the federal arrestee DNA databasing statute, as well as many arrestee state statutes, is unconstitutional. This constitutional defect is easily remedied, however, by adding two conditions to receiving federal DNA database funding: requiring *judicial* probable cause before DNA is admitted into CODIS and state databases; and rewriting state statutes to place the burden of expungement on the *state* instead of the arrestee.[144] Under this proposed scheme, constitutional rights of those who are not found guilty are safeguarded and protected from suspicionless searches, while the governmental interest of expanding databases and catching criminals in DNA collection is promulgated through a mutually beneficial statutory scheme.

Notes

* J.D. Candidate, 2013, Georgia State University College of Law. Thanks to Professor Jessica D. Gabel for all of her advice and friendship, and thanks to Daniel French for his support and encouragement through the development of this Note.

1. United States v. Kincade, 379 F.3d 813, 871 (9th Cir. 2004) (Kozinski, J., dissenting) (discussing the Ninth Circuit's majority holding that DNA sampling is constitutional).
2. *See, e.g.*, Al Baker, *In Manhattan, District Attorney Sees DNA as Tool to Solve Cold Cases*, N.Y. TIMES (June 14, 2011), http://www.nytimes.com/2011/06/15/nyregion/district-attorney-vance-sees-dna-as-tool-to-solve-cold-cases.html; Colin Moynihan, *Cold Case DNA Unit Links Rikers Inmate to '86 Murder*, N.Y. TIMES (July 6, 2011), http://www.nytimes.com/2011/07/07/nyregion/ny-cold-case-unit-links-dna-to-86-murder.html; Michael Stetz, *Cold Case Murder Solved After 31 Years*, SAN DIEGO UNION-TRIB. (Feb. 10, 2008), http://www.signonsandiego.com/uniontrib/20080210/news_1m10carrier.html.
3. To date, in the United States, 306 convictions have been overturned based on DNA evidence. *DNA Exonerations Nationwide*, INNOCENCE PROJECT, http://www.innocenceproject.org/Content/Facts_on_PostConviction_DNA_Exonerations.php (last visited Mar. 21, 2013). The 306 exonerees served an average of over thirteen years, and eighteen served on death row. *Id.*

   > DNA is a powerful component of the forensic science and criminal justice systems; it can link seemingly unrelated crimes, resolve cold cases, track violent offenders both in and out of the penal system, solve crimes which would have been previously unsolvable, and prevent innocent people from going to prison. Currently, DNA is also being used to exonerate the innocent.

   DNA Evidence, Cases of Exoneration, ENOTES, http://www.enotes.com/forensic-science/dna-evidence-cases-exoneration (last visited Mar. 21, 2013).
4. United States v. Kriesel, 508 F.3d 941, 948 (9th Cir. 2007). The possible future developments in DNA:

   > raise[] questions both about the kind of personal and private information that may be derived from the DNA samples in the DOJ's possession, and the uses of that biometric data as scientific developments increase the type and amount of information that can be extracted from it. For example, commentators have discussed the potential for research to identify genetic causes of antisocial behavior that might be used to justify various crime control measures.

   People v. Buza, 129 Cal. Rptr. 3d 753, 769 (Ct. App.), *cert. granted*, 262 P.3d 854 (Cal. 2011) (note that under California Rule of Courts 8.1105(e)(1), an opinion is no longer considered published if the Supreme Court grants review). *See generally* Dorothy Roberts, *Collateral Consequences, Genetic Surveillance, and the New Biopolitics of Race*, 54 HOW. L.J. 567 (2011) (discussing the fear of using DNA as a new form of Jim Crow racial profiling).
5. Jessica D. Gabel, *Probable Cause from Probable Bonds: A Genetic Tattle Tale Based on Familial DNA*, 21 HASTINGS WOMEN'S L.J. 3, 5 (2010) ("High profile paternity and criminal cases become part of water cooler conversation, and the 'ripped from the headlines' approach of popular television programs (such

as NCIS, Criminal Minds, Forensic Files, and, of course, the various incarnations of CSI and Law & Order) continue the soap opera where reality left off.").

6. This demand for DNA evidence has been coined the "CSI effect." *E.g.*, Tom R. Tyler, *Viewing CSI and the Threshold of Guilt: Managing Truth and Justice in Reality and Fiction*, 115 YALE L.J. 1050, 1050 (2006). Mr. Tyler defined the term:

> The "CSI effect" is a term that legal authorities and the mass media have coined to describe a supposed influence that watching the television show CSI: Crime Scene Investigation has on juror behavior. Some have claimed that jurors who see the high-quality forensic evidence presented on CSI raise their standards in real trials, in which actual evidence is typically more flawed and uncertain.

Id.

7. 42 U.S.C. § 14135a(a)(1)(A) (2006). For examples of state laws, see: ARIZ. REV. STAT. ANN. § 13-610 (West, Westlaw through 1st Reg. Sess. of 51st Legislature (2013)); MINN. STAT. § 299C.155 (West, Westlaw through 2013 Reg. Sess. through ch 10).

8. Leigh M. Harlan, Note, *When Privacy Fails: Invoking a Property Paradigm to Mandate the Destruction of DNA Samples*, 54 DUKE L.J. 179, 186 (2004). The original DNA Identification Act included mandatory samples from only those persons convicted of a felony. The act was amended in 2005 to include arrestees. H.R. REP. NO. 109-218(I), at 38 (2005); *see also* 42 U.S.C. § 14135a(a)(1)(A) ("The Attorney General may, as prescribed by the Attorney General in regulation, collect DNA samples from individuals who are arrested, facing charges, or convicted or from non-United States persons who are detained under the authority of the United States."); David H. Kaye, *Two Fallacies About DNA Data Banks for Law Enforcement*, 67 BROOK. L. REV. 179, 180–81 (2001); *State that Have Passed Arrestee DNA Database Laws*, DNARESOURCE.COM (Sept. 2011), http://www.dnaresource.com/documents/ ArresteeDNALaws-2011.pdf [hereinafter *States with DNA Arrestee Laws*]. Twenty-five states have passed arrestee DNA database laws as of September 2011. Id. For example, California's law states:

> Each adult person arrested for a felony offense ... shall provide the buccal swab samples and thumb and palm print impressions and any blood or other specimens required pursuant to this chapter immediately following arrest, or during the booking or intake or prison reception center process or as soon as administratively practicable after arrest, but, in any case, prior to release on bail or pending trial or any physical release from confinement or custody.

CAL. PENAL CODE § 296.1 (West, Westlaw through Ch. 3 of 2013 Reg. Sess.).

9. *States with DNA Arrestee Laws, supra* note 8 (diagram with states that require application for expungement); *see also, e.g.*, CAL. PENAL CODE § 299(a) (West, Westlaw through Ch. 3 of 2013 Reg. Sess.); *Buza*, 129 Cal. Rptr. 3d at 758–59 (reviewing expungement procedures in California).

10. *Buza*, 129 Cal. Rptr. 3d at 759–61. For further discussion on the constitutionality of DNA samples, see generally D.H. Kaye, *Who Needs Special Needs? On the Constitutionality of Collecting DNA and Other Biometric Data from Arrestees*, 34 J.L. MED. & ETHICS 188 (2006).

11. *See generally Buza*, 129 Cal. Rptr. 3d. 753.

12. *See* discussion *infra* Part I.
13. *See* discussion *infra* Part II.
14. *See* discussion *infra* Part III.
15. Robert Wright, *Molecular Biologists Watson & Crick*, TIME, Mar. 29, 1999, at 172, *available at* http://www.time.com/time/magazine/article/0,9171,990626,00.html (discussing the lives and scientific discoveries of James Watson and Francis Crick). For more information on the discovery of DNA, see Leslie A. Pray, *Discovery of DNA Structure and Function: Watson and Crick*, NATURE EDUC. (2008), http://www.nature.com/scitable/topicpage/discovery-of-dna-structure-and-function-watson-397.
16. J.D. Watson & F.H.C. Crick, *Molecular Structure of Nucleic Acids: A Structure of Deoxyribose Nucleic Acid*, 171 NATURE 737, 737 (1953).
17. *See generally* A. JAMIE CUTICCHIA, GENETICS: A HANDBOOK FOR LAWYERS, 8-16 (2009).
18. *See generally id.* at 8–11.
19. *Id.*
20. *Id.* at 7.
21. ANDREI SEMIKHODSKII, DEALING WITH DNA EVIDENCE: A LEGAL GUIDE 12 (2007). "It is these individually varying regions, known as polymorphic loci, that are used in DNA profiling and identification techniques." Harlan, *supra* note 8, at 185; *see also* Gabel, *supra* note 5, at 9 (referring to the regions of DNA that house individual identity as "junk DNA").
22. *Cf.* SEMIKHODSKII, *supra* note 21, at 12.
23. *Id.* at 21-22. British scientist Dr. Alec Jeffreys first used DNA to identify a rapist in a police investigation in 1986. Debra A. Herlica, Note, *DNA Databanks: When Has a Good Thing Gone Too Far?*, 52 SYRACUSE L. REV. 951, 952 n.8 (2002) (describing the first use of DNA in a criminal investigation); Heidi C. Schmitt, Note, *Post-Conviction Remedies Involving the Use of DNA Evidence to Exonerate Wrongfully Convicted Prisoners: Various Approaches Under Federal and State Law*, 70 UMKC L. REV. 1001, 1002 (2002) (discussing Alec Jeffreys's discovery).
24. Gabel, *supra* note 5, at 11 ("The process of collecting and analyzing a DNA profile is often referred to as DNA 'typing,' 'fingerprinting,' or 'profiling.'"); *see also* SEMIKHODSKII, *supra* note 21, at 12 (arguing that the use of the term "DNA fingerprinting" may be widely accepted but is "somewhat confusing" and that "the analogy between conventional and DNA fingerprinting is not helpful").
25. Andrews v. State, 533 So. 2d 841, 843 (Fla. Dist. Ct. App. 1988). In 1987, Tommie Lee Andrews was convicted of rape after a DNA match was made between his blood sample and semen recovered from the victim. *Id.*; *see also* Michelle Hibbert, *DNA Databanks: Law Enforcement's Greatest Surveillance Tool?*, 34 WAKE FOREST L. REV. 767, 773 (1999); *supra* note 24.
26. RON C. MICHAELIS, ROBERT G. FLANDERS & PAULA H. WULFF, A LITIGATOR'S GUIDE TO DNA xiii (2008); Gabel, *supra* note 5, at 12.
27. SEMIKHODSKII, *supra* note 21, at 2. "No two people, with the single exception of idential twins, have identical DNA." *Id.* Therefore, "every DNA profile obtained is virtually unique" to an individual. *Id.*

28. *Id.* DNA's "biometrical parameters" for an individual do not change as that individual grows older, and the DNA profile remains the same regardless of what kind of biological sample is obtained. *See id.*
29. *Id.* Family members have similar DNA profiles, which has led to controversial "familial DNA searches" of databased DNA. Erin Murphy, *Relative Doubt: Familial Searches of DNA Databases*, 109 MICH. L. REV. 291, 294–301 (2010) (discussing the mechanics of DNA databasing and familial searches). Familial DNA searches, which cross-reference two persons to see if they are related based on their DNA, is beyond the scope of this Note. For more information on familial DNA searches, see generally Gabel, *supra* note 5, at 19.
30. *See* SEMIKHODSKII, *supra* note 21, at 2. DNA is resilient, "can be produced from very old and decayed biological samples," and "withstand[s] both natural and man-made environmental injury." *Id.*
31. *Id.* ("[A] single hair, skin flake or small droplet of sweat left at the crime scene is often sufficient to obtain a full DNA profile ..."); Gabel, *supra* note 5, at 13 ("As DNA harvesting went beyond the bounds of blood, evidence took the form of semen, saliva, hair, tissue, bones, teeth, and sweat found on or in clothes, soda cans, hairbrushes, toothbrushes, stamps, envelopes, Kleenex, chewing gum, cigarette butts—anything a person would come in contact with.").
32. Paul C. Giannelli, *Wrongful Convictions and Forensic Science: The Need to Regulate Crime Labs*, 86 N.C. L. REV. 163, 171 (2007) (noting DNA profiling as "the current gold standard in forensic science"); *see also* 8 AM. JUR. 3D *Proof of Facts* § 749 (1990) ("[T]he validity of the underlying principles of DNA identification testing is perhaps the easiest hurdle to overcome for the proponent of that evidence."); William C. Thompson & Simon Ford, *DNA Typing: Acceptance and Weight of the New Genetic Identification Tests*, 75 VA. L. REV. 45, 60 (1989) ("There is nothing controversial about the theory underlying DNA typing. Indeed, this theory is so well accepted that its accuracy is unlikely even to be raised as an issue in hearings on the admissibility of the new tests.").
33. Paul E. Tracy & Vincent Morgan, *Big Brother and His Science Kit: DNA Databases for 21st Century Crime Control?*, 90 J. CRIM. L. & CRIMINOLOGY 635, 649 (2000).
34. SEMIKHODSKII, *supra* note 21, at 23. Other type of DNA samples analyzed include "semen, saliva, hair, tissue, bones, teeth, and sweat found on or in clothes, soda cans, hairbrushes, toothbrushes, stamps, envelopes, Kleenex, chewing gum, cigarette butts—anything a person would come in contact with." Gabel, *supra* note 5, at 13. For deeper analysis on how various biological samples are analyzed, see generally SEMIKHODSKII, *supra* note 21, at 21–26.
35. Robert Berlet, Comment, *A Step Too Far: Due Process and DNA Collection in California After Proposition 69*, 40 U.C. DAVIS L. REV. 1481, 1486 (2007).
36. Harlan, *supra* note 8, at 186–87.
37. *Id.* DNA dragnets collect samples from a large group of people who may have had the ability to perpetrate the crime. *Id.* Dragnets do not require warrants since the samples are typically voluntarily given; however, some scholars have argued against their constitutionality. *Id.* For more on DNA dragnets and challenges to their constitutionality, see generally Fred W. Drobner, Comment, *DNA Dragnets: Constitutional Aspects of Mass DNA Identification Testing*, 28 CAP. U. L. REV. 479 (2000).
38. Harlan, *supra* note 8, at 186–87.

39. Kaye, *supra* note 8, at 180.

40. *Id.* at 180–81; *see also, e.g.*, MINN. STAT. § 609.117 (West, Westlaw through 2013 Reg. Sess. through Ch. 25) (requiring that a person who has been convicted of a misdemeanor submit a DNA sample when that misdemeanor "aris[es] out of the same set of circumstances" as a felony that the person was also charged with); H.B. 483, 2011 Gen. Assemb., Reg. Sess. (N.C. 2011) (proposing expanding list of felonies required to submit DNA samples at arrest to include "assault on handicapped persons" and child abandonment). Minnesota's statute was upheld as constitutional in *State v. Johnson*. State v. Johnson, 813 N.W.2d 1, 11 (Minn. 2012) ("[W]e conclude that when a person is convicted of a misdemeanor offense that arises out of the same set of circumstances as a felony charge and that person's sentence includes probation with conditions such as random urinalyses, there is a significant reduction in that person's expectation of privacy in his or her identity.").

41. 42 U.S.C. § 14135a(a)(1)(A) (2006) ("The Attorney General may, as prescribed by the Attorney General in regulation, collect DNA samples from individuals who are arrested, facing charges, or convicted or from non-United States persons who are detained under the authority of the United States."); Kaye, *supra* note 8, at 180; *States with DNA Arrestee Laws*, *supra* note 8; *see also* CAL. PENAL CODE § 296.1 (West, Westlaw through Ch. 3 of 2013 Reg. Sess.). The statute reads:

> Each adult person arrested for a felony offense ... shall provide the buccal swab samples and thumb and palm print impressions and any blood or other specimens required pursuant to this chapter immediately following arrest, or during the booking or intake or prison reception center process or as soon as administratively practicable after arrest, but, in any case, prior to release on bail or pending trial or any physical release from confinement or custody.

Id.

42. *See States with DNA Arrestee Laws*, *supra* note 8. The twenty-five states that have passed arrestee DNA database laws are: Alabama, Alaska, Arizona, Arkansas, California, Colorado, Florida, Illinois, Kansas, Louisiana, Maryland, Michigan, Missouri, New Jersey, New Mexico, North Carolina, North Dakota, Ohio, South Carolina, South Dakota, Tennessee, Texas, Utah, Vermont, and Virginia. *Id. See also, e.g.*, KAN. STAT. ANN. § 21-2511(e)(2) (West, Westlaw through 2012 Reg. Sess.) ("[A]ny adult arrested or charged or juvenile placed in custody for or charged with the commission or attempted commission of any felony ... shall be required to submit such specimen or sample at the same time such person is fingerprinted pursuant to the booking procedure."); N.C. GEN. STAT. § 15A-266.3A(b) (West, Westlaw through S.L. 2013-36 of 2013 Reg. Sess.) ("The arresting law enforcement officer shall obtain, or cause to be obtained, a DNA sample from an arrested person at the time of arrest, or when fingerprinted. However, if the person is arrested without a warrant, then the DNA sample shall not be taken until a probable cause determination has been made pursuant to [the statute]."); N.D. CENT. CODE § 31-13-03(1) (West, Westlaw through 2011 Reg. and Spec. Sess.) ("An individual eighteen years of age or over who is arrested ... for the commission of a felony shall provide to a law enforcement officer ... at the time of the individual's arrest ... a sample of blood or other body fluids for DNA law enforcement identification purposes and inclusion in the law enforcement identification databases.").

43. The most common form of DNA collection is buccal swabbing, where the "inside of a suspect's cheek is briefly and painlessly brushed with cotton." Harlan, *supra* note 8, at 187.

44. *Id.*; *see also* People v. Buza, 129 Cal. Rptr. 3d 753, 757 (Ct. App.) *cert. granted*, 262 P.3d 854 (Cal. 2011). The court held:

> Analysis of the DNA may be "only for identification purposes." A genetic profile is created from the sample based on 13 genetic loci known as "noncoding" or "junk" DNA, because "they are thought not to reveal anything about trait coding"; the resulting profiles are so highly individuated that the chance of two randomly selected individuals sharing the same profile are "infinitesimal."

Id. (citations omitted).

45. *Buza*, 129 Cal. Rptr. 3d at 757; Harlan, *supra* note 8, at 186–88. *See also Frequently Asked Questions (FAQs) on the CODIS Program and the National DNA Index System*, FED. BUREAU INVESTIGATION, http://www.fbi.gov/about-us/lab/codis/codis-and-ndis-fact-sheet (last visited Mar. 14, 2013) [hereinafter *CODIS FAQs*]. The Federal Bureau of Investigation explains:

> No names or other personal identifiers of the offenders, arrestees, or detainees are stored using the CODIS software. Only the following information is stored and can be searched at the national level:
>
> (1) The DNA profile—the set of identification characteristics or numerical representation at each of the various loci analyzed;
>
> (2) The Agency Identifier of the agency submitting the DNA profile;
>
> (3) The Specimen Identification Number—generally a number assigned sequentially at the time of sample collection. This number does *not* correspond to the individual's social security number, criminal history identifier, or correctional facility identifier; and
>
> (4) The DNA laboratory personnel associated with a DNA profile analysis.

Id. (footnote omitted).

46. Gabel, *supra* note 5, at 13.

47. Harlan, *supra* note 8, at 188. However, the states vary on what kinds of crimes require DNA samples and if arrestees will be included in the database. *See supra* Part I.B.1.

48. *See* Gabel, *supra* note 5, at 13. "State [and] local law enforcement agencies are rapidly developing their own DNA testing laboratories and looking to the Federal Government for potential financial support." 138 CONG. REC. H11737-01 (daily ed. Oct. 5, 1992), 1992 WL 280161 (Westlaw).

49. Gabel, *supra* note 5, at 13. The FBI's website provides the CODIS mission statement:

> The CODIS Unit manages the Combined DNA Index System (CODIS) and the National DNA Index System (NDIS) and is responsible for developing, providing, and supporting the CODIS Program to federal, state, and local crime laboratories in the United States and selected international law enforcement crime laboratories to foster the exchange and comparison of forensic DNA evidence from violent crime investigations. The CODIS Unit also provides administrative management and support to the FBI for various advisory boards, Department of Justice (DOJ) grant programs, and legislation regarding DNA.

Combined DNA Index System (CODIS), FED. BUREAU INVESTIGATION, http://www.fbi.gov/about-us/lab/biometric-analysis/codis (last visited Mar. 31, 2013).

50. Gabel, *supra* note 5, at 13. The Debbie Smith DNA Backlog Grant Program lays out the eligibility requirements for a state to receive federal funding for its DNA sampling and database system, which includes quality controls and inclusion of the samples into CODIS. 42 U.S.C. § 14135 (2006); Jonathan Kimmelman, *Risking Ethical Insolvency: A Survey of Trends in Criminal DNA Databanking*, 28 J.L. MED. & ETHICS 209, 210 (2000); *see also Buza*, 129 Cal. Rptr. 3d at 759 ("In 2004, Congress expanded the definition of 'qualifying federal offenses' to include all felonies. In 2006, Congress further expanded the reach of the 2000 act by allowing the Attorney General to 'collect DNA samples from individuals who are *arrested*, facing charges, or convicted ... .'" (alteration in original) (citations omitted)).

51. *CODIS—NDIS Statistics*, FED. BUREAU INVESTIGATION, http://www.fbi.gov/about-us/lab/biometric-analysis/codis/ndis-statistics (last visited Apr. 6, 2013). Professor Gabel describes the CODIS architecture:

> This three-tier structure functions as a food chain, where information at the lowest level is fed into larger mouths (databases). It begins at the local level ("LDIS"—Local DNA Index System) where local laboratories take samples from both crime scenes and offenders and generate them into CODIS profiles. At the second level ("SDIS"—State DNA Index System), state law enforcement agencies input this information into their statewide databases. At the top of the database food chain—the national level—state profiles are uploaded into NDIS.

Gabel, *supra* note 5, at 14 (citations omitted); *see also CODIS Brochure*, FED. BUREAU INVESTIGATION, http://www.fbi.gov/about-us/lab/biometric-analysis/codis/codis_brochure (last visited Mar. 31, 2013) (detailing the CODIS hierarchy).

52. *Buza*, 129 Cal. Rptr. 3d at 758; *see also* Haskell v. Brown, 677 F. Supp. 2d 1187, 1190–91 (N.D. Cal. 2009).

53. *Buza*, 129 Cal. Rptr. 3d at 758; *see also* Gabel, *supra* note 5, at 16 ("A 'hit' occurs when an offender profile matches a crime scene sample at all thirteen CODIS markers. A 'cold hit' occurs when an offender profile is linked to a cold case years after the crime was committed." (citations omitted)).

54. *CODIS—NDIS Statistics, supra note 51*.

55. The FBI provides information regarding the expungement requirements:

Laboratories participating in the National DNA Index are required to expunge qualifying profiles from the National Index under the following circumstances:

1. For convicted offenders, if the participating laboratory receives a certified copy of a final court order documenting the conviction has been overturned; and
2. For arrestees, if the participating laboratory receives a certified copy of a final court order documenting the charge has been dismissed, resulted in an acquittal or no charges have been brought within the applicable time period.

CODIS FAQs, *supra* note 45.

56. Alabama, Arizona, Arkansas, California, Colorado, Florida, Illinois, Kansas, Louisiana, Michigan, New Jersey, New Mexico, North Carolina, North Dakota, Ohio, South Dakota, Texas, and Utah require a request for expungement. *States with DNA Arrestee Laws*, *supra* note 8.

57. Alaska, Maryland, Missouri, South Carolina, Tennessee, Vermont, and Virginia expunge DNA samples and profiles upon non-conviction. *Id.*
58. CAL. PENAL CODE § 299(a) (West, Westlaw through Ch. 3 of 2013 Reg. Sess.); *see also Buza*, 129 Cal. Rptr. 3d at 758-59 (reviewing expungement procedures in California).
59. CAL. PENAL CODE §§ 299(b)(1), (c)(2)(B).
60. *Buza*, 129 Cal. Rptr. 3d at 758.
61. *Id.*; *see* CAL. PENAL CODE § 299(c)(1).
62. CAL. PENAL CODE § 299(d) ("Any identification, warrant, probable cause to arrest, or arrest based upon a data bank or database match is not invalidated due to a failure to expunge or a delay in expunging records.").
63. Harlan, *supra* note 8, at 191; Drobner, *supra* note 37, at 510 (explaining that the collection of DNA samples requires Fourth Amendment analyses because it implicates privacy interests). Defendants have also used the First Amendment, Eighth Amendment, Fifth Amendment, Due Process Clause, and the Equal Protection Clause to raise constitutional challenges to DNA sampling and databasing. Aaron P. Stevens, Note, *Arresting Crime: Expanding the Scope of DNA Databases in America*, 79 TEX. L. REV. 921, 937-38 (2001).
64. U.S. CONST. amend. IV.
65. *Buza*, 129 Cal. Rptr. 3d at 759. "Searches" include the collection of blood and urine, performing a breathalyzer test, fingernail scrapings, and buccal swabbing for the collection of saliva. *Id.* The test for what falls under constitutional scrutiny has been defined as the searches of parts of the body that are "beyond mere physical characteristics ... constantly exposed to the public." Cupp v. Murphy, 412 U.S. 291, 295 (1973) (alteration in original) (internal quotation marks omitted).
66. United States v. Mitchell, 652 F.3d 387, 406 (3d Cir. 2011) (holding that "[t]he collection of DNA under § 14135a entails two separate 'searches'"), *cert. denied*, 132 S. Ct. 1741 (2012) (mem.). Some scholars have asserted that there are actually three searches in the DNA databasing process: collection of the sample, initial entrance into the database, and the "multiple, recurrent searches" of the DNA against new entries into the database. Ashley Eiler, Note, *Arrested Development: Reforming the Federal All-Arrestee DNA Collection Statute to Comply with the Fourth Amendment*, 79 GEO. WASH. L. REV. 1201, 1209 (2011).
67. Eiler, *supra* note 66, at 1209.
68. Katz v. United States, 389 U.S. 347, 361 (1967) (Harlan, J., concurring) ("My understanding of the [reasonableness] rule that has emerged from prior decisions is that there is a twofold requirement, first that a person have exhibited an actual (subjective) expectation of privacy and, second, that the expectation be one that society is prepared to recognize as 'reasonable.'").
69. *Buza*, 129 Cal. Rptr. 3d at 760 ("Prior to expansion of the scope of the Federal DNA Act in 2006 to include the taking of DNA samples from arrestees, the constitutionality of that act was upheld by every federal circuit presented with the issue." (citations omitted)); *id.* at 760 n.7 ("Comparable state statutes authorizing collection of DNA samples from persons convicted of qualifying offenses were also universally upheld by federal circuit courts." (citations omitted)). For further discussion of the constitutionality of DNA samples, see generally Kaye, *supra* note 10.

70. *See* Eiler, *supra* note 66, at 1213-16. "[T]he majority of circuits—the First, Fourth, Fifth, Sixth, Eighth, Ninth, Eleventh, and District of Columbia—[use the] totality of the circumstances approach." *Mitchell*, 652 F.3d at 403. "Only the Second and Seventh Circuits have consistently held otherwise, employing the special needs exception in every case concerning the constitutionality of a DNA indexing statute." *Id.* at 403 n.15. The Tenth Circuit has used both tests but, most recently, has used the totality of the circumstances analysis. *Id.*
71. Tania Simoncelli, *Dangerous Excursions: The Case Against Expanding Forensic DNA Databases to Innocent Persons*, 34 J.L. MED. & ETHICS 390, 391 (2006); Eiler, *supra* note 66, at 1212.
72. New Jersey v. T.L.O., 469 U.S. 325, 351 (1985) (Blackmun, J., concurring). For examples of courts upholding certain regimes of suspicionless searches where the program was designed to serve special needs beyond the normal need for law enforcement, see *Vernonia School District 47J v. Acton*, 515 U.S. 646 (1995) (upholding random drug testing of student athletes) and *National Treasury Employees Union v. Von Raab*, 489 U.S. 656 (1989) (upholding drug tests for United States Customs Service employees seeking transfer or promotion to certain positions).
73. United States v. Amerson, 483 F.3d 73, 81 (2d Cir. 2007). For more examples of courts upholding DNA databasing under the special needs test, see *United States v. Hook*, 471 F.3d 766, 771- 72 (7th Cir. 2006) and *Nicholas v. Goord*, 430 F.3d 652, 667 (2d Cir. 2005).
74. *Nicholas*, 430 F.3d at 669 (citations omitted).
75. People v. Buza, 129 Cal. Rptr. 3d 753, 760-61 (Ct. App.), *cert. granted*, 262 P.3d 854 (Cal. 2011).
76. "In evaluating the totality of the circumstances, we must balance the degree to which DNA profiling interferes with the privacy interests of qualified federal offenders against the significance of the public interests served by such profiling." United States v. Kincade, 379 F.3d 813, 836 (9th Cir. 2004) (challenging a DNA collection statute).
77. *Buza*, 129 Cal. Rptr. 3d at 761.
78. Eiler, *supra* note 66, at 1226; *see* Samson v. California, 547 U.S. 843, 846, 848-49 (2006) (upholding a statute that requires every prisoner eligible for release on state parole to agree in writing to be subject to search or seizure by a parole officer or other peace officer with or without a search warrant and with or without cause).
79. *Samson*, 547 U.S. at 846, 848-49.
80. *Kincade*, 379 F.3d at 834. "[C]onvicted offenders have been held to have no reasonable expectation of privacy in their identity." *Buza*, 129 Cal. Rptr. 3d at 761 (citations omitted).
81. *See, e.g., Samson*, 547 U.S. at 853 (finding that the state's combined interest in the supervision of its parolees, the reduction of recidivism, and the effective reintegration of parolees into society justified the suspicionless search at issue); United States v. Knights, 534 U.S. 112, 120-21 (2001) (holding that the state had dual interests in reintegrating the probationer into society and in preventing recidivism).
82. *See* United States v. Kriesel, 508 F.3d 941, 947 (9th Cir. 2007) ("As a direct consequence of [Defendant's] status as a supervised releasee, he has a diminished expectation of privacy in his own identity specifically, and tracking his identity is the primary consequence of DNA collection."); *Kincade*, 379 F.3d at 837.

83. In upholding the constitutionality of sampling convicted individuals in *Kriesel*, the Ninth Circuit clarified: "We emphasize that our ruling today does not cover DNA collection from arrestees or non-citizens detained in the custody of the United States, who are required to submit to DNA collection by the 2006 version of the DNA Act." *Kriesel*, 508 F.3d at 948–49.
84. *See* Bail Reform Act, 18 U.S.C. § 3142(b), (c)(1)(A) (2006); DNA Fingerprinting Act, 42 U.S.C. § 14135a (2006).
85. 85. United States v. Pool, 645 F. Supp. 2d 903, 909 (E.D. Cal. 2009).
86. *Id.* ("The judicial or grand jury finding of probable cause within a criminal proceeding is a watershed event which should be viewed differently from mere pre-judicial involvement gathering of evidence.").
87. United States v. Mitchell, 652 F.3d 387, 410 (3d Cir. 2011) (calling DNA profiles "fingerprints for the twenty-first century"), *cert. denied*, 132 S. Ct. 1741 (2012) (mem.).
88. *Id.* at 412; *see also Pool*, 645 F. Supp. 2d at 910 ("An arrestee has a diminished expectation of privacy in his own identity. Probable cause has long been the standard which allowed an arrestee to be photographed, fingerprinted and otherwise be compelled to give information which can later be used for identification purposes." (citations omitted)).
89. The court in *Buza* explained:

> [I]n both *Pool* and *Mitchell*, the defendants had been indicted before law enforcement officers sought to obtain DNA samples. Whereas Pool grounded its analysis on the fact that the defendant's DNA sample was collected after a judicial or grand jury determination of probable cause for felony charges had been made, Mitchell expressly left open the question whether an arresting officer's probable cause determination could be sufficient.

People v. Buza, 129 Cal. Rptr. 3d 753, 765 (Ct. App.) (footnote omitted) (citations omitted), *cert. granted*, 262 P.3d 854 (Cal. 2011).

90. *See id.* In October 2011, the Arizona Court of Appeals reviewed ARIZ. REV. STAT. § 8-238, a statute requiring juveniles to submit to DNA sampling following arrest for certain offenses. Mario W. v. Kaipio, 265 P.3d 389, 393 (Ariz. Ct. App. 2011), *vacated*, 281 P.3d 476 (Ariz. 2012). While this Note does not distinguish between juvenile and adult arrestees in its analysis, the Arizona Court of Appeals found that sampling juveniles who were arrested on an officer's probable cause alone would be unconstitutional. *Id.* at 400. The court held:

> For the two juveniles ... who have been arrested or accused but for whom there has been no judicial finding of probable cause to believe that the juveniles have committed the offenses for which they are charged, evaluating the totality of the circumstances leads me to the opposite result. Without the watershed event of a judicial finding of probable cause, I conclude that application of A.R.S. § 8-238 to take DNA samples from these two juveniles would be unconstitutional.

Id.; *see also In re* Welfare of M.L.M., 813 N.W.2d 26 (Minn. 2012) (examining constitutionality of MINN. STAT. § 609.117, subdiv. 1(2) (2010) from juvenile arrestee perspective).

91. In October 2011, the California Supreme Court granted review of *Buza*, and as of May 2013, the case was fully briefed but no opinion had been issued. *See Appellate Courts Case Information*, CAL. COURTS, http://appellatecases.courtinfo.ca.gov/search/case/mainCaseScreen.cfm?dist=0&doc_id=1990653&doc_no=S196200 (last updated May 24, 2013).

92. *Buza*, 129 Cal. Rptr. 3d at 766 (citing Haskell v. Brown, 677 F. Supp. 2d 1187 (N.D. Cal. 2009)).
93. The *Haskell* court examined the continuum of privacy rights:

> Arrestees undoubtedly have a greater privacy interest than convicted felons, but Plaintiffs have not shown that that interest outweighs the government's compelling interest in identifying arrestees, and its interest in using arrestees' DNA to solve past crimes. Accordingly, based on the evidence presently before the Court, California's DNA searching of arrestees appears reasonable.

Haskell, 677 F. Supp. 2d at 1201. The denial of the injunction by the Northern District of California in *Haskell* was upheld by the Ninth Circuit in *Haskell v. Harris*, 669 F.3d 1049, 1051 (9th Cir.) (concluding "that the Government's compelling interests far outweigh arrestees' privacy concerns"), *reh'g en banc granted*, 686 F.3d 1121 (9th Cir. 2012).
94. *See generally Buza*, 129 Cal. Rptr. 3d at 761–68.
95. *Haskell*, 677 F. Supp. 2d at 1197 (rationalizing that "everyday 'booking' procedures routinely require even the merely accused to provide fingerprint identification, regardless of whether investigation of the crime involves fingerprint evidence." (citations omitted)).
96. *Id.* at 1190. DNA profiles that have the thirteen "junk" DNA are made from DNA samples taken at arrest. *See* H.R. REP. NO. 106-900, pt. 1, at 27 (2000) ("[T]he genetic markers used for forensic DNA testing were purposely selected because they are not associated with any known physical or medical characteristics ... ."). *See also* discussion *supra* Part I.B.1 for more information on the sampling process.
97. United States v. Mitchell, 652 F.3d 387, 407 (3d Cir. 2011) ("[The court is] also reassured by thenumerous protections in place guarding against [the] possibility [of misuse] ... . [T]he [DNA] Act criminalizes the misuse of both the sample and the analysis generated from the sample." (citing 42 U.S.C.§ 14135e(c))), *cert. denied*, 132 S. Ct. 1741 (2012) (mem.). "By using only so-called 'junk DNA' to create the profile, the Government ensures that meaningful personal genetic information about the individual is not published in CODIS." *Id.* at 400.
98. *Buza*, 129 Cal. Rptr. 3d at 767–68.
99. DNA can be recovered from crime scenes in many forms, such as hair, skin, and even sweat. *See supra* note 24. DNA can also reveal information about family members and is used in familial database searches. *See generally* Gabel, *supra* note 5, at 19.
100. *Buza*, 129 Cal. Rptr. 3d at 768; *see also* United States v. Kincade, 379 F.3d 813, 850 (9th Cir. 2004) ("[N]ew discoveries are being made by the day that challenge the core assumption underlying junk DNA's name—regions of DNA previously thought to be 'junk DNA' may be genic after all."). Some scholars have asserted that DNA may reveal personality traits that lead to criminal behavior and that, therefore, everyone should be sampled to identify these traits early on in life. Simoncelli, *supra* note 71, at 392.
101. While a DNA sample is turned into a DNA profile for entry into the database, almost every state law and the federal DNA law require the laboratory to keep part of the original DNA sample that contains the human genome for an unlimited length of time. *Buza*, 129 Cal. Rptr. 3d at 769. Today, junk DNA samples may indicate an individual's race or sex, and in the near future, DNA samples promise to reveal more about an individual's medical characteristics. Eiler, *supra* note 66, at 1211.

102. "That DNA is used most commonly, both in the public perception and in reality, to detect more heinous crimes such as rape and murder [] speaks to this negative perception." Corey Preston, Note, *Faulty Foundations: How the False Analogy to Routine Fingerprinting Undermines the Argument for Arrestee DNA Sampling*, 19 WM. & MARY BILL RTS. J. 475, 496 (2010). However, fingerprinting has long been accepted without such a negative social stigma. *Id.* at 495–96.

103. Fingerprints have become part of the American way of life, without hesitation by the public:

> Because the great expansion in fingerprinting came before the modern era of Fourth Amendment jurisprudence ushered in by *Katz v. United States*, it proceeded unchecked by any judicial balancing against the personal right to privacy. As a consequence, we have become accustomed to having our fingerprints on file in some government database. The suggestion that law enforcement agencies, including the FBI, must destroy the fingerprints of those who were wrongfully arrested and booked, and were later released, would today be greeted by reactions ranging from apathy to a disdainful snigger. Why? Because we have come to accept that people—even totally innocent people—have no legitimate expectation of privacy in their fingerprints, and that's that.

Kincade, 379 F.3d at 874 (Kozinski, J., dissenting) (citations omitted).

104. *Buza*, 129 Cal. Rptr. 3d at 770 (finding that routine fingerprinting without Fourth Amendment analysis cannot lead to the conclusion that DNA sampling survives without a separate constitutional analysis).

105. Haskell v. Brown, 677 F. Supp. 2d 1187, 1199 (N.D. Cal. 2009). The court stated:

> Who the person is can often be checked using fingerprints, but that does not preclude the government from also checking that individual's identity in other ways. An individual might wear gloves at some point, thwarting fingerprint identification, or wear a mask, thwarting the use of photographs. The more ways the government has to identify who someone is, the better chance it has of doing so accurately.

Id. The court in *Buza* considered that the use of DNA for more accurate identification goes to the actual "*investigatory* value," not the identification value as *Haskell* claims. *Buza*, 129 Cal. Rptr. 3d at 774.

106. *Buza*, 129 Cal. Rptr. 3d at 772–73. DNA profiles, once in the database, do not contain any identifying personal information such as the name of the individual that the sample was collected from. *Id.* at 1448; *see also* discussion *supra* Part I.B. (explaining the DNA sampling and profile creation process).

107. The court explained:

> The first step in collecting a DNA sample by means of the "standard DNA collection kit" provided by the DOJ to local and state law enforcement agencies is to "identify the subject," indicating the immediate means of "identification" is *not* the subject's DNA. Further demonstrating this point, since DNA samples are not taken from arrestees who have already had samples taken, the arrestee's identity must be verified by other means before a DNA sample can be collected.

Buza, 129 Cal. Rptr. 3d at 773 (citations omitted).

108. *Id.* at 770–77. When a DNA sample is taken and a profile is created, it is checked against a database of unsolved crimes. *See* discussion *supra* Part I.B.2. "There can be no doubt that this use of DNA samples is for purposes of criminal investigation rather than simple identification." *Buza*, 129 Cal. Rptr. 3d at 774; *see*

also Haskell v. Harris, 669 F.3d 1049, 1080 (9th Cir. 2012) (Fletcher, J., dissenting) ("Proposition 69 does not authorize the taking of DNA samples from felony arrestees for identification purposes. Rather, it authorizes the taking of DNA samples for solely investigative purposes. Such takings are unconstitutional ... ."), *reh'g en banc granted*, 686 F.3d 1121 (9th Cir. 2012); King v. State, 42 A.3d 549, 580 (Md. 2012) (holding the Maryland DNA arrestee sampling act constitutional in the narrow use "as a means to identify an arrestee, but not for investigatory purposes, in any event").

109. *See Buza*, 129 Cal. Rptr. 3d at 774–75. The *Buza* court also questioned the actual success rates of DNA databasing given a recent California Department of Justice study and averred that many of the people arrested are already convicted and have their DNA in the database. This would logically result in only a minimal increase in the success of the database with the inclusion of arrestee DNA. *Id.* at 776–77. For more on the governmental interests behind the federal DNA Act and the expansion of CODIS at the federal level, see Eiler, *supra* note 66, at 1221 nn.126–27.

110. *Buza*, 129 Cal. Rptr. 3d at 776.

111. *Id.* This is similar to the Supreme Court's finding in *City of Indianapolis v. Edmond*, 531 U.S. 32 (2000), in which the Court struck down a roadblock checkpoint program designed to "detect evidence of ordinary criminal wrongdoing," as it could not qualify as a special need. *Id.* at 38. Ordinary investigations do not satisfy the special needs test, and a warrant with sufficient probable cause is required. Eiler, *supra* note 66, at 1220 ("The special needs exception[] ... presents an insurmountable obstacle for the federal all-arrestee law because the law enforcement rationale behind expanding CODIS is so obviously paramount."); *see also King*, 42 A.3d at 578 ("A finding of probable cause for arrest on a crime of violence under the Maryland DNA Collection Act cannot serve as the probable cause for a DNA search of an arrestee.").

112. United States v. Weikert, 504 F.3d 1, 10–11 (1st Cir. 2007); Banks v. United States, 490 F.3d 1178, 1185 (10th Cir. 2007); United States v. Kincade, 379 F.3d 813, 839 (9th Cir. 2004); *see also* Bina Ghanaat, Comment, *Technology and Privacy: The Need for an Appropriate Mode of Analysis in the Debate over the Federal DNA Act*, 42 U.C. DAVIS L. REV. 1315, 1341-43 (2009) (asserting that courts now have the opportunity to potentially uphold all-arrestee DNA statutes given the Supreme Court's failure to articulate a clear rule regarding the totality of the circumstances test).

113. *Buza*, 129 Cal. Rptr. 3d at 761. *But see* Lockard v. City of Lawrenceburg, 815 F. Supp. 2d 1034, 1049 (S.D. Ind. 2011) ("[A]lthough an arrestee may have a larger expectation of privacy than a prisoner, the arrestee's expectation of privacy is still shrunken compared to society at large.").

114. Eiler, *supra* note 66, at 1218.

115. *Id.* at 1226. Thus, an officer can churn up probable cause to arrest an individual to collect a DNA sample to confirm a suspicion on an entirely separate case that lacked the requisite probable cause for arrest. *Id.*

116. 42 U.S.C. § 14135a(a)(1)(A) (2006) ("The Attorney General may, as prescribed by the Attorney General in regulation, collect DNA samples from individuals who are arrested, facing charges, or convicted or from non-United States persons who are detained under the authority of the United States."); *see also, e.g.*, CAL. PENAL CODE § 296.1(a)(1)(A) (West, Westlaw through Ch. 3 of 2013 Reg. Sess.) ("Each adult person arrested for a felony offense ... shall provide the buccal swab samples and thumb and palm print impressions and

any blood or other specimens required pursuant to this chapter immediately following arrest, or during the booking or intake or prison reception center process or as soon as administratively practicable after arrest, but, in any case, prior to release on bail or pending trial or any physical release from confinement or custody.").

117. *Buza*, 129 Cal. Rptr. 3d at 780 (noting that the use of the profile in the database will continue until the arrestee has it successfully expunged from the database).

118. Some scholars have proposed that a judicial remedy may be achieved by the Supreme Court modifying the special needs test back to a "barebones version of the special needs doctrine" that does not consider "law enforcement purpose" or else establish a new exception to the warrant requirement for DNA searches. Eiler, *supra* note 66, at 1229. Others have asserted that the Supreme Court will find DNA arrestee laws unconstitutional and will strike them down, but this would not clarify the Fourth Amendment standard to be applied to DNA sampling and would offer little guidance to legislatures as to what expansions of DNA sampling are constitutional. *Id.* at 1230.

119. The Debbie Smith DNA Backlog Grant Program lays out the eligibility requirements for a state to receive federal funding for its DNA sampling and database system, which includes quality controls and inclusion of the samples into CODIS. 42 U.S.C. § 14135a (2006). Modification of the program requirements would be the most efficient way to ensure state compliance because the majority of state databases rely on federal funding programs to finance their crime labs and DNA databasing systems. *See* LISA HURST & KEVIN LOTHRIDGE, 2007 DNA EVIDENCE AND OFFENDER ANALYSIS MEASUREMENT: DNA BACKLOGS, CAPACITY AND FUNDING 9 (2010), *available at* www.ncjrs.gov/pdffiles1/nij/grants/ 230328.pdf (finding that when surveying publicly funded crime laboratories that were accredited and operating forensic DNA analysis programs, "[n]early 90%, or 133 laboratories, responded that they would not have sufficient funding" if federal funding were no longer available).

120. 42 U.S.C. § 14135a(a)(1)(A) (2006); *see also, e.g.*, CAL. PENAL CODE § 296.1 (West, Westlaw through Ch. 3 of 2013 Reg. Sess.) ("Each adult person arrested for a felony offense ... shall provide the buccal swab samples and thumb and palm print impressions and any blood or other specimens required pursuant to this chapter immediately following arrest, or during the booking or intake or prison reception center process or as soon as administratively practicable after arrest, but, in any case, prior to release on bail or pending trial or any physical release from confinement or custody."); FLA. STAT. § 943.325(3)(a) (West, Westlaw through 1st Reg. Sess. of 23d Leg.) ("Each qualifying offender shall submit a DNA sample at the time he or she is booked into a jail, correctional facility, or juvenile facility.").

121. *See* United States v. Mitchell, 652 F.3d 387, 415–16 (3d Cir. 2011), *cert. denied*, 132 S. Ct. 1741 (2012) (mem.); United States v. Pool, 645 F. Supp. 2d 903, 917 (E.D. Cal. 2009); People v. Buza, 129 Cal. Rptr. 3d 753, 783 (Ct. App.), *cert. granted*, 262 P.3d 854 (Cal. 2011).

122. The "totality of the circumstances" test weighs the interest in the "individual's privacy against the government's interest in conducting a search." *Buza*, 129 Cal. Rptr. 3d at 760–61; *see also* discussion *supra* Part II.

123. When considering the continuum of privacy expected by individuals—from convicts to parolees to arrestees—arrestees' determinations of probable cause create separate "categories." *See Buza*, 129 Cal. Rptr.

3d at 782 ("[W]ithin the category of arrestees, an individual ... who has not yet been the subject of a judicial determination of probable cause, falls closer to the ordinary citizen end of the continuum than one as to whom probable cause has been found by a judicial officer or grand jury.").

124. N.C. GEN. STAT. § 15A-266.3A(b) (West, Westlaw through S.L. 2013-36 of 2013 Reg. Sess.).

125. *Id.* § 15A-511(c)(1). "A judicial official may issue a warrant for arrest only when he is supplied with sufficient information, supported by oath or affirmation, to make an independent judgment that there is probable cause to believe that a crime has been committed and that the person to be arrested committed it." *Id.* § 15A-304(d). Probable cause in North Carolina must be established by affidavit or by sworn oral testimony. *Id.*

126. "[T]he [DNA Fingerprinting] act will allow the creation of a comprehensive, robust database that will make it possible to catch serial rapists and murderers before they commit more crimes." 151 CONG. REC. S9472, 9528 (daily ed. July 29, 2005) (statement of Sen. John Kyl), 2005 WL 1797658 (Westlaw).

127. VA. CODE ANN. § 19.2-310.3:1(A) (West, Westlaw through 2013 Reg. Sess. cc. 2 and 3) ("The sample shall be secured to prevent tampering with the contents and be accompanied by a copy of the arrest warrant or capias.").

128. 42 U.S.C. § 14135(a) (2006).

129. *See* U.S. CONST. amend IV.

130. 42 U.S.C. § 14132(d) (2006).

131. *See, e.g.*, HAW. REV. STAT. § 844D-72(a) (West, Westlaw through Act 5 of 2013 Reg. Sess.) (requiring the arrestee to submit a "written request for expungement"; "[a] certified copy of the court order" or a "letter from the prosecuting attorney certifying that ... the case [was] dismissed"; proof that "written notice [of the request for expungement] has been provided to the prosecuting attorney and the department"; "[a] court order verifying that no retrial or appeal of the case is pending"; and that at least 180 days have passed since the prosecuting attorney received notice of the request for expungement and has not objected); VA. CODE ANN. § 19.2-310.7 ("A person whose DNA profile has been included in the data bank ... may request expungement on the grounds that the felony conviction on which the authority for including his DNA profile was based has been reversed and the case dismissed."); see also People v. Buza, 129 Cal. Rptr. 3d 753, 758–59 (Ct. App.), cert. granted, 262 P.3d 854 (Cal. 2011).

132. *See, e.g.*, O.C.G.A. § 35-3-165(b) (2012) (West, Westlaw through 2012 Reg. Sess.) ("A DNA sample obtained in good faith shall be deemed to have been obtained in accordance with the requirements of this article and its use in accordance with this article is authorized until a court order directing expungement is obtained and submitted to the bureau."); HAW. REV. STAT. § 844D-72(d) ("Any identification, warrant, probable cause to arrest, or arrest based upon a data bank match shall not be invalidated due to a failure to expunge or a delay in expunging records.").

133. N.C. GEN. STAT. § 15A-266.3A(j) (2011) (West, Westlaw through S.L. 2013-36 of 2013 Reg. Sess.); *see also* VA. CODE ANN. § 19.2-310.2:1 ("The *clerk of the court* shall notify the Department of final disposition of the criminal proceedings. If the charge for which the sample was taken is dismissed or the defendant is acquitted at trial, the Department shall destroy the sample and all records thereof, provided there is no

other pending qualifying warrant or capias for an arrest or felony conviction that would otherwise require that the sample remain in the data bank." (emphasis added)).

134. N.C. GEN. STAT. § 15A-266.3A(k).

135. *Id.* § 15A-266.3A(k)(3).

136. *Id.* § 15A-266.3A(l)–(m).

137. *See* discussion *supra* Part II.

138. 42 U.S.C. § 14135(a) (2006).

139. See discussion *supra* Part I.

140. Preston, *supra* note 102, at 475.

141. People v. Buza, 129 Cal. Rptr. 3d 753, 783 (Ct. App.), *cert. granted*, 262 P.3d 854 (Cal. 2011).

142. *See* discussion *supra* Part II.

143. *See* discussion *supra* Part II.

144. *See* discussion *supra* Part III.

Culture Clashes

Freedom, Privacy, and Government Surveillance Issues Arising in Relation to National Security and Internet Use

BY PAULINE C. REICH

Fourth Amendment

Although the Fourth Amendment does not guarantee complete privacy (Kerr, 2010), there has been some jurisprudence developed concerning what constitutes a search. Just as the *Katz* case discusses what a person can expect in the way of privacy in one's home or use of a public telephone booth, for example, the Internet cases look at the difference between content (protected-but what is content of an email, for example?) and non-content communication. The analogy of the address on the outside of an envelope is used—it is not protected from public view, e.g. by the post office when delivering it. On the other hand, the contents inside the envelope are considered private, however, "Whether Internet users have a reasonable expectation of privacy in their emails and web surfing data is largely unresolved. Unlike traditional letters, emails and web surfing communications are often copied in transit by Internet Service Providers (ISPs) and are (in theory) easily accessed by ISP employees. Because emails and other forms of Internet communications are arguably exposed to third parties during transmission, it remains controversial whether the Fourth Amendment protections that apply to the contents of letters and telephone calls can apply to them. Yet, an emerging body of case law suggests that the content/noncontent distinction is crucial in determining whether Internet communications are protected by the Fourth Amendment" (Kerr, 2010).

The Fourth Amendment third-party doctrine says that "a person does not retain a reasonable expectation of privacy in information disclosed to a third party. An Internet user discloses both content and non-content information together to third-party network providers" (Kerr, 2010).

How have content and non-content been defined?

"Contents" have been defined quite broadly in the ECPA as "any information concerning the substance, purport, or meaning of (a) communication" (Tokson, 2009).

When can emails be intercepted?

"The body of an email is considered content under the Wiretap Act, and thus capable of interception. However, email content, which is generally copied by ISP servers in the course of transmission to the recipient's ISP, is highly unlikely to be intercepted under the Wiretap Act. Any 'intercept' under the ECPA must occur contemporaneously with transmission, andcourts applying the Wiretap Act to the acquisition of emails have concluded that even email stored temporarily on an ISP's servers is in storage and not in transmission within the meaning of the Act. As a result of this interpretation, the government has little motive to capture emails during the fraction of a second when they are transmitted to or from the ISP. By waiting until they are in storage on the ISP server, the government can acquire the contents under the less stringent standards of the Stored Communications Act" (Tokson, 2009).

As for noncontent information, the sparse case law indicates that there is no Fourth Amendment protection for such information, e.g. in *United States* v. *Hambrick,* "the Fourth Circuit held that there was no Fourth Amendment [protection] for subscriber information that a user submitted to an ISP in order to set up an email account ..." and in *United States* v. *Forrester,* "the Ninth Circuit directly held that there was no Fourth Amendment interest in the to/from addresses of emails, Internet Protocol (IP) addresses of websites, or the total volume of file transfers associated with an Internet user's account ... According to the court, surveillance techniques that capture IP addresses relating to Internet communications were constitutionally indistinguishable from the pen registers approved in *Smith,* because the IP addresses obtained were no more private or intimate than phone numbers" (Tokson, 2009).[14]

Another question that has beenposed is whether there is content in certain aspects of e-mail and Internet use, and how this compares to searching physical space vs. cyber space. The author of that article has provided a chart comparing physical searches with Internet content as well as other characteristics (Tokson, 2009).[15]

Freedom, Privacy, and Civil Liberties in a Democracy

People in the United States and in other countries worldwide view the United States as a democracy that provides and protects the constitutional rights of its people by ensuring freedom, privacy and other rights. The advent of the Internet brought about the export of certain Wild West metaphors for the Internet, and countries worldwide interpreted the culture of the Internet to be thus. The following excerpt from an article published by a scholar in the former Soviet bloc gives an example of a view of Internet use and its culture from abroad.

A View of Exported American Culture from Outside: Comment from the Former Soviet Bloc

The internet is a socially constructed technological system. The culture of internet producers shaped the internet as a medium. Castells (2001) conceptualises internet culture as a quadripartite structure joined by the ideology of freedom. At the initial phase of internet development, the internet was governed by the techno-meritocratic culture and the hacker culture, the first two parts of Castells theoretic four-part model. Both technocrats and hackers shared the faith that the scientific and technological development was inherently positive. The hacker culture originated from academic culture, where the distinctive features were and continue to be open communication and peer-based control. Hence, hacker culture had already marked the beginning of the cyberspace development that was to follow in the next few years when it bridged the knowledge of the techno-meritocratic culture with that of the business sector, (Zavrsnik, [2008])[23] thus enabling widespread expansion of the commercial use of information technology': this commercial and financial sector formed the third part of the internet culture recognisable today. The last part of the internet culture comprises what Castells describes as a "virtual community" (Rheingold) that represents the users of cyberspace. This consists of the values of the users of which these cyber communities are made up and who shape the various social processes connected to IT usage.

The essential cultural elements and values of the internet communities are to be found in the 1960s and in the counter-culture movement. Historical analyses of the internet show early online conferences as attempts to form a community after the counter-culture movement had failed in the physical world. Hacker culture is therefore imbued in values that were exiledfrom the physical world in a response to the emancipative movements of the sixties, in a "counter-revolution" carried out by the capitalist conservative powers. The values of the counter-culture united with the technological knowledge of techno-meritocratic culture, then found a productive base for development conducive to the form the hacker culture then took. The latter allowedfor the incorporation of highly developed technological knowledge with freedom, pleasure, creativity and respect among peers. It also introduced an informal organisational structure, (Zavrsnik, [2008]*)*[24] *the ideology of the gift culture, the principle of reciprocity and the principle of cooperation. But the commercialisation of various outcomes arising from computer programming was performed only on condition that all information regarding intellectual products (i.e. computer software) was to be freely accessible and that the free modification of products should also be allowed. These values were (and still are) in direct opposition to the prevailing logic in the contemporary' world; namely, the logic of privatisation, profit orientation, formal legal protection and economic power. Within hacker culture, however, the commercialisation of and direct economic benefit from one's intellectual activity is only allowed to a partial extent. Hacker culture, then, is a typical post- modern paradigm that incorporates values of equality, independence, freedom of expression and communication. It is a paradigm that creates a free space for new ideas* (Zavrsnik, n.d., Fontaine & Rogers, 2011).

Comments of the United States Supreme Court (Different Context): Issues of Constitutional Rights of Citizens in a Democracy

The U.S. judiciary "has wrestled with constitutional tensions created by the spate of legislative and executive actions in response to the current terrorist menace in basically four scenarios: (1) the gathering and use of foreign intelligence information; (2) the designation of individuals and groups as terrorists ..."[25] TheU.S. government "is being challenged, as never before, to determine to what extent civil liberties should be compromised when the nation's security is atrisk" (Block, 2005).

As Supreme Court Justice Sandra Day O'Connor remarked soon after September 11, 2001, "we're likely to experience more restrictions on personal freedom than has ever been the case in our country." She posed an important question that continues to be the subject of debate and litigation:

> At what point does the cost to civil liberties from legislation designed to prevent terrorism outweigh the added security that the legislation provides? (Block, 2005)

Former President George W. Bush, “citing the National Emergencies Act, declared a national emergency on September 14,2001, ‘by reason of the terrorist attacks at the World Trade Center... and the Pentagon, and the continuing and immediate threat of further attacks on the United States’. There are currently sixteen declarations of national emergency in force. Twenty others, dating back to President Wilson, have been terminated” (Block, 2005).

The question of the power of the Executive in such circumstances (national emergencies) to suspend the usual application of the United States Constitution arises in various cases, for example:

Hamdi v. Rumsfeld

In this June 28, 2004 decision by a plurality of the United States Supreme Court, the threshold question was “whether the Executive has the authority to detain citizens who qualify as ‘enemy combatants’. The plurality ruled that the Due Process Clause of the U.S. Constitution entitled the U.S. citizen to a ‘meaningful opportunity to challenge the factual findings justifying the detention, either before a criminal court or a military tribunal’. In their holding, the Justices rejected the Government’s assertion that separation of powers principles mandate a heavily circumscribed role for the courts in such circumstances. Indeed, the position that the courts must forego examination of the individual case and focus exclusively on the legality of the broader detention scheme cannot be mandated by any reasonable view of separation of powers, as this approach serves only to condense power into a single branch of government. *We have long since made it clear that a state of war is not a blank check for the President when it comes to the rights of the Nation’s citizens* [emphasis added]. Whatever power the United States Constitution envisions for the Executive in its exchanges with other nations or with enemy organizations in times of conflict, it most assuredly envisions a role for all three branches when individual liberties are at stake” (Block, 2005).

Justice Souter, in the Opinion Concurring, Dissenting and Concurring in the Judgment stated :

> The defining character of American constitutional government is constant tension between security and liberty, serving both by partial helpings of each.
>
> In a government of separated powers, deciding finally on what is a reasonable degree of guaranteed liberty whether in peace or war (or some condition in between) is not well entrusted to the Executive Branch of Government, whose particular responsibility is to maintain security ... (Block, 2005).

Justice Stephen Breyer in his book, *Active Liberty: Interpreting our Democratic Constitution* (2005), addresses the complexity brought into constitutional discussions about privacy due to our reliance on technology. He defines privacy as "a person's power to control what others come to know about him or her. It illustrates constitutional decision-making under conditions of uncertainty-uncertainty brought about by rapid changes in technology[26]. Whenever technological advance means significant change in the régula- tory environment, Americans normally search pragmatically for new legal answers, and they often participate in a democratic conversation along the way ... (Breyer, 2005). To explain the constitutional matter, I must begin by describing the privacy-related legal problem. I believe that the problem arises out of three factors: the variety of values implicated by our concern for privacy; the need for already complicated legal regimes to accommodate new technologies; and the difficulty of balancing competing (sometimes conflicting) concerns in this complex area of law" (Breyer, 2005).

Ensuing litigation over Internet surveillance in the United States has attempted to address the powers of the Executive branch.

Electronic Privacy Information Center v. Department of Justice

In this consolidated action brought in the United States District Court in the District of Columbia in October 2008, plaintiffs the Electronic Privacy Information Center (EPIC), the American Civil Liberties Union Foundation, and the National Security Archive Fund, Inc. brought suit against the U. S. Department of Justice regarding the prior policy of the Bush Administration "to conduct, under certain circumstances, surveillance of domestic communications without the prior authorization of the Foreign Intelligence Surveillance Court" ("FISA Court") (2008). The Department of Justice moved for summary judgment and EPIC moved for *in camera* review of records requested under the Freedom of Information Act. After consideration of the motions, the court held that twelve documents withheld by the FBI were properly withheld under Exemptions 1 and 3 of FOIA, which provide:

> *5 U.S.C. 552(b)(1), EXEMPTION 1 Classified secret matters or national defense or foreign policy—protects from disclosure "national security information concerning the national defense or foreign policy, provided that it has been properly classified in accordance with the substantive and procedural requirements of an executive order.*[27]

> *5 U.S.C 552(b) 3 EXEMPTION 3 Information Specifically Exempted by Other Statutes.*[28] *Allows the withholding of information prohibited from disclosure by another federal statute provided that one of two disjunctive requirements are met: the statute either (A) requires that the matters be withheld from the public in such a*

manner as to leave no discretion on the issue, or (B) establishes particular criteria for withholding or refers to particular types of matters to be withheld.[29]

Although EPIC argued under Exemption 5 against the deliberative process privilege, the attomey-client privilege and the presidential communications privilege, however the court did not uphold its view.[30]

It also ordered that DOJ's motion for summary judgment be granted in part and denied in part, and that EPIC's motion for *in camera* review be granted in part and denied in part. The same court also granted in part and denied inpart DOJ's previous motion for summary judgment in September 2007. This time it ordered DOJ to produce those documents for which it had not been granted summary judgment for *in camera* review.

As seen in previous sections of this chapter, recent court decisions have shown inconsistency in the courts in their interpretation of the constitution and the respective electronic surveillance laws related to government agencies.

Bush Administration Policies: CNCI

In January 2008, the Bush administration launched a classified cyber policy called the Comprehensive National Cybersecurity Initiative (CNCI) that was outlined in the Homeland Security Presidential Directive (HSPD-23). CNCI was to be a multiyear $ 17 billion program (Senkowski & Dawson, 2009). Details were only released in March 2010 by the Obama administration.

According to the summary released in 2010, the 12 initiatives are to:

1. Manage the federal enterprise network as a single network enterprise with Trusted Internet Connections to reduce access points to and from the Internet.
2. Deploy an intrusion detection system of sensors, known as Einstein 2, across the federal enterprise.
3. Pursue deployment of intrusion prevention systems, Einstein 3, across the federal enterprise.
4. Coordinate and redirect cybersecurity research and development efforts.
5. Connect current cyber ops centers to enhance situational awareness.
6. Develop and implement a government-wide cyber counterintelligence plan.
7. Increase the security of our classified networks.
8. Expand cyber education.
9. Define and develop enduring "leap-ahead" technology, strategies, and programs.
10. Define and develop enduring deterrence strategies and programs.

11. Develop a multi-pronged approach for global supply chain risk management.
12. Define the federal role for extending cybersecurity into critical infrastructure domains (Chabrow, 2010).

Obama Administration Policies: Privacy and Civil Liberties

The Cyberspace Policy Review

The above policy, formerly classified, arose during the Bush administration, but was only released during the Obama administration. Another significant policy document was issued by the White House in May 2009. The Cyberspace Policy Review—Assuring a Trusted and Resilient Information and Communications Infrastructure-states that (1) the Federal government needs to be better organized to address cyber issues; (2) there is a need for a national dialogue on cyber security; (3) *there needs to be a balance between national security and the protection of privacy and civil liberties guaranteed under the U.S. Constitution;* [emphasis added]; (4) the U.S. government needs to cooperate with the private sector and other countries to resolve cybersecurity issues. It points to the need for addressing a number of issues, such as defining acceptable legal norms about territorial jurisdiction, sovereign responsibility, and the use of force, and states the challenges arising in prosecuting cybercriminals and data preservation (whitehouse.gov, 2009).

Department of Homeland Security Privacy and Civil Liberties Policies

The author contacted the Department of Homeland Security (DHS) in January 2011, and requested information about the nature of privacy policy reviews under the Obama administration, i.e., who conducts them in each government agency and under what guidelines, regulations, policies or standards privacy reviews are conducted. The following are the responses from the Senior Privacy Officer at the National Protection and Programs Directorate of U.S. Department of Homeland Security:

1. Who does the privacy reviews? Name of office, agency (not only DHS, but also NSA, military), who is the contact person? Responses:
    a. The Chief Privacy Officer or its equivalent for each agency is responsible for reviewing and approving privacy compliance documentation for their agency.

   b. The Chief Privacy Officer for DHS is Mary Ellen Callahan. Information on Ms. Callahan can be found at http://www.dhs.gov/xabout/structure/editorial_0510.shtm#contact
   c. Contact information on DHS component offices can be found at http://www.dhs.gov/xabout/structure/gc_1285774534288.shtm
   d. Alist of DoD, includingNSAprivacy points of contact can be found at http://privacy.defense.gov/dpo_points_of_contact.shtml

2. Under what guidelines, regulations, policies or standards do they conduct the privacy reviews?
   a. Section 208 of the E-Govemment Act of 2002 requires federal agencies to conduct Privacy Impact Assessments (PIAs) for any new or substantially changed technology that collects, maintains, or disseminates Personally Identifiable Information (PII). The DHS Privacy Office also has its own statutory authority under section 222 of the Homeland Security Act to require PIAs.
   b. M-03-22-OMB Guidance for Implementing the Privacy Provisions of the E-Gov Act of 2002 can be found at http://www.whitehouse.gov/omb/memoranda_m03-22. This link provides information on government agency requirements for privacy compliance and guidance on its implementation.
   c. An excellent example of how DHS has implemented privacy can be found in its implementation guide that can be found at http://www.dhs.gov/xlibrary/assets/privacy/privacy_implementation_guide_June2010.pdf (E. Andrews, personal communication, January 10, 2011)

The Director of Communications in the Office of the Under Secretary of the National Protection and Programs Secretariat of DHS provided additional information in response to a similar inquiry:

1. Who does the privacy reviews? Name of office, agency (not only DHS, but also NSA, military), who is the contact person?
2. Under what guidelines, regulations, policies or standards do they conduct the privacy reviews?

Response: There is quite a bit of information publicly available on the DHS.gov web site regarding Cybersecurity and Privacy. The link to the site is http://www.dhs.gov/files/publications/editorial_0514.shtm#4.

Information and resources that can be found on the DHS web site provided by DHS follow.

Cybersecurity

The Privacy Office works closely with the Office of Cybersecurity & Communications (CS&C), and, within CS&C, the National Cybersecurity Division and the United States Computer Emergency Readiness Team (US-CERT), to integrate privacy protections into the Department's cybersecurity activities. The following resources provide background on these efforts:

EINSTEIN Program Privacy Impact Assessments

- **US-CERT:** Initiative Three Exercise. March 18, 2010 (*PDF 19 pages—457 KB*) Pursuant to Initiative Three of the Comprehensive National Cybersecurity Initiative, DHS is engaging in an exercise to demonstrate a suite of technologies that could be included in the next generation of the Department's EINSTEIN network security program. This demonstration, (commonly referred to as the "Initiative Three Exercise" or, more simply, as "the Exercise") will use a modified complement of system components currently providing the EINSTEIN 1 and EINSTEIN 2 capabilities, as well as a DHS test deployment of technology developed by the National Security Agency (NSA) that includes an intrusion prevention capability (collectively referred to as "the Exercise technology"). The purpose of the Exercise is to demonstrate the ability of an existing Internet Service Provider that is a designated as a Trusted Internet Connection Access Provider (TICAP) to select and redirect Internet traffic from a single participating government agency through the Exercise technology, for US-CERT to apply intrusion detection and prevention measures to that traffic and for US-CERT to generate automated alerts about selected cyber threats. This PIA is being conducted because the Exercise will analyze Internet traffic which may contain personally identifiable information (PII).
- **EINSTEIN 1 PIA Update:** February 19, 2010 (*PDF, 12 pages—194 KB*) DHS and the State of Michigan ("Michigan") plan to engage in a 12-month proof of concept to determine the benefits and issues presented by deploying the EINSTEIN 1 capability to Michigan government networks managed by the Michigan Department of Information Technology (MDIT). This PIA updates the previous EINSTEIN PIAs listed below in one narrow aspect: the use of EINSTEIN 1 technology in a proof of concept with Michigan.
- **EINSTEIN 2 Privacy Impact Assessment:** May 19, 2008 (*PDF, 23 pages—423 KB*). This is the Privacy Impact Assessment (PIA) for an updated version of the EINSTEIN System. EINSTEIN is a computer network intrusion detection system (IDS) used to help protect federal executive agency information technology (IT) enterprises. EINSTEIN 2 will incorporate network intrusion detection technology capable of alerting the US-CERT to the presence of malicious or potentially harmful computer network activity in federal executive agencies' network traffic.

- **EINSTEIN 1 Privacy Impact Assessment:** September 2004 (*PDF, 12 pages—153 KB*) This PIA examines the privacy implications of US-CERT's EINSTEIN Program. The EINSTEIN Program is an automated process for collecting, correlating, analyzing, and sharing computer security information across the federal civilian government. By collecting information from participating federal government agencies, US-CERT builds and enhances our nation's cyber-related situational awareness.

Other Cybersecurity Privacy Impact Assessments

- **Malware Lab Network:** May 4, 2010 (*PDF, 13 pages—172 KB*) The goal of the Department of Homeland Security (DHS or Department) National Protection and Programs Directorate (NPPD) is to advance the risk-reduction segment of the Department's overall mission. To meet this goal, the NPPD/U.S. Computer Emergency Readiness Team (US-CERT) provides key capabilities in four cyber mission areas: 1) Alert, Warning, and Analysis; 2) Coordination and Collaboration; 3) Response and Assistance; and 4) Protection and Detection. The Malware Lab Network (MLN) contributes critical support to existing tools used by US-CERT to better meet these cyber mission areas. The MLN collects, uses, and maintains analytically relevant information in order to support the Department's cyber security mission, including the prevention and mitigation of cyber attacks, protection of information infrastructure, the assessment of cyber vulnerabilities, and response to cyber incidents. DHS is conducting this PIA to publicly analyze and evaluate the personally identifiable information (PII) within the MLN.
- **24 × 7 Incident Handling and Response Center:** April 2, 2007 (*PDF, 17 pages—265 KB*) The 24 × 7 Incident Handling and Response Center ("24 × 7") focuses on ways to gather cyber information prior to attacks and to use that information to prevent attacks, protect computing infrastructure, and respond/restore where attacks are successful. 24 × 7 serves as a communication hub for the United States Computer Readiness Team (US-CERT) program, issuing regular security and warning bulletins, serving as a gateway for public contribution and outreach, and also serving as a ticketing center through which tasks may be delegated out to the various US-CERT programs.

Other Cybersecurity Resources

- **White Paper on Computer Network Security and Privacy Protection:** February 19, 2010 (*PDF, 11 pages—114 KB*). Provides an overview of the Department's cybersecurity responsibilities, the role of the EINSTEIN system in implementing those responsibilities, and the integrated privacy protections.

- **White House Cybersecurity Site:** The White House recently launched a site dedicated to the federal government's cybersecurity efforts, www.whitehouse.gov/cybersecurity, including the declassified description of the Comprehensive National Cybersecurity Initiative.

Link to DHS's Privacy site: http://www.dhs.gov/xabout/structure/editorial_0338.shtm
A search of the White House Website came up with several resources, some of which are listed below:

- White House Council Launches Interagency Subcommittee on Privacy & Internet Policy (Posted on October 24, 2010 at 10:10 AM EST.)
    - Type: Office of Science and Technology Policy, Blog Post http://www.white-house.gov/search/site/ Privacy

As part of the Obama Administration's commitment to promoting the vast economic opportunity of the Internet and protecting individual privacy, the National Science and Technology Council has launched a new Subcommittee on Privacy of individuals' private information and the ability of governments to meet their obligations to protect public safety. Recognizing the global nature of the digital economy and society, the Subcommittee will monitor and address global privacy policy ... privacy and innovation policies. Such policies are essential to the health of competitive marketplaces for online goods and services. The public policy direction developed by the Subcommittee will be closely synchronized to privacy practices.

- DARPA Develops New Privacy Principles. (Posted on August 09, 2010 at 03:34 PM EST)
    - Type: Office of Science and Technology Policy, Blog Post

The value of having access to information and the importance of respecting personal privacy. To address that tension, DARPA recently released a thoughtful set of Privacy Principles to help ensure that any future research and development programs that raise privacy issues are designed and implemented in a responsible and ethical fashion. As one expression of those principles, DARPA resolves, among other things, to consistently examine the impact of its research and development programs on privacy. And it commits to analyze the privacy dimension of its ongoing research endeavors with respect to their ethical, legal and societal implications. DARPAhas also outlined a number of specific steps already launched in areas such as research, internal controls ...

- M-03-22, OMB Guidance for Implementing the Privacy Provisions of the E-Government Act of 2002. (Posted on May 25, 2010 at 05:40 PM EST)

  - Type: Office of Management and Budget

SUBJECT: OMB Guidance for Implementing the Privacy Provisions of the E-Govemment Act of 2002. The attached guidance provides information to agencies on implementing the privacy provisions of the E-Govemment Act of 2002, which was signed by the President on December 17,2002 and became effective on April 17,2003. The Administration is committed to protecting the privacy of the American people. This guidance document addresses privacy protections when ... that personal information is protected. The privacy objective of the E-Govemment Act complements theNational Strategy to Secure Cyberspace. As the National Strategy indicates, cyberspace security programs that strengthen protections for privacy and other. (T. Livick, personal communication, January 8, 2011)

While the above information provides increased transparency concerning DHS policies and those of other Federal agencies, the intelligence and military agency privacy and civil liberties protections are not as clearly delineated.

Privacy Vs. Security: Legal and Policy Issues in a Number of Democracies

K.A. Taipale, Executive Director of the Center for Advanced Studies in Science and Technology, noted in an article published in 2003:

> Privacy and security are often seen as being in tension and requiring balance. The metaphor of balance suggests that when new developments create disequilibrium, a new fulcrum needs to be sought to restore balance. Privacy advocates believe that new information technologies have upset the balance and that stronger protection for individual privacy is the required response they would move the fulcrum towards "more privacy." Those concerned with security argue that global terrorism has upset the balance and that new methods and technologies, even if they impact on historic privacy concerns, need to be employed—they would move the balance towards "more security." The metaphor of balance has led to the dichotomous

> ideological choice being presented as privacy or security ... However, privacy and security might be more properly considered dual obligations—to protect civil security and to preserve civil liberty. Then, achieving security while also protecting privacy means recognizing 'that security need not be traded off for liberty in equal measure and that the 'balance' between them is not a zero-sum game (Taipale, 2003).

Speakers at the East West Institute First Worldwide Cybersecurity Summit held in Dallas from May 3–5, 2010, noted the complexity of this endeavor, and "identified the lack of attribution as a key weakness in cybersecurity, calling for a global electronic architecture that allows cyber attacks to be traced back to their sources. Response to hostile acts is impossible without such clarity, they said. "You need to be able to define who you're declaring a war on," said retired Lieutenant General Harry Raduege, Chairman of the Deloitte Center for Cyber Innovation.

But efforts towards clearer attribution must be approached with caution. "How muchprivacy are you ready to delegate to the government?" asked Andrei Korotkov of the Moscow State Institute of Foreign Affairs."[31]

As of 2012, there is ongoing grappling in the courts and in policy and law circle discussions about the need to balance concerns about security with traditional constitutional protections of privacy, human rights and civil liberties in many democracies worldwide. Some of these discussions are included in this chapter so that readers will be familiar with the varying perspectives in countries other than the United States.

Europe, Data Privacy, and Concerns

Professor Francesca Bignami compares the legality of a government maintaining an antiterrorism database containing call records, for example, in Europe and the United States, where the concepts of data privacy are quite different. She refers to the history of the Nazi occupation of Norway, when Norwegian government files containing names, addresses, gender, dates of birth and other personal information about the population were demanded. The Norwegian resistance destroyed the only two machines capable of being used to sort the files. She notes, "Without the ability to tabulate the population data, a Norwegian draft was too difficult to put into effect and the Nazi plan had to be dropped."[32]

Professor Bignami proposes an overhaul of the U.S. Electronic Communications Privacy Act to put the U.S. into a closer alignment with the EU and other allies with respect to citizen Internet use and data privacy.[33]

In actuality, given recent developments in the UK and EU, there are now exceptions to the strict data privacy regime in Europe, with attempts to override existing privacy law in the name of national emergency necessity.[34]

Further Developments: Europe

In 2008, the Council of Europe adopted Voluntary Guidelines providing for collaboration between ISPs and law enforcement in connection with Cybercrime investigations.[35] There has been some litigation in various countries (e.g., UK, Germany, Poland) concerning the privacy implications of such collaboration.[36]

Germany

On February 27, 2008, the German Federal Constitutional Court recognized in a landmark ruling a new constitutional right in the confidentiality and integrity of information technology systems.[37] The primary issue was the constitutionality of a law authorizing the secret services of the German state of North Rhine-Westphalia to "surreptitiously monitor and investigate the Internet. In particular, the law would have granted the secret services the right to clandestinely intercept and search for communication via the Internet, and to secretly access its information technology systems. This law had been introduced as an amendment to Art 5.2 no. 11 of the Act on the Protection of the Constitution in North Rhine-Westphalia" (Abel and Schaefer, 2009, p. 107) as of December 20, 2006. The Federal Court held that such investigative acts interfere with constitutional guaranteed rights, and that any such legislation would have to demonstrate that "such an interference is justified by the protection of other constitutional rights, necessary to achieve this protection and proportionate in its impact" (Id., 107). The Court held the legislation to be unlawful and not in accordance with the constitution (Id.).

The amendment of Section 5.2 of the Act on the Protection of the Constitution was one aspect of a Federal discussion about the legality of a new type of investigative technique, the remote searching of computers and laptops. The discussion was triggered by the application of a State prosecutor to the German Federal Court of Justice for a warrant to remotely search the computer of a suspect in a terrorism investigation. The search entailed the covert installation of a surveillance program similar to a Trojan. The intial application was rejected on November 25, 2006. The prosecutor appealed, arguing that articles of the Criminal Code permitted such a search, and assuming a similarity to the physical search of premises permitted in the Code. The Court rejected the analogy between the code provisions permitting physical search of premises and clandestine search of a computer (Id., 108).

The Act on the Protection of the Constitution in North Rhine-Westphalia "outlines the rights of, and establishes a legal basis for operations by the Constitution Protection Agency, Germany's main secret service for internal affairs. Art. 5.2 ... defines permissible actions to acquire information and private data from suspects. The amendment in question, of Article 5.2 (11) of the North Rhine-Westphalia Constitution Protection Act, empowered the Constitution Protection Agency to carry out two types of investigative measures: Firstly, secret monitoring and other reconnaissance of the Internet (alternative 1), and secondly secret access to information technology systems (alternative 2). Secret monitoring of the Internet is ameasure by which the Constitution Protection Agency obtains information about the content of Internet communication using the communication technology in the way it was intended to be used. These can be measures such as accessing an open website, participation in chats or online, but also accessing an email inbox or accessing restricted websites using a password obtained elsewhere, for example from an informant. By contrast, the secret access to an information technology system is understood to be its technical infiltration, by taking advantage of the security loopholes of the target system, or by installing a spy program ... The method at the core of the decision, infiltration of a computer through technical means, also referred to as 'online search,' 'Federal Trojan' or 'remote searching,' is one specific form of such information gathering ..."(Id., 108).

To accomplish the remote search, "a specifically designed computer program, a 'remote forensic software' (RFS) tool, is planted on the suspect's computer without his knowledge. This program is then able to copy all data stored on the computer and subsequently transfer it back to the investigation authority for evaluation. Such a program shares crucial features with well-known malware, in particular viruses and Trojans. The latter in particular can be used to access and extract personal data from targets, and hence is equally suitable for data collection by police authorities .... The advantage of using these technologies is that they can be installed clandestinely, and without access to the suspect's house or physical premises. They are designed to resemble harmless applications and therefore trick the suspect into installing them. Therefore, as with their criminal counterparts, police Trojans require the unwitting cooperation of the target .... Furthermore, it allows collecting encrypted data in an unencrypted form as the investigating authority can access the data while the user is typing it. Moreover, passwords and further information on the usage pattern of the suspect can be collected ..." (Id., 109).

The regional government (*Land*) argued that the RFS tools were similar to existing police powers in the offline world so that analogous application of relevant constitutional provisions was appropriate. It stated that the constitutional right guaranteeing the privacy of telecommunications in Art. 10.1 of the German Basic Law (*Gundgesetz-GG*) was applicable law, arguing that remote online search was "essentially a new form of wiretapping" and its proposed legislation extended the safeguards in place for wiretapping to new technologies.

(Id., 111) On the other hand, the Federal Government argued that this form of search paralleled search of one's home.

Both the regional government and the Federal Government agreed that the "right to informational self-determination as derived from Article 2.1 GG in connection with Article 1.1 GG could serve as a standard for an online search." This argument was similar to that in an earlier decision of the Constitutional Court that had "shaped Germany's data protection law in the past" (Id.).

Article 10.1 of the GG protects the "nonphysical transmission of information to individual recipients with the aid of telecommunication devices," and covers any type of telecommunication regardless of the type of transmission or the type of data transmitted. It states that, "The privacy of correspondence, posts and telecommunications shall be inviolable." Not only are the contents of the communication protected by this right, "but also details about their general circumstances, such as details about the communication partners, and the transmission type (by email, chat, VoIP). Particularly important for online contexts, metadata generated as a result of communication has been included into the scope of the article by the courts in previous decisions" (Id. at 112).

France

The French Association of Internet Community Services (ASIC), including 26 companies, among them Google and eBay, have reportedly expressed "strong opposition" to a new French law requiring that Internet service providers "keep user names, passwords, dates and times of online phone activity, phone numbers, email addresses and home addresses of all customers for 12 months. The records can then be made available to the police and other government agencies ... "[38]

Anglo-American System Constitutions and Privacy Concerns Related to Government Internet Surveillance

A number of countries with legal systems in the Anglo-American tradition have Privacy Commissioners, e.g. Canada, Australia, New Zealand. (The United States does not have a Privacy Commissioner, however the Federal Trade Commission has played an important role in the protection of consumer privacy in the United States, and as discussed above in this chapter, other individual Federal agencies have privacy and civil liberties officials).[39] The Canadian Privacy Commissioners in particular have expressed concern about government surveillance of Internet use and other issues in light of their traditional constitutional protections. *See* Appendix II to this chapter for some of their comments.

Canada

Privacy advocates in Canada had taken issue with the USA PATRIOT Act provisions that impact on Canadian entities as well as other post-September 11, 2001 legal measures. "An overall concern is that some of the measures do not meet the test of a demonstrated clear and compellingneed, balanced with the least possible intrusion on the rights and freedoms of people in Canada ... .The Information and Privacy Commissioner has on many occasions acknowledged that the rights and freedoms which we have come to expect will be upheld in Canada, including privacy rights, are not absolute. It is imperative, however, that government abridgements of privacy rights in the name of protection against terrorism not be intended merely to assuage fears by making people feel more secure, as opposed to effectively and rationally addressing real risk."[40]

In August 2004, Canada's Minister of Justice:

> affirmed the imperative of crafting security measures that complement rather than conflict with fundamental rights and freedoms:
>
> The underlying principle here is that there is no contradiction between the protection of security and the protection of human rights. In a word, anti-terrorism law and policy itself is anchored in a twofold human rights perspective: first, transnational terrorism—the slaughter of innocents—constitutes an assault on the security of a democracy and the most fundamental rights of its inhabitants-the right to life, liberty and security of the person ... Accordingly, antiterrorist law and policy should be seen as the promotion and protection of the security of a democracy and fundamental human rights in the face of this injustice-the protection, indeed, of human security in the most profound sense ...
>
> At the same time, the enforcement and application of counterterrorism law and policy must always comport with the rule of law ... .[41]

Two bills introduced in the House of Commons in 2010 are the Investigative Powers for the 21st Century Act and the Investigating and Preventing Criminal Electronic Communications Act.

The 2012 version of the legislation, now entitled the "Protecting Children from Internet Predators Act," is described by the Conservative government as "a new tool to end frustrating delays police face when they seek to track suspects' online activities," however the opposition say that police should be required to obtain a warrant to prevent authorities from abusing "their new powers and snoop on anyone without any oversight or justification." The Government's response is that the police "will still need a warrant to actually read the online communications of suspects," however the Assistant Privacy Commissioner of Canada "left the door open to a constitutional challenge of the law, pending further study."[42]

Other views of earlier proposed legislation were that its passage would result in:

- "Enabling police to identify all the network nodes and jurisdictions involved in the transmission of data and trace the communications back to a suspect. Judicial authorizations would be required to obtain transmission data, which provides information on the routing but does not include the content of a private communication;"
- "Requiring a telecommunications service provider to temporarily keep data so that it is not lost or deleted in the time it takes law enforcement agencies to return with a search warrant or production order to obtain it;"
- "Making it illegal to possess a computer virus for the purposes of committing an offence of mischief;" and
- "Enhancing international cooperation to help in investigating and prosecuting crime that goes beyond Canada's borders." The introduction and first reading in the House of Commons occurred on November 1, 2010.43 (Library Boy blog, 11/2/10).

The latter bill "would require ISPs to include interception capability in their networks, making it easier for law enforcement and national security agencies to intercept suspicious information. The proposed Act also calls for service providers to supply basic subscriber information upon request from law enforcement, Competition Bureau and national security officials." It is a réintroduction of Bill C-47 from the previous session of Parliament (Library Boy blog, 11/2/10).

A more detailed analysis by Professor Michael Geist of the University of Ottawa, one of Canada's leading Cyberlaw experts, notes that the new "lawful access initiatives" followed a three pronged approach: information disclosure, mandated surveillance technologies and new police powers. "The first prong mandates the disclosure of Internet provider customer information without court oversight. Under current privacy laws, providers may voluntarily disclose customer information but are not required to do so ... The new system would require the disclosure of customer name, address, phone number, email address, Internet protocol address, and a series of device identification numbers ... the ability to link it with other data will often open the door to a detailed profile about an identifiable person ... The second prong requires Internet providers to dramatically re-work their networks to allow for real-time surveillance. The bill sets out detailed capability requirements that will eventually apply to all Canadian providers. These include the power to intercept communications, to isolate the communications to a particular individual, and to engage in multiple simultaneous interceptions ... . Having obtained customer information without court oversight and mandated Internet surveillance capabilities, the third prong creates several new police powers designed to obtain access to the surveillance data. These include new transmission data warrants that would grant real-time access to all the information generated during the creation, transmission or reception of a communication including the type, direction, time, duration, origin, destination, or termination of the communication ... . Law enforcement could then obtain a preservation order to require providers to preserve subscriber information, including specific communication information, for 90 days. Finally, having obtained and preserved the data, production orders can be used to require the disclosure of specified communications or transmission data ... While Internet providers would actively work with law enforcement in collecting and disclosing the subscriber information, they could also be prohibited from disclosing the disclosures as [sic] court may bar them from informing them that they have been subject to surveillance or information disclosures."[44]

The official government view of the proposed legislation indicated that in part it was being initiated in order to enable Canada to ratify the Council of Europe Cybercrime Convention. [45]

The Canadian Privacy Commissioners had announced their concerns about the proposed legislation in a letter to Public Safety Canada from Canada's Privacy Commissioners and Ombudspersons on the (2011) "lawful access" proposals. [See Appendix II to this chapter]

Australia

On June 22, 2011, the Australian government was due to introduce legislation entitled the Cybercrime Legislation Amendment Bill 2011 which would enable it to join the Council of Europe Cybercrime Convention. Under current Australian law, "authorities can only order phone companies to hold data after a warrant is issued, often leading to the loss of crucial evidence in live cases."[46] Under the new amendments, law enforcement and intelligence agencies would be able to issue "an immediate 'non-destruction' order of cyber and phone data to phone and internet companies. It would allow them to preserve personal records of suspects before a formal warrant can be issued ... The laws would apply to all electronic data including calls, text messages, emails and computer or internet activity, and will require changes to both the cyber crimes laws and telephone intercept legislation...However the laws would prevent agencies from actually accessing the seized information until the warrant was issued. If the warrant failed, the data would be ordered destroyed."[47]

United Kingdom

In April 2012 it was announced that the United Kingdom will have new legislation that will allow "the Government to monitor calls, emails, texts and website use of everybody in Britain. The new law was due to be announced in the Queen's Speech in May, but "would not allow GCHQ unprecedented access without a warrant .... But intelligence officers would be allowed to examine material if someone came under suspicion." An MP stated, "This is not focusing on terrorists or criminals, it's absolutely everybody's emails, phone calls and web access."[48]

On May 9,2012 the Queen's Speech indicated the "communications data" includes information such as "timing and duration of telephone calls, the email address communications are sent to as well as the location of the person initiating the communications," however not the content of the communications. Safeguards would require that Communication Service Providers (CSPs) would have to delete communications data they store after one year "as well as measures to protect the data from unauthorized access or disclosure."[49]

Where Have We Been? Where Are We Going?

United States

Overbreadth of Investigations? U.S. v. Google

On January 19,2006, the U.S. Department of Justice announced that it had subpoenaed four major Internet companies (Google Inc., America Online Inc., Microsoft Network and Yahoo Inc.) for data about what people search for on the Internet. Three of the companies responded to some degree, but Google, Inc. announced that it was resisting the demand. Privacy organizations stated that the government subpoenas "raised deep concerns about the government's ability to track what ordinary people view on the Internet." The government had asked Google, Inc., which operates "the world's most popular search engine" "to turn over every query typed into its search engine over the course of one week without providing identifying information about the people who conducted the searches ... It also asked for a random sample of 1 million Web pages that can be searched in the vast databases maintained by Google." Privacy experts stated that although the requests seemed tailored to try to protect the privacy of millions of people who conduct Google searches, "it could set a precedent for more intrusive future government demands." Several privacy advocates said "they did not object to government subpoenas in criminal cases in which someone is suspected of a crime, but they suggested that the latest demand was sobroaditamountedto a fishing expedition."[50]

In a more recent change of policy direction, on February 4, 2010 the *Washington Post* reported that Google has agreed to partner with the National Security Agency to analyze certain cyberattacks on Google and other large American companies in mid-December 2009. Google's new policy is that it "will share personal information when there is a good faith belief that access, use, preservation, or disclosure of such information is reasonably necessary to (a) satisfy any applicable law, regulation, legal process or *enforceable government request,* (b) enforce applicable Terms of Service, including investigation of potential violations thereof, (c) detect, prevent or otherwise address fraud, security, or technical issues, or (d) protect against harm to the rights, property, or safety of Google, its users or the public as required or permitted by law."[51]

On the other hand, it was reported that under the terms of the alliance "Google will not be sharing proprietary data and the NSA will not be viewing users' searches or e-mail accounts."[52]

Liberty Vs. Security, Balancing Competing Interests

Some Proposals and Opinions

K.A. Taipale proposed in a law journal article published some time ago that there are ways to separate the various entities that conduct data analysis and law enforcement functions, to separate domestic from international intelligence functions, and to create a separate agency with a "narrow charter to process intelligence for domestic security, no independent law enforcement powers, and subject to strict oversight."[53] He also proposed "a distributed architecture with local responsibility and accountability for data and access, together with strong credential and audit functions to track usage" to provide " protection from a centralized expansion of power or use." He noted, too, that the same information systems that cause concern can also be turned on the watchers to monitor their proper use of the technology, e.g. through "real time automated monitoring of system usage and post usage analysis and review, together with oversight of systems logs ... and organizational structures to ensure such results should be devised as part of systems implementations ."[54] Although it may be more theoretical than practical, he suggests that "technological systems should conform to existing (or evolving) notions of due process and technical features and implementations should be designed to support those procedures." [55]

Thus, it may be possible to program the monitoring and investigation technology to encompass the legal protections expected under various constitutions worldwide, and to develop a system of checks and balances on abuse, as Taipale points out, and as does Catherine Lotrionte in her chapter in this book.

On the other hand, Professor Susan Brenner questions whether we can construe Fourth Amendment privacy in "a fashion that is expansive enough to encompass life in a society where physical barriers have little, if any, meaning? If we cannot, we will have little, if any privacy" (in light of ubiquitous technology).[56]

James A. Lewis of the Center for Strategic and Intelligence Studies states more forcefully that existing privacy policy may be obsolete in light of cyber security issues:

> ... privacy has come to mean preserving an unconstrained space for individual action andprotecting the original sense of unlimited opportunity the Internet seems to offer ... The expansive definition focuses privacy policy on three issues. The first is grounded in the traditional understanding of privacy and seeks to limit the effect of network technologies on individual control over personal data, which retains as much as possible of our pre-Internet seclusion. The second is to reduce or constrain the role of government in cyberspace in order to protect civil liberties. The third is to safeguard the Internet's potential for innovation. Privacy policy advocates assert that these three issues are linked and depend on defending an open and free Internet ... Many assumptions underpin these ideas. The most problematic are that we can restrict or eliminate government involvement in the Internet without risk; that anonymity is always beneficial; that an open, unsecure Internet is crucial for innovation; and that digital technologies have not eroded earlier conceptions of privacy as they have done with so many other concepts in business and politics. In looking at these assumptions, we must ask if trends in technology and governance have made some aspects of privacy policy obsolete.[57]

James Lewis dismisses the role of legal precedent in American law and the shaping of American policy, as he minimizes the effect of the U.S. civil rights movement and its impact on American law and policy, as well as the effect of the privacy and civil liberties organizations and the culture of freedom in the Internet pioneering days, characterizing them as "outdated". He states that since the American constitution is an anomaly in comparison with those in other countries around the world, e.g. our First Amendment provisions guaranteeing freedom of speech, future American cyber security policy should take this into account. He notes: "The larger problem, however, is that the American perspective on privacy and Internet governance is unique. The United States once dominated the governance of the Internet. But that governance is shifting to a global community of nations, and so the United States must do away with old ideas in order to retain its influence to defend core values for the rules, institutions and technologies of the Internet."[58] Is he saying that the United States should do away with its history and democratic values and get into step with policies adopted by non-democratic countries or democratic countries with fewer constitutional and legal rights in order to stay up to date with cybersecurity issues?

Professor Jack Goldsmith also seems initially to have adopted an ironic view about the possibility of retaining the Fourth Amendment as we have known it in light of cyberthreats and the maintenance of cybersecurity:

> The purpose behind the cybersecurity collection and analysis scheme would not be law enforcement but rather the protection of the critical infrastructure that undergirds our military and economic security. For a nationwide intrusion-detection system to have a chance at legality, the government, backed by express congressional findings, would need to establish that (a) network-wide coverage is necessary because deadly computer attack agents are tiny needles hidden inside giant haystacks consisting of billions of innocent communications that each travel at the speed of light and are often designed to learn from computer defense systems—automatically and at computer speed-and morph to exploit their vulnerabilities; and (b) only comprehensive, speed-of light collection and analysis will enable the government to find and thwart this threat and keep the network and the infrastructure connected to it safe.[59]

He then provides "A Model for Constitutional Cybersecurity Surveillance" that reflects anumber of the safeguards that have in fact been put into effect by the FISA Amendments of 2008, which enable the "targeting of persons reasonably believed to be located outside the United States to acquire foreign intelligence information." The four safeguards are (1) the requirement of an independent *ex ante* scrutiny by the Foreign Intelligence Surveillance Court "that results in a certification that the government's general targeting procedures are reasonably designed to stay within statutory guidelines"; (2) applying "*various privacy and Fourth Amendment-protecting requirements,* most notably 'minimization procedures' that are themselves subject to *ex ante* review and approval by the FISC"; (3) "a variety of *ex post oversight mechanisms:* The AG and DNI must assess legal compliance and report to Congress every six months, and inspectors general across the intelligence community and DOJ must perform annual reviews for legal compliance and effectiveness"; 4) the 2008 FISA amendments contain a 2012 sunset provision "that requires Congress to revisit and reapprove (if it so desires) the entire scheme after four years of operation." Professor Goldsmith states that the four above mechanisms "would inform the proportionality and reasonableness of the scheme and could form the foundation of any aggressive government cybersecurity activity in the domestic network."[60]

The debate is heated and active among U.S. and other academics, think tanks, in the courts and elsewhere. Stay tuned for further policy developments, legislation, and court holdings on these issues .... The jury is still out.

References

Abel, W., & Schafer, B. (2009, April) The German Constitutional Court on the Right in Confidentiality and Integrity on Information Technology Systems, a case report on BVerfG, NJW 2008, 822. *SCRIPTed,* (5(1).

ACLU. (2011). *Amnesty et al. v. Clapper.* FISA Amendment Act Challenge. *Civil Freedoms: Promoting & Protecting Civil Freedoms in the US.* Retrieved from http://www.civilfreedoms.org/?p=1605

ACLU. (2012). *Amnesty et al. v. Clapper:* FISA Amendment Act Challenge. Retrieved from http://www.aclu.org/national-security/amnesty-et-al-v-clapper

Associated Press. (2005). FBI tosses Carnivore to the dogs. *Wired.com.* Retrieved June 26,2012, from http://www.wired.com/politics/security/news/2005/01/66327

Bagley, A. W. (2011). Don't be evil: The Fourth Amendment in the age of Google, national security and digital papers and effects. *Albany Law Journal of Science & Technology,* 27(153), 155.

Baker, S. (2010). *Skating on stilts: Why we aren't stopping tomorrow's terrorism.* Stanford, CA: Hoover Institution Press.

Balkin, J. M. (2008). Essay: The Constitution in the National Surveillance State. *Minnesota Law Review.* Retrieved from www.minnesotalawre-view.org/articles/essay-constitution-national-surveillance-state/

Bazan, E. B. (2008). *The Foreign Intelligence Surveillance Act: An overview of selected issues.* Congressional Research Service. Retrieved from http://www.fas.org/sgp/crs/intel/RL34279.pdf

Bazan, E. B., & Elsea, J. K. (2006). *Presidential authority to conduct warrantless electronic surveillance to gather foreign intelligence information.* Congressional Research Service. Retrieved from www.fas.org/sgp/crs/intel/m010506.pdf

Bellia, P. L. (2005). Spyware and the limits of surveillance law. *Berkeley Technology Law Journal, 20,* 1283–1287.

Bemers-Lee, T. (2010). Long live the web: A call for continued open standards and neutrality. *Scientific American.* Retrieved from http ://www.scientificamerican.com/article.cfm?id=long-live-the-web

Block, F. (2005). Civil liberties during national emergencies: The interaction between the three branches of government in coping with past and current threats to the nation's security. *NYU Review of Law & Social Change, 29,* 459.

Bradshaw, T. (2011). Sarkozy riles Internet CEOs at e-G8. *Financial Times.* Retrieved from http:// blogs.ft.com/tech-blog/2011/05/sarkozy-riles- intemet-ceos-at-e-g8/#axzzlxmLUN7tQ

Brenner, S. W. (2011). Fourth Amendment future: Remote computer searches and the use of virtual force. *Mississippi Law Journal, 81*(1).

Breyer, S. (2005). *Active liberty; Interpreting our democratic constitution.* New York, NY: Vintage Books.

Castells, M. (2001). *The Internet galaxy: Reflections on the Internet, business, and society.* New York, NY: Oxford University Press.

Center for Democracy and Technology. (2012). *Existing federal privacy laws.* Retrieved from https://www.cdt.org/privacy/guide/protect/laws.php

Center for Democracy and Technology. (2012). *Security and surveillance.* Retrieved from https://www.cdt.org/issue/wiretap-ecpa?order=field_ date_value&sort=asc

Chabrow, E. (2010). White House partially lifts CNCI secrecy. *Government info security news, training, education—GovInfoSecurity.* Retrieved from http://www.govinfosecurity.com/articles.php?art_id=2257

Cheng, J. (2010). Appeals court: Warrant required before Feds can read e-mail. *Ars Tech-nica.* Retrieved from http://arstechnica.com/tech-policy/2010/12/appeals-court-warrant-required-before-feds-can-read-e-mail-mail/

Continuing attention to privacy concerns is needed as programs are developed, Testimony before the Subcommittee on Homeland Security, Committee onAppropriations, House of Representatives, Homeland Security. (2007) (Statement of Linda D. Koontz.)

Couts, A. (2012a). CISPA supporters list: 800+ companies that could help Uncle Sam snag your data. *Digital Trends.* Retrieved from http://www.digitaltrends.com/web/cispa-supporters-list-800-companies-that-could-help-uncle-sam-snag-your-data/

Couts, A. (2012b). Watch out, Washington: CISPA replaces SOPA as Internet's enemy no. 1. *Digital Trends.* Retrieved from http://www.digitaltrends.com/web/watch-out-washington-cispa-replaces-sopa-as-internets-enemy-no-1/

Congressional Research Service (CRS). (2011). Amendments to the Foreign Intelligence Surveillance Act (FISA) Extended Until June 1, 2015. *Full Text Reports.* Retrieved from http://fulltextreports.com/2011/06/28/amendments-to-the-foreign-intelligence-surveillance-act-fisa-extended-until-june-1-2015/

Dempsey, J. X. (2010, September 22). *The Electronic Communications Privacy Act: Promoting security and protecting privacy in the digital age.* Retrieved from https://www.cdt.org/files/pdfs/20100922Jxd_testimony_ecpa.pdf

Digital Due Process, (n.d.). Digital due process. *Resources.* Retrieved from http://digitaldueprocess.org/index.cfm?objectid=FE5C92F0-2552-11DF-B455000C296BA163#3

Downes, L. (2012). Why CISPA can't be fixed. *Forbes.com.* Retrieved from http://www.forbes.com/sites/larrydownes/2012/04/25/why-cispa-cant-be-fixed/

Doyle, C. (2009). *National security letters in foreign intelligence investigations; Legal background and recent amendments.* Congressional Research Service. Retrieved from http://www.fas.org/sgp/crs/intel/RL33320.pdf

Electronic Communications Privacy Act Amendments Act of 2011. (2011). Retrieved from http://thomas.loc.gov/cgi-bin/query/z?c 112:S.1011

Electronic Communications Privacy Act: Government perspectives on protecting privacy in the digital age, Statement before the Committee on Judiciary, United States Senate. (2011). (Testimony of James A. Baker) Retrieved from www.judiciary.senate.gov/pdf/11-4-6 Baker Testimony.pdf

Electronic Frontier Foundation. (2005). *Communications Assistance for Law Enforcement Act (CALEA).* Retrieved from https://www.eff.org/issues/calea

Electronic Frontier Foundation, (n.d.). *EFF's case against AT&T.* Retrieved from https://www.eff.org/nsa/hepting

Electronic Privacy Information Center v. Department of Justice, American Civil Liberties Union etal v. Department of Justice, Memorandum Opinion and Order (2008). (Civil Action)

Elias, P. (2010). Judge orders feds to pay $2.5M in wiretapping case. *The Washington Times.* Retrieved from www.washingtontimes.com/news/2010/dec/22/judge-orders-feds-pay-25m-wiretapping-case/

European Parliament, Draft Report on the Existence of a Global System for the Interception of Private and Commercial Communication (2001).

Executive Office of the President. (2012). *Statement of administration policy H.R. 3523: Cyber intelligence sharing and protection act.* Retrieved from http://www.whitehouse.gov/sites/default/files/omb/legislative/sap/112/saphr3523r_20120425.pdf

FISA Sunsets Extension Act of 2011, S. 289, 112th Cong., 1st Sess. (2011). Retrieved from http://www.openeongress.org/bill/112-s289/show

Fontaine, R., & Rogers, W. (2011). Internet freedom and its discontents: Navigating the tensions with cyber security. In K. M. Lord & T. Sharp (Eds.) *America's cyber future: Security and prosperity in the Information Age* (Vol. 2.). Washington, DC: Center for a New American Society.

Foreign Intelligence Surveillance Act of 1978. (1978). Retrieved from http://www.law.comell.edu/uscode/text/50/chapter-36

Former Attorneys General urge dismissal of constitutional challenge to foreign surveillance statute (*Clapper v. Amnesty International USA,* No. 11-1025). (2012). *Washington Legal Foundation News Release.* Retrieved from www.wlf.org/upload/litigation/pressrelease/032012RS.pdf

Full text ofH.R. 3523: Cyber Intelligence Sharing and Protection Act. (2012). *GovTrack.us: Tracking the U.S. Congress.* Retrieved from http://www.govtrack.us/congress/bills/112/hr3523/text

Garvey, T., & Liu, E. C. (2011). *The state secrets privilege: Preventing the disclosure of sensitive national security information during civil litigation.* Congressional Research Service. Retrieved from www.fas.org/sgp/crs/secrecy/R41741.pdf

General Accounting Office. (2004). *Data mining: Federal efforts cover a wide range of uses.* Retrieved from http://www.gao.gov/new.items/d04548.pdf

General Accounting Office. (2008). *Agencies have taken key steps to protect privacy in selected efforts, but significant compliance issues remain.* Retrieved from http://www.gao.gov/new.items/d05866.pdf

General Accounting Office. (2011). *DHS needs to improve executive oversight of systems supporting counterterrorism.* Retrieved from http://gao.gov/products/GAO-11-742

Geolocational Privacy and Surveillance Act, 112th Congress. (2011). Retrieved from http://www.gpo.gov/fdsys/pkg/BILLS-112s1212is/pdf/BILLS-112sl212is.pdf

Going dark: Lawful electronic surveillance in the face of new technologies, Hearing before the Committee on the Judiciary Subcommittee on Crime, Terrorism and Homeland Security (2011). (Testimony of Mark A. Marshall, Valerie E. Caproni and Susan Landau)

Granick, J. (2011). Court holds ECPA allows Myspace to disclose private messages pursuant to out of state warrant. *Center for Internet and Society.* Retrieved from http://cyberlaw.stanford.edu/node/6687

Grazzini, M. (2010). U.S. vs. Warshak; The constitutionality of search and seizure of E-mails. *Berkeley Technology Law Journal.*

Hafetz, J. (2011). No exemption from judicial review for national security surveillance. *Concurring Opinions.* Retrieved from http://www.concurringopinions.com/archives/2011/03/noexemption-from-judicial-review-for-national-security-surveillance.html

Harris, L. (2012). Cyber security: Civil liberties threatened in effort to protect Internet, electric grid, comm unications? *ABCNews.com.* Retrieved from http://abcnews.go.com/Technology/cyber-security-civil-liberties-threatened-effort-protect-internet/story?id=l 6104680#.T-n-A5H091K

Harris, S. (2010). *Thewatchers: The rise of America s surveillance state.* New York, NY: Penguin.

Harvard Law Review. (2009). Recent legislation: Electronic surveillance—Congress grants telecommunications companies retroactive immunity from civil suits for complying with NSA terrorist surveillance program—FISA Amendments Act of 2008 8, Pub. L. No. 110-261, 122 Stat. 2436. Retrieved from http://www.harvardlawreview.org/media/pdf/FISA_amendments_act.pdf

Henning, A. C., & Liu, E. C. (2011). Amendments to the Foreign Intelligence SurveillanceAct (FISA). *Knowledge Empire.* Retrieved fromhttp://knowledgeempire.wordpress.com/2011/02/15/amendments-to-the-usa-patriot-act-fisa/

Hepting v. AT&T Corp, United States Court of Appeals for the Ninth Circuit. (2011). Retrieved from www.ca9.uscourts.gov/datastore/opinions/2011/12/29/09-16676.pdf

Hibbard, C. M. (2012). Wiretapping the Internet: The expansion of the Communications Assistance to Law Enforcement Act to extend government surveillance. *Federal Communications Law Journal, 64,* 372–399.

Homeland Security & Governmental Affairs Committee. (2012). Lieberman, Collins, Rockefeller, Feinstein offer bipartisan comprehensive bill to secure Federal and critical private sector cyber systems. Retrieved from http://www.hsgac.senate.gov/media/majority-media/lieberman-collins-rockefeller-feinsteinoffer-bipartisan-comprehensive-bill-to-secure-fed-and-critical-private-sector-cyber-systems

H.R. 3523: An act, 112th Congress, 2nd Session. (2011). Retrieved from http://www.gpo.gov/fdsys/pkg/BILLS-112hr3523eh/pdf/BILLS-112hr3523eh.pdf

Information sharing, monitoring and countermeasures in the cybersecurity act, S. 2105, and the SECURE IT Act, S. 2151. (2012). Retrieved from http://www.cdt.org/files/pdfs/analysis_senate_cyber-bills_2012.pdf

James R. Clapper, Jr., Director of National Intelligence v. Amnesty International USA et al, No. 11-1025. Supreme Court of the United States. (2011). retrieved from http://www.supremecourt-preview.org

James R. Clapper v. Amnesty International USA et al., Petition for Writ of Certiorari to the United States Court of Appeals for the Second Circuit, No. 11-1025. Supreme Court ofthe United States. (2011). Retrieved from www.justice.gov/osg/briefs/2011/2pet/7pet/2011-1025.pet.aa.pdf

James R. Clapper, Jr., Director of National Intelligence, etal. v. Amnesty International USA, No. 11-1025. Supreme Court ofthe United States. (2012). Retrieved from http://www.supremecourt.gov/Search.aspx?FileName=/docketfiles/11-1025.htm

Jewel v. NSA. (2011). *Electronic Frontier Foundation.* Retrieved from https://www.eff.org/cases/jewel

Jewel v. NSA Full Complaint. (2011). *Electronic Frontier Foundation.* Retrieved from https://www.eff.org/files/filenode/jewel/jewel.complaint.pdf

Johnson, E. (2010). Surveillance and privacy under the Obama administration: The Foreign Intelligence Surveillance Act of 1978 Amendments Act of 2008 and the Attorney General's guidelines for domestic FBI Operations. *I/S: A Journal of Law and Policy for the Information Society,* 6(1), 419–446.

Jonas, J., & Harper, J. (2006). *Effective counterterrorism and the limited role of predictive data mining.* Cato Institute. Retrieved from http://www.cato.org/publications/policy-analysis/effective-counterterrorism-limited-role-predictive-data-mining

Kerr, O. S. (2010). Applying the Fourth Amendment to the Internet: A general approach. *Stanford Law Review, 62,* 1005–1029.

Knapp, J. (2006). CC adopts order to enable law enforcement to access certain broadband and VoIP providers. *Cybertelecom: Federal Internet Law and Policy.* Retrieved from http://www.cybertelecom.org/voip/fcccalea.htm

Kravets, D. (2011). Appeals court revives lawsuit challenging NSA surveillance of Americans. *Wired.com.* Retrieved from http://www.whed.com/threatlevel/2011/03/warrantless-eavesdropping/

Library Boy Blog. (2010, November 2). *Canadian Government Re-Introduces Internet Surveillance Bills.* Retrieved from http://micheladrien.blogspot.com/2010_11_0 1_archive.html

Liu, E. C. (2011). *Amendments to the Foreign Intelligence Surveillance Act (FISA) extended until June 1, 2015.* Congressional Research Service. Retrieved from www.fas.org/sgp/crs/intel/R40138.pdf

Lynch, J. (2011). Newly released documents detail FBI's plan to expand federal surveillance laws. *Electronic Frontier Foundation.* Retrieved from https://www.eff.org/deeplinks/2011/02/newly-released-documents-detail-fbi-s-plan-expand

McCullagh, D. (2011). FBI to announce new Internet-wiretapping push. *CBS News.* Retrieved from http://www.cbsnews.eom/8301-501465_162-20032695-501465.htm

Minow, N. N., & Cate, F. H. (2008). Government data mining. In Kamien, D. (Ed.), *The McGraw Hill Homeland Security Handbook.* New York, NY: McGraw Hill.

Morrison, S. R. (2011). What the cops can't do, internet service providers can: Preserving privacy in email contents. *Virginia Journal of Law and Technology,* 16(253), 297.

Nagesh, G. (2011). Sen. Leahy introduces update to digital privacy law. *TheHill.com.* Retrieved from http://thehill.com/blogs/hillicon-valley/technology/161691-sen-leahy-introduces-update-to-digital-privacy-law

Nojeim, G. (2011). Cyber intelligence bill threatens privacy and civilian control. *Center for Democracy and Technology.* Retrieved from https://www.cdt.org/blogs/greg-nojeim/112cyber-intelligence-bill-threatens-privacy-and-civilian-control

Office ofthe Director of National Intelligence Data Mining Report. (2008, February 15). Retrieved from http ://www.au.af.mil/au/awe/awegate/dni/data_mining_report_feb08.pdf

Ohm, P. (2009). The rise and fall of invasive ISP surveillance. *University of Illinois Law Review, 1417.*

Opderbeck, D. W. (2012). Cybersecurity and executive power. *Washington University Law Review, 89*(4), 795.

Oza,A. (2008). Amend the ECPA: Fourth Amendment protection erodes as e-mails get dusty. *Boston University Law Review, 88,* 1043–1072.

Perera, D. (2011). Book excerpt: 'Surveillance or Security' by Susan Landau. *Fierce Gov IT.* Retrieved from http://www.fiercegovernmentit.com/story/book-cxccrpt-survcillancc-or-sccurity-susan-landau/2011-04-14

Royalty, D. H. (2011). CALEA II–Bigger and badder? *TMT Law Watch.* Retrieved from http://www.tmtlawwatch.com/2011/01/articles/calea-ii-bigger-and-badder/

Rule 41. (2009). Search and seizure. *Legal Information Institute.* Retrieved from http://www.law.comell.edu/rules/frcrmp/rule_41

Sasso, B. (2012). Senators float compromise on cybersecurity mandates. *TheHill.com*. Retrieved from http://thehill.com/blogs/hillicon-valley/technology/231601-senators-float-compromise-on-cybersecurity-mandates-

Schwartz, M. J. (2012). CISPA Bill: 5 main privacy worries. *InformationWeek*. Retrieved from http://www.informationweek.com/news/security/privacy/232900418

Schwartz, P. M. (2008). Reviving telecommunications surveillance law. *The University of Chicago Law Review, 75,* 287.

Scientific American. (2012). *Read my e-mail? Get a warrant.* Retrieved from http://www.scientificamerican.com/article.cfin?id=read-my-e-mail-get-a-warrant

Senkowski, R. M., & Dawson, M. W. (2009). Cybersecurity: A briefing—Part II. *Metropolitan Corporate Counsel,* 77(8), 13.

Shank, S. (2011). Cybersecurity: Domestic and legislative issues. *National Security Law Brief, 1*(1).

Shanker, T. (2010, September 24). Cyberwar chief calls for secure computer network. *The New York Times.* Retrieved from http://www.nytimes.com/2010/09/24/us/24cyber.html?_r= 1

Smith v. Maryland, 442 U.S. 735 (Cert, to Ct. of App. Md.). (1979).

Steinbock, D. J. (2005). Data matching, data mining, and due process. *Georgia Law Review, 40*(1), 10.

Stem, J. (2012). CISPA: What you need to know about the cybersecurity bill Congress just passed. *ABCNews.com.* Retrieved from http://abcnews.go.com/Technology/cispa-cybersecurity-bill-congress-passed/story?id=l 6230902#.T-n8EJH091I

Stevens, G. M., & Doyle, C. (2009). *Privacy: An overview of federal statutes governing wiretapping and electronic eavesdropping.* Congressional Research Service. Retrieved from www.au.af.mil/au/awc/awcgate/crs/98-326.pdf

Taipale, K. A. (2003) Data mining and domestic security: Connecting the dots to make sense of data. *Columbia Law Review,* 1(70), 22.

Taipale, K. A. (2005). Technology, security and privacy: The fear of Frankenstein, the mythology of privacy and the lessons of King Ludd. *Yale Journal of Law and Technology, 7*(123), 174.

Taipale, K. A. (2007). *The privacy implications of government data mining programs, Hearing before the United States Senate Committee on the Judiciary.*

Tew, S. (2012). Major CISPA opponent steps down, jeopardizing White House's veto promise. *RT.com.* Retrieved from rt.com/usa/news/white-cispa-security-house-535/

The Cato Institute. (2006, December 11). *Data mining doesn't catch terrorists: New Cato Study Argues it Threatens Liberty.* Retrieved from http://www.cato.org/pressroom.php?display=news&id=73

The Cybersecurity Act of 2012, S.2105, 112th Cong, 2nd Sess. (2012).

Title III of the Omnibus Crime Control and Safe Street Act of1968 (Wiretap Act). (1968). Retrieved from http://cyber.law.harvard.edu/privacy/Statutory%20Summaries%20for%20Module%20IV.htm

Tokson, M. J. (2009). The content-envelope distinction in internet law. *William and Mary Law Review, 50*(6), 2105–2176.

Tokson, M. J. (2011). Automation and the Fourth Amendment. *Iowa Law Review, 96,* 49.

United States Court of Appeals for the Third Circuit. (2010). *In the matter of the application of the United States of America for an order directing a provider of electronic communication service to disclose records to the government.* Retrieved from www.ca3.uscourts.gov/opinarch/084227p.pdf

United States v. Forrester, 09-50029 U.S. (2010).

United States v. Hambrick, 99-4793 U.S. (2000).

Unites States v. Warshak, 631 F. 3d 266 (2010).

US Department of Justice Office of Information Policy. (2010). *Congress passes Amendment to Exception 3 of the FOIA.* Retrieved from http://www.justice.gov/oip/foiapost/2010foiapost7.htm

WhiteHouse.Gov. (2009). *Cyberspace policy review-Assuring a trusted and resilient information and communications infrastructure.* Retrieved from http://www.whitehouse.gov/assets/documents/Cyberspace_Policy_Review_fmal.pdf

Wikipedia. (n.d.). *Einstein (US-CERTProgram).* retrieved from http://en.wikipedia.org/wiki/Ein-stein_(US-CERT_program)

Wolf, C. (2011). *The role of government in commercial cybersecurity: Public-private partnerships and improvements in government data security rather than government control as the optimal model.* Paper presented at 2011 Technical Symposium at ITU Telecom World (ITU WT). Washington, DC: IEEE Press.

Zavrsnik, A. (2008). Cybercrime definitional challenges and criminological particularities. *Masaryk Journal of Law and Technology, 2*(2), 21–22.

Notes

1. The latter is a discussion of ISP surveillance rather than government surveillance of email, etc., however it is a foreshadowing of current efforts in the U.S. Congress to pass Cybersecurity legislation. See Section 5 *infra* for an update on the current status of that legislation.
2. It is difficult to clearly understand the evolution of the Stored Communications Act and other laws cited in this chapter, when each is applied and their relationship to the Fourth Amendment. One clarifying statement is found in a court opinion from the Third Circuit: "... The growth of electronic communications has stimulated Congress to enact statutes that provide both access to information heretofore unavailable for law enforcement and, at the same time, protect users of such communications from intrusion that Congress deems unwarranted. The Stored Communications Act ('SCA') was enacted in 1986 as Title II of the Electronic Communications Privacy Act of 1986 ('ECPA'), Pub. L. No. 99-508, 100 Stat. 1848 (1986) (codified as amended at 18 U.S.C. Sections 2701-2711) (2010), which amended the Omnibus Crime Control and Safe Streets Act of 1968 (the 'Wiretap Act'), Pub. L. No. 90-351, 82 Stat. 197 (1968). In 1994, Congress enacted the Communications Assistance for Law Enforcement Act ('CALEA'), Pub. L. No. 103-414, 108 Stat. 4279,4292 (1994) (codified in relevant part at 18 U.S.C. Sec. 2703 (2010), part to amend the SCA." *In the Matter of the Application of the United States of America for an Order Directing a Provider of Electronic Communication Service to Disclose Records to the Government,* United States of America, Appellant, No. 08-4227, 9/7/2010 (United States Court of Appeals for the Third Circuit, 2010), page 4. "Title II of the ECPA was formally entitled 'Stored Wire and Electronic Communications and Transactional Records Access,' Pub. L. No. 99-508,100 Stat. 1848 (1986)."
3. With the adoption of the ECPA, Congress enabled the law to "govern the interception of electronic communications." *See* Paul Ohm (2009), noting, "The Fifth Circuit has complained that the Act 'is famous (if not infamous) for its lack of clarity,' a statement which the Ninth Circuit rejoined 'might have put the matter too mildly.'" Professor Orin Kerr blames this confusion on the unfortunate combination of 'remarkably difficult statutory language' … .

   Better precision in the drafting of cybersecurity legislation might allay the fears of the U.S. civil liberties and privacy communities and the general public, and could be applied in other countries as well, where there is a need for national cybersecurity but concern about protecting constitutional rights in democracies as well as reasonable use of government surveillance to protect the general public, private sector, critical information infrastructure.

4. *Warshak* was subsequently vacated on the ground that the case was unripe, then relitigated.
5. Of course, given recent pending legislation related to cybersecurity in the House and Senate in 2012, the existing privacy and warrant legislation might become null.
6. For the background of ECPA and criminal penalties for interception of "electronic communications," defined as "any 'transfer of signs, signals, writing, images, sounds, data, or intelligence of any nature transmitted in whole or in part by a wire, radio, electromagnetic, photoelectronic orphotooptical sysem' which is not a wire or oral communication," see Tokson, (2009) and Hibbard, (2012).
7. The same conceptual emphasis on reporting to the government information about cyberattacks without obtaining a court order is found in the House CISPA legislation passed on April 26,2012 (version sent to the Senate on May 7, 2012). For analysis of that bill and Senate bills, see Section 5 *infra.*

9. For the FISA amendments up to 2006, *see* http ://www.fas.org/sgp/crs/intell/mO71906.pdf
10. *In re Sealed Case,* 310 F. 3d 717 (Foreign Intell. Surveillance Ct. Rev. 2002).
11. See *U.S. v. AbuJihaad,* 630 F. 3d 102 (Ct. of App. 2d Cir. 2010) for discussion of Fourth Amendment warrant requirements in light of FISA certification of a "significant" rather than a "primary purpose" of obtaining foreign intelligence information when it applies for a warrant to conduct surveillance based on joint investigation by law enforcement and intelligence officials.
12. Orin S. Kerr offers the view that, "Courts should hold that Internet users ordinarily have a reasonable expectation of privacy in the contents oflntemet communications but not innon-content information." He also distinguishes content fromnon-content, saying, "The addressing (or 'envelope') information is the data that the network uses to deliver the communications to or from the user; the content information is the payload that the user sends or receives."
13. See Tokson (2011), citing a proposal by Christopher Slobogin that "courts should hold that the Fourth Amendment applies to noncontent information but that law enforcement officials can obtain it with a court order issued upon a demonstration of reasonable suspicion, rather than a warrant based on probable cause."
14. *See Smith v. Maryland,* 442 U.S. 735 (1979) which held that phone numbers dialed are noncontent information and not protected by the Fourth Amendment, but telephone call contents are.
15. Courts may see this issue differently than the author of that chart when it comes to deciding what aspect of email and website search is content.
16. This author does not agree with Prof. Ohm on this point—who is to decide the implications of content and their meaning? What is important to me may be banal to someone else, and vice versa, and may result in censorship and loss of freedom of speech if a third party is to make that decision about one's content.
17. At the end of each recommendation, there is the comment, "When we confirm what actions the agency has taken in response to this recommendation, we will provide updated information."

18. It notes that the House Homeland Security Committee's PRECISE Act, H.R. 3674, "appropriately permits information shared for cybersecurity purposes to be used to prosecute cybersecurity crimes but not other crimes."

19. Id. In a recent ruling, for example, *Electronic Privacy Information Center* v. *National Security Agency,* U.S. C.A. 11-5233 (D.C.) decided on May 11, 2012, the Appellate Court upheld a ruling that EPIC could not obtain under the Freedom oflnformationAct requested disclosure of any communications between NSA and Google, Inc. regarding encryption and cybersecurity. According to a footnote to the decision, "Prior to January 2010, Google allowed Gmailusers to encrypt the email thatpassedthrough Google servers using Secure Hypertext Transfer Protocol (HTTPS), but it did not provide encryption by default. Id. note 1. "Google subsequently changed Gmail's privacy settings to automatically encrypt all traffic to and from its servers" after a January 10, 2010 attack on Google "that primarily targeted the Gmail accounts of Chinese human rights activists." Id. at 2. On February 4, 2010, "EPIC submitted a FOIA request to NSA, specifically requesting three categories of records: (1.) All records concerning an agreement or similar basis for collaboration, final or draft, between the NSA and Google regarding cyber security; (2.) All records of communication between NSAand Google concerning Gmail, including but not limited to Google's decision to fail to routinely encrypt Gmail messages prior to January 13, 2010; (3.) All records of communications regarding NSA's role in Google's decision regarding the failure to routinely deploy encryption for cloud-based computing service, such as Google Docs." Id. at 3. NSA then issued a *"Glomar* response" in which the agency "neither confirmed nor denied the existence of any responsive records," under the purview of Section 6 of the National Security Agency Act, which provides that "nothing in this Act or any other law ... shall be construed to require the disclosure of the organization or any function of the National Security Agency, [or] of any information with respect to the activities thereof ..." Pub. L. No. 86-36, Section 6(a), 73 Stat. 63,64 (1959). Id. at 3, note 2. Essentially, the Appeal Court upheld the lower court ruling that NSA should be granted summary judgment.

20. Citing Cybersecurity Act, Section 708(5), stating that an "information system" is "a discrete set of information resources organized for the collection, processing, maintenance, use, sharing, dissemination, or disposition of information ..." Cybersecurity Act, Section 708(10). The CDT analysis notes that, "It seems that under this definition, every computer and smart phone is an 'information system,' as is every website. In fact, it would seem that every student term paper with a list of references is a 'discrete set of information resources organized for the ... sharing of information.'"

21. Such precision in the drafting of cybersecurity legislation might allay the fears of the U.S. civil liberties and privacy communities and the general public, and could be applied in other countries as well where there is a need for national cybersecurity but concern about protecting constitutional rights in democracies as well as reasonable use of government surveillance to protect the general public, private sector, critical information infrastructure.

22. *But see* Jennifer Granick, citing a Southern District of New York dismissal of the complaint in *Hubbard v. Myspace.* The court rejected the "claim that a social network violated the Stored Communications Act ... by disclosing certain user information pursuant to law enforcement demands." The claim relied on SC A

provisions stating that "electronic service providers may not disclose the contents of user communications, except to law enforcement with a valid warrant. Specifically, Section 2703 (e) provides that: 'No cause of action shall lie in any court against any provider of wire or electronic communication service, its officers, employees, agents, or other specified persons for providing information, facilities, or assistance in accordance with the terms of a court order, warrant, subpoena, statutory authorization, or certification under this chapter.'" The demand was made by faxed legal process.

Other ISPs and social media companies also report law enforcement demands for user information. "Google reports that U.S. government agencies send it nearly 1,000 requests for information every month; the company complied with 93 percent of them between January and June of last year ... Verizon executives told Congress in 2007 that law-enforcement agencies send the company 90,000 requests for user details a year, including information on the specific locations of cell-phone customers." As a result, a coalition of "technology companies, think tanks and privacy advocates called Digital Due Process has formed to ask Congress to update the ECPA for the modem age. Its demand is simple enough; if a law-enforcement agency wants to look at private user data—whether e-mails, documents or cell-phone location information—it needs a warrant. This reasonable demand for clarity is fully in keeping with the spirit of the original ECPA, as well as the Fourth Amendment of the Constitution's prohibition 'against unreasonable searches and seizures.'"

It is unclear at this time whether all members of the Digital Due Process coalition are still on board; some are among the 800+ companies listed as supporting CISPA.

23. "The business sector changed the internet into a so-called 'new economy'. The driving power of the internet economy became business's innovation-led approach and not capital itself—which is to say that the ideas that could be realised as a business venture were the driving power of the 'new economy'. The only goals that should in theory have made new companies successful and freed them from the bounds of traditional corporative capital, were the expected levels of pro fit and the speed at which they could be reached. Internet entrepreneurs thus had to unite the figure of the innovator, technologist and venture capitalist. This type of entrepreneur is characterized by excessive consumption, shallow socialisation and is more an artist than a businessman."

24. "Informal organisations are governed by tribal elders (as for instance Linus Torvalds in the Linux system) or by collective authority switching its maintenance, co-maintenance etc. between different members of staff."

25. This wide-ranging piece of scholarship examines "... the scope of powers that the Constitution and Congress have conferred upon the President to act in times of national emergency; ... modem anti-terrorism legislation enacted by Congress before September 11; ... post-September 11 anti-terrorism legislation, and ... judicial decisions addressing the President's war-making powers, historic cases addressing the curtailment of civil liberties during past national emergencies, and decisions concerning the recent terrorist crisis."

26. That is, the use of technology by both law enforcement and national security entities as well as those who may be the actual or potential targets of government surveillance in democracies.

27. See *The Department of Justice Guide to the Freedom of Information Act* (2009 Ed.), http://www.justice.gov/oip/foia_guide09.htm and, for example, http://www.corporateservices.noaa.gov/foia/foiaex.html
28. http://www.justice.gov/oip/.foiapost/2010foiapost7.htm This amendment was signed by President Obama on 10/28/09
29. http://www.justice.gov/oip/foia_guide09/exemption3.pdf
30. *See EPIC v.Dep't of Justice, ACLUv. Dep 'I of Justice,* Civ. Action Nos. 06-0096, 06-00214, DDC, 10/31/08. *See also EPIC v. Dep't of Justice,* 511 F. Supp.2d 56 (DDC) (2007)
31. First Worldwide Cybersecurity Summit, EastWest Institute, http://www.ewi.info/ two-tiered-structure-may-allow-both-security-and-privac y-online-say-experts
32. Francesca Bignami, "European Versus American Liberty: A Comparative Privacy Analysis of Antiterrorism Data Mining," 48 *Boston College Law Review.* 609 at 609-610 (2007), citing Jon Bing, *Smilets Interior,* in Angell 2002, at 114, 114-23) (Lill Granrud et al. eds, 2002). For a fictionalized account of that period in European history and the aftermath in the United States, *see* Ralph Freedman, *Rue the Day* (Twilight Times Books, Kingsport, Tn., 2009).
33. Id. at 691-697.
34. *See, e.g.,* Trevor Timm, "UK Government Proposes Law Monitoring Every Email, Phone Call and Text Message," 4/3/12, EFF, https://www.eff.org/deeplinks/2012/04/uk-govemment-proposes-law-monitoring-every-email-phone-call-and-text-message; EmmaDraper, "Queen's Speech shows British government still intent on ... something to do with communications surveillance," Privacy International, https://www.privacyintemational.org/blasts/queens-speech-shows-british-govemment-still-intent-on-something-to-do-with-communications, 5/10/12; "Draft Communications Data Bill," Press Office Home Office, 5/9/12, at 50-51; Annual Reports of the Art. 29 Data Protection Working Party (most recent one adopted 7/14/10), http://ec.europa.eu/justice/policies/privacy/workinggroup/annual_reports_en.htm
35. Doreen Cavajal, "Tackling cybercrime: guidance on sharing Internet data," *The New York Times,* 4/2/08, http://www.ny-times.com./2008/04/02/technology/02iht-cybercrime.4.11626434.html
36. Europe/Open Net Initiative, *see* "Surveillance," at http://opennet.net/research/regions/europe; Privacy International, PHR 2006, Republic of Poland, http://www.privacyintemational.org/article.shtml/cmd[347]-x-347-559594
37. Wiebke Abel and Burkhard Schafer, "The German Constitutional Court on the Right in Confidentiality and Integrity on Information Technology Systems, a case report on BVerfG, NJW 2008, 822," SCRIPTed,Vol. Issue 1, (April 2009)
38. Matt Liebowitz, "Internet Privacy Sparks Fight inFrance and Canada," *Online Privacy and Security,* 4/11/11, http://www.securityncwsdaily.com/intcrnct-privacy-sparks-fight-in-france-and-canada ... <accessed 7/13/11>

40. *See, e.g.* Information and Privacy Commissioner for British Columbia, *Privacy and the USA Patriot Act; Implications for British Columbia Public Sector Outsourcing,* October 2004, pp. 95-96, and Chapter State Surveillance, Privacy and National Security, Chapter 7 Anti-Terrorism Laws in Canada and Ch. 8 Privacy

under Canadian Charter of Rights and Freedoms, in Pauline C. Reich, Ed., CYBERCRIME AND SECURITY (Oceana Division, Oxford University Press, 2003).

41. Id. *See also* Jason M. Young, Surfing While Muslim: Privacy, Freedom of Expression and the Unintended Consequences of Cybercrime Legislation—A Critical Analysis of the Council of Europe. *Convention on Cybercrime* and the Canadian Lawful Access Proposal, *Yale Journal of Law & Technology* 1 (2004–2005)
42. Louise Egan, "Canada boosts police powers, alarms privacy watchdog," Reuters via Yahoo! News, 2/15/12, http://news.yahoo.com/canada-boosts-police-powers-alarms-privacy-watchdog-22311...
43. LEGISinfo- House of Government Bill C-51, http://www.parl.gc.ca/LegisInfo/BillDetails.aspx?Bill=C51&Language=E &Mode=l& ... <accessed7/13/11>

45. It should be noted that Canada has signed but has not ratified the Council of Europe Cybercrime Convention.
46. Department of Justice (Canada), LawfulAccess Consultation Document, http://justice.gc.ca/eng/cons/la-al.b.html
47. Simon Benson, "Police win phone data-new laws to invade your privacy," The Daily Telegraph, 6/22/11, http://www.dailytelegraph.com.au/news/national/police-win-phone-data-new-laws-to ... <accessed 6/29/11>
48. Id.
49. "Government to monitor email and web use of EVERYONE in Britain," 4/2/12, http:// www.dailyrecord.co.uk/news/uk-world-news/2012/04/02/govemment-to-monit ... *See also* 'Email and web use 'to be monitored' under new laws," BBC News- UK Politics, 4/1/12, http://www.bbc.co.uk/news/uk-politics-17576745. A previous effort to pass such legislation in 2009 met opposition and did not succeed. *See* Dominic Casciani, "Plan to monitor all internet use,," BBC News UK Politics, 4/27/09, http://news.bbc.co.uk/2/hi/uk_news/politics/8020039. stm
50. "Home Office promises 'strict safeguards' over privacy for new laws governing communications datamonitoring," Out-Law.com (Legal news and guidance from Pinsent Masons), 5/9/12, http://www.out-law.com/en/articles/2012/may/home-office-promises-strict-safeguards ... See *also* John P. Heekin, "Leashing the Internet Watchdog: Legislative Restraints on Electronic Surveillance in the U.S. and U.K.," http://works.bepress.com/john_heekin/1
51. Arshad Mohammed, "Google Refuses Demand for Search Information," 1/20/06, http://www.washingtonpost.com/wp-dyn/content/article/2006/01/19/AR200601190333. It must be noted that the government's request for this information was not related to a terrorism issue, but rather to its attempt to revive previously repealed legislation concerning access to child pornography. *See also* Tom Raum, "Google case raises new questions about U.S. spying," SiliconValley.com, 1/20/06, http://www.siliconvalley.com/mld/silicon-valley/news/editorial/13 674298.htm?tem ... (Last accessed 10/01/12); Reuters, "Privacy experts condemn Google subpoena," http://news.com.com/Privacy+experts+condemn+Google+subpoena/2100-1025_3-6029348.html, 1/20/06 <accessed l/25/06>

52. DeVos, Stephanie A., "The Google-NSA Alliance: Developing Cybersecurity Policy at Internet Speed," 21 *Fordham Intellectual Property, Media and Entertainment Law Journal* (211) (2011), note 94 citing *Google Privacy Policy*, March 11, 2009, http://www.google.com/intl/en/privacy_archieve.html
53. DeVos, citing Ellen Nakashima, "Google to Enlist NSA to Ward Off Attacks; Firm Won't Share User Data, Sources Say, But Deal Raises Issue of Privacy vs. Security," *Washington Post,* Feb. 4, 2010 at Al.
54. K. A. Taipale, "Technology, Security and Privacy; The Fear of Frankenstein, the Mythology of Privacy and the Lessons of King Ludd," 9 *International Communications Law and Policy* (Winter, 2004/2005) at 145, 145 note 105.
55. K. A. Taipale, "Technology, Security and Privacy; The Fear of Frankenstein, the Mythology of Privacy and the Lessons of King Ludd," 9 *International Communications Lawy and Policy* 8 (Winter, 2004/2005) at 8.
56. Id., p. 151.
57. Susan W. Brenner, "Symposium: The Search and Seizure of Computers and Electronic Evidence: The Fourth Amendment in an Era of Ubiquitous Technology," 75 *Mississippi Law Journal* 1, 13 (Fall, 2005)

CHAPTER 4

Conclusion, References, and Review

The readings in this chapter were designed to introduce some of the large swath of legal concerns regarding cybercrime investigations and forensic examinations of digital evidence. As technology continues to develop at an exponential rate, the debate continues as to how we as a society balance personal privacies and freedoms on the Internet with online security and safety. As these issues are brought before the courts, decisions are handed down that differentially impact the way police and forensic examiners collect and store digital evidence; these decisions also provide more clear guidelines as to the extent to which police can "police" the Internet. Over the past fifteen years, we as a society have had to adapt to the new digital environment, and many have learned (or are learning) the hard way that what you put on the Internet stays on the Internet. Even when a comment or picture is "deleted" from your Facebook profile, there is a cache (an archived digital copy) of it that is electronically stored. From law enforcement and forensic standpoints, this may seem like Christmas came early; evidence of digital wrongdoing (particularly content-based crimes) is served on a silver platter. But to what extent can we reasonably expect to have privacy or ownership of our data online, and hence the right to "delete" it, without it being recovered without a warrant by police? These related privacy matters have been discussed in this chapter, but it is important to understand that the discussion has not ended. As more Internet-based cases are brought before the courts in the United States and abroad, we will continue as a society to shape and mold our responses to the "privacy vs. security" debate.

Interestingly, we must remember that laws are man-made; if our courts and legislators do not place legal limits on online behaviors, those behaviors are not illegal and therefore there is nothing for the police to enforce. Selling controlled substances has been legally restricted in the United States in various forms for one hundred years (Lyman, 2011); it makes logical sense to us that selling illegal drugs over the Internet would also be illegal. However, nothing is illegal until legislation is passed or the courts decide it is. The creation of laws in the United States is often a very time-consuming, lengthy process; the wheels of justice indeed turn very slowly, which is why the legal system is often left playing catch-up to events in the cyberworld. As was seen in this chapter, in some countries mere unauthorized access to a computer system is not against the law, nor are generating and disseminating spam emails. Without a unified definition of "cybercrime," countries are able to differentially legally interpret the term; this can be seen as a benefit, since each country's definition will most likely be representative of the cyber issues faced in that country (i.e., what's the point of spending the time to define "cyberterrorism" legally if the country does not have a cyberterror-related problem?) However, the fragmentation of legal interpretations can also be detrimental to international investigations of cybercrime acts.

As this chapter discussed, absent specific laws or precedent governing law enforcement behavior online, law enforcement agencies have simply translated their traditional methods of operation to the online environment until such actions are challenged in court. A good example of this is the recent decision handed down by the Supreme Court in *Riley v. California* and *United States v. Urie*, in which the Court ruled that police can no longer search the cell phones of people they arrest without a warrant. Before this decision in late June of 2014, this was not the case. Police have long been allowed to search arrestees without a warrant upon arrest (i.e., a search incident to arrest) for safety and evidentiary protection purposes. If you have a cell phone in your pocket when you are arrested, that is evidence, and law enforcement officials argued that the right allowing them to search physical evidence without a warrant upon arrest also applied to digital evidence housed on the cell phone. The Supreme Court disagreed. Cases such as these will continue to define the actions of law enforcement for years to come, and the readings in this chapter served as the foundation for understanding the current legislative atmosphere regarding a myriad of digitally-related law enforcement operations (e.g., electronic communications, trap and trace, electronic surveillance, digital forensic evidence processing and storage). Keep a close watch on cyber-related legislative matters in the future; it will impact all of us (law enforcement or otherwise) as our society strives to find that perfect balance between security and privacy in cyberspace.

References

Cohen, Charles, "Growing Challenge of Computer Forensics." *The Police Chief* 74, no. 3 (2007): 6-14.

Drug Enforcement Administration (DEA). Department of Justice Federal Register: 21 CFR Parts 1300, 1301, 1304, 1306: Implementation of the Ryan Haight Online Pharmacy Consumer Protection Act of 2008. *Federal Register* 74, no. 64 (2009): 15596-15625.

Lyman, Michael D. *Drugs in Society: Causes, Concepts and Control* (6th ed). Waltham, MA: Anderson Publishing, 2011.

United Nations Office on Drugs and Crime (UNODC). *Comprehensive Study on Cybercrime*. New York: United Nations Publication, 2013.

Chapter 4 Review

SECTION A

Choose the best match from the list below. Answers are listed at the back of the book.

1. _____ Malware Lab Network
2. _____ *U.S. v. U.S. District Court* (1972)
3. _____ Privilege teams
4. _____ *Olmstead v. United States* (1928)
5. _____ Internet Service Providers (ISP)
6. _____ EINSTEIN
7. _____ 'Sniffer' software
8. _____ *Berger v. New York* (1967)
9. _____ Special master
10. _____ Server

A. A computer network intrusion detection system (IDS) used to help protect federal executive agency information technology (IT) enterprises.

B. The first electronic surveillance case in which the US Supreme Court held that the tapping of telephone wires by federal agents did not violate the Fourth Amendment.

C. The case in which the court found the New York Code of Criminal Procedure to be unconstitutional because it failed to require a description of the place to be searched, the crime to which the search related, and a description of the conversation to be seized.

D. Collects, uses, and maintains analytically relevant information in order to support the Department of Homeland Security's cyber security mission.

E. Government investigators and attorneys who are involved in a case solely to work with the defense to determine, prior to release to the case investigation or prosecution team, whether or not files, data, or other evidence are protected by an evidentiary or testimonial privilege.

F. A computer program running to serve the requests of other programs known as clients and connected through a computer network.

G. The case regarding the President's authority to conduct warrantless wiretaps, in which the court rejected the claim of inherent presidential electronic surveillance authority in domestic national security cases.

H. Software that monitors network packets and can be used to intercept data including passwords, credit card numbers, etc.

I. A court-appointed independent person who assists a judge by deciding which of the files, data, or other digital evidence are indeed protected by a privilege and those which are not.

J. Organizations that provide subscribers with access to the Internet.

SECTION B

Discussion questions. Answer these questions given the context of the readings in the chapter.

1. In Young's (2011) reading, respond to the amendments proposed by the author to the specific statutes cited. Do you think these amendments would help to solve the problems mentioned? Specifically list 1) the benefits of such amendments and 2) the potential harms or risks by passing these suggested amendments. Do the pros outweigh the cons?

2. In Wehunt's (2013) reading, respond to the issue of long-term electronic storage of DNA evidence. Do you agree with the reading that DNA collection and storage at arrest is an unconstitutional invasion of privacy that should be amended? Why or why not? Use the readings to back up your answer.

3. In light of all of the readings in this chapter, how do you respond to the issue of privacy versus security in regards to electronic surveillance? Do we need to tip the scales more in favor of personal privacy and freedom to use cyberspace as we wish, or do we need to tip the scales more in favor of national and international security? Use the readings to back up your answer.

APPENDIX

Chapter Review Answers

CHAPTER 1 SECTION A

1. F
2. E
3. J
4. G
5. A
6. I
7. B
8. D
9. C
10. H

CHAPTER 2 SECTION A

1. F
2. H
3. D
4. J
5. A
6. C
7. E
8. I
9. G
10. B

CHAPTER 3 SECTION A

1. A
2. D
3. J
4. B
5. G
6. F
7. E
8. H
9. I
10. C

CHAPTER 4 SECTION A

1. D
2. G
3. E
4. B
5. J
6. A
7. H
8. C
9. I
10. F

Printed in the USA
CPSIA information can be obtained
at www.ICGtesting.com
LVHW080732091223
765787LV00010B/44